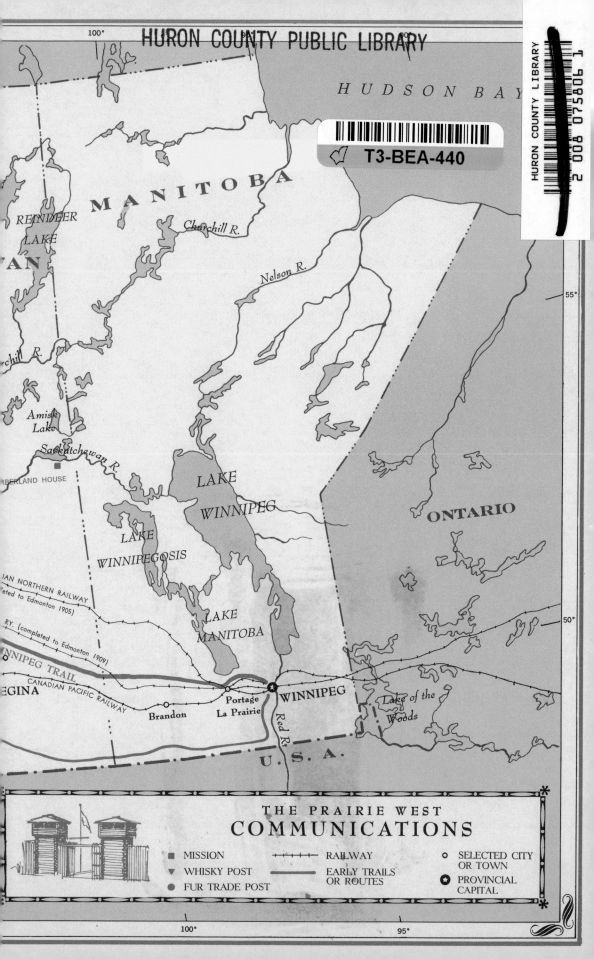

HUDSON BAY

MANITOBA

REINDEER LAKE

Churchill R.

Nelson R.

55°

Amisk Lake

Saskatchewan R.

MBERLAND HOUSE

LAKE WINNIPEG

LAKE WINNIPEGOSIS

ONTARIO

50°

IAN NORTHERN RAILWAY
eted to Edmonton 1905)

LAKE MANITOBA

RY. (completed to Edmonton 1909)

NNIPEG TRAIL

CANADIAN PACIFIC RAILWAY

EGINA

Brandon

Portage La Prairie

WINNIPEG

Red R.

Lake of the Woods

U. S. A.

THE PRAIRIE WEST
COMMUNICATIONS

■ MISSION

▼ WHISKY POST

● FUR TRADE POST

┼┼┼┼┼ RAILWAY

――― EARLY TRAILS OR ROUTES

○ SELECTED CITY OR TOWN

★ PROVINCIAL CAPITAL

a history

EDMONTON

by J. G. MacGREGOR

HURTIG PUBLISHERS

Hurtig Publishers
10560 - 105 Street
Edmonton, Alberta

ISBN 0-88830-100-6

Printed and bound in Canada

Illustrations
and Maps

contents

Introduction

EDMONTON, the Core of Canada's Energy Empire, is the country's seventh largest metropolitan area. Bisected by the twenty-two-mile long park of its magnificent river valley, it sits in the midst of the 50,000 square miles of riches that have created it. At the outermost edge of its ever-expanding network of streets lies rich soil, black and deep. And for fifty and one hundred miles and 150 miles farther out, this soil supports an agriculture wealthy in its varied production. Beyond that, to the west sway the forests of the foothills, while to the north thousands of square miles of forest merge at last into the rich mineralized zone of the pre-Cambrian rocks. Underneath the city, however, extending down for thousands of feet and encircling it for a radius of scores of miles, lies a fabulous store of petroleum wealth.

For eons riches rained on the land we know as Alberta. All the forces of geology working through infinite ages laid down pool after pool of oil and lens after lens of gas. Then, having tucked away these vast stores of energy for future use, they laid over them a thick bed of coal, and in turn covered this with a mantle of clay. To this vast land came glacier-fed streams to mould and shape it, lakes to beautify it, and a moderate rainfall to ripen it into rich soil. In time, it brought forth a mixed forest of spruce and poplar to be the home of countless fowl, multitudes of game animals and millions of fur-bearers.

When, some 10,000 years ago Indians began to work their way into this region, they found it congenial. For hundreds of generations they roamed its forests, having neither inkling of what might be done with this soil nor knowledge of the vast stores of energy beneath their campfires.

Then, a little over two hundred years ago, the first white men came strolling in to see what the area might offer. With their nose for natural resources and their devastating ability never to let well enough alone, they began to develop its riches.

Shortly afterwards, in 1795, on the north bank of the great Saskatchewan River, fur traders erected Edmonton House. Set in the midst of such resources, Edmonton was bound to become a great city. It had only to wait till man's progress up the intellectual ladder should open his eyes to the riches around him and the enormous store of energy beneath his feet.

For a hundred years fur traders ruled the land; for a while gold drew miners to the river's gravels. Then, with increased demand for cereals and great improvements in know-how, the town's tributary soils had been exploited, first by a few, then by hundreds, and finally by thousands. By the early 1940's, based upon the needs of the farming areas, accompanied by some small exploitation of coal and timber, Edmonton grew to 100,000 people. Then, ever extending their field of knowledge and aided by American capital, Albertans found the riches that had always lain beneath their soil — oil and gas — and in the short space of twenty years Edmonton shot up to be a city of 400,000. The riches had always been there, but it took an upwelling of knowledge to perceive them and an upswing in world demand before they bore fruit.

To guide, control and direct the enormous concentration of petroleum products on their way to the markets of the continent came population; labourers and welders, clerks and computers, technicians and engineers, till what had been the city of Edmonton became merely the core of a huge city that went sprawling out for miles. The pre-war population of 90,419 which had crept up to 113,116 by 1946 became insignificant as year by year the new census figures were tallied through the Roaring Fifties; 1951 — 159,631, 1956 — 226,002, and on into the sizzling Sixties; 1961 — 281,027, 1964 — 357,696. And those are city figures only; by 1965 the Edmonton metropolitan area held 385,000 people. Little over sixty years had elapsed since in 1904 Edmonton, with a population of 8,350, had been incorporated as a city.

But this is neither a Chamber of Commerce compilation painting a prideful picture of population nor a compendium of natural resources. It is essentially a history of people, of their reaction to their new environment and of the changes they wrought in a land filled with resources. For it is man who makes cities, and their greatness is a result of his effort and of the resources he has to work. Edmonton then is the result of men working with furs, farms and forests, delving for oil or gas, or toiling to combine these resources into manufactured products.

There are some who profess to believe that because Edmonton's history has been singularly free from bloodshed it must be dull. Since the last Indian battle some ninety-five years ago, Edmonton has been free from wars and invasions (even the Norway rat has not been able to get in). Edmonton has had no Jesse James and no Wild Bill Hickok. It has never been besieged or captured; neither revolution nor rapine has stalked its streets. It has no harbour from which enemy fleets have shelled it, nor from which the armed hosts of a new religion have sailed to conquer the world. But for the very reason that its record is barren of internal or external violence or of gang warfare and gun fighting, it should be admired all the more.

Edmonton's history is that of fur traders venturing far into a wilderness and, by their tact, keeping it friendly; of sturdy pioneers of a rather Puritan persuasion wresting a living from rich though heavily forested soils; of the colourful influx of Scot and Swede, French and Irish, Ukrainian or Hungarian, and their peaceful intermingling; of their forbearance in thinking their way through their problems; and of their free enterprise approach to success. It is a history which the motto of its coat of arms envisaged, "Industry, Integrity, Progress."

So, this is the story of Rowand, the fur factor; Rundle and Lacombe, the missionaries; of Irish Jim Gibbons, the miner; McQueen the "meenister", and McDougall, the merchant; of Abe Cristall and Emily Murphy; of Mayors Matt McCauley, McNamara and fighting Joe Clarke, Elmer Roper and Bill Hawrelak; of the fighting 49th Battalion, of "Wop" May and Punch Dickins, the bush pilots, and of Henry Marshall Tory, father of the university.

Unfortunately, when the history of so many decades has to be compressed into one volume, the story has to hurry along from movement to movement and the painting has to be done with a broad brush. Lack of space prevents following anyone's career too closely or pausing to note the many and varied contributions of hundreds of individuals who in their day played a major part in Edmonton's development. Unfortunately too, while it is desirable to bring the story up as close to Canada's centennial year as possible, that also presents problems. It is most difficult to interpret recent movements or to write objectively of current events, as Sir Walter Raleigh realized when he said: "Whosoever, in writing a modern history, shall follow truth too near the heels, it may haply strike out his teeth."

EDMONTON
a history

Earliest Years
1795-1809

chapter *I*

GREAT CITIES grow only where resources abound and only when men are ready to use them. By 1795 fur traders were clamouring for Edmonton's first resource, and that year Hudson's Bay men erected Edmonton House, a sturdy log building sixty feet by twenty-four feet, and roofed it with sods. A stone's throw away some weeks previously the rival North West Company traders had started their Fort Augustus. Duncan McGillivray, a Northwester, explaining why his company had decided to build at this location, said: "This is described to be a rich and plentiful Country, abounding with all kinds of animals especially Beavers and Otters, which are said to be so numerous that the Women and children kill them with Sticks and hatchets. . . ." The first of the Edmonton area's many resources was about to be tapped.

These fort builders, however, were not the earliest Europeans to pass this way, for on March 5, 1754, Anthony Henday, the first white man to visit Alberta, walked downstream over the ice-locked North Saskatchewan River past the future site of these posts. Then, somewhat below the mouth of the Sturgeon River, he spent the next seven weeks waiting for the river ice to go out so that he could set out by canoe. On April 23, the day the ice broke up, he celebrated St. George's Day, for his diary says: "Displayed my Flag in Honour of St. George; and the Leaders did the same, after acquainting them and explaining my reason . . ."

Even in Henday's time, however, paddling downstream with a load of furs, Alberta's earliest exports destined for Europe, was nothing new. For over half a century the Crees of the Edmonton area had been doing just that. Each spring they took advantage of another of Edmonton's rich resources, the mighty North Saskatchewan River, to take their furs to sell to the Hudson's Bay Company, which had been trading with them since it had been organized in 1670.

Within a few years after the company's ships began trading in Hudson Bay, the Crees in the Edmonton area began to hear of the strange white men who each year crossed the ocean in great ships seeking furs to buy. These men, though undoubtedly gifted with great magic, having ships, guns, steel axes and copper kettles, were as moon-struck as they were magical. According to the talk around campfires where Alberta's Legislative Building is now, these white men would actually trade priceless axes and other tools for the useless furs that lay around Indian tepees. Surely, thought the Indians, they must be soft in the head, but nevertheless, the astute natives set off down the river to get their share of these tools before the naive white men came to their senses. In doing so, they started a trade which survives to this day. In doing so, they gave the white man all the encouragement he needed not only to come in to look at their country and in the course of time to build Edmonton House, but in the end to take their lands away from them. The white man was not so naive as he appeared.

The Crees and the Saskatchewan River were the keys that unlocked the riddle of the unknown West. This tribe's homeland extended from the vicinity of modern Edmonton all the way downstream to Hudson Bay. The North Saskatchewan and its continuation, the Nelson River, was destined to form the major waterway by which white men penetrated the West. Then too, because its waters paused temporarily in Lake Winnipeg, which also received the Winnipeg River from the south-east, they led to a connecting link which by way of the Great Lakes and the St. Lawrence River, opened the way to tidal waters in French Canada. Because of this fortunate configuration, both the Hudson's Bay men and the French and their successors, the North West Company traders, were able to travel far inland. Because of the Saskatchewan River, Edmonton is where it is, and perhaps of more interest, because of the Saskatchewan River, Edmonton is located in a beautiful setting.

During the four decades following Henday's visit to the mouth of the Sturgeon River, several traders, mainly Hudson's Bay men, came out year by year to visit the Alberta Indians. It was not until 1792, however, that the North West Company built Fort George, the first fur post on the Alberta portion of the Saskatchewan River. From then on, in bitter competition, the traders of both companies started leap-frogging posts up the river; Fort Augustus (North West Co.) and Edmonton House side by side, and then rival posts at Rocky Mountain House.

Within the space of twenty-five years the impetus of the intense competition between the two great fur trading companies gave them a fair knowledge of Alberta's geography and spurred them on to discovering all the main waterways of Western Canada. It is noteworthy that Alexander Mackenzie, the Northwester, was the first white man to cross the continent anywhere north of Mexico, and that Edmonton House, when it was built in 1795, was over 1,500 miles farther west than any American post in the Dakotas and Montana. Mackenzie's trips to the Arctic and the Pacific, and America's tardiness in trading along the upper Missouri, were both to have their influence on Edmonton's later history.

When, therefore, it came time to move far up the Saskatchewan and establish a post near modern Edmonton, Alberta's hills, lakes and rivers were well known to white men. As early as 1793 the Hudson's Bay Company sent Peter Fidler to see about a site for this new post, and in a day or so Angus Shaw of the North West Company followed him. Nevertheless, two more years went by before on May 11, 1795, Duncan McGillivray, entering up his diary at Fort George, let us in on a secret.

"Mr. Shaw has projected a plan of erecting a House farther up the River, in course of the Summer. For this purpose Mr. Hughes has received directions to build, 12 or 14 days march from this by Water, on a spot called the Forks . . . it is carefully concealed from every person that a step of this kind is intended . . ."

The forks to which McGillivray refers was the mouth of the Sturgeon River. That summer John MacDonald, James Hughes, and perhaps twenty men, came upstream to build the North West Company's Fort Augustus on the west bank of the river, on NE 9-55-22-W.4th and about two miles due north of the heart of modern Fort Saskatchewan.

By this move the North West Company caught the Hudson's Bay Company napping. When, however, the dour Scotsman, William Tomison, returned from the Bay that fall, he dashed on to the mouth of the Sturgeon, and on October 5, 1795, set his men to building Edmonton House within a musket shot of his rivals. As Peter Fidler had reported, the site lacked suitable timber, but since Fort Augustus was already well advanced, Tomison was forced to build beside it. In his journal for October that year Tomison bemoans this lack of building material and states that suitable logs had to be cut upstream and floated down. He hurried his men along, and on November 7, reported that the roof had now been covered with turf. From then on, Edmonton was a name on a map.

Two plausible explanations are given as the reason why Edmonton was chosen as the name for the post. The first, and least likely, is that Edmonton, at that time a town on the outskirts of London, England, was the birthplace of John Peter Pruden, a clerk working under Tomison. The fact that Pruden first saw Edmonton House in May 1796, that is, several months after it had been built and named, puts that explanation at a discount. The second is that Tomison, wishing to honour the Deputy-Governor of the Company, Sir James Winter Lake, but finding it impractical to call his new post Lake House, named it Edmonton after an estate owned by that gentleman.

The name itself, however, has a long history, and was first applied to the English hamlet near London in 793 A.D. In that year it was called Edelmentuna, which is believed to be the Latinized form of the Saxon word derived from "Eadhelm", meaning Happy Hamlet. Over the years the form of the name changed, until by 1589 it was spelled Edmonton.

Angus Shaw and William Tomison, who as commanders of Fort Augustus and Edmonton House opposed each other, were experienced foemen. Shaw was a relatively young but forceful man, who as early as 1787 became a clerk in the North West Company's service. Before coming to build Fort Augustus, he established a post on Moose Lake near modern Bonnyville in 1789 and three years later played a large part in building Fort George, near modern Elk Point. Eventually he rose to be a partner in the North West Company.

William Tomison, a grizzled, loyal old veteran of fifty-six years, who had spent thirty-five of them in the Hudson's Bay Company's service, knew all the tricks of the trade and of his rivals, as well as those of his sometimes belligerent customers. For the previous twenty years his high ability and his truculence had supplied the drive which had successfully swept the Hudson's Bay Company forces across Manitoba and Saskatchewan and far into Alberta. After establishing Edmonton House, this purposeful Scot spent another sixteen years working for his company before returning to his birthplace in the Orkney Islands, where he remained until his death in his ninetieth year.

Though these two were the rival leaders, several of the members of their staffs at Fort Augustus and Edmonton House were already well known in fur trade circles, or else rose to prominence later on. Of these we may mention the Northwesters, John MacDonald of Garth, and Duncan McGillivray, both of whom wrote interesting accounts of their experiences. Of the Hudson's Bay Company men, George Sutherland, John Peter Pruden and Mitchell Oman, all spent their lives in the fur trade. And all these five have many descendants living in the Edmonton area today.

Both companies had hoped that the war-like Plains Indians, the Blackfoot, Blood, Piegans and Gros Ventres, would continue to trade two hundred miles downstream at Fort George and Buckingham House, while the Crees and Assiniboines would come to Fort Augustus and Edmonton House. Bad blood always existed between the Plains Indians and these Woods Indians, and whenever they met at trading posts they fought. Usually the Crees and Assiniboines came off second best, so it was highly desirable to have a place where these tribes might bring their furs with a reasonable expectation of safety.

The traders' hopes, however, were doomed to disappointment. The Crees and Assiniboines were willing enough, but the Plains Indians would not let the white men push them around. They would trade where they wished, and since to those who lived in southern Alberta Edmonton House was closer to home, they came to it in droves. To confuse the situation even more, the Gros Ventres showed up too. No one had expected to see them. Within the previous few years they had sacked North West and Hudson's Bay Company posts farther east in Saskatchewan and officially no one was talking to them any more. Nevertheless, they had furs to trade, and furs were the reason for all this laborious business of building posts and manning them.

In the fall of 1795 they showed up. According to John MacDonald of Fort Augustus, "When there appeared on the opposite (the South) side of the River a large Band of Indians with Horses in numbers, women and all other accompaniments, who they were was the question. We were not picketed, merely log Houses in a Square Shape with a gate between the two Houses. Shortly some chiefs came to the bank of the River and held a Parley, saying they came to sue for peace. . . .

"As we required all the help we could give one another Mr. Hughes and myself held a Council of war with Mr. Thompson (Tomison). He told us that after destroying their establishment and killing their men . . . he could not receive them as friends. . . ."

Then having made sure that Tomison would stand by them in case of trouble, MacDonald went out to meet the Gros Ventres, and did not overlook the opportunity of telling them that Tomison would not trade with them. As Mac-Donald continues the story: "They loaded me with kindness and Buffaloe fur Robes—they had by this time pitched their tents. They told me they would willingly make peace and not molest the Hudson's Bay establisht,—but would trade all they had with me—and was glad that I met them without any fear of any harm—and I placed confidence in them. They accordingly came on and we made a good Trade. Mr. Thompson (Tomison) biting his fingers at the result. . . ."

One up for the North West Company.

As MacDonald had said, the arrival of the Gros Ventres had caught them with their palisades down. Each of the companies had been too busy putting up buildings to spend time enclosing their establishments with a stockade.

Even though the staffs of the two companies were often bitter in their rivalry and regarded each other as enemies, nevertheless they were aware that by combining forces they were still but a handful of white men facing hundreds of savages. At any time the war-like Plains Indians might fall upon them as swiftly as the thunder clouds that swept across the parklands. As A. S. Morton, the great historian of the West, said: "Those were brave men and masterly who faced these perils, maintained their supremacy over swarms of savages, sober and drunk, and returned safely, bringing their rich harvest of pemmican and furs with them."

One way to reduce the peril of attack by the Plains Indians was to build the fur trade posts on the north bank of the Saskatchewan River, and invariably they were so located. That way, before attacking the post, any tribe had to cross the swift stream. Another way to protect each of the posts was to build them side by side and then surround them with a common stockade made of logs set on end and rising some fifteen feet above the ground. In such a manner Fort Augustus and Edmonton House were built and protected.

We do not know how big the staffs at these two posts were, but they would have been much the same as Fort George and Buckingham House had a few years earlier when they were the most westerly posts on the river. In 1793 the Northwesters at Fort George had eighty men, while the Hudson's Bay Company's staff at Buckingham House was thirty-nine. During these early years the North West Company invariably had about twice as many employees as its rival.

The North West Company's larger staff enabled it to secure more furs, and to this extent it outshone its rival in the fur country. The trade was, nevertheless, a very expensive business. It is commonly said that the fur trading companies made exorbitant profits by giving the Indians a mere pittance for their furs. A closer examination of the affairs of these two companies during the years of unbridled competition around 1800, however, shows that they made very little profit.

Keen rivalry existed between Angus Shaw and William Tomison, who lived side by side on the banks of the forest-clad Saskatchewan River nearly two hundred canoe-miles farther west than any other traders. When the Gros Ventres had come to trade, Shaw had pulled a fast one on his opponent. Tomison, however, was to suffer other vexations, and one of them concerned rum kegs. On October 13, 1795, when writing up his journal, he waxed sarcastic, in the hope that the London officials would get a better grasp of the situation:

"At 5 P.M. two young Indians arrived for Tobacco and Powder and also Brandy, the former they got but the latter I could not give without I had given the whole Keg such as it was, not being master of one small (?) to Distribute the Brandy in, my Neighbours have got two Coopers at work daily making Kegs from 2 qt. to 6 Gallons which saves them a great quantity of liquor and brings them many Skins, I desired a Cooper myself when Inland several years ago but none has been sent as yet. It must be a silly notion to send Strong Liquor Inland without a Cooper to make small Kegs to divide it in, it is well known that natives have no Kegs of their own."

Although Tomison had not traded with John MacDonald's Gros Ventres and then afterwards they would not trade with him, both companies did a good business that winter. In the spring of 1796, Tomison took his furs down to Hudson Bay and then took a year's leave in Britain. For the summer of 1796 he left John Peter Pruden in charge of the six men who remained at Edmonton House. That fall George Sutherland returned from the Bay to take over the responsibility of this far western post.

During December the Gros Ventres again rode in from the remote hills of the prairies. Sutherland, perhaps less truculent than Tomison, made friends with them. All winter the rival companies' traders did an amazingly large business, an indication that the Edmonton area was fulfilling its promise of abundant resources. Then in the fall of 1797 William Tomison, refreshed by a year's sojourn amidst the peat smoke and the heather of Scotland, came back to Edmonton to take over. His journal for that winter keeps us abreast of affairs there, and on February 10, 1798, points out one of the good practices of the fur trade companies and the responsibilities they, and in particular the Hudson's Bay Company, assumed in extending benevolence to the Indians who traded with them. The Indian in question had been a staunch customer and the company felt responsible for the welfare of his family.

"Buried one of the best Indians, this country can produce, he departed this life in the night, after a long lingering Disorder of 16 Months, brought on by immoderate drinking at Both Houses, in the fall of '96, he has left a wife and six Children which has been very expensive for the last 12 Months and will be for Some time to Come. He traded at the Honourable Company's Settlements since Hudson House was Settled."

All through the following winter Angus Shaw at Fort Augustus and William Tomison at Edmonton House were well pleased with their location. In the fall of 1798, however, one of his customers gave Tomison a painful wound. Not inclined toward the modern namby-pamby that the customer is always right, he got the worst of an encounter with two bad tempered Gros Ventres. These arrived at Edmonton House and, even though they had no furs to trade, demanded goods. Crusty old Tomison, expressing his opinion of them, turned them away empty handed. As they were leaving, one of them gave him "a Cruel Stab in the inside of the left knee, which almost went through". In spite of Tomison's suffering, business was good at the two posts. It was so good that a new Montreal company, which for a few years flashed across the fur trade sky, built a post nearby. This was the X.Y. Company in which Sir Alexander Mackenzie had a hand. Moreover, another Montreal outfit, the Ogilvie Company, also built some minor posts along the Saskatchewan.

The two older companies were also busily expanding in the region which we now call Edmonton's trading area. For one thing, still trying to keep the Piegans and the other war-like Plains Indians from battling with the Crees at the older posts, both of them set up outposts to serve the Piegans much farther up the Saskatchewan at Rocky Mountain House. Furthermore, in 1798 David Thompson, who a year earlier had left the Hudson's Bay Company's service under somewhat of a cloud, started Greenwich House on Lac La Biche for the North West Company. He decided that the mouth of the Lesser Slave Lake River near modern Smith would also be a good place for a post, and accordingly that fall the North West Company sent men there to build. Peter Fidler, who had stepped into David Thompson's shoes as the Hudson's Bay Company's surveyor, followed his old associate and in the fall of 1799 also built at Lac La Biche.

Except for Rocky Mountain House, all these were mere outposts of the two main houses. So too were Pembina House (H.B.Co.) and Boggy Hall (N.W.Co.), both some six miles south-east of modern Lodgepole, together with Nelson House (H.B.Co.) and Whitemud House (N.W.Co.), both at the mouth of Wabamun Creek south of Duffield, as well as some shacks put up by the winterers for the Ogilvie and X.Y. Companies. During the four years since Edmonton House had been built, these little outposts had multiplied, and yet in spite of fierce competition the two old companies did a reasonable business.

Even as early as 1800, though in a very small way, Edmonton was beginning to be a depot for the trans-shipment of goods to the far north. The same year too the two old companies and the X.Y. organization decided to see what luck they would have trading farther out on the baldheaded prairies and accordingly each of them set up a post at the junction of the Red Deer and the South Saskatchewan rivers, near modern Empress. Peter Fidler, who was in charge of the Hudson's Bay Company's fort there, occasionally sent to Edmonton House for additional trade goods. In November, he sent there asking if Sutherland could spare him some cloth suitable for making coats to present to Indian chiefs and "other goods to rig chiefs". On January 7, after a bitterly cold trip across the blizzard-swept prairie, his men returned with some goods and a letter from George Sutherland saying: ". . . there not being one single feather to go round hatts in the house . . . have sent you instead of the former, ostrich feathers. . . ." Included with the other goods were forty-one ostrich feathers.

These ostrich feathers add an incongruous touch to our picture of life far out in the western wilderness. Here were some three or four white men accompanied by one or two Blackfoot Indians, battling through blizzards and hurrying towards the relief of Chesterfield House, carrying not food nor ammunition nor even trade hardware, but forty-one ostrich feathers to decorate Indians' hats. Here was the master of Edmonton House, a remote outpost nearly 3,000 route-miles west of the nearest Canadian village large enough to have a main street, busying himself picking out forty-one ostrich feathers to despatch nearly three hundred miles over the trackless snows to meet the latest demands of fashion.

Though Edmonton House fell far short of being any great emporium of the West, it could nevertheless produce ostrich feathers on demand. Actually, Edmonton had already become the headquarters of the West. From it the crudest of trails, mere traces left by the hooves of pack-horses, spread out south to Rocky Mountain House and Chesterfield House, north to reach the Peace River country and Lac La Biche, and west and east up and down the river. Over these trails all the men of the opposing outfits kept in touch with each other. All told, they could have crowded into a small mess hall. But these few men emanating from the Edmonton forts knew Alberta like the backs of their hands. To these men on the job, busy with these every-day tasks at their posts, where each man knew every other in the whole country, life held a deep satisfaction. They knew their business, they knew each other, and they knew the country; to them it was neither strange nor remote.

The Indians too regarded these Edmonton houses as part of the landscape. Off to the south-east, directly across the river and rising gradually to a height of some five hundred feet above it, stood the wooded Beaver Hills. To the Crees, these posts were the Beaver Hill Houses which, rendered into their language, became *Amisk Wutchee Waskahegan,* a name with which for the next century every resident of Edmonton was to be familiar.

Then in 1802 Fort Augustus and Edmonton House, situated as they were in the midst of an illimitable forest, ran out of firewood. As the years went by, the circle chopped out of the forest grew larger, and the business of hauling in logs became more and more onerous and took up time that should have been devoted to business. The chief traders of both houses decided that it would be easier to build new ones than to spend so much of their men's time hauling wood.

Accordingly, James Bird, who had replaced Tomison, and James Hughes, the new North West Company's man, decided to move some twenty miles up the river and to build immediately downstream from Edmonton's present 105th Street bridge. With all their goods and chattels, they brought along the old names, Fort Augustus and Edmonton House. Once everything was moved out of the old establishments, the Indians gathered around, and, after rummaging for any objects overlooked by the traders, they set the buildings on fire and stood gleefully watching the spectacular blaze.

Fortunately we have a plan of the two new posts, Fort Augustus and Edmonton House. It shows the two houses side by side and enclosed in one palisade with a dividing stockade between them, and gives interesting details of typical fur trade posts.

For some years conditions at the two new houses remained more or less static. Plains Indians continued to come in to trade and clashed with Crees. Because as well as the two old companies the X.Y. and the Ogilvie traders were also in the area, the use of liquor in bribing the Indians increased. The natives, sharp traders in other respects, thirsted for liquor above all else, and dealt with whoever would dish out the most grog.

With four companies competing, the profits from furs decreased year by year until by 1804 the X.Y. Company amalgamated with the North West Company, and the Ogilvie outfit disappeared. Even though the new companies had been put out of business and, therefore, many of the small outposts of former years could be closed, the rivalry between the North West Company and the Hudson's Bay Company men increased. The North West Company, which had been a strong rival, was now more formidable than ever. In spite of all Bird could do, his opposition got the lion's share of the furs.

Map showing the various locations of Edmonton House and Fort Augustus from 1795 to 1813.

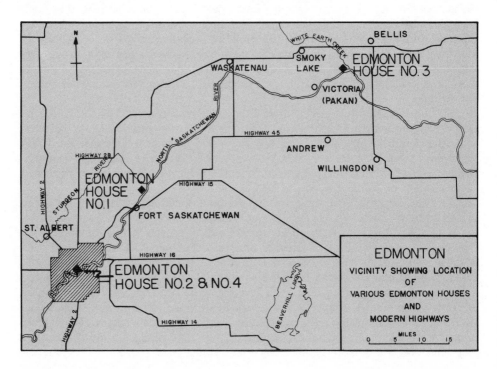

By this time, however, another of Alberta's early exports was regularly sent off down river each spring. This was meat pounded up and mixed with grease to form bags of pemmican. Because the canoe trip to Hudson Bay or Montreal had to be made as speedily as possible, the brigades had no time to hunt as they went along. It was necessary, therefore, for either the North West Company's French voyageurs bound for Montreal or the Hudson's Bay Company's Orkney boatmen to carry food with them, and no other concentrated food packed the punch that pemmican did. Moreover, with the North West Company operating another large transport route from central Saskatchewan north to beyond Lake Athabasca, the boats from Edmonton took down extra pemmican to supply the voyageurs on that route. Before long, Fort Augustus and Edmonton House began buying tons of pemmican from the Plains Indians.

During the years that the two forts did business on the site now occupied by the Edmonton power house, four significant events took place. The first was that in 1805 on the Peace River the North West Company established Fort Dunvegan, which, except for a short interval about twenty years later, remained in operation until 1918. Fort Dunvegan became the headquarters of the Peace River country, and much business was transacted between it and Edmonton.

The Blackfoot Indians brought in news of the second event for they told of a great party of Americans which, starting at the mouth of the Missouri, had rowed arduously upstream in a keel boat fifty feet long, fitted with sails, and carrying some thirty men. This boat, they said, was accompanied by two smaller craft carrying a total of fourteen more men. They had started in the spring of 1804, spent the winter in a camp near the Mandan villages, and by mid-summer 1805 were at the Great Falls of the Missouri. Then, more or less on foot, they had disappeared westward over the mountains and had wintered at the Pacific, whence during the following summer they reappeared in modern Montana on their way eastward. That summer they had fought with the Blackfeet at a point four hundred miles south of Edmonton House and then went home down the Missouri. This party, of course, was what we know as the Lewis and Clark Expedition, the first American group to go down the Columbia River to reach the Pacific. James Hughes and James Bird and their associates listened attentively to this news and discussed it carefully. Up to this time Edmonton House had regarded the Blackfeet of Montana and Idaho as their customers and now the Americans were making contact with them.

The third significant event was a move on the part of the North West Company to find a shorter route to Oregon than the one it had worked out by the way of Lake Athabasca, the Peace River, and up it to the mountains and thence down the Columbia to the Coast. The task of finding such a route fell to David Thompson. After 1806, when he made his headquarters at Rocky Mountain House, he was a frequent visitor at Fort Augustus. Though he was dilatory in accomplishing his task of finding a route across the mountains west of Edmonton and in descending the Columbia to its mouth, Fort Augustus and Edmonton House followed his efforts with rising interest during the years 1806 to 1810.

The fourth event, and one in which Edmonton House had a supporting hand, was the Joseph Howse Expedition across the Rockies. Howse, a Hudson's Bay man with an education much better than average, had been at Carlton House in 1799. In 1809, with ten years' experience along the Saskatchewan behind him, he set out with one white helper and one Indian and crossed the Rockies by the pass which now bears his name. On his way back to spend the winter of 1809-1810

Paul Kane's painting of Edmonton House made during his visit in 1846.

at Edmonton House, he met David Thompson in the vicinity of Kootenay Plains. Then, starting out with nine white men and half a dozen Indians in the spring of 1810, and crossing Howse's Pass once more, he built a post on Pend d'Oreille Lake. After wintering there he came back with a good load of furs.

Though the pass he used to cross the mountains from the headwaters of the Saskatchewan River to the Columbia bears his name, it should be remembered that David Thompson had travelled it two years before he did. For some years more Howse and one of his brothers were active along the Saskatchewan, and today there are many Métis families in the Edmonton area whose name the passing of generations has changed into House. It was only natural that nearly all the early traders should enter into conjugal alliances with the beautiful and loyal Indian girls, and the Howses, like so many others, appear to have done that.

Hugh Munro was another man who worked at Edmonton and married an Indian girl. As a youth of 18 he came west about 1802 to serve the Hudson's Bay Company. James Bird, who in 1807 was in charge of Edmonton House, felt that he had to have men on his staff who had a thorough knowledge of the Blackfoot language, and picked Munro and Big Donald MacDonald to go and live with the Piegan branch of that tribe for three years to learn it. To further this aim,

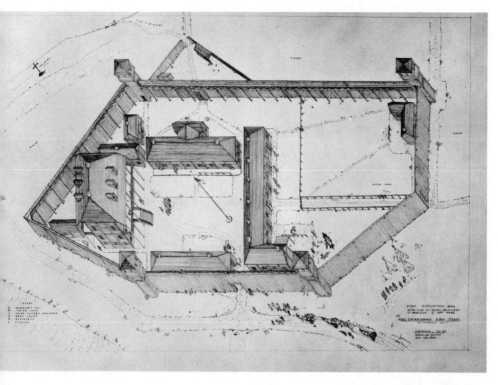

Aerial perspective view of Edmonton House based upon Lieutenant Vavasour's plan drawn 1846.

he made an agreement to pay Chief Painted Feather goods to the value of £100 per year for looking after Munro and MacDonald. These two had many adventures, including taking part in a battle between the Piegans and the Crows, Snakes and other enemies from the south. This fight took place in 1808 near the Old Man's Bowling Green on the headwaters of the Old Man River. About this time Munro married a Blackfoot woman and eventually went to live and trade in Montana, where he became the first white man to see one of the most beautiful lakes of the American Rocky Mountains. Overlooking this he erected a cross and named the lake St. Mary's. This early, men from the Edmonton posts were playing a part in Montana.

Dealing with the Peace River country in the north, reaching out over the mountains to the west and down into Montana in the south, Edmonton House and Fort Augustus dominated a large area. Within the space of a dozen years the Amisk Wutchee Waskahegan had established itself as a key point in the far west. Moreover, situated at the upper end of easy navigation on the great Saskatchewan waterway which gave access both to Hudson Bay and to Montreal, Edmonton was beginning to flex its muscles.

Widening Horizons
1810-1830

chapter 2

THEN IN 1810, after spending eight years on the flats now covered by the Edmonton power house, the two forts moved again. This time they went downstream about sixty-five miles to the mouth of White Earth Creek not far from modern Smoky Lake. Because they were in the same general area as the older sites, it was good business for them to retain the same names. Once more these rival houses were built side by side within a common stockade, and although we do not have a plan of them, we do have Alexander Henry's account of building his company's Fort Augustus, which was sometimes called the Lower White Earth Post. Since they shed light on the details of building a post, the following extracts are quoted from his journal.

"June 7th (1810). The bastion being finished, we put our property under lock and key. Men began to make the separation between us and the H.B. Co., by erecting a range of stockades; others covered the house, and others worked on the E. wing. . . . Sent women for gum to daub the covering of the house, and men to collect stones for the chimneys. . . .

"Men off to raise bark to cover the small houses. . . .

"I sent for white clay, of which there is plenty near a small lake about two miles from here. . . .

"I sent Hamel to sow turnips and radishes in the woods. . . .

"Lussier finished hauling planks from the woods, where they had been sawed—193 of 20 feet, and 104 of 12 feet. . . . Lussier hauled stones up the hill, which the men had found in a quarry, of an excellent kind for chimneys, about a mile up the S. side of the river, only 100 yards from the water's edge, where any quantity may be had. . . .

"Men finished covering the house with mud, earth, and pine bark; not a drop of water penetrated. . . ."

Alexander Henry planted some barley at his new Fort Augustus, but it was hailed out. Since similar grain had also been sown on the river flat at the end of today's 105th Street bridge, Henry sent men back to that field to cut it. While gardens and perhaps grain crops had undoubtedly been sown in previous years, this is the earliest record of grain grown at Edmonton. When the men came to cut the barley, they found that once more the Indians had burned the empty buildings of the two former forts.

That September, on another of his trips westward over the mountains, David Thompson called at Fort Augustus. Many weeks later word reached the fort that he was having trouble with the Piegans. They had put their collective feet down and declared that no more white men, not even their former friend Thompson, were to cross the mountains and arm their enemies, the Kootenay Indians. In the face of their opposition, Thompson had to make a long end run to avoid them. Returning downstream from Rocky Mountain House to a point near modern Lodgepole, he set off north-westerly, and after a terrific struggle through fallen timber and muskeg, he reached the Athabasca River in the vicinity of Hinton. Working his way up as far as Jasper, he set off over the Athabasca Pass during the first week of January 1811. In making this detour around the angry Piegans, he discovered the pass which for the next seventy years was to be used as the main highway to the coast. Thereby, all unwittingly, he was paving the way for Edmonton's importance and growth.

Earlier that fall the war-like Blackfeet called at Edmonton House, bringing the news that American traders in the wake of Lewis and Clark were at last working their way up the Missouri River and indeed had built a fort at the Three Forks of the Missouri. Near this point, about five hundred miles due south of Edmonton, these Indians reported catching some American traders off their guard, killing them, and making off with a rich booty in furs and trading goods. At Edmonton House James Bird kept a watchful eye on the Americans, who of late had been invading the area now known as Montana, Wyoming and Idaho, which up till now had marketed its furs at Edmonton. The news the Blackfeet brought bothered him, but the furs they had captured and now sold at Fort Augustus and Edmonton House rested lightly on his conscience.

That the Blackfeet brought more than furs, to Fort Augustus at least, is shown by a newsy letter which Bird sent to his friend Peter Fidler, saying: ". . . the Muddy river Indians have massacred an American officer and eight men near the sources of the Missouri River last fall and scalped the whole and brot to the Canadian house in the Saskatchewan river 110 Trenton Bank Notes of Three Dollars each—which the Canadian master (at Fort Augustus) got from them for very little. . . ."

Occasionally Alexander Henry's new Fort Augustus journal mentioned young John Rowand, who by his masterful leadership during the next four decades, was to make Edmonton the foremost settlement in the West. As a husky lad of fourteen, Rowand, the son of an Irish Montreal surgeon, entered the service of the North West Company in 1803, spent some years along the Saskatchewan River, and from time to time visited Fort Augustus. Sometime in 1811 he wed in the fashion of the country. Years later, Colonel Lefroy, who visited Edmonton in 1842, entered into his journal all the details we have of this interesting romance, which led to a life-long attachment that was terminated only by Rowand's wife's death in 1848.

"I was received by Mr. Rowand, widely known among the Plains Indians as the 'Big Mountain'; he was a powerful but not very tall man of rough determined aspect and very near lame from an early accident. Hunting alone as a young man he had been thrown from his horse and had broken his leg. By some means intelligence reached the fort of what had occurred and before the whites could do anything an Indian girl had mounted and galloped off in the direction indicated. She found him, nursed him, and saved his life and he married her."

This is a charming story, and as far as the romantic rescue is concerned it is undoubtedly true. But the girl was only half Indian, for she was Louise, the daughter of Edward Umfreville, who in 1784 was operating a post for the North West Company on the Saskatchewan River slightly downstream from the present Alberta-Saskatchewan border.

Shortly after Rowand's marriage, the fur traders on the upper Saskatchewan found that moving their fort to the mouth of White Earth Creek had been a mistake, so during the summer of 1813 Fort Augustus and Edmonton House were moved once more. This time they came back to the site they had left three years earlier and started afresh. From that day to this, Edmonton has been continuously occupied, and the Hudson's Bay Company, one of the world's longest lived companies, has done business in the city.

Since Edmonton House was moved about so frequently during the first seventeen years of its existence, its peregrinations are hard to follow. On the map on page 24 its various sites have been marked "Edmonton House Nos. 1 to 4" in chronological order.

If the movements of Edmonton House are hard to follow, keeping track of the wanderings of Jean-Baptiste Lagimodière, one of its employees, is also difficult. Besides being an exceptionally capable frontiersman, he is of particular interest to us because he was the father of the first all-white child born in wedlock in the West. Within two or three years of the time that baby, which was named Renè, was born at Pembina in January 1808, the Lagimodières moved to the Edmonton area where they lived for four years. Undoubtedly during that time the couple were blessed with one or two other children and these would be the first all-white children born in Alberta. What is also most interesting is that later on, after the Lagimodières settled down in Selkirk's Red River Settlement, Julie, their sixth child arrived, and she was destined to become the mother of Louis Riel.

Though once more in 1813 Fort Augustus and Edmonton House were built within a common stockade as a defense against the Indians, it soon began to look as if they were to need defence against each other. The strong rivalry of former years began to grow into a bitterness that in many other parts of the West brought on bloodshed. The Northwesters' belligerence reached its maximum about 1815 after the appearance of Lord Selkirk's Colony at what is now Winnipeg, and until then the houses on the upper Saskatchewan were spared its worst extremes.

Selkirk's settlers began to arrive in 1812, and immediately the North-westers, who saw them as a threat to their trading position all over the West, took steps to stamp out the colony. By destruction of their crops, burning their buildings, and some killing, they achieved their end, and in 1815 the colonists left. In concentrating their hostility against the Selkirk Settlement, they recruited men from many of the western posts. John Rowand, for instance, took a force of canoes and half-breeds from the Edmonton area and reached Winnipeg on May 29, 1815, in time to be in on the rape of the colony a couple of weeks later. He was still in that area when on June 19, 1816, the so-called Massacre of Seven Oaks killed the Selkirk Colony's Governor, Robert Semple, and twenty of his men, and once more caused the settlers to abandon their colony.

This attack on Selkirk's Colony, together with the virtual warfare practised against the Hudson's Bay Company all the way from Saskatchewan to Great Slave Lake, marked the beginning of the end for the North West Company. By

1816 it had passed its peak, and due to its heavy expenditure on the campaign and its over-expansion in western Canada, bankruptcy began to stare it in the face.

With all the recent movement of men and news back and forth from the Red River Settlement as far west as Edmonton House, the beginning of a fairly definite trail came into being across the prairies. It ran from Brandon House up the Assiniboine and then, cutting across the parklands to Fort Carlton on the North Saskatchewan River near the Forks, it continued to Edmonton. Along it carts became a significant feature of travel on the prairies.

In 1820, amongst other adjustments that were following in the wake of the recent troubles, John Rowand returned to the land of his choice, and once more concerned himself with affairs at Fort Augustus and Rocky Mountain House. That summer a new Scot fresh out from the Hudson's Bay Company's London office arrived in the West. This dapper little snip of a man, who at Chipewyan during the winter of 1820-21 cut his fur trade teeth by opposing the North West Company, was George Simpson. Neither he nor the dour old Scottish traders with whom he came to associate and to command could possibly have foreseen that Simpson was to rise rapidly and that for some thirty-four years he was to govern all the company's business spread over the vast area of Canada and over much of the western United States.

Before Simpson emerged from the far north in the spring of 1821, the North West Company and the Hudson's Bay Company amalgamated, and the former passed out of existence. Actually, the agreement came as a great relief to the Hudson's Bay Company, which, though it was still paying dividends, had its back to the wall. After the pact, the Hudson's Bay Company, utilizing the best of the many good wintering partners of the North West Company, and using George Simpson, a genius of its own finding, to manage the whole, operated as a monopoly. Simpson's efforts immediately after the union were directed towards the sorely needed rehabilitation of the fur trade, so badly crippled by the preceding strife.

As a result of the amalgamation of the two companies and because James Bird was on the point of retiring, John Rowand, the strong man of the West and a former Northwester, rose to well-deserved prominence. He was now a mature man of thirty-two, with sufficient of a reputation to be admitted to the new concern as a Chief Trader. For a short time he was posted to Rocky Mountain House.

Simpson's sizing up of the situation in Alberta, however, nearly meant curtains for Edmonton House, which now, of course, included the combined buildings of the two former establishments looking south over the magnificent Saskatchewan valley. According to the records he studied, it had been a dangerous post to maintain and a costly one. Moreover, it lay off the main route via the Beaver River which the Northwesters had been in the habit of taking to cross Alberta on their way to the Coast.

In Edmonton's place Simpson advocated using the more northerly posts for trading with the Crees and establishing a new one on the Bow River some-where in the vicinity of modern Calgary. He hoped that the Plains Indians would take such a post under their wing. But Simpson always looked before he leaped, and in looking, he sent out the famous Bow River Expedition of 1822 under Donald Mackenzie, a cousin of Sir Alexander. John Rowand was appointed second in command, and he assembled the staff of nearly one hundred men, which, from a rendezvous on the Bow River, was to take part in the venture. John Harriott, who was later to take command at Edmonton House, went along as one of the clerks.

Attached to it as a labourer was Pierre Bungo, possibly the first negro to spend some time at Edmonton and working out from there. He evidently was a favourite with the Indians, for George Simpson, writing of him some years later, said: "These unsophisticated savages, however, had their curiosity most strongly excited by a negro of the name of Pierre Bungo. This man they inspected in every possible way, twisting him about and pulling his hair, which was so different from their own flowing locks; and at length they came to the conclusion that Pierre Bungo was the oddest specimen of a white man that they had ever seen. These negroes, of whom there were formerly several in the company's service, were universal favorites with the fair sex of the red race; and, at the present day, we saw many an Indian that appeared to have a dash of the gentleman in black about him. . . ."

While the Bow River Expedition was abroad, battling the winds and snows of the prairies, and while Pierre Bungo was seeking shelter and solace in tent and tepee, Simpson came out west for the first time. After spending a few days at Edmonton in March 1823, he went on to Rocky Mountain House, where he discussed the problems of the West with John Rowand. By this time it was evident that the Bow River Expedition had been a failure and Rowand had returned to Rocky Mountain House. With his background of nearly twenty years spent in Alberta, Rowand was able to show Simpson that, while business with the Plains Indians was profitable, the best way to conduct it was from Edmonton House and from its subsidiary post two hundred miles upstream. By the time Simpson returned to Edmonton where he remained till May 10 when the brigade was able to float downstream with the furs, he had ample time to realize that Edmonton was the focal point of the West. By this time too he had decided to put John Rowand in charge of it.

During his stay at Edmonton, Simpson decided to build Fort Assiniboine on the Athabasca River some eighty miles north and west of Edmonton. This post, which would serve as a stopping place for brigades going up or down the Athabasca on their way to or from the Pacific Coast, would also serve as a half-way house for traffic between Edmonton and Lesser Slave Lake and the Peace River country in general. For at this time the Athabasca River formed part of the only trans-Canada water highway, and all traffic to Oregon and the Coast passed up or down it. The route in use came from the east through Lake Winnipeg and up the Saskatchewan River as far as Cumberland House in eastern Saskatchewan. From there it left that river and detoured over to the Churchill, which the brigades ascended as far as its most westerly headwater, the Beaver River. Then by pushing their canoes up its tortuous and often nearly dry meanderings in eastern Alberta until they neared Lac La Biche, they made a short portage to that lake. Once they reached it, they struck out for its north-west corner and paddled down its frustrating s-curved outlet to the Athabasca River. Then they headed upstream past the site of modern Athabasca town and on to Fort Assiniboine, and then upstream to Jasper. From there, by crossing the Athabasca Pass, they reached the mighty Columbia, which they followed to the Coast.

In 1824, following this route, Simpson set out for the Coast. On such trips he was a furious traveller, pushing his men to exert themselves to the utmost. Leaving York Factory on August 15, he reached Fort Assiniboine on October 2.

There, to his surprise, he found that Rowand, who had left York Factory a couple of weeks before him and who had paddled up the Saskatchewan to Edmonton and then set out for Fort Assiniboine, had been there four days earlier, and, thinking he had missed Simpson, had returned to Edmonton. Though Rowand had made an earlier start from York Factory, he had had to travel far more slowly with his laden boats than the swift-journeying Governor with his light canoes. Even though two months earlier Simpson had been ready to swear that the route he had followed would prove the most economical one, now at Fort Assiniboine, faced with the evidence Rowand had provided, he was quick to change his mind.

With that convincing proof of its superiority, he ordered that the Saskatchewan route be used exclusively from then on. His initial move was to construct the first long road to be made in Alberta: "Sept. 21st, 1824. With Cardinal the Freeman I made an agreement that he should in the course of this ensuing Winter and Spring get a Horse track or road cut from Fort Assiniboine to Edmonton House. . . ." He estimated that by using the route the company would save one thousand pounds a year.

Once more John Rowand had served Edmonton well. Early in 1823 he had convinced Simpson that Edmonton should be the most important point in the West. Now, a year and a half later, he had raised its status by showing that the most practical route across Canada to the Coast should pass through Edmonton. Striking while the iron was hot, he took steps to capitalize on this new advantage and set to work to make Edmonton House the most important post west of York Factory and to build it up into the main depot for brigades heading west for the Pacific Coast and for those heading north into the Mackenzie River Basin.

Under his prideful eye, aided at times by his forceful fists, Edmonton House prospered. Prior to the amalgamation of the two companies, Rowand, as a Northwester, had always been a thorn under the nails of all Hudson's Bay Company men. Now that that company, the victor in the recent fray, had recognized his great ability and had set him up as its leading man in the Edmonton area, he turned all his many talents towards its interests and not only became its most capable employee but also its most loyal.

In the same way that the amalgamation had brought about a major change in Rowand's attitude and a change for the better, it likewise revolutionized the fur trade. Prior to 1821 competition had kept the West turbulent. The Indians, foolish indeed in the matter of liquor but otherwise shrewd traders, took advantage of the split in the white men's ranks. In those days the West had only one resource, and since its utilization required a far-flung, expensive organization, the facts of economics dictated that its successful exploitation could be carried out only by a monopoly. In the year 1822, before the benefits of amalgamation had time to take effect, the loss on the Saskatchewan River operations was £4,000. This had been one of the reasons why Governor Simpson had toyed with the idea of abandoning Edmonton House.

With John Rowand's ham-like fists holding the reins, and with Governor Simpson's fine Italian hand guiding the whole monopolistic Canadian fur trade chariot, the situation was about to change. First of all, many of the old competing posts were closed down, and those which, like Edmonton House, were left, rose in importance. Next, as soon as possible, the number of men employed during the days of competition was reduced to the bare minimum. Then Governor Simpson reorganized the transportation system, substituting York boats for the more romantic but more costly canoes, and went on to re-orient the routes of transport. All of these moves cut down expenses.

Now that monopolistic control could be exercised nearly all over Canada, the Hudson's Bay Company returned to its old-time practice of treating the natives well. In the matter of liquor, in 1822 the London Committee wrote Simpson, saying: "In the course of 2 or 3 years at farthest we think the use of spirits among the Indians of all the best fur countries may be entirely given up, and that the quantities given to them may safely be reduced immediately to one-third."

While these instructions applied all over Canada, conditions along the Saskatchewan River, which ran along the north side of the prairies, made it impractical to enforce them there. For some five hundred miles to the south the Missouri River brought American traders into contact with the Plains Indians. And when a roaring thirst parched Blackfeet or Gros Ventre, five hundred miles was regarded as a mere jaunt if a skinful of fire water lay at the end of it. So, though liquor was kept from Indians in the regions where the Hudson's Bay Company had no competition, it could not be cut out entirely at Edmonton House.

The Hudson's Bay Company's paternalistic attitude towards its Indians in the matter of liquor was, of course, as good for business as it was for the Indians; it cut costs. But the company's injunction to its traders to treat Indians as if they were human beings and to deny them grog was not founded solely on the matter of profits. At that time a wave of humanitarian sympathy had swept over Britain to such an extent that made it politic, if nothing else, for the Committee in London to lay down this course. Whatever may have been its cause, however, the regulations prevailing during Simpson's regime mark a great contrast to the period of violence that preceded the amalgamation. The repeated injunction that the Indians must be treated with civility goes far towards explaining the control the company exercised over them. The consequent comparative orderliness of life in Rupert's Land was in marked contrast to the era of hatred and bloodshed which reigned south of the international boundary.

For the next three decades under Rowand's careful supervision the Edmonton area enjoyed a period of relative calm. It was hard to rule the Plains Indians and impossible to deny them some liquor, but on the whole, peace and quiet settled over the area. During Rowand's regime, which ended only with his death in 1854, he contributed as much to Edmonton's development as any other man in its history.

Perhaps because of the centuries of pomp and circumstance that lay behind the Hudson's Bay Company employees, its English and Scottish traders were past masters at impressing the Indians. With the deep love of ceremony as manifested in all their dances, secret societies and religion, the natives could appreciate and applaud similar ceremony when conducted by white men. Rowand, for instance, as head of the district, adhered to the ceremonial by which his chief factor's position was exalted. Like similar chief factors, and usually dressed in a suit of black or dark blue, white shirt, collars to his ears, frock coat and so on, he rarely ventured out of doors without his black beaver hat worth forty shillings.

When travelling by boat, he, like other chief factors, was lifted out of the craft by the crew. In camp, his tent was pitched apart from the shelter given his boatmen. Salutes were fired on his departure from a fort or on his return. And all this ceremony was thought necessary because it did impress the Indians, and in the eyes of his subordinates it added to his dignity.

If, however, John Rowand played his part in impressing the Indians, his boss, Governor Simpson, on his occasional visits to Edmonton, also put on a magnificent show. He travelled in a style befitting the stature to which he and his office had grown. After 1826, when Colin Fraser, a Highlander whom he had recruited, came out specifically to act as his piper, his arrival at a post was an event to be remembered.

Piping away as the canoes slipped along, or by the campfires in the evenings, Fraser also played a full part in the ceremonial approach to the posts. In full Highland costume he marched between the guide bearing the company's flag and the Governor, playing Highland marches which not only stirred the souls of the Scots, but as well moved the Indians deeply.

But there was far more to Simpson or to John Rowand than empty ceremony. At Edmonton House, for instance, Rowand had to get more land under cultivation, and soon, as Alexander Ross, who passed there in 1825, said, there were "two large parks for raising grain, and, the soil being good, it produces large crops of barley and potatoes; but the spring and fall frosts prove injurious to wheat, which, in consequence seldom comes to maturity".

In 1825 one of the recurring high floods drove the traders out of their buildings. The river rose high enough to spread out over the flat on which hitherto the two forts had reposed high and dry. Since the amalgamation of the companies, the Northwesters' buildings had been relegated to living quarters and Edmonton House carried on as the trading establishment. While the flood drove everybody out, nevertheless, the staff reoccupied the fort as soon as it subsided and Rowand carried on at the old stand.

Now that Edmonton, at the end of practical navigation on the upper Saskatchewan, was being built up to become the main depot in Western Canada, it was a busy place. Early in October each year some ten boats manned by fifty men arrived from York Factory. Immediately the goods were carried into the store and everything wet was set out to dry. Then the crews appeared for their *regale*— a quart of rum to steersmen, a pint to the men at the bow, and half a pint to the middlemen. Beginning in this manner, the merry-making culminated in the dance in the chief factor's house where eight- and four-hand reels and single and double jigs were the favourites. Everyone from the chief factor's family to the Orkney blacksmith and his household, and the middleman's squaw, took part in this joyous opening of the season at the fort.

But the fur trade was a stern master, and the outfits for the upper posts must be hurried onward over the portage to Fort Assiniboine. For this purpose, the company kept two "horse-guards" where it pastured these animals. A large one lay beyond the Sturgeon River north of St. Albert, while another was located at Lac La Nonne. It says much for the relations of the company with the Indians that some four hundred horses could be kept safely at these distances from the fort, guarded only by a man or two.

Within three or four days of the dance, the trains of pack horses would be off. In a normal year the first to leave consisted of twenty-eight horses carrying goods and provisions. It was taken overland to Fort Assiniboine and then by boat upstream to the post on Jasper Lake.

The next outfit was loaded on forty-three horses. At Fort Assiniboine it would be stowed into boats, which slipped down the Athabasca as far as present day Smith, and then with mighty effort were towed up the fast-water portion of

Lesser Slave Lake River and then rowed the remainder of the way to Lesser Slave Lake House at the north-westerly corner of the lake.

Having seen these two pack trains off, the staff at Edmonton House then loaded seven horses with the supplies needed at Fort Assiniboine, and it too moved out along the way, which some years later was to become known as the St. Albert Trail.

With these outfits on their way, the chief factor would then turn his attention to the Indians, who, in anticipation of the arrival of a fresh supply of goods, had come in to trade. When they arrived in a band, they too observed due ceremony. As they saluted those in the fort by a friendly discharge of firearms, the old guns in the bastions of Edmonton House burst forth with a salvo perhaps more potentially dangerous to those who fired than to any enemy against whom they may ever have been directed. Following these salutes which echoed and re-echoed from the wooded banks of the valley, the Indians marched in procession through the widely thrown gate and up to the great hall, where the chief factor met them. Then, for hours, amidst sedate smoking, traders and chiefs in solemn council discussed the happenings in the trade and the luck or misadventures the Indians had experienced since their last visit. Next day the actual trading started, and one band after another would be given goods and ammunition on credit and allowed to go north, south, east or west to hunt furs or pemmican to bring in later to pay off the credit given them.

About the same time, several servants had their hands full bringing in the crop. Barley and oats were not too much of a problem, but since the wheat of that era took about 135 days to ripen, and, therefore, usually froze, it was rarely sown. It appeared quite certain that the Edmonton area would never be a wheat growing country. But potatoes were another matter, and each year, to feed the staff during the coming season, hundreds of bushels were dug up and stored.

Meat was another problem. Several half-breeds and Indians attached to Edmonton House regularly contracted to bring in buffalo meat from the prairies. The roving Indians also brought in fresh or dried meat, as well as grease and pemmican. In addition, men were sent out to the fishery at Lac Ste. Anne to catch thousands of fish to add to the food supply. For at Edmonton House the large staff of perhaps fifty men and their native families consumed immense piles of provisions. Then too, starving Indians who came in had to be fed, and so did some of their old or infirm, who soon found the fort a haven in their distress. Furthermore, the staff had to make enough pemmican to provision the brigades which swept up or down the river every spring and fall and were in too much hurry to depend upon the uncertainty of hunting as they sped along.

To keep the place warm during the winter, several men were sent upstream to raft down firewood. Undoubtedly, too, the blacksmith gathered coal from the river bank to mix with charcoal for his forge. At the same time, other men working at the saw-pit whip-sawed lumber; one man standing on the log, while the other below drew the saw down to cut.

Most of the year, therefore, Edmonton House was a busy place. The company's carpenter was kept at the usual repairs and alterations necessary in an establishment of this size. Furthermore, he had to supervise the boat building, because Edmonton House turned out not only the York boats needed to carry its own goods and supplies, but most of those used all along the Saskatchewan. The blacksmith made nails and iron-work, mended plough shares, and on occasion made sheet-iron stoves.

Spring too was a busy time, with its heavy trade in pemmican, dried meat, grease, and furs, and the packing and pressing of the "pieces" for their long journey to the sea. The staff hastily ploughed and seeded the farm. Then the trains of horses began to arrive with the furs from Fort Assiniboine and the boats arrived from Rocky Mountain House. All the incoming furs were inspected, packed, and loaded into the boats, while some of the staff were selected and additional help in the shape of half-breeds hired for the long trip to York Fort. About the middle of May the brigade set off down the river with most of the men of the fort. Now that the busy season was over, the long summer's quiet settled down on the post, only to be broken by occasional visits of the Blackfeet.

As Rowand carried out Simpson's able policies and improvised some of his own, prosperity returned to Edmonton House. Its expenses fell, and its profits rose. The once-risky Saskatchewan District was now back on the even keel which only a monopoly could ensure.

Once more, in May 1825, Governor Simpson visited Edmonton, and being well pleased with what he saw, commented in his diary: "Mr. Rowand up to his ears in business as usual and without exception he is the most active and best qualified person for the troublesome charge he has got of any man in the Indian country."

On another occasion he described Rowand as: "One of the most pushing and bustling men in the Service whose zeal and ambition in the discharge of his duty is unequalled, rendering him totally regardless of every personal comfort and indulgence. Warm hearted and friendly to an extraordinary degree where he takes a liking, but on the contrary his prejudices exceeding strong. Of a fiery disposition and bold as a Lion. An excellent trader who has the peculiar talent of attracting the fiercest Indians to him while he rules them with a rod of Iron and so daring that he beards their chiefs in the open Camp while surrounded by their warriors; has likewise a Wonderful influence over his people. . . . Will not tell a lie publick (which) is very common in this country but has sufficient address to evade the truth when it suits his purpose; full of drollery and good humor and generally liked and respected by Indians, Servants and his own equals."

So much was Simpson impressed with Rowand's merit that in 1826 he promoted him to chief factor of the whole Saskatchewan District with his headquarters in Edmonton. This district extended from Rocky Mountain House far into Saskatchewan, as well as including Jasper House, Fort Assiniboine and Lesser Slave Lake. Between them, Simpson and Rowand had set Edmonton on its course.

Rowand's Big House completed 1832 and torn down 1875. Photo taken 1871.

John Rowand's Regime
1830-1854

chapter 3

I N 1830 ANOTHER FLOOD, worse than the previous one, made it advisable to move Edmonton House to higher ground. The old buildings had been getting into poor shape anyway, and Rowand was glad of the opportunity of laying out a better and more commodious establishment. The work of rebuilding was not completed until 1832, but everyone was so pleased with the new fort that for a while they renamed it Fort Sanspareil. This change appears to have been viewed coolly in London and the new name was dropped.

While the new fort was under construction, Rowand and his men built the imposing "Big House," or "Rowand's Folly," as some of his critics called it. It appears to have been finished early in 1832. It was about thirty by eighty feet, having three stories in addition to a basement. Along the front and back, galleries ran the full length of the building. The Big House, by far the largest west of York Factory, was well provided with windows made up of panes of glass about seven inches by eight inches. To the Indians, this glass, the first to be used in the West, was a seven days' wonder. With his unrivalled grasp of Indian psychology, Rowand saw how this mansion would impress them. But it also impressed all white visitors, including George Simpson, who, when he visited it in 1841, wrote:

"Edmonton is a well-built place, something of a hexagon in form. It is surrounded by high pickets and bastions, which, with the battlemented gateways, the flagstaffs, etc., give it a good deal of a martial appearance; and it occupies a commanding situation, crowning an almost perpendicular part of the bank of about two hundred feet in height . . .

"This fort, both inside and outside, is decorated with paintings and devices to suit the taste of the savages that frequent it. Over the gateway are a most fanciful variety of vanes; but the hall, of which both the ceiling and the walls present the grandest colors and the most fantastic sculpture, absolutely rivets the astonished natives to the spot with wonder and admiration. The buildings are smeared with a red earth, found in the neighborhood, which, when mixed with oil, produces a durable brown."

With such a fortress as Edmonton House and with its monopoly firmly established, the Hudson's Bay Company was in a position to rule the West. The monopoly aspect was most important. Now, the company could take steps to

John Rowand — Entered North West Company's service in 1803. At amalgamation of companies in 1821 he became an employee of the Hudson's Bay Company, and two years later became Chief Trader at Edmonton House, where, except for holidays, he remained until his death in 1854. During half a century he exerted a mighty influence towards Edmonton's progress.

conserve the beaver. The London Committee kept hammering away at this desirable objective. Each year after the amalgamation it sent out various directives to this end. In 1841, for instance, it said: "That the Gentlemen in charge of Districts and Posts be strictly enjoined to discourage the Hunting of Beaver by every means in their power; and that not more than half the number collected Outfit 1839 be traded during the Current and two ensuing Outfits . . . That the Governor and Committee be respectfully advised to give notice of retirement from the Service to such Gentlemen as may not give effect to the spirit and letter of the Resolutions . . ."

These steps towards conservation taken well over a century ago are certainly amongst the early, if indeed they are not the first, such measures applied anywhere in Canada. Having then been in business some 170 years, the Hudson's Bay Company had learned lessons which another century later were only beginning to be perceived in Canada.

By now, because it was one of the company's important depots and because it was on the trans-Canada route, Edmonton House kept in touch with almost half a continent. The Hudson's Bay Company supplied its posts along the Pacific Coast from San Francisco to Alaska by sea, but, when messages had to be sent rapidly, they sped through Edmonton. So did the personnel for these posts, which were ever changing as new recruits went west and time-expired men came back across the mountains. And all these, when they reached Edmonton House, had some news to tell John Rowand.

While he could bring efficiency to bear on the operations along the Saskatchewan and to the north, where the company had no competition, the situation to the south constantly worried him. There, the Americans on the Missouri were steadily encroaching on territory and dealing with Plains Indians which the Hudson's Bay Company regarded as in its bailiwick. To try to counter them, Rowand sent men out to live with the Piegans in southern Alberta. In 1826 and again in 1827, William McGillivray, a half-breed, led these men. Then in 1831 Rowand sent out a colourful character called Jamey Jock, a half-breed son of James

Bird. Jamey was given a large quantity of goods and told to oppose the Americans well out towards the Missouri River in Montana. Alas, for Rowand's hopes, the American Fur Company, which was busy setting up a post where the Yellowstone River joins the Missouri, near Williston, North Dakota, proved able to buy Jamey Jock lock, stock and barrel, including some three or four thousand beaver pelts which really belonged to Edmonton House.

Rowand's next move was to send out a strong force in 1832, under J. E. Harriott, to build what was called Piegan Post on the north side of the Bow River, not far east of Canmore. Sometime previously Harriott had married his cousin, Margaret Pruden, and in 1829, when he was in the general area of Prince George, she had an attack of insanity. The next year at Fort Vancouver the couple had a daughter Margaret. Harriott's trip east that year, on which he was accompanied by his wife and infant daughter, was a tragic one. Mrs. Harriott, possibly because of her mental state, became lost in the mountains and no trace of her was ever found. The infant Margaret was kept alive with difficulty until the party reached Edmonton.

Scarcely a year went by but what some tragedy occurred in the mountains or on the rapid water of the Columbia River. About this time, a harrowing experience befell A. C. Anderson, who in September 1835 set out from Edmonton for Prince George. Taking forty packs of dressed moose skins needed for leather in British Columbia, the party ran into disastrous storms in the Yellowhead Pass and had to fall back on Jasper House. Shortage of provisions there, however, made them return half-starved to Edmonton House, from whence they set out west once more. For many years cargoes of leather similar to this one were sent from Edmonton through the Yellowhead Pass, and before long, all the traders referred to it as the Leather Pass.

But getting back to Harriott, his post on the Bow River was not a success, because the Piegans, in whose territory it was built, regarded it as an unwelcome intrusion. As a result, after struggling along for two winters, Harriott closed it in 1834. He then assumed charge of Rocky Mountain House, and the company had to content itself with what trade the Piegans and other Plains Indians would bring there. As a rule, though Harriott remained in charge there until 1841, Rocky Mountain House was closed each summer.

Because of the turbulence of the Blackfeet and other Plains Indians, Edmonton House was indeed a troublesome charge. In a letter which John Rowand wrote in January 1840, he revealed some of his tribulations. Speaking of American competition, he said:

". . . But I am sorry to say we are losing ground with the Slave (Blackfoot) tribes who laugh at the poverty of our shops and who do not hesitate to remind one of the old times before they got introduced to the American traders when they had but one shop to go to. . . . What they speak most of is about the presents the Indians receive from the Americans twice a year. . . . The Peigans who are the worst of all the Slave tribes to please expect a great many things for nothing. They are all Chiefs who must be dressed as such, Gratis of course. If not, off they go back to the Americans where they say they are sure of being well received for their few furs, Buffalo Robes, Wolves and their Horses. (These) form one of their principle articles of trade with the Americans and us too, to enable us to keep up the number of Horses so much required for the Company's work and for sales to our men and Indians, etc. . . ."

Then, as an example of the difficulty of dealing with the Plains people, he tells how out on the prairies, when on their way to Edmonton, some Gros Ventres and Blackfeet who had been induced to "turn their backs on the Americans" were slaughtered by some Crees and Saulteaux. Out of thirty-eight tents of Gros Ventres and Blackfeet "only six Crees and two Soteaux remained upon the place of bloodshed. The others after taking the scalps of more than one hundred men, women and children got off with upwards of two hundred horses and everything else they found worth carrying with them. Not very long ago another small camp of Cercees was attacked by some plain Crees and Stone Indians who killed a few of them also and took their horses. For all these misfortunes we are the ones who get blamed for it for inviting them back to us."

Poor Rowand was indeed having his troubles, and others were in store for him. Like Tomison years before him, he had repeatedly and unsuccessfully asked to have a cooper attached to Edmonton House. He pointed out that the Blackfeet "who get as much liquor as they like from the Americans and who are becoming most determined drunkard dogs as ever was, of late feel not a little displeased with us because they cannot get liquor to take away with them, as with the Americans, all for the want of small kegs. As ridiculous as this may appear to someone it is of more consequence to us here than they may suppose. Kegs would prevent quarrels and save goods in scarce times. You may all think as you like but the Americans give more liquor to the Indians than we ever did here; we have proof enough to make me say so".

During all of Rowand's long sojourn at Edmonton, the Plains Indians and the Americans were never far from his mind. A year or so earlier than this letter, however, he forgot them for a while, because from September 6 to 10, 1838, Edmonton House placed itself at the disposal of the first two missionaries ever to reach Alberta. On that occasion Fathers François Blanchet and Modeste Demers, acting under the orders of Bishop Provencher of St. Boniface on the Red River, stopped at Edmonton on their way to open a mission at Fort Vancouver. During their stay they performed thirty-seven baptisms and three marriages.

Most of the names in the register of baptisms were, of course, French, an indication of the preponderance of that race amongst the voyageurs and laborers in the service of the fur trade. Since so many of these surnames occur and reoccur in the history of the West, it might be well to list them here: Saloy, Patenaude, Banquet, Parisien, Jacques, Berlant, Paulet, Auger, Leblanc, Racette, Vilneuve, Boucher, Lucier and Hibert. The non-French names include children of Hugh Munro and grandchildren of John Ward, who, with Peter Fidler, around 1792 spent so much time in the Alberta area. Then too, the names of Rowand and Harriott were prominent in the list.

Of the three marriages recorded in this register, two concerned the Rowand family. The priest baptised Nancy Rowand and her two children and then gave church sanction to her marriage of three or four years' standing to Edward Harriott, son of Chief Trader J. E. Harriott. John Rowand, who for so long had lived happily with Louise Umfreville since their union in 1811, took advantage of the Reverend Fathers' presence to tidy up some of his family affairs. With his son John Junior acting as godfather, three of his other daughters were baptised; Sofie, born August 30, 1814; Marguerite, born July 5, 1825; and Adelaide, born February 8, 1832. Hardy old John Rowand seems to have run heavily to daughters.

Pleased as he must have been to set his family affairs in order, this visit of missionaries provided food for thought. Hitherto no one not directly concerned with the fur trade had ever visited the Edmonton area, and now these priests, the narrow edge of the wedge of civilization, had put in an appearance. Rowand had always felt that in the matter of religion the Hudson's Bay Company was sufficient unto itself. As chief factor, he had dutifully followed the company's instructions in providing a sincere religious service for the employees every Sunday. But now with this visit of Fathers Blanchet and Demers, Edmonton House had its first official service with candle and book.

And yet he must have wondered too if it were not time to have a few missionaries to keep some semblance of religious order. Around Edmonton House and the other posts along the river, the tally of half-breed children of voyageurs and of Hudson's Bay Company laborers and traders was growing apace. Some lived and traded with the Indians, and some had already moved out to support themselves as fishermen at Lac Ste. Anne and Lac La Nonne, but since they were increasing far more rapidly than the company could employ them, they were a growing problem. Maybe if missionaries came out, they could settle these people into something approaching an agrarian life.

In any event, Rowand had mixed feelings as he watched the two fathers fashion a crude cross and plant it on the point of the hill above the fort and within the space now occupied by the Legislative Building. Having done that, they went on their way with the annual westward Columbia Brigade, which, with more than a hundred pack or riding horses, set out over the eighty-mile portage to Fort Assiniboine.

But the winds of change were blowing, and about two years later, on October 18, 1840, the Reverend Robert Terrill Rundle, the first missionary to reside in the Edmonton area arrived. As a result of co-operative action between the old fur trading company and the Wesleyan Society of London, England, Rundle, a man of great zeal and fortitude, crossed the sea to face conditions of which he had only a vague conception. Though he arrived under the handicap of being a "greenhorn," he remained until the spring of 1848, and during that interval proved to be a man of rare courage. Going out to find and to tend his flock, he ranged from modern Saskatoon on the east to Jasper on the west, and from Banff in the south where now the impressive mountain bears his name, to Lesser Slave Lake in the north. Suffering great hardship at times, and once returning to Edmonton House alone with an arm that had been broken days before, he nevertheless made a mark upon Cree and Stoney that persisted for generations.

John Rowand, though of the Roman persuasion and at times a difficult man to like, nevertheless treated Rundle well, afforded him the hospitality of the fort and gave such assistance as he could. Before long, however, Rowand, still wondering what to do with one missionary, found that he had another on his hands when the Reverend Father A. Thibault, an Oblate from St. Boniface, arrived on June 19, 1842. This worthy man, who travelled hither and yon serving the natives and Métis, covered the same territory as Rundle. A year or so later, after sizing up the situation, he established a mission amongst the half-breeds at Lac Ste. Anne. Here, in a soil that could be cultivated and near the Hudson's Bay Company's old fishery station, he hoped to induce the Métis to settle down to farm. He hoped also that here, back in the bush, far removed from the reach of attacking Plains Indians, the Crees could worship in peace.

But John Rowand, with his joints stiffening after some forty years in the fur trade and his mind settling down into a pattern that looked back upon the good old days, was doubtful of the value of the missionaries. Writing to a friend in

1843, he expressed the opinion that: "The worst thing for the trade is those ministers and priests—the natives will never work half so well now—they like praying and singing. Mr. Thingheaute (Thibault) is allowed to go back again to the Saskatchewan. We shall all be saints after a time. Rundle says that all Catholics will go to . . . for himself he is sure of going straite to heaven when he dies, but he longs to get a wife. . . ."

Presiding over such a far-flung empire kept Governor Simpson running hither and thither around the continent at a sort of dog trot. In 1839 the British government, realizing the stupendous effort he was putting forth on behalf of the empire, elevated him to the rank of knight. This recognition spurred him to even greater heights. Since his company was also dealing with Russians in Alaska and Mandarins in China, and had way stations at Honolulu and the Sandwich Islands, he decided in 1841 to take a trip around the world.

In doing so, he visited Edmonton once more, and, accompanied by John Rowand, who went to meet him, he started from Fort Garry on July 3. The party had about thirty horses and one light cart, and they planned to change horses at the Hudson's Bay Company's main posts at Forts Ellice, Carlton, Pitt and Edmonton. Although Simpson rode, he was probably the first to bring a wheeled vehicle all the way from Winnipeg to Edmonton along the trail which came to be known as the Carlton or Edmonton Trail. Covering forty or fifty miles a day, he made the trip in twenty-two days.

When Sir George's party left Edmonton, they travelled by pack horses along a new route, which took them south past Gull Lake to Lake Minnewanka and on through what is now Banff and the pass that now bears Simpson's name. They were twenty-one days on the trail before reaching Fort Colville, which was a few miles upstream from the Grand Coulee Dam of modern times. From there Simpson and Rowand floated down the Columbia to Fort Vancouver, which was located on the right bank of the river across from the modern city of Portland. Ultimately the two men sailed across the Pacific to Honolulu, and then at the Sandwich Islands, while Simpson went on to Russia and then via London to Canada, John Rowand turned back towards Edmonton. By spending the winter at Honolulu, he must surely have been the first Edmontonian to swelter under palm trees during January and February.

One interesting episode took place while Sir George was at Edmonton. Though John Rowand may have had his difficulties with the Blackfeet, Bloods and Piegans, they came in to greet Simpson, whom they knew was ruler of all the West. The missionaries who had but recently appeared in the country might talk to them of a Supreme Being or of the Great White Mother overseas, but to them Simpson was an all-powerful Manitou. On this occasion he was here in person, and they did not miss the opportunity to wait on him. Quoting Simpson again:

" These chiefs were Blackfeet, Piegans, Sarcees and Blood Indians, all dressed in their grandest clothes and decorated with scalp locks. I paid them a visit, giving each of them some tobacco. Instead of receiving their presents with the usual indifference of savages, they thanked me in rotation, and, taking my hand in theirs, made long prayers to me as a high and powerful conjuror. They implored me to grant, that their horses might be swift, that the buffalo might constantly abound, and that their wives might live long and look young."

These chiefs were clear headed. What greater good could Plains Indians want—or for that matter, their white brothers?

Simpson's trip seemed to be the signal that set loose a comparative flood of travellers upon Edmonton House. During the next decade, many strangers, either not connected with or only remotely related to the fur trade, availed themselves of Edmonton's hospitality.

Even when he was on his jaunt around the world, his main worry went with him. England and the United States were competing for the possession of the territory which we know as the states of Washington and Oregon. Britain rightfully claimed all of the west coast between the limits set by the Russians in Alaska and the Mexicans in California, and based her claim upon the fact that the Hudson's Bay Company traders had occupied the country and traded in it for years. America, however, was casting longing eyes on it. In the fall of 1841 a few American families completed the long trek over the Oregon Trail. In 1842 one hundred and fourteen people reached Oregon by the same route. The rush of Americans to the coast was on, and increased in tempo year after year. Before leaving Edmonton, Simpson did what he could to fill Oregon with Canadians, and took steps to send twenty-three families of Red River half-breeds out there. He had arranged that they were to be given land, livestock and implements, and that generally the company would take them under its wing. These emigrants set out from Fort Garry, and when they reached Edmonton House found J. E. Harriott in charge during Rowand's absence. Leaving there, they too took the same general route Simpson had taken, but instead of following exactly in his steps, James Sinclair, their guide, took them through the pass we still know as Sinclair Pass.

Sinclair's party of Canadians was soon swallowed up by the much greater influx of Americans to Oregon, and for the next few years settlers from the easterly United States continued to pour in. By 1844, the year of the presidential election, a great clamor arose to drive the British and the Hudson's Bay Company out. During the whole of the winter of 1844-1845 Sir George Simpson remained in London to advise the British government. By spring, the possibility of war was very real. As a result, Lord Metcalfe, Governor-General of Canada, working with Simpson, sent two military men, Lieutenants H. J. Warre and M. Vavasour, across Canada to Fort Vancouver. They were to study the line of communication across the country to see what could be done to fortify it, as well as Fort Vancouver, and to make recommendations for garrisoning such places as Fort Garry and Edmonton House. So as not to arouse suspicion, they were to travel in the guise of a hunting party.

Our interest in this pair is that Lieut. Vavasour drew a plan of Edmonton House as it was in mid-summer 1845, and suggested that as a military post it left much to be desired. A copy of this plan is shown on page 27.

Of all the travellers who spent some time at the Edmonton House of those early days, Paul Kane has left us the best picture we have of the state of affairs there. Now regarded as one of Canada's great early artists, he persuaded Sir George Simpson to let him accompany one of the brigades to Oregon. On this trip he painted innumerable pictures of Indian life in the far West, and later on wrote one of Canada's most interesting travel books, which he called *Wanderings of an Artist*.

Somewhere not far from present day Vermilion, Kane came upon one of the usual sights of the prairies:

"Sept. 24th [1846] — We passed through what is called the Long Grass Prairie. The bones of a whole camp of Indians, who were carried off by that fatal scourge of their race, the small-pox, were here bleaching on the plains, having fallen from the platforms and trees on which it is their custom to suspend their dead, covered with skins,—which latter, as well as the supports, time had destroyed."

In travelling through the country south of modern Willingdon, Kane ran into buffalo, for he said: "We had much difficulty that evening in finding a place to encamp away from the immense number of buffaloes that surrounded us, and we found it necessary to fire off our guns during the night to keep them away. . . ."

Then on September 26, Kane and Rowand forded the river to Edmonton House. The artist's description of the fort gives a good idea of the conditions there.

"Edmonton is a large establishment . . . with forty or fifty men with their wives and children, amounting altogether to about 130, who all live within the pickets of the fort. Their employment consists chiefly in building boats for the trade, sawing timber, most of which they raft down the river from ninety miles higher up, cutting up the small poplar which abounds on the margin of the river for fire-wood, 800 cords of which are consumed every winter, to supply the numerous fires in the establishment. The employment of the women, who are all, without a single exception, either squaws or half-breeds, consists in making moccasins and clothing for the men, and converting the dried meat into pemmican."

Writing about the plentiful provisions of the post, Kane said they consisted "of fresh buffalo meat, venison, salted geese, magnificent whitefish, and rabbits in abundance, with plenty of good potatoes, turnips and flour. . . ."

Continuing, he described the storing of meat and the great ice house, which was a feature common to all the forts which collected meat from the plains. "This is made by digging a square hole, capable of containing 700 or 800 buffalo carcases. As soon as the ice in the river is of sufficient thickness, it is cut into square blocks of uniform size with saws; with these blocks the floor of the pit is regularly paved, and the blocks cemented together by pouring water in between them, and allowing it to freeze solid. In like manner, the walls are solidly built up to the surface of the ground. The head and feet of the buffalo, when killed, are cut off, and the carcase, without being skinned, is divided into quarters, and piled in layers in the pit as brought in, until it is filled up, when the whole is covered with a thick coating of straw, which is again protected from the sun and rain by a shed. In this manner the meat keeps perfectly good through the whole summer and eats much better than fresh killed meat, being more tender and better flavoured."

Kane left us a description of Christmas dinner at Edmonton, which, though often quoted, will bear repetition.

". . . No tablecloth shed its snowy whiteness over the board; no silver candelabra or gaudy china interfered with its simple magnificance. The bright tin plates and dishes reflected jolly faces and burnished gold can give no truer zest to a feast. . . .

"At the head, before Mr. Harriett was a large dish of boiled buffalo-hump; at the foot smoked a boiled buffalo calf. Start not, gentle reader, the calf is very small, and is taken from the cow by the Caesarean operation long before it attains its full growth. This, boiled whole, is one of the most esteemed dishes amongst the epicures of the interior. My pleasing duty was to help a dish of mouffle, or dried moose nose; the gentleman on my left distributed, with graceful impartiality, the white fish, delicately browned in buffalo marrow. The worthy priest helped the buffalo tongue, whilst Mr. Rundell cut up the beavers' tails. Nor was the other gentleman left unemployed, as all his spare time was occupied in dissecting a roast wild goose. The centre of the table was graced with piles of potatoes, turnips, and bread conveniently placed, so that each could help himself without interrupting the labours of his companions. Such was our jolly Christmas dinner at Edmonton; and long will it remain in my memory, although no pies, or puddings, or blanc manges shed their fragrance over the scene. . . ."

On January 6, 1848, the Harriott and Rowand families were drawn still closer by the marriage of Rowand's son John, who was in charge of Fort Pitt, to Margaret, daughter of J. E. Harriott. This was the girl who was brought to Edmonton House as a babe in arms when in 1830 her mother had perished in the Yellowhead Pass. Participants at the wedding must have recalled the day some nine years earlier when Harriott's son had married Rowand's daughter Nancy. On that occasion young Harriott, a Protestant, was united in marriage with Nancy, a Roman Catholic, by a priest of that faith. Now, at the time of Kane's visit, young Rowand, a Catholic, was wed to Margaret, a Protestant, by the Rev. Mr. Rundle, a Methodist.

Along the same lines, when on November 8, 1840, the infant daughter of Harriott Jr. and Nancy Rowand was baptised, the Rev. Mr. Rundle performed the ceremony. When the second child, a son, came along in 1842, however, Rev. Father Thibault was there to christen him.

At the time of Paul Kane's visit, Rundle was nearing the end of his mission to the Edmonton area. In July 1848, worn to a skeleton after nearly eight years of hardship, he returned to England, and for the next few years the Methodists had no ordained missionary in the area. Time and time again, we read of missionaries breaking down under the continual hardship. Father Thibault's health gave way under the load imposed on it, and in 1852 he returned to St. Boniface. By this time, however, Father Bourassa was at Lac Ste. Anne, so that the Edmonton area was not totally bereft of priestly consolation.

Though a few years in the Edmonton area was all these missionaries could stand, nearly five decades seemed to merely whet John Rowand's appetite for more. Even at that, by 1851 Rowand, then over sixty, was beginning to notice his age. In writing to a friend from Edmonton on December 28 that year, he said: "I make difficulties where there are none; people after being so long in the service get useless. . . ." There was also, as always, the other side of the story. Eden Colvile, deputizing for Governor Simpson, made several references to Rowand. At times this young man, so recently arrived on the scene, must have found the old chief factor a bit difficult. Thus, in the summer the same year as Rowand's letter quoted above, Colvile wrote:

"He does not seem to have the least intention of retiring, though I think it would be almost as well for the concern. . . . At the same time I should be sorry to turn (him) out, though perhaps this visit to Red River may put it into his head to retire to that place." And again, ". . . I cannot make out what (he) will do. . . . I think he will be an unhappy creature, whenever he leaves Edmonton." Finally, apparently making the best of it, he said: "I suppose old Rowand will hang on for a while yet."

To take Father Thibault's place in the Edmonton area and at Lac Ste. Anne came a young Canadian priest sponsored by the Oblate Order. In 1852, Father Lacombe, then twenty-five years old, left St. Boniface with the Hudson's Bay brigade, bound for Edmonton. At Cumberland House he met Chief Factor Rowand and travelled with him to their common destination. These two men, the old factor nearing the end of his life, and the young priest just entering on his, were the two outstanding figures along the Saskatchewan, each dominating his field for half of the nineteenth century. The old man represented the best traditions of the Hudson's Bay rule, the young man foreshadowed the life that was to be along the Saskatchewan.

For the next two years, there was intimate contact between these two, as Father Lacombe lived in Edmonton House that first winter and was a frequent visitor after his removal to Lac Ste. Anne. That he learned much from the older man cannot be doubted. One of his first lessons concerned the sacredness of the fur trade, on which there must be no trespass. One day he appeared with a couple of out-of-season muskrat skins sewn on the cuffs of his coat. Rowand was furious, and bellowed at the young priest for daring to touch any of the furs in the country. Father Lacombe, all unconscious of any wrong-doing, became enraged, tore off the skins, and threw them in the factor's face. Though both were hot-tempered, nevertheless, a great bond grew up between them.

As the years went by, Father Lacombe's name was to become a by-word in the Canadian West. His was a name to open doors and to work wonders. Along the trails of the West for the next sixty-five years, at any time, one might meet the priest in his tattered robe, or see his red and white banner around the next bend. All the West was his battleground, but particularly so were Edmonton and Calgary. All the people of the West were his charge, whites, half-breeds, Crees, Piegans; but, above all, he gave his life to the Blackfeet.

As Colvile had guessed, John Rowand did hang on. He remained until the spring of 1854. That May, as he had so often done, he attended to the assembling of the brigade bound for Norway House, and once more set out along the route which after fifty years of journeying was so intimately familiar. Upon arriving at Fort Pitt, where his son John was in charge, his own sixty-five years must have felt heavy, because he told the young man that when his time came he wished to be buried among his kin at Montreal. It was a premonition. Next day, when a violent quarrel broke out amongst the boatmen, John Rowand, his ready temper flashing, rushed out to quell it, and fell dead. His death marked the closing of an era. Sir George Simpson, when he heard the news, wrote:

"With him, it may be said, the old race of officers is extinct, he being the last in the list who held a commission at the date of the Coalition. . . . He was a man of sterling integrity and a warm heart and was not surpassed by any officer in the service for unswerving devotion to the public interest."

But still Rowand's story was not closed, and a bizarre chapter was to be written before the chief factor's bones reached their final resting place. He was buried at Fort Pitt, but when his old friend Governor Simpson heard of his last request, he had the body disinterred, so that the bones might be buried in Montreal, and thereby hangs a true tale, attested by W. E. S. Gladstone, who arrived at Edmonton in 1848. In a letter describing this event, he said: "Well the next spring they tolded to dig up the body and send the bones to St. Boniface on red river so they got an indian to dig it up and boil the flash of. it was sayed that the wemmen of the fort made soap with the fat of the pot . . . the indian was drunk all the time he was boiling it."

Further adventures, however, were to befall the old trader's remains, for Sir George Simpson, in a letter to Rowand's doctor son in Montreal, told more of the story.

"I directed that (the package with the bones) should be brought out this summer (1856) to Norway House, from whence I conveyed it this summer in

Rev. Father Lacombe, who reached Edmonton 1852 and devoted his next 65 years to the West.

my own canoe to Red River, but some of the crew having discovered the contents of the package, I was afraid they might from a superstitious feeling drop it overboard at some time and therefore had it repacked and sent to York Factory for transmission to England by ship, from whence it will be forwarded to this place (Lachine)."

Finally, on November 10, 1858, over four years after his death, Rowand's bones were buried in Montreal's Mount Royal Cemetery. Subsequently, a red granite monument, costing some £500, was erected over them. Thus ended the career of one of the great men of the early West, son of a physician and father of another, who gave half a century of his life to Edmonton and enjoyed every hour of it.

Palliser, Gold Miners,
And Grey Nuns
1854-1862

chapter 4

AS CHIEF FACTOR at Edmonton, William Sinclair took John Rowand's place, and for a few more years the fur trade carried on much as it had in the past. And yet, even in 1854, there were signs that worried all devoted Hudson's Bay Company men. In what we may call the western province of the fur trade, that area west of the Rocky Mountains, as well as in the eastern area centering around the Red River Settlement the company's worries came in the form of American traders and settlers.

In Oregon, at the far end of the long line of communication across the continent, Simpson's efforts had met defeat. American settlers had flooded in there, and a militant United States, puffed up with the doctrines of *Manifest Destiny,* threatened war if British interests did not pull out of Oregon. Canadians were not interested in Oregon; if war came, Britain would have to wage it under a heavy disadvantage and would risk an aroused America gobbling up the Maritimes and Upper and Lower Canada. The gamble was too great, so in June 1846, by the Treaty of Oregon, the Hudson's Bay Company was in effect kicked out and the boundary between Canada and the United States set at the 49th Parallel west to the Pacific.

For the last decade, at the Red River Settlement rumblings against the company had risen to an outcry. Because it was an agricultural settlement of sorts, and because it was not very far north of the rampaging Americans, the situation there worsened year after year. From the ranks of the Red River half-breeds an occasional free trader popped up his head and other traders from the United States showed up. In 1849, when at the trial of a free trader named Sayer open rebellion of the half-breeds was averted only by a narrow squeak, the Hudson's Bay Company's hitherto legal monopoly was broken.

Then, to add to the company's other worries, hundreds of settlers began to move into Minnesota, and by 1854 some 30,000 of these enemies of the fur trade were squatting about the country. Not only was the company's monopoly at Red River distorted to a mere semblance of its former self, but across the border to the south hordes of unspeakable dirt farmers were starting to till land and to break up beaver dams.

The tide of militant American expansion had set farther west, and each month saw it lap even higher. Unless it could be deflected, the vast open prairies of the Hudson's Bay Company's Rupert's Land in modern Manitoba, Saskatchewan and Alberta, would be flooded with Americans and lost to Canada. Statesmen in the Canadas and in Britain became alarmed and were on the point of taking steps which the fur traders in their remote posts knew would sooner or later catch up with them and their livelihood.

At Edmonton House William Sinclair pondered this problem. Though Edmonton was protected by a thousand miles of prairie, empty except for buffalo and brown-eyed susans and useless except for buffalo grass or barley, nevertheless, from the back of his mind this carking worry came to spoil his quiet moments. Some day this cloud on his horizon, now a mere misty puff, might swell up to overwhelm even far away Edmonton. Reason said, No, it could never do that, for in those days Edmonton was so utterly remote. Why, at George Simpson's furious pace, it was twenty-two days away from Winnipeg, and no one but a mad man would ever equal Simpson's record time. Edmonton was indeed far more remote from the Red River than Aklavik is now from Edmonton. And yet from time to time Sinclair's nagging little voice came to remind him that a few years back even Edmonton's isolation had not saved it from smallpox. Would its remoteness be any better shield from this new infection which had overtaken the Red River Settlement or from the creaking cart wheels of settlers advancing west of the Mississippi?

Perhaps it was better not to think of these things. In the meantime, Sinclair had to see that the brigades for the west and north were sent off. Then with their departure Edmonton settled gradually into its winter routine, and the weeks slipped by till the main event of the year, the New Year's Ball. Since mainly French and Scottish blood ran in the veins of the staff, New Years was the chief celebration, although as a rule the festive season started at Christmas and continued till then. At midnight, as the old year expired, every hand, whose elbows could still raise an old flintlock, fired salute after salute to the new one. In 1854, however, the three-pound cannon was not fired. In fact, no one had touched it since the New Year's Eve three years earlier when the blacksmith had gone into a bastion, loaded one of the guns, and set it off. As the blast echoed from the south shore and rolled up and down the valley, everyone cheered and rejoiced. Only next morning did anyone realize what had happened. The blacksmith being missing, a search revealed his body beside the burst barrel.

But New Year's Day 1855, with its good feeling, its good cheer, hand-shaking, kissing, and foot races, was its usual happy time. That evening, as was customary, the chief factor gave a dance, and the belle of the ball was a tall blonde Blackfoot woman, who had been left temporarily with Mrs. Sinclair. Her skin was white and she wore a gown loaned for the occasion by the factor's wife. Undoubtedly she was of all white parentage, one of those girls adopted by the Blackfeet and well cared for when they had massacred all the rest of an Oregon-bound wagon train.

During the following summer, Edmonton House became the headquarters of its second Methodist missionary, the Rev. Thomas Woolsey, a brother-in-law of Rundle. This saintly man, fervent and faithful, but incompetent when it came to adjusting to the way of life in the West, remained in the area about nine years. From time to time, fortunately, he had the consolation of being able to consult with another minister of his own faith, because the Rev. Henry B. Steinhauer had accompanied him west.

Steinhauer, who was to spend some time at Lac La Biche and then in 1860 was to open a mission for the Crees at Whitefish Lake, was to serve his people in Alberta for nearly thirty years. The Crees were indeed his people, for he was a full-blooded Indian of the Ojibway tribe, which is of a stock closely related to them. As a youth he was taken in hand by a Methodist named Steinhauer, who provided funds for the bright boy's education and by whose name he came to be called. Once he settled at Whitefish Lake, he turned his great talents not only in the direction of Christianizing the Crees, but to inducing them to form an agricultural settlement around the shores of that lovely lake. With much merit, his contribution has been called the most impressive single achievement in Alberta's history. In due course, his son followed in his steps, and today many of his descendants, although still proudly preferring to remain treaty Indians, are making significant contributions to the white man's world.

If the arrival of several missionaries, either Roman Catholic or Methodist, gave the Hudson's Bay Company traders at Edmonton House food for thought, another event also made them sit back and ponder. In England and in the Canadas statesmen continued to worry about the imperialism of the aggressive Americans. Though a boundary had been drawn across the prairies on the 49th Parallel of latitude, there was the suspicion that the unrest at the Red River Settlement was partly due to American influence and the certainty that the United States would soon show its hand there. More than that, it appeared that, if steps were not taken soon by British or Canadian authorities to settle the Canadian Prairies, the Americans would do the job for them and the screaming eagle would do away with the more industrious though less bombastic beaver. There were some in Britain, of course, who correctly felt that Canada was a greater financial burden than a blessing and incorrectly would have been more than willing to let the prairies fall into American hands. There were many in Canada who had either never heard of the prairies or who likewise cared nothing for them. But in each country there were statesmen who thought that something should be done. There were also many in each country who, although they themselves had no solution for the problems of ruling such an empty hinterland, had their knife into the Hudson's Bay Company because it was big and because it was a monopoly. Between them all, they wished to take the company's Canadian property away from it.

In general, that property was known as Rupert's Land. Originally it had consisted of all the land drained by the rivers which ultimately flowed into Hudson Bay. With the amalgamation of the North West Company and the Hudson's Bay Company in 1821, it came to include two other vast areas; all the watershed of the Mackenzie River, as well as practically all the area which is now included in the province of British Columbia and the States of Idaho, Washington, Oregon and Northern California.

Though the recent Treaty of Oregon had lopped off everything south of the 49th Parallel, the Hudson's Bay Company was in effect left with all of Canada west of Ontario and much of Northern Quebec. Now, a decade later, there was talk of taking away Vancouver Island. Furthermore, due to the troubles at Red River, there were many advocates of taking over the rest of the company's property.

The time was ripe for such discussions, because the Hudson's Bay Company's charter, which had been renewed in 1838, was due for reconsideration in 1858. In 1857, with this in mind, the Imperial Government set up its Select Committee of the House of Commons to consider the whole matter of what to do with Western Canada. Essentially, it had to find answers to two questions. Should the ownership and hence the government of Rupert's Land be taken away from the Hudson's Bay Company? If so, who could take it over and govern it?

Behind these two questions, of course, lay one of the facts of life; unless either Canada or Britain took more active steps to populate the prairies, the Americans would. Among thoughtful Canadians the real trouble was not how Canada might acquire Rupert's Land, but how she should then administer and defend it. As eagerly as the slow transmission of news would permit, the Hudson's Bay Company's factors at places like Edmonton House waited news of the proceedings of the Select Committee.

Their Governor, Sir George Simpson, was one of the first witnesses the Committee called. Though seventy now, he was not only still vigorous but still wily and wise. Because, of all men, he knew most about the country, his evidence, in fact, was the most important information laid before the Committee. Among other things, he gave it as his opinion that the prairies and parklands of the West were "not well adapted for settlement".

Many modern critics have seized upon his evidence bearing on the agricultural possibilities of the West and have said that with ulterior motive, he deliberately beclouded the issue. In this the critics have been unfair. It is true that even had the Hudson's Bay Company known that the West could be farmed profitably, their spokesmen, anxious not to lose their fur trade business, would not have pushed the truth forward. They honestly believed, however, that, due to early frosts, grain growing would be too hazardous. And at the time they were right. With our hindsight, we know that some 200,000 farmers now cultivate the three Prairie Provinces. Very few of us, however, realize that all this has been made possible by the improvements plant scientists have made since that time in developing strains of wheat that will ripen in our climate. Wheat of that era took from 135 to 155 days to ripen, while our modern wheats take some 105 days.

On the one hand, the Select Committee had men like Simpson giving factual information, but fortunately on the other it had a man like Canada's Chief Justice Draper, who, while requesting the right for Canada to explore and settle the lands west of Lake Superior, had vision. For he said: "I hope you will not laugh at me as very visionary, but I hope to live to see the time . . . when there is a railway going all across that country and ending on the Pacific."

The upshot of the Committee's efforts was to grant Canada the right to settle and to take over the Red River, as well as to take steps to create the colonies of Vancouver Island and of British Columbia. The question of the Hudson's Bay Company's charter was left in the air, and this was tantamount to continuing it. One of the recommendations in the Committee's report read as follows:

". . . the opinion at which your Committee have arrived is founded on the following considerations: 1st. The great importance to the more peopled portions of British North America that law and order should, as far as possible, be maintained in these territories; 2nd. The fatal effects which they believe would infallibly result to the Indian population from a system of open competition in the fur trade, and the consequent introduction of spirits in a far greater degree than is the case at present; and 3rd. The probability of the indiscriminate destruction of the more valuable fur-bearing animals in the course of a few years. . . . For these reasons your Committee are of opinion that whatever may be the validity or otherwise of the rights claimed by the Hudson's Bay Company, under the Charter, it is desirable that they should continue to enjoy the privilege of exclusive trade, which they now possess. . . ."

Sitting remotely in this far-flung land which, as yet, no one fully comprehended and over which no one but the Hudson's Bay Company had any means of governing, the men at Edmonton House were relieved when the Committee's report came out. They knew, of course, that it did not end their worries, but for the time being at least, so long as the land remained under the Hudson's Bay Company's jurisdiction, they could carry on in an orderly manner.

Of far more interest to Edmonton House, however, was another step taken by the British Government even before the Select Committee had time to act. That was to send out the Palliser Expedition to gain some factual scientific information about Western Canada. On March 31, 1857, Palliser was commissioned to undertake this study, and before long some of his party reached Edmonton. The letter of instructions the captain received stressed the importance "of regularly recording the physical features of the country through which you will pass, noting its principal elevations, the nature of its soil, its capability of agriculture, the quantity and quality of its timber, and any indications of coal or other minerals."

At last someone had been delegated to study the prairies with an eye to seeing what resources, other than fur, lay in them. While Palliser performed his duty well, two of his very capable staff were exceptionally well fitted to recognize and report on the bounties which for a century the fur traders had seen but had noticed not. The first of these was Dr. James Hector, a physician and a geologist, who proved to be both gifted and versatile. The second was Eugene Bourgeau, a French botanist, who turned out to be a "prince of botanical collectors."

For two years, sometimes splitting up into different parties, sometimes travelling together, the Palliser Expedition in one group or another roved the prairies, explored the Rockies, wandered through the parklands, and took a look at the edge of the boreal forest. During the winter of 1857-1858, Fort Carlton was their base camp, while the next year most of the party wintered at Edmonton.

Within the limits of the scientific knowledge of the day and the capacity of a small party to study a vast area, the Palliser Expedition did a good job. When its various members' reports were compiled, they provided much level-headed information about the prospects for agriculture. Palliser singled out the most arid area of the plains, which is still known as Palliser's Triangle. Dr. Hector, perhaps the most valuable member of the group, considered the Triangle to be practically useless, for he said: "The arid district, though there are many fertile spots throughout its extent, can never be of much advantage to us as a possession."

He thought the parkland and the rich soils adjoining the North Saskatchewan River to be eminently fit for cultivation. Turning his attention to Alberta's boreal forest, he was disparaging, calling its spruce timber "coarse and worthless" to the point where it was only good for "a very inferior quality of firewood."

Palliser drew attention to the abundance of coal in Alberta, and in summing up the expedition's work, presented a very favourable assessment of the prairies and of the Edmonton area. Incidental to his stay at Edmonton House during the winter of 1858-1859, he left us several interesting bits of information.

First of all, in the fall of 1858, assisted by W. J. Christie, who that year had assumed the office of chief trader, he paid off a number of his men and sent them home. Telling of the complicated business of giving them their wages, he said:

"All payments in this country being made in kind . . . Mr. Christie, who understood the pricing and value of the articles, very kindly undertook the payment of the men, which is thus conducted:—Mr. Sullivan made out account of wages due to them, deducting advances, &c. I then signed this, and each man presented it to Mr. Christie, who sat in my shop in the fort, surrounded by ready-made clothes, blankets, beds, axes, knives, files, kettles, tea, sugar, tobacco, &c, and the man kept taking what he wanted till Mr. Christie called out 'assez', upon which the account closed. Frequently Mr. Christie would say, 'Now you have but half a skin left,' when his customer would immediately turn to the ribbons or beads for an equivalent of the difference."

The missionaries at Edmonton rejoiced at the rare pleasure of being able to spend some time in the company of the educated men of the expedition. That the pleasure was mutual is evident in the kindly references to missionaries in the various reports. Palliser thought Father Lacombe to be not only a kindly man but a most valuable missionary. In his opinion, that black-robed voyageur had been more successful up to that time with the half-breeds than with the Indians. The Captain was equally complimentary to the Methodists, for he said: "Mr. Rundle, who must have been a very able and influential man, is spoken of among them with reverence and enthusiasm to this day. Mr. Woolsey also, the present missionary, is a most excellent benevolent person. . . ."

In the fall of 1859 the various leaders of the expedition crossed the mountains, made their way to the Coast, and eventually sailed for England. They had done a good job of sizing up the prairies from the Red River to the Rockies, and had also studied and mapped several mountain passes. To Palliser, the possibility of a railroad across Canada seemed too remote to warrant serious study. He concluded that a wagon road might be worked out through the Vermilion Pass, but felt that any such work would be a long way in the future.

While from time to time during 1857-1858 the staff at Edmonton House had welcomed various members of the Palliser Expedition and had helped them along, this study, aimed mainly at finding out what possibilities the prairies had for settlement, had no apparent effect on the Edmonton area. Actually, it had been a good study, and in Palliser's Report Eastern Canada and Britain had a reliable document which showed for the first time that the prairies were reasonably well fitted for settlement. It called attention to another resource of the Edmonton area—almost unlimited square miles of arable soil. But even then the time was not ripe and no one was particularly interested. Edmonton's soil was left unmolested to nurture its rich vetches, its wild roses and its blue saskatoons. Chief Trader W. J. Christie and his cohorts breathed a sigh of relief—for the time being at least, the fur trade was to be left in peace. No meddlesome farmers peered over the horizon. Palliser had piped, but no one had danced.

If, however, all fear of farmers was still far away, a new breed of adventurers was on its way to disturb the tranquility of Edmonton House. In the spring of 1857 when Dr. Hector had mushed his dog-teams to Fort Pitt, he saw his first trifling amount of Saskatchewan River gold. It had been secured by a party from

Minnesota, which had set out across the prairies bound for the Fraser River Gold Rush and had wintered at Fort Pitt.

One of the first of the miners to reach Edmonton House was C. A. Loveland of Wisconsin, who, in March 1858, worked his way west from Fort Pitt. At that time he had no inkling that gold might be found in the Saskatchewan River. He had plenty of American money and wished to buy supplies and to hurry on west through the mountains. Chief Trader Christie, however, would not accept his money but put him to work at finishing a church for Father Lacombe within the palisades of the fort, and paid him a shilling a day. Many years later, in telling of his experiences at Edmonton House, Loveland said: ". . . . a band of about 3,000 Blackfeet Indians arrived from the south to trade at the fort. The first morning after their arrival a chief came down in full dress accompanied by 50 or 100 of his followers, bringing a present for the H.B. Co.'s chief factor. When the present had been made the cannons of the fort fired a salute, which was answered by the Indians firing their guns. Then the chief retired and another came, and the ceremony was repeated, until all had greeted the factor. Then six of the Indians were told off to take care of the arms of all the others, and trading commenced. . . . The Indians got considerable rum and had a carousal. The six guardians were compelled to keep sober. At nightfall the Indians came and fired at the fort, but were not answered and did no damage. When the trading was ended the six sober Indians were taken into the fort and treated to drink and the best of what was going. The party remained about three or four days and then returned south."

During 1859, parties of gold seekers continued to cross the Canadian plains on their way to the diggings on the Fraser River. One of these parties, of whom a record remains, consisted of Messrs. Colville, Reid, Dickman, Hind and two or three others. Then in the fall of 1860, or the spring of 1861, some American prospectors discovered gold, in what was considered to be paying quantities at Rocky Mountain House, but whether these prospectors were going westward on their way to the Fraser River or to the newly discovered diggings at Cariboo, or had come eastward across the mountains from British Columbia, is not certain.

Under John Rowand, Edmonton House had been concerned solely with the fur trade, but now, almost immediately after his death, a plague of strangers began wandering in and out of the fort; first, more missionaries, then Palliser and his people, and now these unwelcome fools with the glint of gold in their eyes. Times were changing.

During the summer of 1860 a party consisting of Timolean Love, D. F. McLaurin, A. Perry and Tom Clover, for instance, ascended the Fraser, came through the Yellowhead Pass and arrived at Edmonton. Along with Perry, Tom Clover remained to prospect the Saskatchewan from Fort Edmonton to Rocky Mountain House. His name is perpetuated in a suburb on Edmonton's eastern outskirts, which eventually grew up adjacent to the bar he worked, known first as Tom Clover's Bar, but now shortened to Clover Bar. His partners McLaurin and Love, went east to Winnipeg and on to Minnesota for supplies. On their return to Fort Garry, McLaurin died. While Perry and Tom Clover were practical working miners, Love was a talker who basked in the acclaim accorded his exaggerations. At Fort Garry he aroused a lot of interest in the mines on the Saskatchewan. From time to time Clover wrote to Love at Fort Garry. By a discriminating use of these letters there, Love convinced the unwary that with his extensive knowledge of gold mining on the Saskatchewan, he was a man to heed. Based on Love's information, the Toronto *Globe* criticized the Government of Canada for not hastening to encourage gold mining on the rich Saskatchewan River. It said:

"If anything can rouse the representatives of the people of Canada to action on the question of opening up the North West Territory, it will surely be done by the intelligence from Red River which we furnish below. There seems to be no doubt whatever that the streams to the east of the Rocky Mountains water a gold region as large as those of the west. The precious metal is there, and speedily thousands will occupy the territory and develop its resources. . . .

"There are now organizing at Fort Garry two parties under the leadership of Mr. George Flett and Mr. Timolean Love, men fully competent to take charge of the task they have undertaken. Canadians getting through to Red River about the middle of May or June will be in time to join one of these parties."

By this means, and others, great interest was aroused in Ontario. One manifestation of this was the organization of several groups of miners who planned to go overland from Fort Garry to the Cariboo. Ultimately these groups more or less coalesced at Fort Garry and became known as the Overlanders of 1862. Timolean Love, with his ready tongue, soon latched onto them and for a while became the leader of one of the groups. Fortunately, however, they had another leader in the person of John Whiteford, a reliable Red River Métis.

The Overlanders, consisting of about 175 men, set forth in two main parties, which both left Fort Garry early in June 1862. Travelling by carts, they made poor time, but at that reached Edmonton about the end of July. There they left their carts and, still in two parties, continued their trip west to St. Albert, Lac Ste. Anne and Jasper. At Edmonton House, Timolean Love, who was still with them, met his partner Tom Clover. The latter's report of the prospects along the Saskatchewan were rosy enough so that over sixty men deserted the Overlanders to try their luck at Edmonton.

On June 11, 1862, the *Nor'-Wester* of Fort Garry mentioned the men who were leaving Winnipeg for the goldfields, saying: "Besides 200 foreigners who pass through the settlement enroute to the Saskatchewan and B. C. Mines, several of our own settlers are going. George Flett, George Gunn, John Atkinson, George Sutherland, Hector McBeath, Donald Mathewson and others."

In the same issue, the paper published a letter from the Rev. Mr. Woolsey at Edmonton hastening to disclaim that he had held out any inducement for miners to come to Edmonton. Presumably he had sized up the prospects of mining on the Saskatchewan and was pessimistic, even though men like Timolean Love may have tried to use Woolsey's name in their advertising.

At Edmonton House, however, Chief Trader Christie had to deal with missionaries as well as miners. In 1857, as a special favour to his friend Father Lacombe, he started to build a little chapel for his use. This friendly gesture he set on foot with both eyes open. With one of them he saw the pleasure it would give the good Father, but with the other he saw the Blackfeet, whom he noted were coming to respect the priest whose friendly overtures to them might ease the tension of Blackfeet visits. Recently, when a mysterious illness fell upon their camps, these mighty plainsmen had sent for the missionary, and he had gone among them. Though helpless to stem the tide of an epidemic of scarlet fever, which in camp after camp carried off scores of victims, he nevertheless extended the hand of sympathy in their time of need, and pagan though they remained, they responded to the kindness in the priest's heart. W. J. Christie's chapel would be a good investment.

PALLISER, GOLD MINERS AND GREY NUNS — 1854-1862

Father Lacombe's next move was a bit of a surprise, for he announced that he hoped to obtain the services of three Grey Nuns from Montreal to assist at his mission at Lac Ste. Anne. The old traders shook their heads. This was no place for white women, and particularly for delicately reared convent women. What indeed was the world coming to?

But they came. In 1859, under the protection of Father Remas, a small train of carts drew up to the fort—twelve horses, six carts, and a wild dog. And stiff and bruised from their long trip from Fort Garry, the three Grey Nuns climbed down from the cart. In due course they hastened to Lac Ste. Anne, but their coming marked a new milestone in the opening up of the West. Moreover, although the first white woman to visit Edmonton, Marie-Anne Lagimodière, had preceded them by some fifty years, the three nuns were the first educated women to come to Edmonton.

That same year the first of the peering world travellers, Lord Southesk, stopped at Edmonton House for a while and then went on to the mission at Lac Ste. Anne, and thence west and south along the foothills to the Bow River.

Times were indeed changing, and news of one of the most significant changes arrived in the fall of 1860 with a letter, saying that the great Sir George Simpson had died at his home near Montreal.

With his death an era closed. Forty years earlier, when he had first set foot in Canada, the fur trade was in a chaotic condition, with two great companies battling each other to the brink of bankruptcy. With their amalgamation, he had assumed the reins of power over nearly half a continent. Under his guidance, the trade had settled into an orderly and a profitable pattern, and the Hudson's Bay Company's name became synonymous with greatness, order, and law. During his regime, but in spite of his best planning and of his mighty efforts, the area of Oregon and Washington had fallen before American expansion. Even then he had regrouped his forces and carried on a most successful business all over Western Canada. Among the men we look upon as Makers of Canada, Sir George Simpson ranks high.

During his regime too, Edmonton House had grown in importance and had become the headquarters of the prairies and the gateway to the north. Working with and influenced by his friend John Rowand, Simpson had devoted much thought to Edmonton's interest. Now, at his death, this important fortress, looking south over its magnificent river valley, stood ready for the changing era, which, though but dimly perceived, lay ahead of it.

Edmonto

Enters Confederatio

1862-186

chapter 5

FURTHER FINGERS OF CIVILIZATION were soon clawing at the rents in the fur trade cloak. In September 1862, a school invaded the fort, when at Father Lacombe's instigation Brother Scollen taught some twenty pupils in a log building within the palisades, a labour he continued until 1871.

The early 1860's was a busy time for Father Lacombe. In 1861, some ten miles away from Edmonton House he started the mission of St. Albert which down the decades was to contribute so much to the West. Two years later, the Grey Nuns, who had been stationed at Lac Ste. Anne, moved over to the new establishment, and about the same time the good father got his horse-driven grist mill into operation.

In 1862 also, two Methodist missionaries, George and John McDougall, father and son, arrived at Edmonton House. After visiting the Rev. Henry Steinhauer's mission at Whitefish Lake and coming on to Edmonton, the Rev. George McDougall set John to work building a new mission at Victoria, some seventy river miles downstream from Edmonton. To this mission the father returned in 1863, bringing his wife and family, and here he became fast friends with Pakan and Maskepetoon, two famous Cree Chiefs. In remembrance of one of them, the old settlement of Victoria is today called Pakan.

In 1864, McDougall established the first Protestant schools west of Portage la Prairie, starting one at Victoria and one at Whitefish Lake. The same year, because the mission at Victoria had attracted so many Indians and half-breeds, the Hudson's Bay Company opened an outpost there.

By this time there was sufficient interest in the West that parties of sports-men and globe trotters were including Edmonton in their itineraries. In 1863 Lord Milton and Dr. Cheadle, on their way across the continent, called at Edmonton. Both Southesk, who had arrived four years earlier, and Dr. Cheadle wrote entrancing books about their experiences, and both these books were widely circulated in Britain. Through them, the West and the Edmonton area became known to a widening circle of interested readers.

Totally indifferent to English readers, however, the mighty Blackfeet still rode and ruled the endless rolling plains. Once or twice a year a large party would descend on Edmonton House to trade. In the spring of 1864 such a party,

Rev. George McDougall, who arrived in Edmonton 1862 and later built first house· in hamlet.

seven hundred strong, crossed the river and camped on the hill behind the fort. For a few days the great smoke-stained tepees glowed in the sun. While the men were trading and carousing, the busy life of a great camp went on. Horses were picketed all about or grazed freely farther back, dogs and children ran barking and shouting hither and yon, while the women folk, gathered into laughing groups about the campfires, sewed and cooked.

Then one morning the lodges were pulled down, and in marching order, led by the warriors, they filed down the steep path to the fort. A writer of the time said that "They made a picturesque array—lusty strong-featured bronzed men and women with lithe half-naked bodies and faces streaked with vermilion. The leaders wore eagle-feathers in their hair: the men were for the most part naked but for a buffalo-robe caught around them; the women wore decorated tunics of antelope-skin or blue cloth and richly beaded gaiters. Men and women alike sat upon their sure-footed bronchos with the ease of the plainsmen, their primitive chattels fastened to travoix dragged behind the ponies."

Once more the Hudson's Bay traders and staff breathed a sigh of relief. The Blackfeet had come and gone and all had passed off quietly, and now the bulk of the band could be heard climbing the hill on the south side of the river. Unfortunately a Sarcee, who had come with them, had lingered and was bartering with "Flatboat" McLean for a horse. Joe MacDonald, half-breed son of Big Donald, who for so long had lived with the Piegans, and a man named Smith, watched with interest as the Sarcee demanded more whisky in exchange for his horse. Suddenly a group of Crees slipped around the south bastion and, before anyone was able to stop him, Little Pine, their leader, shot the Sarcee through the thighs. Flatboat McLean pulled the wounded man inside the gates, while the other hastened to shut them. Malcolm Groat and Brazeau, one-time chief trader at Rocky Mountain House, did all they could for the stricken man, but he died.

When they heard of the killing, the departing Blackfeet overlooked it temporarily and kept on their way. A few weeks later, however, they returned, intent on revenge. Brazeau, Christie and Father Lacombe pacified them, and, loading them with gifts, sent them away without open hostilities. But it had been a near miss.

In this case the Crees had stirred up the Blackfeet, but nearly every day somewhere in Alberta the miners irritated them all over again. For there was a fundamental difference between the outlook of the fur traders and the miners, whom the Hudson's Bay Company men regarded as mere interlopers with no long-range interest in the country. For over half a century the company had dealt honourably with the Crees of the forests and the Blackfeet of the plains, providing a market for their furs, and, applying the views on conservation that were ever the outlook of the London Committee, they did what they could to ease the lot of their native customers.

Added to the miners' complete disregard for both the Blackfeet and the company and the long established way of life at Edmonton House, was the demand they placed upon it for supplies. They felt that since the company had a post at Edmonton it was duty bound to keep sufficient supplies to sell to them. Chief Trader Christie, sorely torn between wishing that all miners would starve and seeing that none of them did, had a difficult time.

Moreover, many of the company's servants, lured by the prospect of gold, left its service. In the report of the *Nor'-Wester* in 1863, George Gunn stated that at Edmonton House "no less than eight Company servants left during the winter to join the miners." He added that the company was "bitterly opposed to mining." Amongst the men who had quit were "Wm. Gladstone and Nils Martinsen who left the Cos. service at Edmonton on May 20th and arrived at Fort Garry June 19th." Gladstone, taking a wise course, visited Fort Garry with the sole purpose of obtaining supplies and then returned immediately to the Saskatchewan River bars.

In an optimistic letter dated Saskatchewan, May 10, 1863, published in the *Nor'-Wester,* George Flett gave news of affairs at Edmonton. He mentioned a wise move he had taken which had a direct bearing on the food supply. "Geo. Gunn and I left the miners to farm. We seeded 9 bushels of wheat and barley." After mentioning their agricultural activities and what was probably the first commercial farm in Alberta, he noted the fact that he had gone to hear the Rev. Mr. Woolsey preach to the Indians, even though the minister could not speak Cree. William Monkman, a half-breed, was Woolsey's interpreter. Flett commented, "it seems strange to see a minister so excited, preaching to people that do not understand him."

The miners' reports were mainly optimistic. W. J. Christie, however, viewed their goings and comings in a different light. Miners and other idlers were influencing his men and they were deserting, and he was having trouble getting the work of the fort done. The miners, moreover, were in a constant state of flux, some coming in from across the mountains, some from Fort Garry, and others from Fort Benton or even from the Peace River, while still others returned to all of these places. By August 1863, many of them and many of the Over-landers who had stayed at Edmonton had decided that the gold in the Saskatchewan River was not worthwhile, and for a spell their departure comforted W. J. Christie. One of the difficulties the miners experienced was the fact that they could only work when the water in the river was low. For a period in the springtime they could work. Then during the high water of June they had to lie by until they could resume work later in the fall. When the water was low, however, if they were diligent and lucky, they could pan out between $10 and $20 a day.

But to Christie's dismay, a few days after one batch of miners got dis-couraged and left, another batch arrived. In the fall of 1863, one group of miners from Fort Benton brought him some pleasant news. They told him that four steamboats had come up to Fort Benton that year and each of them was loaded with men going to the Beaverhead mines. So many had arrived in the country that the free traders in Fort Benton found it much more profitable to trade with them than with the Blackfeet that prices had gone sky high. When the Blackfeet complained, they discovered that the white traders didn't care whether or not they continued to deal with them.

Christie cannily concluded that their action would result in the Blackfeet returning north to resume trading with the Hudson's Bay Company. Acting on this reasoning, he decided to re-establish Rocky Mountain House as a year round venture, and sent Richard Hardisty there to take charge.

Christie had other problems too. The Blackfeet, ever intransigent, were at odds not only with the Crees and the miners but also with the Métis, whose numbers were increasing. Up to this point the Métis were mainly under the company's thumb, and even though Christie would have preferred to see them in Halifax, they brought in the furs they obtained from the Indians. Furthermore, they hunted buffalo and, though that brought down on them the further wrath of the Blackfeet, they were a large factor in keeping Edmonton House supplied.

The Métis, however, were always more than a match for the Indians. While they suffered casualties, they invariably inflicted much heavier losses on their enemies. One of their leaders in the Edmonton area was James Whiteford, a brother of the man who guided the Overlanders. Another was young Gabriel Dumont.

When Gabriel was a year or two old, his father, Isadore, had come to live in the Fort Pitt-Edmonton area as a trader and remained there for some ten years. By 1860 young Gabriel himself was the recognized leader of a large band of Métis who wandered and traded over the length and breadth of the Canadian prairies. That year he led his people to establish the first of the Métis settlements on the South Saskatchewan River, at St. Laurent, Duck Lake, and Batoche. These settle-ments, together with those at Lac Ste. Anne, St. Albert and Lac La Biche, soon became focal points for the "New Nation," as the Métis, with some justice, were beginning to call themselves.

More and more the Hudson's Bay Company and W. J. Christie were becoming aware of these people and worrying about their effect on the Indian trade and their frequent skirmishes with the Blackfeet. In the middle of the winter of 1863-1864, the local Métis came in to Edmonton to announce that the Blackfeet had stolen fifty-seven of their horses and asked Christie's advice. He tried to calm them and told them to demand their horses back. In due course they did, and regained most of them. Even the Blackfeet knew when to fight and when to give in.

With Métis and miners stirring up the Blackfeet, and with the growth of raiding between the Crees and the plains people, times were becoming difficult for the Hudson's Bay Company. To venture out into the plains began to be risky even for the company's men. Travellers moving in small parties without the protection of the company took their lives in their hands, and yet one day in the spring of 1864, when the Blackfeet visited Edmonton House, they brought along an American miner who had become lost and had stumbled along on the verge of starvation until they found him and harbored him.

About this time Flatboat McLean, who had dragged the stricken Sarcee into the fort when the band of Crees had shot him, set out to prospect for gold in the Kootenays. On his way over the mountains he fell in with two of the most interesting miners who ever came to Edmonton. These were Jim Gibbons and Sam Livingstone, both old 49'ers and both fascinating characters. After talking to McLean, these two decided to try their luck at Edmonton. On their way in the fall of 1864, their food ran low, but before they perished Father Lacombe found them and took them to Rocky Mountain House.

In the spring of 1865, Jim Gibbons moved on to Edmonton, where, except for occasional absences of a year or so, he remained till his death in 1933. In his reminiscenses, he left us some interesting comments on Edmonton House as it was that spring.

"Christie was in charge at Edmonton. There were about twenty-five families about the place. They were French Canadians, half-breeds, and Highland Scotch. William Borwick was the blacksmith. William Lennie was also a blacksmith; there were in those days two kinds of Scotch—those who could speak English and those who could not. Jimmie Gullion was the boat builder assisted by his brother, George. Pig Kenny was in charge of the pigs. Malcolm Groat was in charge of the men. There were two clerks in the post—McAulay and McDonald. Sandy Anderson was the saddler and made the dog harness. John Norris was dog runner. Donald McLeod was in the Company service at that time and I remember that he spoke very little English. Gilbert Anderson was whip sawing lumber for the Company, and William Meavor was getting out the logs."

Three of the men Jim mentioned loomed large in Edmonton's affairs. Malcolm Groat at that time was a recent arrival in the West. Born in Glasgow, he had left Scotland in 1862 and that fall found himself in Edmonton House. John Norris left Scotland in 1846, and then spent some time at Fort Pitt, where, in 1852, he had married a half-breed woman, Mary Pelletier, who as the years went by bore him thirteen children. As recently as 1864 he and George Flett had taken a brigade of two hundred Red River carts from Fort Garry to Fort Carlton. In the company's service Kenny McDonald had been transferred to Edmonton in 1860, and the next year he built a house near Rat Creek and in effect homesteaded what was later to become River Lot 20. This house is believed to be the first one built east of 101 Street.

Of the crops grown around the fort, Gibbons said: "In 1865 oats were grown on the Hudson's Bay field where the present power house now stands, and potatoes had been grown on the same ground for some eighty years previously. This was the talk of the men around the fort. The oats had become very light owing to inbreeding and the potatoes from the same cause were not much bigger than my fingers. . . . The barley was the best crop. A bag of potatoes and a bag of imported flour was the Hudson's Bay ration to each man. There was another field just behind the Hudson's Bay store which was called the 'New Field.' This field afterward became the race track. The Hudson's Bay Company had a horse-power flour mill for grinding."

When the river froze over, Jim Gibbons, Sam Livingstone and Mike Shannon, good Irishman all, decided to go downstream to Victoria. Before leaving they could not resist the chance to pull Malcolm Groat's leg.

"Malcolm," said Jim, "this is the queerest place I've ever been in. It's a perfect babble of tongues, Cree, French and Gaelic. Is there no place in these British possessions where us Englishmen can speak our own language?"

Malcolm, perhaps rejoicing at the chance to rid Edmonton of three more miners, recommended that they go downstream to Victoria.

Though Jim Gibbons undoubtedly exaggerated the babble of tongues at Edmonton and the absence of the English language, nevertheless, in Chief Trader Christie's opinion, that state of affairs was infinitely preferable to a spate of miners speaking English with an Irish brogue. Whether he liked it or not, however, he had to endure this influx of miners. They were a sign that there were other resources in the Edmonton area as well as furs, and a sign too that Edmonton must sooner or later lose its isolation.

One straw in the wind blowing Edmonton's way was Dr. John Rae, who in 1864 had called at Edmonton House on his walking tour from Fort Garry to the Pacific Coast by way of Tête Jaune Cache and the Fraser River. For Dr. Rae came at the instigation of the great bankers, Baring Brothers, who were involved in the Hudson's Bay Company and in financing the Grand Trunk Railway. Rae was to report on the feasibility of building a wagon road and a telegraph line west along the Saskatchewan River.

Because Dr. Rae was a man of great repute, Edmontonians were more interested in him than in any of the implications of his visit. And yet, however dimly the fur trade inhabitants in Edmonton may have perceived it, the English, the Americans and the Eastern Canadians were looking in their direction. To these Englishmen, Yankees and Canucks, Edmonton itself may have been a fuzzy spot on a map, but the great prairies and parklands stretching for four hundred miles south and one thousand miles east of it had begun to come into focus. Now, for the first time, and for a variety of motives, they began to have value.

Listening to John A. Macdonald during 1865, however, would have led an observer astray, for he said that the prairie "country is of no present value to Canada." In that opinion, as this great statesman was soon to learn, he was as wrong as he had been on many other occasions. Soon the British, the Americans and his compatriots were to shape up a set of circumstances that quickly changed his mind.

At the time he expressed the unfortunate opinion, John A., of course, was far too busy with Canada east of Lake Superior to worry about the prairies. He was then in the midst of dipping into his bag of tricks and using all his wiles to pull together the various colonies from the bleak shores of Newfoundland to the bare rocks of Lake Superior into a venture called Confederation.

Two years later he succeeded, and on July 1, 1867, Confederation became a fact, with John A. Macdonald at the zenith of his career as Prime Minister of Canada. His dominion included the four provinces of Nova Scotia, New Brunswick, Quebec and Ontario. Prince Edward Island and Newfoundland had stayed out. Two thousand miles away to the west, beyond the prairies "of no present value" and beyond the formidable wall of the Rocky Mountains, British Columbia watched the new Dominion with a cool eye. Nevertheless, Canada, with its 3,300,000 people and its 662,148 square miles, had come into being. With luck, and John A. the procrastinator was as lucky as he was astute, Canada's area could expand six times. Confederation had been achieved.

But towards it, Edmontonians, remote in the bleak wilderness, were totally indifferent. Their thoughts ran to furs and gold and to buffalo wandering in their millions over the vast untilled prairies. For though more than a century had passed since the first white man had tramped along Edmonton's eastern outskirts, neither he nor his successors had laid grasping hands on Alberta's natural beauty. Outside of Edmonton the only evidences of the white man's caress were some missions and ten fur trade posts, of which all but Chipewyan and Fort Vermilion came under the direct supervision of Edmonton House. These points were: Rocky Mountain House, Jasper, Fort Assiniboine, Lesser Slave Lake, Fort Vermilion, Chipewyan, Lac Ste. Anne, Lac La Biche, Victoria and Dunvegan. At the last five, missions of either or both the Wesleyan or the Roman Catholic faith had church structures, or were more or less in residence. As well as these places, there were three separate mission stations, St. Albert, the headquarters of the Roman Catholics, and Whitefish Lake and Pigeon Lake, where the Wesleyans were working.

At six of the far-flung missions, St. Albert, Lac Ste. Anne, Lac La Biche, Victoria and at Whitefish and Pigeon lakes, the half-breeds and Indians formed fairly large communities. At St. Albert, for instance, some seventy families of these wanderers were trying to settle down, while at Victoria perhaps thirty had dotted the river bank with shacks.

Of all these settlements, Edmonton, of course, with its population of about 150, was the largest. The old fort perched at the edge of the bank, with its bastions and palisade frowning on the river, was a busy place. Some remodelling had gone on shortly before 1867 and the stockade enclosure, dominated by Rowand's Big House, was crowded with large log buildings. Here and there outside the fort a few half-breed shacks peered out of the bush, while a handful of hovels housed an itinerant population of perhaps fifty gold miners. The bulk of these lived on Miners' Flats, where the modern zoo is, although some had chosen to work Tom Clover's gravel bar a few miles downstream, while here and there for all of the seventy river miles to Victoria an occasional miner's shack sent its blue smoke curling up into the heavy woods behind it.

In 1867, then, Edmonton House, three isolated mission stations and ten outlying fur posts more or less tributary to Edmonton, were all that the white man had to show for a century of occupation of Alberta. In the whole province the total half-breed and white population would be some two thousand. Because at times smallpox had got in its deadly work and because the fact that the natives had been armed with guns increased the deadliness of their inter-tribal warfare, the Indian population, which may have been ten thousand when the white man came a century before, had been reduced to five or six thousand. As recently as the winter of

1864-1865, scarlet fever and measles, for instance, had been on the rampage, and in what is now the Provinces of Alberta and Saskatchewan, killed about twelve hundred of the native population.

Since, however, each of these communities occupied such a little space compared to the vast silent forest that encompassed all of them, they had made no appreciable mark on Alberta. To all appearances, it was almost exactly the same beautiful wilderness that it had been for thousands of years. The white man's fourteen settlements had marred it as little as fourteen tiny fly specks upon a huge and otherwise clean window-pane.

These settlements, of course, had to communicate with each other. Along the Saskatchewan, Athabasca and Peace rivers this communication was by canoe or boat, and left no mark of its passing. Moreover, the Saskatchewan River was the great highway across Canada, and most of the commerce of the day floated down or poled its way up its broad bosom. Since at times it was convenient to transport goods by pack horses, a few trails had come into being, all radiating out from Edmonton. The two oldest, dating back before 1800, were the ones on each side of the river, which eventually led to Fort Garry. They were each known as Fort Garry Trails, but since John McDougall had started his mission seventy miles downstream from Edmonton, they had also come to be known as the Victoria Trails.

The next oldest pack trail west and north went through modern St. Albert to Fort Assiniboine as the eighty-mile portage connecting the Saskatchewan and Athabasca rivers and thus formed part of the first trans-Canada highway. Since in recent years Father Lacombe had started his mission eight miles north of Edmonton House, it came to be known as the St. Albert Trail. Beyond St. Albert the trail forked, and the left branch followed up the Sturgeon River to Lac Ste. Anne. Ten years previously, in 1857, Henry Moberly, when in charge of Jasper House, had been the first white man to break a trail from there to Jasper House. This was the route the Overlanders had followed in 1862.

The last trail emanating from Edmonton was that to the south, to the mission at Pigeon Lake and to Rocky Mountain House. Beyond that it led southwest and crossed the mountains in the vicinity of modern Banff.

Along the trails to Fort Garry, carts had been passing and re-passing for a few years. Along one of them in 1841 George Simpson and the Oregon-bound settlers had brought carts from Fort Garry. More recently, in 1862, Father Lacombe had sent the first organized brigade of freighting carts to Fort Garry for his mission's supplies, and in 1867 began annual freight shipments along this thousand-mile trail.

This, then, was Alberta in 1867, the same beautiful and rich land it had been for thousands of years, which, except for a total of fourteen specks of civilization all. tributary to Edmonton, was still unscarred by the white man's grasp. This too was Edmonton in 1867, a cosy spot in which to live, the key spot in the trans-Canada highway, the gateway to all the vast northland, and the point of contact between white men and the war-like Plains Indians.

The docile Crees and the other Indians of the forests to the north were no problem, but the Blackfeet out on the prairies continued to be a headache. Sometimes they came in to trade and sometimes they never showed up. Now that the Americans were crowding into Montana and pushing hard against the invisible boundary of the 49th Parallel, these Plains Indians had become even more unpredictable. Chief Trader Christie, relatively untroubled otherwise, had more worries on that score than on any other.

But, if Christie at Edmonton only had to worry about Americans in Montana, his superiors in London were gravely concerned on a much wider front. So were a few statesmen in Canada. For in the United States *Manifest Destiny* was champing at the bit, ready to charge into Canada. By a narrow squeak during its 1858 gold rush, British Columbia had escaped American annexation, and now in 1867, fresh fears of a move in that direction had reared their heads. Now, too, the anarchy prevailing in Montana was threatening to spill over into Alberta. But worst of all, *Manifest Destiny* in the shape of directed settlements was forming ranks to descend upon the Red River Colony in Manitoba.

Watching all this, Canadian statesmen worried. With its two maritime provinces and its long, skinny provinces of Ontario and Quebec forming a narrow fringe along the St. Lawrence and lakes Erie and Ontario, mere miniatures of their present day large areas, Canada was a pitifully small and weak country to hold off the Americans. The Hudson's Bay Company owned all the vast prairies and much of the rest of modern Canada, and as owners, they were governing this tremendous empty region. If Canada took over these prairies, how could it finance their development, and how could it govern them?

Many influential Canadians, exhibiting a not unusual but nonetheless remarkable generosity toward someone else's property, advocated seizing the Hudson's Bay Company's prairie lands without compensation. On November 1, 1869, however, Macdonald's government concluded an agreement with the company. Under it, the Hudson's Bay Company was to receive a cash payment of £300,000 and be left with some three thousand acres around each of its posts, as well as to retain some seven million acres of land which were to be allocated on a systematic basis whenever the land should be surveyed. It was naturally permitted to continue its fur business. By this agreement, as John A. said, Canada had "quietly annexed" all the land lying on its western flank as far as the Rocky Mountains. Once this claim should be implemented, Edmonton would be part of the Dominion of Canada.

But when John A. spoke, the wedding had yet to be consummated, and, through an oversight, the consummation was far from quiet. For he and everyone else had forgotten the 11,500 British or French half-breed settlers in the Red River Colony, and no one had consulted them. Suffering from an inferior status and struggling with an inferiority complex for which there was no cure, they defied Canada and the Hudson's Bay Company. In their just fight, Louis Riel, partly a selfless patriot and partly the leader of a riot that got out of his hands, led them.

In 1869, before all the fuss started, the Red River Colony had stretched for a few miles up and down that river. In it the old mission colony of St. Boniface faced a newer hamlet of Winnipeg across the river, a hamlet that was growing by leaps and bounds now that steamboats from the United States were plying the Red River. It was a roistering frontier town, cooled down only slightly by the law and order imperfectly imposed by a Hudson's Bay Company, which was rapidly losing its legal potency.

Being so close to Minnesota, many of Winnipeg's new citizens were Americans, who naturally did all they could to see that as soon as possible the Red River Settlement should have the opportunity of becoming a part of the United States. Opposed to them was a Canadian faction with leanings toward the

Orange order. Caught between these two on the one hand were the more staid Selkirk Settlers and the British half-breeds, and on the other, the French half-breeds, who were soon to be led by Louis Riel, grandson of the first white woman ever to live in the Edmonton area. Winnipeg was a powder keg to be handled respectfully.

Instead of fondling it with diplomatic hands, John A. blundered against it. Some months before the deal had actually been consummated, acting as if the transfer of the territories to Canada had really been made, his government sent surveyors to Winnipeg to lay out the land into a rectangular system of sections and quarter sections. These surveyors were the sparks ready to fall into the powder. And when they drove pegs into André Nault's "hay privilege," he, brave man that he was, and made doubly brave by the justice that sat on his side, ran out to stop them. Then when the surveyors stretched their steel chain out from that peg, Louis Riel, hitherto an unnoticed settler, whose blood was one-eighth Indian, trod on it, and in so doing, stepped into history and into legend. The powder keg had gone off.

Even Ottawa heard its bang. There it hit a surprised John A. Macdonald and banished any chuckling over how "quietly" Canada had "annexed" the prairies. Its echoes reached London and rejoiced Washington, where sabre-rattling *Manifest Destiny* was introducing impudent bills to Congress destined to release the prairies from the heels of monarchs and tyrants.

In the end, after a winter of near anarchy at Red River, and after Donald Smith, who was later to become Lord Strathcona, had cut Riel's feet from under him, order was restored. The prairies were legally transferred to Canada, and by the Manitoba Act assented to on May 12, 1870, Manitoba, a pocket-size province of 11,000 square miles, was created. Canada now stretched from Halifax to the Rockies. Edmontonians, smelling the balm of new buds and looking across the spate of spring run-off in the mighty Saskatchewan River to the verdant loveliness of new leaves clothing their valley, were now citizens of Canada.

Red River Cart

Looking north across the river to Fort Edmonton 1879. Outside the palisade and up the hill from the fort is Hardisty's Big House. Buildings on the skyline are the hamlet of Edmonton near Rev. George McDougall's church. John Walter's house is on the south bank.

Smallpox, Mounties And Earliest Settlers 1868-1879

chapter **6**

A T ST. ALBERT, where the Oblate Fathers were making mighty progress, they too watched the marvel of spring sweep across their river valley. Father Lacombe, who had opened the mission in 1861 and who two years later had started a horse-driven grist mill, found that it worked indifferently. To replace it he built a dam just below Big Lake in 1864 and erected a new mill there to supply flour to the three hundred souls who even this early looked upon St. Albert as their home. In the spring of 1868, Father Leduc, another of the great Oblate priests and another of Alberta's great men, took charge of St. Albert. While he continued to carry the burden of this mission for another quarter of a century, Bishop Vital Grandin arrived in the fall, and henceforth this was his episcopal seat. Then in the spring of 1870 men were set to work to replace Father Lacombe's old church with one worthy of a bishop, one eighty-four feet long and thirty-two feet wide, with transepts extending on either side.

Meanwhile, missionaries, both Roman Catholic and Methodist, were doing all they could to bring about peace between the Blackfeet and the Crees who were ever at each other's throats. In this work, Father Lacombe and both the McDougalls strove incessantly, making infinite sacrifices and exposing themselves to many an Indian battle.

The fur traders, case-hardened by extensive exposure to natives, were apt to be cynical. Their journals paid more regard to Indians who caused them trouble and overlooked the fact that they were, after all, human beings with their own private woes and public problems. The missionaries on the other hand were apt to think of the Indians in the plane of a Sunday school class. Some Indians scoffed at them, and were recorded as being inspired by the devil. Others succumbed to their blandishments and were reported as angelic souls whose true identity was hidden under the disguise of a red skin and buckskin clothes. The Indians, of course, were neither angels nor devils, but human beings sorely pressed by a changing environment.

Maskepetoon, one of the Methodist protégés, however, whose life ran its course in the Edmonton area, deserves more attention than he has been given. In spite of the fact that most of our information about him comes to us through the missionaries' writings, which smack of the fondness lavished upon a neophyte, he appears to have been a great man. Undoubtedly amongst the wide variety of chiefs there were other Indians of his ilk, but they must have been few and far between. Even though we discount some of his recorded saintliness, his story is worth telling.

Born sometime around 1810, he first enters our ken when in January 1848 Paul Kane met him near Fort Pitt. He was then a chief, and hence a man given to meditation. At that time the missionaries with their inter-faith bickering confused him, and he explained to Kane that: "Mr. Rundell has told him that what he preached was the only true road to heaven, and Mr. Hunter (Anglican) told him the same thing, and so did Mr. Thebo, and as they all three said that the other two were wrong, and as he did not know which was right, he thought they ought to call a council among themselves, and that then he would go with them all three; but that until they agreed he would wait." In spite of their differences, however, he had spotted a philosophy common to them all—that of turning the other cheek and requiting evil with good.

In pursuit of it, sometime about 1850, under dramatic circumstances, he brought about a peace which is commemorated in the name of the Peace Hills near modern Wetaskiwin. Finally, in April 1869, still following his peace-oriented philosophy, he walked into a treacherous Blackfoot trap and was shot and horribly dismembered.

His untimely death set off a fresh burst of Blackfoot and Cree killings. On April 13, 1870, the Rev. Peter Campbell, who was stationed at Pigeon Lake, wrote: "Of late we have become painfully familiar with deeds of cold-blooded butchery and unpitying revenge. . . . On the 8th inst. two men, three women, and one child, belonging to the Blackfoot tribe were also killed at Edmonton by the Crees and Stoneys. . . . The triumph of the Crees is great. They now possess the savage satisfaction of killing a Chief of the tribe who struck down their beloved Chief, Mas-kee-pe-toon, nearly one year ago. Such is savage warfare, merciless cruelty, deathless hate."

Lieutenant W. F. Butler, who had accompanied Wolseley's expedition to Red River and then had been commissioned to visit Edmonton to report on conditions there, mentioned this battle. "This attack occurred after the safety of these Indians had been purchased from the Crees by the officer of the Hudson's Bay Company in charge at Edmonton, and a guard provided for their safe passage across the rivers. This guard, composed of French half-breeds from St. Albert, opened up to right and left when the attack commenced, and did nothing towards saving the lives of the Blackfeet, who were nearly all killed or wounded. . . ."

In retaliation, the Blackfeet soon mustered a large force and returned to attack Edmonton House, its Crees and its misguided half-breeds. When in April 1870 Chief Factor Christie heard of their approach, he put the fort into a state of defence, and at the same time sent to St. Albert for Métis reinforcements and for Father Lacombe, who might be able to talk the angered plainsmen into calming down.

While the good Father was on his way, corpulent Christie started to gird himself for the fight by putting on his wide sword belt, which he had not worn for many a year, and thereby provided a moment of laughter that helped to cut the tension. Due to his increased girth, it took all the tugging and pinching that Malcolm Groat and Harrison Young could do to squeeze his fat figure into the outgrown belt.

SMALLPOX, MOUNTIES AND EARLIEST SETTLERS — 1868-1879

When the Blackfeet descended the long hill on the south side of the river opposite the fort, they found the Rev. Peter Campbell of Pigeon Lake, David McDougall, and the Hudson's Bay man from Rocky Mountain House, and a few others, waiting to ford the river. To save their lives, these men had to abandon their carts and hurriedly cross over to the fort, leaving a fine assortment of trade goods on the south bank.

Rejoicing in their windfall of blankets and prints, tea and sugar, the Blackfeet quickly looted the goods and then made a bonfire of the carts. From their position on the flats opposite the fort, they peppered the post with rifle fire. Everyone braced for the attack which was expected when after dark the Indians could cross the river unobserved. At midnight Father Lacombe arrived, and by walking around outside the palisade and calling out in Blackfoot, he helped to persuade the angry Indians to call off their attack. Next morning they had vanished.

As it turned out, this was to be the last time Edmonton House was ever in any danger from a concerted attack. That this was so was merely fortuitous because the Hudson's Bay Company's power had been eroded away. No longer could it keep the peace, and unfortunately no other constituted government had come along to assume its former authority. Theoretically, the Dominion of Canada should have taken over the heavy responsibilities which the company had carried, but because the West was in transition, the government had not had time to decide what to do. A whole chain of events occupying the next five years had to work itself out before Canada rose to the occasion. Links in this chain were the inroads of free traders, the influx of Métis, the invasion of American whisky traders, and the eruption of smallpox. And during a period of three or four years all these came piling in on top of each other to create incredible confusion.

By this time free traders, that is, individuals mainly from the Red River, came in to compete with the Hudson's Bay Company. Having no responsibility for maintaining order or for the welfare of the Indians, they undersold the Hudson's Bay Company and indiscriminately dished out liquor. To compete, the company increased its outpouring of rum, and soon every man's hand was against every other and a wave of turbulence swept over the West.

During this period, the population of the Métis settlements at Lac La Biche, Victoria, St. Albert and Lac Ste. Anne increased rapidly. Many of the Red River half-breeds, fretting over the increasing encroachment of white adventurers and apprehensive of what might happen when that settlement became part of Canada, decided to move a thousand miles west to join their relatives.

With Indians stirred up by free traders and firewater, and with an incursion of Métis, the Hudson's Bay Company maintained its lessening grip on the Alberta area under conditions that were most insecure and unsatisfactory. Its old rule had gone. As Lieutenant Butler said: "As matters at present rest, the region of the Saskatchewan is without law, order, or security for life or property; robbery and murder for years have gone unpunished; Indian massacres are unchecked even in the close vicinity of the Hudson's Bay Company's posts, and all civil and legal institutions are entirely unknown."

Moreover, due to the presence of free traders and the resultant heavy expense, the Hudson's Bay Company was taking a large loss at Edmonton House, a loss estimated to be from £2,000 to £6,000 a year. While, of course, this was partly offset by profits coming in from Lesser Slave Lake and the Peace River, nevertheless, the company would have liked to have abandoned the heavy liability of Edmonton. Everyone knew, however, that, if it did, the American fur traders would come whooping in.

As a matter of fact, they did enter Alberta, and came as far north as they dared. In 1869 the traders from Fort Benton, Montana, came in and built the first Fort Whoop-Up, near modern Lethbridge. That same year, Dave Akers and Liver-Eating Johnston built the Spitzee Post on the Highwood River. Other so-called whisky forts were added during the next year or so, including a post built within the present limits of the City of Calgary. Not content with that advance, however, the American whisky traders brought cart loads of liquor and other trade goods to Tail Creek, near Buffalo Lake, and on occasion traded in the vicinity of Edmonton.

In general, the American adventurers were of Anglo-Saxon or Irish stock, but occasionally rare individuals of other races showed up. Such a rarity was a man named Silverman who spent the summer of 1869 searching for gold along the Saskatchewan River, and thereby became the first recorded person of Jewish descent to reach Edmonton.

Then in 1869, Father Lacombe, with three Métis and a cart, set out for Fort Benton to investigate the feasibility of getting goods for St. Albert through American channels. Now, on top of the comings and goings of gold miners and the incursion of whisky traders, even Canadian clerics were setting their thoughts towards Montana. For a time too, the Blackfeet quit trading at Edmonton while they experimented with the guns and booze the Montana traders held out to them. The country was rapidly being oriented towards the Americans.

But then, just as this American trade was getting a foothold, another import from the United States, a totally unplanned one, bowled over the Blackfeet and other Indians. It reached Edmonton shortly after the Blackfeet besieged the fort in the spring of 1870, and went on to devastate the Métis. That was smallpox, the terrible plague of 1869-1870.

Like a prairie fire it swept north over the plains, licking up the natives as it bore onward, leaving bleaching skeletons and stark tepee poles as souvenirs. The chain of infection splashed up the Missouri in a steamboat, made a bee-line for the Crow lodges, and leaped over the Piegans, whom it hit in the winter of 1869-1870. By the spring of 1870 it had swept on to the Bloods, the Blackfeet and the Assiniboines, and by June it was clutching at the half-breed camp at Tail Creek, where the Métis hunters from St. Albert and Edmonton House were assembled for their annual spring buffalo hunt. Chief Factor Christie, in reporting the progress of the plague, said that "it spread through the whole (camp), and in the early part of September their situation was most pitiful, small-pox of the worst form in every tent, with deaths daily. . . ."

East and west and north it swept, to Lac Ste. Anne, Victoria, Fort Pitt and Fort Carlton. From there it was carried to Lac La Biche, because a brigade of carts went from the lake to Fort Carlton for the usual supplies. Of the fourteen cart drivers who left Lac La Biche, eight died on the way or immediately after getting home.

Amongst Alberta Indians about one-half died of the disease. The official figures for the Saskatchewan District show that 2,686 of the Plains Indians were swept away, while 485 Crees and 373 half-breeds died.

But these are just statistics. Various writers tried to portray the stark tragedy of the plague. Of these, perhaps, Lieutenant Butler, who toured the prairies on a commission of enquiry, gave the clearest description.

SMALLPOX, MOUNTIES AND EARLIEST SETTLERS — 1868-1879

". . . By streams and lakes, in willow copses, and upon bare hill-sides, often shelterless from the fierce rays of the summer sun and exposed to the rains and dews of night, the poor plague-stricken wretches lay down to die—no assistance of any kind, for the ties of family were quickly loosened, and mothers abandoned their helpless children upon the wayside, fleeing onward to some fancied place of safety. . . ."

The smallpox smote St. Albert in its most virulent form. There, six hundred souls out of nine hundred caught the disease, and in spite of the untiring devotion of priests and nuns, 320 died. Father Lacombe, who laboured at his outpost at St. Paul de Cris and travelled out to stricken Indian camps, lost many of his flock.

At Victoria, perhaps because it was a much smaller settlement than St. Albert, and perhaps because of the policies adopted by the Rev. George McDougall, the native mortality was proportionately less. All the missionary's family, except Mrs. McDougall, caught the disease, and two of her children, Flora and Georgina, died. So did her adopted Indian girl Anna. Then, some weeks later, during his absence, John McDougall's wife contracted the disease and died.

Fortunately, due to the care exercised by the fur traders, Edmonton House came through the epidemic unscathed. The scare, however, was great enough that Edmontonians sent for the nearest physician. This was the famous Dr. W. M. Mackay, who later became a citizen of the growing city but who at the time was stationed a thousand miles away at Fort Simpson on the Mackenzie River. By the time he made his way into Edmonton House, the plague was over.

In 1871, then, with the Indians devastated by smallpox and with an increasing influx of American whisky traders, the western prairies and Edmonton their capital were on the verge of change. In the forefront of the movement for a better deal for the West and its Indians stood the missionaries, led by Father Lacombe and the two McDougalls, while taking up a position to support them stood an aroused eastern Canada. All of them demanded more education, more missions and some military intervention.

On the scene of education in 1868, as a supplement to Brother Scollen's school, A. J. Snyder, under the eye of the Rev. Peter Campbell, operated a Methodist day school at Edmonton until he moved away to the mission at Whitefish Lake. In respect to more missions, in 1870 Rev. Mr. Campbell arranged to have logs cut for an Edmonton mission house to be built the next year. The Rev. George McDougall moved his family to Edmonton in June 1871 and lived at the fort until December when his house was finished. With him he brought a small organ, the first such musical instrument west of Winnipeg.

His new and comfortable parsonage, twenty-three by thirty-three feet, two stories high and with a board ceiling, was the first building to be erected along the high bank in what, to distinguish it from the immediate environs of the fort, we may call the Hamlet of Edmonton. It was situated immediately east of the Hudson's Bay Company's land on what is now McDougall Church property. Shortly afterwards, Mrs. McDougall conducted a day school, while her husband set about building Edmonton's first Protestant church, which was to be consecrated in 1873. Meanwhile, in 1872, down at the fort, Chief Trader Richard Hardisty, who had married one of John McDougall's sisters, had succeeded Chief Factor Christie. With a foot in both camps, he helped in getting the church built and in fact fashioned its pulpit.

At the time the McDougall house and church were built, not a single parcel of land had been surveyed in the Edmonton area. By the terms of the agreement by which the Hudson's Bay Company had ceded its old territory to Canada, the company was to retain three thousand acres of land around each of its posts. Shortly after the agreement was signed, surveyors started the task of fixing the boundaries of these parcels of land, but it was not till 1873 that W. S. Gore reached Edmonton and actually staked out the Hudson's Bay Company's Reserve.

Even though a few squatters had built shacks along the river bank, prior to this everyone had a rough idea of what land would be included in the official survey, and, if he had any notion of settling down and claiming land for himself, he tried to locate so as to be outside the reserve. The only two serious squatters near it were George McDougall, who, as we have seen, built to the east of the fort, and Malcolm Groat, who settled down on land west of it. Each expected that when the boundary lines came to be drawn their establishments would be well clear of them. As we have seen, over the years other squatters, most of them transients, built shacks all the way from Miners' Flats downstream for some miles. If, however, we were to try to designate a point in time when what we know as the Edmonton Settlement began, we should give credit to Malcolm Groat and George McDougall for starting it.

With the appearance of Groat's house and McDougall's mission the nucleus of the new Edmonton had appeared. As it turned out, several other squatters settled down east of the church and soon this area assumed the stretched out appearance of a typical fur trade settlement. From it was to grow the city which would outshadow the fort, overwhelm it, and finally erase it.

Not all of the new arrivals, however, chose to squat in this hamlet, and during the next few years some of them selected sites which suited them at various points up and down the river and on each side of it. Of some of these we have fairly definite information, as in the case of Dr. George Verey, Edmonton's first resident physician. Though a member of the Royal College of Surgeons, he was somewhat of a wanderer and in 1873 he came to work as a clerk at Edmonton House. The following year he went to help the McDougalls at their new Morley Mission for a while and then returned to Edmonton to build a house on the present Municipal Golf Course near the Groat Ravine. There he farmed and practised medicine until his death in 1881. From 1874 to 1876, as well as carrying on these other activities, he taught Edmonton's first real school. It was for the children of Hudson's Bay Company employees and held forth in a house on Ross Flats east of the fort.

While Edmonton was getting its small but vastly significant start, many other developments, all devoted to foisting civilization on the surrounding prairies, were stirring. The first was the force of Dominion Land Surveyors sent to parcel out the West. After a slight pause, when they fired the fuse of Riel's Rebellion, they resumed work in 1871 and gradually spread west from Manitoba. Not only did they divide the land, but like Joshua, the son of Nun, and Caleb, the son of Jephunneh, they spied it out and reported to Ottawa and to all men on what land it was, whether it was fat or lean, and whether there was wood therein or not.

Hard on their heels came the North American Boundary Commission Survey of 1872-1874, which, with pits and cairns, marked the boundary between Saskatchewan and Dakota, Alberta and Montana. Now the whisky traders of Fort Whoop-Up, stepping over it, could be certain that it was Canadian Indians they were debauching.

Neither the Dominion Land Surveyors nor the boundary commission, however, focused as much attention on the West as the CPR surveyors. When in 1871

SMALLPOX, MOUNTIES AND EARLIEST SETTLERS — 1868-1879

John A. Macdonald swung his confederation noose and caught British Columbia's head in it, his Canada truly stretched from sea to sea. But since his taut lariat was already overstressed, he promised to set to right away to replace it with a more permanent though equally stretched-out railway, and undertook to complete it to British Columbia within ten years. Now he found both his hands full trying to hold a wild, struggling British Columbia with one and with the other urging his bucking CPR horse to hurry west to take the strain off his rope.

As a start he made Sandford Fleming engineer-in-chief of his visionary CPR. Fleming went right to work, and by 1872, sparing neither money nor vigour, he had surveyors fanning out all over. That year he had twenty-five parties in the field, and six of them studied various routes, such as the Yellowhead, Athabasca, Howse and Peace River passes. Many of these paused in Edmonton and recruited men, horses and supplies in the frontier settlement. In August, Fleming, making a personal inspection, reached Edmonton, accompanied by a Presbyterian, the Rev. George M. Grant. About this trip Grant wrote an interesting book, "Ocean to Ocean," commenting on Edmonton, praising the work of the McDougalls at their Victoria mission, and speaking in glowing terms of the Roman Catholic mission at St. Albert.

During 1872 the Federal government, spurred on by the missionaries' representations and by Captain Butler's report of what he saw on his trip to Edmonton, sent out Colonel P. Robertson-Ross to study the situation in the West and to bring back recommendations on how best to establish law and order. In his report, Robertson-Ross said: "The demoralization of the Indians and injury to the country from this illicit traffic (liquor) is very great. It is stated on good authority that last year eighty-eight of the Blackfeet Indians were murdered in drunken brawls among themselves. . . ." He reported that Americans from Fort Benton made their way to Edmonton, where they openly sold whisky, declaring that "as there was no force to prevent them, they would do just as they pleased." Amongst other things, Robertson-Ross recommended stationing troops at Edmonton, saying: "With regard to the accommodation of Troops, they should be hutted outside the H.B. Fort in log huts of their own on the high ground at the Back of the Fort but temporary accommodation could be found for them in the H.B. Fort for about 6 officers and 120 men."

After considering this report, the Dominion government brought the North West Mounted Police into being. In due course, this military body set out on its memorable trek from Fort Garry to southern Alberta. From Roche Percée in southern Saskatchewan on August 1, 1874, "A" Division, under Inspector W. D. Jarvis, Sub-Inspector Gagnon, and Sergeant-Major Sam Steele, split off from the main body and struck out for Edmonton. They "took with them six men from other divisions and 12 half-breeds, 24 wagons, 55 carts, about 55 sick or tired horses, 62 oxen, 50 cows and calves, as well as the agricultural implements and general stores (including over 25,000 lb. of flour) not essential to the main body."

Travelling by way of Fort Ellice and Fort Carlton and reaching McDougall's mission at Victoria on October 19 almost in a state of collapse, they struggled on. One of the men's diaries shows how they stumbled on from there to Edmonton.

"October 26. Reached Sturgeon Creek by noon. All horses close to exhaustion. Crossed the creek at 'The Rapids'. Great difficulty getting the wagons across. One horse, unable to make it, died in the stream. Weather cold. . . . The trail grew worse, sloughs across it every few hundred yards; men and animals struggled knee-deep in black mud. Time and again the wagons had to be unloaded and dragged out by hand. On every side were small ponds covered with thin ice, which proved to be a menace. The horses and oxen, feverish and thirsty, would rush to the ponds, crash through and wait to be hauled out with ropes. Some were so exhausted they had to be held up by the head while the ropes were being attached."

Next day they straggled into Edmonton House, where they were quartered for the winter and where shortly before they arrived Richard Hardisty had vacated John Rowand's Big House for a new one he built higher up the hill and outside the stockade. In its turn it came to be known as the Big House.

Meanwhile, the CPR surveyors going out to study alternative routes through remote canyons passed and repassed through Edmonton. During 1873-1874 they concentrated on the Yellowhead Pass as Sandford Fleming tried to compare the merits of seven different routes from Edmonton to the Coast. While this survey work continued to be carried on in various parts of the West, by 1875 the line was actually located from the east to the vicinity of Edmonton. Amongst the very few white traders living at Edmonton a new confidence began to reign; before long they hoped to find themselves on the transcontinental railroad with all that would mean to their future. Edmonton's prospects appeared excellent.

Even though the arrival of the railway surveyors was an encouraging indication of a future easing of the burden of the long freight haul that summer saw an actual milestone in transportation progress. For, on July 22, 1875, the "Northcote," the first steamer to ascend the river as far as Edmonton, arrived. From then on, whenever the depth of the water in the river permitted, Edmonton formed the upper terminus of a line of steamboat communication starting at Winnipeg. From that town steamers churned their way north along Lake Winnipeg to the mouth of the Saskatchewan River at Grand Rapids. To circumvent the three miles of rough water there, the Hudson's Bay Company built a tramway and once goods from Winnipeg had passed over it they could be carried the hundreds of miles upstream to Edmonton by steamboat.

Inspector Jarvis had been instructed to set up his North West Mounted Police fort on the south side of the river anywhere between Edmonton House and the mouth of the Sturgeon River. As a suitable spot for the police post, Richard Hardisty, on his own authority, had already selected the area now occupied by the university. Jarvis, however, preferred a site some twenty miles farther downstream, partly because at the time the railway survey was not finished and it was the general opinion that because of the low river banks there as compared to the deep valley at Edmonton, the railway would cross the river that far downstream. It was common gossip in those days that Jarvis and Hardisty had quite an altercation on the subject, and that Jarvis chose the site downstream to show the Hudson's Bay Company factor who was boss. Accordingly, in the spring of 1875 the police started to build their post, which at first they called Sturgeon Creek Post, but soon changed its name to Fort Saskatchewan.

With the arrival of the police, regardless of whether or not the headquarters of "A" Troop actually remained in Edmonton, and with all the activity engendered by the railway surveyors, business began to look up. Commencing in July 1876, the police detachment at Edmonton operated a semi-official post office called Edmonton. It was not till March 1, 1878, however, that a fully official post office opened under the name of Fort Edmonton, with Richard Hardisty as its properly appointed postmaster.

SMALLPOX, MOUNTIES AND EARLIEST SETTLERS — 1868-1879

In 1876, to accommodate the many men who were coming and going, Donald Ross, who had come to Edmonton four years earlier, started Edmonton's first and famous hotel. The small settlement was also served by clerics of three faiths, the Roman Catholic and the Methodists, who had long been there, and by an Anglican, the Rev. Wm. Newton. The transcontinental railway was on its way. Its actual route was still a little vague, but it appeared that it was to approach Edmonton from the south-east, because in 1877 the contractors had strung a telegraph line, which for the moment terminated at Hay Lakes. If it continued west from there the railway would pass some twenty miles south of Edmonton, but since the route farther west was still uncertain, there was every chance that it would swing north to the hamlet. It appeared that at last Edmonton's place in the sun was assured.

Ever since 1875 when the "Northcote" had reached Edmonton, steamboats plying the river brought in goods for the Hudson's Bay Company. Then at least as early as 1879, the old pack trail to Athabasca Landing had been cut out to permit the passage of carts. Recently too, a new trail had come into use to the Mounted Police post established on the Bow River in 1875 and called Fort Calgary. This was an extension of the one that had been used for decades to reach Rocky Mountain House and Lake Minnewanka. While there had been a shack or so on the site of Calgary for some years and as early as 1871 an American whisky post had been located some miles up the Elbow River, no permanent settlement had taken place at its junction with the Bow until 1875.

One of the early men to use the new trail to Calgary was John A. Mc-Dougall, the young trader, when in 1877 he accompanied some Methodist friends to Calgary, where his namesake the missionary was building a church. John McDougall, who was to rise to such prominence in Edmonton's business world, was not unduly impressed by the hamlet of Calgary and preferred to set up shop in Edmonton. In the near future, as he sized up the situation, trains would deliver truck of all kinds to Edmonton, which, acting as a distribution centre, would trans-ship goods by freight teams to the north and to all such hamlets as Calgary. That point, which had come into being as a mere police outpost, lay two hundred miles south of Edmonton, and, therefore, its future was strictly limited.

While the end of the telegraph was still at Hay Lakes, some twenty miles away, it was nevertheless a great convenience. There was no actual office there, but young James McKernan, who had first seen the West in 1874 as a member of the North West Mounted Police and then three years later had helped his brother Robert to build the line, and who had settled down at its end, operated it to send messages for Edmontonians. He sent the first such message on November 20, 1877.

Shortly afterwards his brother Robert moved up to Hay Lakes, and in 1879 moved once more to build his home on the lake on the south side which came to be called after him. In doing so, he became one of Edmonton's earliest farmers.

By this time, several half-breeds, who were still casually employed by the Hudson's Bay Company or who had left its service, and an occasional miner or other white man, had selected choice spots along the river's bank and had settled down there. One of these was Thomas Smith, who came to Edmonton in 1875 and who was destined in 1881 to go back to Winnipeg to purchase the first steam thresher ever to appear in the settlement and to haul it with oxen all the way along the old Winnipeg trail. Another was John Walter, an Orkney boat builder, who, starting when he was twenty-one, had worked for the company since 1870. Early in 1876 he decided to live in a place of his own, and accordingly built a house facing the fort across the river. In due course, he obtained title to this land, which turned out to be River Lot 9 and extended east and west from 107 Street to 109 Street and south as far as University Avenue.

Any settlers such as Smith or the McKernans raised some grain for a cow or two and for their horses and were able to sustain themselves by agriculture alone if they had to. Most of them, however, found other work either with the Hudson's Bay Company or as packers and guides with the railway surveyors. Although Edmonton's soil was rich enough for farming, there was no export market for any grain or other produce and no practical way of shipping it. While these farmers managed to get along, the question of whether or not most of Alberta's soil could be turned into successful farms, however, was still a matter of speculation.

About this time, Ottawa loosed a host of scientists and surveyors on the West, and each of them, after scurrying about, sent an increasing store of knowledge back east. One of these, the famous G. M. Dawson, who had gone on from working for the boundary commission to join the Geological Survey of Canada, had several parties working in the West. In 1879 he stopped at Edmonton for a day or so and took one of the earliest photos of the fort which appears on page 73. Another was the eminent botanist John Macoun, whom Sandford Fleming employed and who on occasion visited Edmonton. He was far more optimistic about much of the West than Palliser had been. His reports were the means of convincing eastern Canada that the West, and particularly Alberta, was capable of supporting an untold number of settlers. In spite of these reports, however, which induced an immigration into Manitoba, Alberta's lands had to await the arrival of the railway, and even then their time had not really come. Even in Manitoba the first wheat was not exported until 1876.

Even though Edmonton was far removed from Manitoba, occasional settlers like the McKernans began to come out to have a look, and, having come, usually stayed. In 1878 Jim Gibbons, the roving 49'er, who at times had panned gold up and down the Saskatchewan and had interspersed that with trading trips all over the prairies, decided to make his permanent home in Edmonton. That year he made formal application to homestead the land on Miners' Flats on which he had lived for some time. This is the land in Laurier Park on which the Storyland Valley Zoo is now located. At the same time, his old mining crony, Charles Stephenson (English Charlie) filed on the land north of his. That year too, Malcolm Groat made formal entry for his land, which we know as the Groat Ravine area.

In 1878 William Bird, a descendant of the original Hudson's Bay Company's J. B. Bird, imported a flour mill from England. When its machinery reached Edmonton by steamboat, he erected it beside what, because of it, came to be called Mill Creek. Since the flow of that creek is most erratic, the mill's years were numbered, but for a while Bird served the surrounding farmers.

Out of the handful of curious adventurers who came at this time, three o her individuals stand out; Dr. Newton, Frank Oliver and Alex Taylor. Of these, Dr. Newton, the diminutive but irascible Anglican minister, arrived first in September 1875, after being five months on the journey from Toronto. As soon as he sized up Edmonton, he went some seven miles downstream from the fort and there at what he called the Hermitage he built his church. Later on, when he could, he homesteaded most of the land which is directly across the river from the Canadian Chemical Company. When by 1877 the site of his church proved

*Frank Oliver whose Edmonton Bulletin,
started in 1880, was a potent force in the
West. Always active in politics, Oliver rose
to be Minister of the Interior in the Federal
Cabinet in 1905.*

to be impractically remote, Malcolm Groat gave him five acres of land west of
124 Street and there he erected another edifice. Though the learned Dr. Newton
was to serve his Edmonton flock for twenty years, there were times when his
parish disappointed him. Writing of it on November 1, 1879, he said:

"We have nothing like a town. As we said, there is the fort, then if you
had a telescope and could look around the corner into a valley you would see a
hotel. Then if there was no fog you could see the Methodist chapel and parsonage
and scattered houses on that side; and on the other, All Saints English Church,
a few Indian tents and again a few settlers' houses up the river. This is Edmonton
proper."

Frank Oliver, after a sojourn in Winnipeg where he worked for one of the early newspapers, loaded a few trade goods into an ox-drawn Red River cart, and in 1876 set out for Edmonton. After weeks on the old Carlton Trail, he camped for the night on the south side of the river in sight of the fort. He spent most of the next day lashing a raft together to cross the stream. Though when he was half way over it upset, Oliver and his ox made it to the Edmonton shore and he was able to save some of his goods. In a day or so, after he got his bearings, he built a shack two or three hundred yards east along the trail from the McDougall Mission, and for four years did some trading or took a hand in any other gainful employment he could come by.

In 1879, Alex Taylor, an ingenious individual, caught the public eye when he became the telegraph operator. Ever since the end of the CPR construction telegraph line had been at Hay Lakes Edmontonians had made various attempts to have it extended to the fort. This step was finally approved and Mr. Fuller, the telegraph contractor, offered to supply the wire free of charge if the people of Edmonton would provide the poles and defray the labour costs. On October 6, according to the *Saskatchewan Herald,* a subscription was started. In the end, the Hudson's Bay Company put up most of the cost of the line and it was extended to a building owned by John Walter, across the river from the fort, and Alex Taylor moved in as operator. Inspector Jarvis received the first message over the extended line on January 1, 1880.

At last Edmonton was beginning to take shape as something more than a mere fur trade post. Some settlers had come in, the NWMP had established a post in the area, steamboats plied between Winnipeg and the hamlet, and the telegraph connected it with the outside world. Best of all, a railway was soon to keep the telegraph line company. It was to this promise of a railway that Edmontonians pinned their hopes. In fact, the confident expectation that this promise would be fulfilled and that Edmonton would soon be on the transcontinental railway, had induced many a trader to settle there. Edmonton's prospects looked good.

A group including some N.W.M.P. in front of Commanding Officer's house inside Fort Edmonton, 1884, showing cannon available for defense.

Riel Rebellion
1879-1885

chapter 7

IN AUGUST 1879 John A. McDougall, who had visited Edmonton two years earlier, brought his young wife to the hamlet and set up as a trader close to Frank Oliver. Many years later, when reminiscing, he gave a picture of what the settlement was like when they arrived.

". . . Edmonton was then nothing but a Hudson Bay Company post surrounded by a high stockade with bastions at each corner . . . Outside the fort and where the Parliament Buildings now stand was the 'big house,' the residence of the Chief Factor.

"The Hudson Bay Company owned a reserve of 3,000 acres of land at this place which today is in the heart of the city. To the west and east of this reserve a few farmers — former employees of the Hudson Bay Company — had taken up claims upon which they had settled.

". . . After getting their little crop in in the spring they would generally go down to Winnipeg with a string of ponies and carts after freight for the Company and in the fall after their return and when their small crop was gathered in, they would all start for the plains for a buffalo hunt and to lay in a winter's supply of meat. . . .

"Down on the flat a little north west of the power house was a small cemetery where many of the Company's employees were buried. It was enclosed by a picket fence. There were quite a number of very fine Scotch granite tombstones and monuments which had been brought all the way from Scotland to mark the graves . . . Across the river at the mouth of Mill Creek there was a small flour mill run by water power which ground what little wheat there was raised here.

". . . There was no settlement of any kind or no one living between here and Calgary except a small half-breed settlement on the Battle River and the telegraph operator at Hay Lake. . . ."

When speaking of Edmonton House, McDougall called it the fort. This was a change which crept into common usage about this time, with the result that thenceforth the older appellation was dropped.

In 1878 an unofficial census, which counted only adult whites and half-breeds but left out treaty Indians, gave the population of the five principal settlements tributary to Edmonton as follows:

1878 population	
Fort Saskatchewan	59
St. Albert	178
Lac Ste. Anne	58
Lac La Biche	102
Victoria	58
	455

As for the Edmonton settlement itself, including Hudson's Bay Company employees, the miners and the squatters stretched out along the river, and the forty souls in the little hamlet by McDougall Church, the combined population was 148. To this strung-out settlement with its homes in isolated spots or in little groups cleared out of the enveloping bush, came one trail from the east, and from it led three other trails, and up the river to it, two or three times a year, puffed a steamer. Through a gash in the woods but dead-ending at Hay Lakes, wound the survey line for the proposed railway, while beside it hung the telegraph line. Three miles south of the settlement and just beyond McKernan's Lake, lay the recently surveyed Papaschase Indian Reserve, while seven miles west the Stony Plain Reserve endeavoured to reconcile its foot-loose denizens to living in one spot.

The west boundary of the hamlet — downtown Edmonton of 1879 — was a slash cut through the trees by W. S. Gore, when in 1873 he surveyed the three thousand acre Hudson's Bay Company Reserve. Defined in terms of modern streets, the reserve was bounded on the east by 101 Street, on the west by 121 Street, and extended from the river to a line near 127 Avenue.

With the prospect that Edmonton would grow rapidly, John Norris, Donald McLeod and the Belcher Brothers, started to build a saw and grist mill on Kenny Macdonald's property east of the hamlet. Then in October James McDonald and Matt McCauley came in by cart from Winnipeg. McCauley, after looking around, set his heart on some land at Fort Saskatchewan and went there to farm. That fall too, the Hendersons, coming over the mountains, settled down on land west of Whitemud Creek and about two miles south of today's Grandview Heights. In November the Edmonton Agricultural Society held its first exhibition at the fort, while three months earlier the Hudson's Bay Company boats, which hitherto had restricted themselves to carrying company freight only, began carrying passengers.

The West was a man's world. Few white women were willing to face its hardships, its loneliness and its lack of female companionship. When young Mrs. John A. McDougall came, her arrival in the hamlet adjacent to the Methodist Mission brought the number of white women there to four. The other three were Mrs. Donald Ross, Mrs. Coleman and Mrs. Whiteside. Down at the old fort, however, lived the three other white women, Mrs. Taber, and the daughters of the Rev. George McDougall; Mrs. Hardisty, wife of the factor, and her sister Mrs. Leslie Wood.

Most of the white men who had spent many years in the West were married to Indian or Métis women. They invariably found these women to be fine wives, obedient, chaste, able to cope with pioneer hardships, and infinitely loyal. Among these men were John Norris and Ed Carey who operated the store over near the fort, Colin Fraser, Dan Noyes, Jim Gibbons, Malcolm Groat, the Gullions from the Orkneys, and many others. These men, together with Richard Hardisty, John Walter, Donald Ross, Frank Oliver and John A. McDougall, formed the aristocracy of early Edmonton — an aristocracy of accomplishment.

Prominent in Edmonton society, of course, were the Métis, who were having a difficult time adjusting to the economic situation they faced. Where hardihood was essential, they had no superiors, and of the things that counted between man and man: loyalty, courage, friendliness and affection, they had good measure. Lucky was the white man who, similarly endowed, merited the full friendship of a Métis. They were proud of their blood and of their identity as a separate race combining many of the Indians' virtues with much of the white man's culture. Many of the half-breeds or "the people," as they called themselves, were moderately well educated and adhered to their own strict code.

When embryo Edmonton was taking its first halting steps, the Métis far outnumbered those whose skins were all white. Then they had a most useful place in the hamlet's society. On every hand they made a major contribution towards opening up the West. Unfortunately, they could not keep up with the speed of the change to an agricultural and a mercantile economy and dropped so far behind that their contribution of those days has been overlooked.

While in most ways Edmonton was a self-contained community making its way on the resources at hand, nevertheless the difficulty of keeping in touch with the rest of Canada always amazed newcomers. Writing in March 1880, Mrs. John A. McDougall pointed up Edmonton's isolation, when she said: "It is now six weeks since we have had any mail here or any communication with the outside world. The mail is at a stand still on account of the man who had the contract dying last winter $20,000.00 in debt and until that is settled we do not expect much news. The telegraph line is down some place and that throws us completely out of civilization. . . ."

During the summer of 1880, Frank Oliver made a return trip over the trail to Winnipeg. When he got back in November, one of his carts carried a second-hand press which he had bought for $20. Though it was only a miniature press, so small that for a long time Oliver could boast of producing the world's smallest newspaper, one of four pages each five inches wide and six inches deep, nevertheless, in his hands Alberta's first paper became a vital new force in the West. Soon his sound sense, his abiding faith in the new country, and his sometimes sharp but always pertinent editorials attracted country-wide attention. The fiery little *Bulletin,* always reflecting his peppery personality and his Liberal political views, grew rapidly in stature. Its threefold policy, damning John A. Macdonald and the Conservatives, battling for the rights of settlers, and lauding the rich possibilities of the prairies, exerted a great influence. It always expressed the utmost confidence in the north-west, but while all pioneer papers considered it their purpose to "boom" the country, Frank Oliver never descended to careless reporting or to painting a "get-rich-quick" picture. His paper never promised the prospective immigrant an easy living in a land of milk and honey, but guaranteed that the land would repay any persevering person who worked hard. For the student of the early days, its unusual wealth of accurate reporting makes it a gold mine of information.

Its birth was linked with Alex Taylor's telegraph line. During the winter of 1879-1880 Taylor had arranged with George H. Ham of Winnipeg to compile and wire him a weekly bulletin of world news. At Edmonton Taylor wrote out the week's news and for this service the handful of businessmen paid a small subscription. Then, after talking it over with Oliver, the telegrapher and the printer combined forces so that on December 6, 1880, the first issue of the *Edmonton*

Bulletin came out. Tiny though the paper was, its first issue had room for advertising matter, and amongst other enterprising businessmen, Donald Ross called attention to his hotel. His advertisement, in which the last two digits of the date were transposed, was as follows:

EDMONTON HOTEL & FEED STABLES
Established 1867

The pioneer house of accommodation this side of
Portage la Prairie. A good game of

BILLIARDS OR POOL
Can be played, and a very social evening can be
spent in the Billiard Room.

DONALD ROSS,
Proprietor

Prior to this time no one had been concerned with titles to property, and so long as he stayed off the Hudson's Bay Company Reserve and so long as he did not interfere with someone else's yard, a newcomer built his house wherever he wished. By 1880, now that the railway was on the way and, therefore, the town would soon start to grow, rights to property began to come into focus. The original settlers started looking about them, and although they had no legal title, they did have a claim to the piece on which they lived. Since land was of such little value, neighbour agreed with neighbour as to what frontage each one owned along the river. Along the trail that people began calling High Street, Frank Oliver and John A. McDougall purchased the first lots that were sold.

Edmontonians are proud of the great width of Jasper Avenue but few of them know that for this they have to thank the Hudson's Bay Company. When in 1880 that company employed a surveyor to subdivide the south end of its reserve, it called a meeting of local residents, asked them to select which of the proposed streets they thought should be the main one, and stated that it planned to make that street one hundred feet wide. The local people asked that as near as possible it should run from McDougall's Methodist Church on the east side of the reserve to Dr. Newton's Anglican Church on the west. Since the 14th Base Line did almost that, it was chosen for the main street and since it headed straight west towards the old fur trade post in the mountains, they called it Jasper Avenue.

By 1881 enough people had come in to make John Walter feel that a ferry would pay, so he strung a cable across the portion of the river between what is now 105 Street and the High Level bridges and rigged up a scow capable of carrying a team and a wagon at one time. About the same time, Donald Ross drove the shaft of his coal mine into the side of McDougall Hill.

Frank Oliver was also keeping track of the number of people coming in to Edmonton, for his *Bulletin* said:

"EDMONTON POPULATION INCREASES TO 263
Edmonton, Jan. 31, 1881 — The unofficial census which has just been completed gives the following as the adult population of the principal settlements in this district, with the increase or decrease since the last census was taken in '78.

> Edmonton settlement 263, increase 115.
> Fort Saskatchewan 60, increase 1.
> St. Albert 292, increase 114.
> Lac Ste. Anne 30, decrease 28.
> Lac La Biche 75, decrease 27.
> Victoria 46, decrease 12.
> Total 766. Total increase 163.

The apparent decrease in some of the settlements is on account of many who formerly were counted as half-breeds taking the treaty, thereby taking rank as Indians. The total population has of course increased much more than is apparent, as children are not counted in this census."

On every hand the signs were encouraging, and particularly with respect to the railway. In February 1881, with John A. Macdonald back in office, the government had come to grips with that problem and passed the act of parliament which brought the CPR one step nearer reality. Edmontonians could now see the prospect of an imminent boom. Looking back east to what was happening in Winnipeg, which, with a population of 10,000 in 1880, had nearly doubled to 18,000 within a year, they rubbed their hands, certain that their hamlet would follow in its footsteps and do so soon. Already too, because settlers in Manitoba could not wait for the railway, they had fanned out for a radius of nearly a hundred miles from Winnipeg. Then, due to Macdonald's new drive, the CPR began actual construction, and by September 1881, was as far west as Brandon. Assuredly, now that the railroad was really being built, Edmonton too might expect an influx of settlers within a year or so.

Almost unnoticed amongst all the other excitements was the fact that, on other fronts quite apart from the railway, scientists and practical men were studying the problems of what kinds of produce this new prairie soil might nurture. Not too long previously, David Fife, an Ontario farmer, had developed his Red Fife wheat, and his discovery provided Manitoba farmers with a wheat which would ripen on the prairies before being ruined by the West's early frosts. But Red Fife was a hard wheat, difficult to grind into flour by any of the conventional methods. Just at the right time, however, the Ogilvie Flour Milling Company came out with a new type of machinery which could cope with this hard northern wheat, and instead of millstones it introduced steel rollers. Although perhaps scarcely noticed by Manitobans, these two developments, Red Fife and a new method of milling, were the bases which permitted farmers to grow a commercial crop on the prairies.

In 1881 Matt McCauley, who had been farming near Fort Saskatchewan, moved into the hamlet and built a house east of the Methodist Church, on the site now occupied by the Edmonton Club. Almost immediately Matt faced up to the problem of a school. It was time, he thought, that Edmonton had a permanent school financed by the citizens. After discussing it with his friends, he set up a board with himself as chairman and William Rowland and Malcolm Groat as trustees, and started canvassing for funds. Before long he had collected $968, and with it he built Edmonton's first all-frame building on what is now 99 Avenue between 104 and 105 Streets on four lots donated by the Hudson's Bay Company. It was twenty-four feet by thirty feet, had twelve forms four feet long, and boasted of a blackboard. He hired a teacher by the name of Harris, whose salary of $500 a year was guaranteed by R. Hardisty, J. Cameron, D. McLeod, J. A. McRae, R. Logan, J. A. McDougall, J. Morris, C. Stewart, K. McDonald and Malcolm Groat.

Shortly after this, in October 1881, the Rev. A. B. Baird, Edmonton's first resident Presbyterian minister, reached the hamlet. He set to work to collect enough money to start building a Presbyterian Church on the north-west corner of 99 Avenue and 104 Street, a project he completed within a year.

With a school, a new minister, several new settlers, and an energetic man like Matt McCauley about, Edmonton assumed a bustle and an air of prosperity. In the West, meanwhile, the CPR crews were racing to outdo each other by laying two or even three miles of track across the open prairie in one day. No matter by what criterion anyone judged Edmonton's prospects, they were good.

But then something happened. Someone decided to change the route of the CPR and to build it straight west across southern Saskatchewan and then to have it run up the valley of the Bow River and to fight its way through Hector's incredibly difficult Kicking Horse Pass. Instead of working its way north and west from Brandon, generally along the decades-old trail from Winnipeg to Fort Carlton and thence up the North Saskatchewan River through Battleford, the erstwhile capital of the western prairies, and finally through the fur traders' old gently sloping Yellowhead Pass, it was to run straight west through the cactus of the Palliser Triangle. The Dominion government, worrying about protecting the prairies' southern border from American invasion, had changed the route!

Edmontonians had looked forward so eagerly to the coming of the railway and all the development it would have started, and when the news leaked out during the summer of 1881, it caught them below the belt. Although for many a month they felt sorry for themselves and for many a year they cursed the CPR and Ottawa's blind stupidity, all they could do was swallow their disappointment.

Instead of a railway, Edmontonians had to get along with a stage coach line. Flatboat McLean took on a mail contract for Prince Albert, Battleford and Edmonton. At intervals of forty miles all along the trail from Qu'Appelle to Humboldt and thence north to Prince Albert and west to Edmonton, he arranged for the erection of stage stations and stopping houses. Passengers, mail, and express were hurried along the road by wagons especially built for the job and drawn by four horses.

In spite of the fact that the CPR had by-passed Edmonton, a few more people came trickling in all the time. Because many of them did not want to buy Hudson's Bay Company lots, some simply squatted here and there along the high bank in the strung-out little hamlet. These newcomers were really trespassers on land which all the older settlers had claimed for several years but to which, because of the lack of any legal survey, they held no official title. Some of the interloping type were not particular where they built their shacks, and in a few cases put them up within a few feet of some of the old timers' buildings. One particularly obnoxious trespasser, J. L. George, built a shack on Richard Hardisty's land on the high bank between today's 96 and 97 Streets. This brought matters to a head in March 1882, and Matt McCauley, leading a vigilante committee, warned George to get out. When he ignored the warning, Matt and his men heaved the shack over the cliff, whence it rolled and rollicked merrily down towards the water. McCauley and his friends were maintaining a clear-cut principle about the sanctity of property rights which could find no legal protection.

Vigilante committees, however, taking the law into their own hands, were a development not to be encouraged in a British Dominion. Consequently, the Mounted Police rounded up McCauley and his friends and fined them. In the end, on one hand the sanctity of property was insured for the interim until legal titles could be obtained, and on the other hand, due warning was broadcast that here in Canada no one should take the law into his own hands.

That fall, M. Deane, a Dominion Land Surveyor, set to work measuring the Edmonton Settlement and laying the framework that was to confirm the early settlers' rights to the land they claimed. In laying out the river lots, he took account of the location of buildings and of any patches of land which they had cultivated, and set the boundaries accordingly. Altogether, his survey stretched along the river from River Lot No. 1 (Joseph Hebert) and No. 2 (Malcolm Groat) in the west and to River Lot No. 40, which was on the south side of the river across from modern Beverly, and No. 45, which included the river flat on the left bank of the river south of the Clover Bar traffic bridge. Moreover, as in the case of all river lot surveys where everyone's land fronted on the river, and where its boundary lines were produced back more or less at right angles from the stream, it was inevitable that whenever there was a bend in the river these lines would not be parallel. Reference to the map on page 96 for instance, shows how these lines which eventually became streets between 97 and 101 Streets ran into each other. Now that the railway had left Edmonton sitting in a backwater, however, and now that the eyes of Canada were focused on the southern prairies, the need for clearly defined titles was not so pressing.

Keeping up with the railway in its haste to cross the plains, settlers started to pour into the Northwest Territories. Over 25,000 came in 1881, and they were followed by 100,000 in 1882, and all of them settled in southern Manitoba or southeastern Saskatchewan. In February 1883 the newly built immigration sheds at Qu'Appelle were crowded with settlers. By December 1883 the steel of the CPR had been spiked down for 121 miles beyond Calgary.

That fall, although Edmonton was a mere two hundred miles away from the end of steel, it was no longer the main depot for all the West. Its upstart rival, Calgary, had sprung into being. All of a sudden too, the Saskatchewan River route to the Coast fell into disuse. As the CPR pushed west into British Columbia, no one had any further need for this old trans-Canada highway, which had been pioneered by David Thompson and put to practical use by George Simpson and had served for some sixty years. For the first time in nearly ninety years, Edmonton had been outranked. So Edmontonians set about improving the old trail south. Then in July 1883, Ad McPherson and John Coleman took a contract to carry mail to Calgary every two weeks and to start a passenger and express service. In August that year also, Donald McLeod announced that his new stage line was "making weekly trips 'between said points. Leaves Jasper House, Edmonton, at 9 and the steamboat dock at 9:30 o'clock every Monday morning, stopping at Peace Hills (Wetaskiwin), Battle River (Ponoka), Red Deer Crossing, and Willow Creek (Olds area), and arriving at Calgary on Friday. Returning, leaves Calgary Monday,

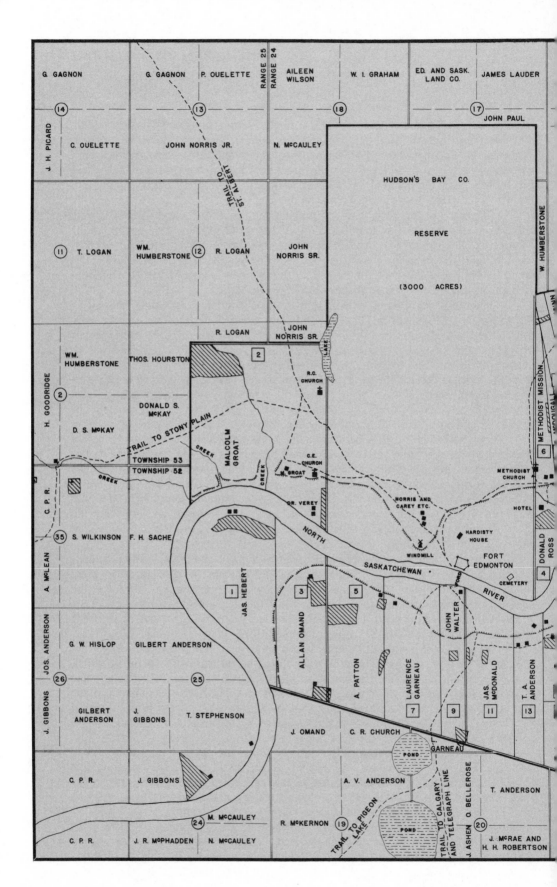

G. GAGNON   G. GAGNON   P. OUELETTE   RANGE 25   RANGE 24   AILEEN WILSON   W. I. GRAHAM   ED. AND SASK. LAND CO.   JAMES LAUDER

(14)   (13)   (18)   (17)   JOHN PAUL

J. H. PICARD   C. OUELETTE   JOHN NORRIS JR.   N. McCAULEY

TRAIL TO ST. ALBERT

HUDSON'S BAY CO.

RESERVE

(3000 ACRES)

(11)   T. LOGAN   WM. HUMBERSTONE (12)   R. LOGAN   JOHN NORRIS SR.

W. HUMBERSTONE

R. LOGAN   JOHN NORRIS SR.

WM. HUMBERSTONE   THOS. HOURSTON   2

H. GOODRIDGE

(2)

D. S. McKAY   DONALD S. McKAY

R.C. CHURCH

TRAIL TO STONY PLAIN   CREEK

TOWNSHIP 53

TOWNSHIP 52   CREEK

MALCOLM GROAT   CREEK

C.E. CHURCH

M. GROAT

METHODIST MISSION

McDOUGALL

(6)

METHODIST CHURCH

C. P. R.   CREEK

DR. VEREY

NORRIS AND CAREY ETC.

HOTEL

(35)   S. WILKINSON   F. H. SACHE

A. McLEAN

NORTH

HARDISTY HOUSE

WINDMILL

SASKATCHEWAN

FORT EDMONTON

DONALD ROSS

(4)

CEMETERY

RIVER

JOS. ANDERSON

G. W. HISLOP   GILBERT ANDERSON

JAS. HEBERT   1

3   5

ALLAN OMAND

A. PATTON

LAURENCE GARNEAU

JOHN WALTER

JAS. McDONALD

T. A. ANDERSON

(26)   (25)

J. GIBBONS

GILBERT ANDERSON   J. GIBBONS   T. STEPHENSON

7   9   11   13

J. OMAND   C. R. CHURCH

GARNEAU

C. P. R.   J. GIBBONS

A. V. ANDERSON

POND

T. ANDERSON

M. McCAULEY

(24)   R. McKERNON   (19)

POND

O. BELLEROSE

(20)

J. ASHEN

TRAIL TO PIGEON LAKE

TRAIL TO CALGARY AND TELEGRAPH LINE

C. P. R.   J. R. McPHADDEN   N. McCAULEY   J. McRAE AND H. H. ROBERTSON

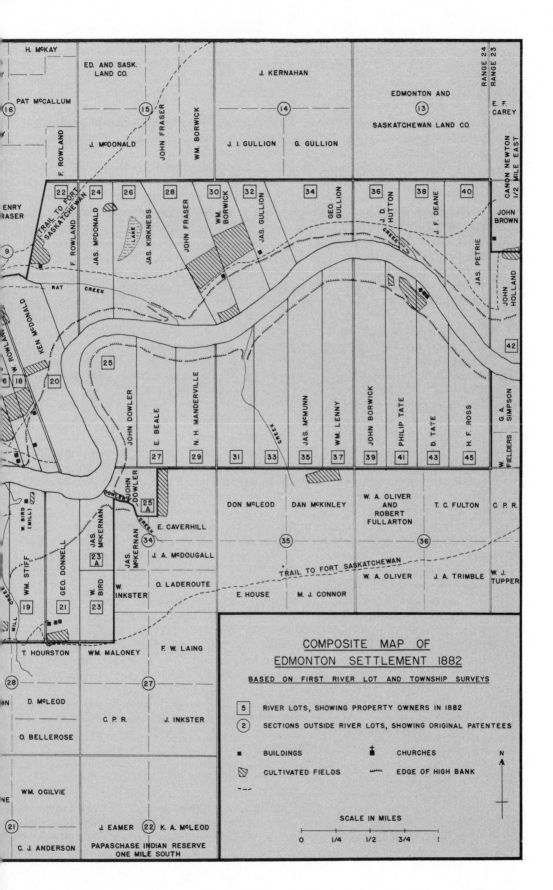

COMPOSITE MAP OF
EDMONTON SETTLEMENT 1882

BASED ON FIRST RIVER LOT AND TOWNSHIP SURVEYS

| 5 | RIVER LOTS, SHOWING PROPERTY OWNERS IN 1882 |
| 2 | SECTIONS OUTSIDE RIVER LOTS, SHOWING ORIGINAL PATENTEES |

■ BUILDINGS   ✝ CHURCHES

▨ CULTIVATED FIELDS   ⌇ EDGE OF HIGH BANK

N

SCALE IN MILES

0   1/4   1/2   3/4   1

stops at same places, and arrives at Edmonton on Friday. Fare each way $25, 100 pounds baggage allowed. Express matter 10 cents per pound. Calgary office in H. B. Co. store."

Even though the southern prairies were now out of bounds to Edmontonians and the territory over the mountains had been taken away from them, they still had their old connections with the Far North. Now, though the freight for these far-off places came by wagon from Calgary, it still passed through Edmonton, and year by year it increased. To keep abreast of it, the Hudson's Bay Company spent considerable money improving the Athabasca Trail, putting in a bridge or two and installing ferries across the Sturgeon and Redwater rivers. The increased volume of freight called for steamboat service on the Athabasca River. On account of the Grand Rapids, the freight had to go by scows from Athabasca Landing to Fort McMurray, but in 1883 the old company built the steamboat "Grahame" to ply from that point down to Fort Smith. Before long, in catering to the Far North, Edmonton found itself busier than ever.

All the while new people were coming to the embryo city. In 1881 Dick Secord, who was later to form a partnership with John A. McDougall, arrived, and as well as doing other jobs, worked for M. Deane in surveying the Settlement. That year too, Scott Robertson came to see what the West was like, and two years later brought out his family. In 1883 Major A. H. Griesbach of the Mounted Police was transferred from Regina to Fort Saskatchewan, and his three year old son William had his first look at Edmonton.

By this time, Frank Oliver's *Bulletin* had become a voice in the land. During 1882 he acquired a larger press and with it he belaboured the far-away Ottawa government. A year later, when, after a sojourn of four years at Battleford, the capital of the Northwest Territories was transferred to Regina, he joined P. G. Laurie, the editor of the Battleford *Herald,* in opposing the move. Then, after winning in the Northwest Territories' election of 1883, he went to Regina as the sole representative for Alberta. There he was vigorous in his demands for enlarged rights for the West. One of his most important contributions in the council was the part he played in designing the School Bill of 1884, which set up the first public school system in the Territories.

As soon as possible, Edmontonians took advantage of this act and relieved the few private patrons of the burden they had carried for three years. At that point, Edmonton (Protestant) School No. 7 became the first legally constituted school in Alberta. While for the next five years Matt McCauley continued as chairman, the make-up of the board changed, and Scott Robertson and Donald Ross became the new trustees. They added another room to the original school, and engaged Dick Secord to teach, at a salary of $800 a year.

Even though Edmonton had an officially recognized public school, it was nevertheless a small straggling settlement and now on the eve of the Northwest Rebellion, when relations with the Métis and the Indians were deteriorating, an awareness of its vulnerable position began to seep in.

The Edmonton hamlet of that time stretched for nearly two miles along the road that everyone called High Street. For the first three-quarters of a mile east from the fort no houses relieved its loneliness until Alex Taylor's and Pierre Gauvreau's homes came in sight. East of these, along the trail were McDougall's Church and the other houses and stores of the village, with Robertson's somewhat off by itself to the north-east. From the *Bulletin* office on the trail near 99 Street a wagon road ran along the recently surveyed Jasper Avenue as far west as 101

Main Street before 1885. Photo taken on Jasper Avenue looking east from just west of modern 98th Street.

Street. West of there, Jasper was marked by a slash cleaving the forest. Intersecting cutlines indicated where other streets would be whenever people came to build along them. Actually the line of Jasper Avenue extended to where Dr. Newton had built his church, but no one else lived along it. About 117 Street, after passing Norris and Carey's store and a few other buildings, the St. Albert Trail crossed the cutline. North along the trail, about 105 Avenue, was Father Blanchet's Roman Catholic Church. The rest of Edmonton was fairly dense forest of the type now found in uncleared sections of the river valley.

Whatever good the railway may have done in opening up the prairies, it had done the Métis a bad turn. In the south it was bringing added business and some demand for labour, but along the Saskatchewan valley at Prince Albert, Fort Carlton and Battleford, where the bulk of the Métis lived, they found little employment. At Edmonton, where the needs of the north kept them relatively much busier than their cousins in Saskatchewan, the situation was not quite so bad.

Because the Indians derived none of their sustenance from freighting, the disappearance of the buffalo hit them a body blow. Though, since the treaties of 1876 and 1877 they had tried to settle on their newly established reserves, they had not had time to make a start in the practice of agriculture. When in 1879 the buffalo vanished, the Indians were in a desperate plight. The white man had an obligation to feed them, and towards that end the Mounted Police and the Indian agents directed strenuous efforts, but the transition had come so rapidly that all their efforts were of little avail. In desperation the once mighty plainsmen began to flock to such places as Battleford and Fort Macleod looking for food, but little could be done for them.

That year several hundred prairie Indians died of starvation, and while during the next five years the government redoubled its efforts to feed them, nevertheless, each year saw many deaths. Faced with such a situation, the Indians became increasingly belligerent. Even on the reserves near Edmonton: Papaschase just south of McKernan's Lake, Stony Plain some six miles west, and Alexander, Alexis and Calihoo. all three just beyond St. Albert, where they could look to the moose, deer and big game of the forests, they became bitter.

In the fall of 1884 an assembly of half-breeds in the vicinity of Batoche in Saskatchewan sent to Montana to bring Louis Riel, the hero of the Manitoba rebellion, back to Canada to advise them. After his arrival the whole situation became dangerous. While men like Frank Oliver and the missionaries implored Ottawa to forget its red tape and its lethargy and to send out help, and to reassure its people of native blood, nothing happened. Edmontonians, aware of how tense the air had become, kept waiting for word to reach Alex Taylor's telegraph office on 103 Street that at last Ottawa was about to do something. Instead, on March 27, the telegraph key tapped out another message: "Métis attacked at Duck Lake yesterday. Ten police killed. Louis Riel and Gabriel Dumont victorious."

Then the telegraph went dead. The wire had been cut. Edmonton, suddenly over-shadowed by imminent disaster, surrounded by hundreds of hostile savages, was isolated from outside contact or help.

Now it was too late; the rebellion had started. The Métis, caught in the web of economic fact and suffering frustrations which their white rulers could neither untangle nor cut, resorted to arms. In Saskatchewan the Indians, starving and suffering similar ills, sided with their half brothers and went to war. The Métis were on the march, and the Crees had danced the war dance.

Fortunately for Edmonton the course of the rebellion was run far away in Saskatchewan and only its echoes stirred the hamlet. But these echoes were spine-chilling. The fight at Duck Lake had shattered the white man's prestige. Now if the Crees of the Edmonton area were to join their cousins farther east, if the Edmonton Métis threw in their lot with those of Batoche, Edmontonians' outlook would be bleak indeed. The railway was two hundred miles away at Calgary, and if the Blackfeet in the south were to rise and cut it, the native peoples could simply snuff out the whites. For eight weeks Edmonton was in a position of defence; for six weeks Edmontonians lived in dread of rifle shots roaring out from the bush which ringed the little settlement; for one week a state of panic prevailed.

For Edmonton was such a little settlement, and so isolated; its white adults added up to 125. Within one day's march lived between five hundred and a thousand Indian men, all practised warriors, and probably ready to join hands with them were some five hundred Métis from St. Albert, Victoria and other nearby settlements.

The Indians and Métis of the Edmonton area had always been more friendly to white people than their counterparts in southern Alberta or Saskatche-wan had been. The flats upstream and the higher ground just north of the fort were rarely without some Indian tepees. So too were the shores of McKernan's Lake on the south side and Drunken Lake near 109 Avenue and 121 Street. With neighbourly gatherings of Indians in all these places, always accompanied by festive dancing, the sound of the Indians' drums had become part of Edmonton's life. How long now would these drums remain friendly?

Years later, Frank Oliver, recalling them, wrote of the evening of March 27, when Edmontonians had heard the fateful news. He walked from the *Bulletin* office near the modern Macdonald Hotel west through one of these camps near 109 Street to reach Norris and Carey's store a couple of blocks farther on along 99 Avenue, and as he walked, the drums kept up their old time chant. Discussing the friendliness of the Indians with some of the old timers like Bill Cust and Jim Gibbons, they pointed out that the presence of the drums indicated peace. Carey said: "When the Indians go to war the first thing they do is to put their families in safety at a distance from the scene of action. If the Indians meant mischief now, the tents would not be in town. So long as you hear the drum, there can be no danger." As Oliver told the story, he said. "That seemed to clinch the matter satisfactorily. I returned home, passing the Indian tents again on the way. I slept without thought of danger, for the drum was the last sound I heard before going to sleep.

"In the morning there was not a tent in sight.

"The removal of the tents was accepted by all parties as notice that a state of war existed."

Discussing the situation a few days later in his April 4 *Bulletin,* he said: "The fort is a fort no longer and yet contains immense value in goods. There are 5 general stores with not less than $50,000 of goods. The police post is 18 miles away and few men in it. This is the most remote settlement in the country and the least protected." It seemed to Oliver that it was only a matter of days before the local Indians would attack.

Preparing to meet the onslaught in every way they could, the men organized the Edmonton Volunteer Company with William Stiff, an old soldier, as captain. Its total strength was about thirty, and it occupied the fort and took charge of the company's three small brass cannons and about a dozen old muzzle loader muskets. Many of the men, of course, had their own relatively modern rifles, and, as a reserve weapon, each man was issued with a brush-hook. Some of them set to work to mould lead balls, while the women made up little sacks of powder.

The Volunteer Company always kept a guard on the gate of the fort, which faced the river, and maintained a line of sentries extending east to Donald Ross's Hotel, thence up the hill and around the settlement. The brush was cleared from a zone around the fort. In charge of the bastions stood Kenneth A. McLeod, James McDonald, and John S. Edmiston, and special "sharp-shooters" were detailed for this duty. Up at the hamlet men turned out and cut the brush far enough back so as to leave a cleared space across which any attacking Indians must charge. This open area extended even north of modern Jasper Avenue, especially in the vicinity of 97 and 98 Streets.

Since the telegraph line had been cut, no one knew what was happening in Saskatchewan, the scene of the fighting. Were the police and the soldiers from Eastern Canada being successful, or had the Indians risen in a concerted effort and made mincemeat of them? For days at a time no news reached Edmonton. Occasionally someone came in from Calgary and brought everybody up to date. And invariably his news was bad — Battleford had been sacked; at the Battle of Cutknife Hill the police had been routed; two priests and seven other white men had been killed at Frog Lake, Alberta, and some wives carried back into the forests as prisoners.

Edmonton's leading men decided to send a messenger to Calgary to ask any relief forces to hurry. After midnight April 7, J. Mowatt set out to brave the hazardous trip through the half dozen Indian reserves which lay across the trail to Calgary. With a knowledge of the trail and of Indian habits, and rare good luck, he completed the two-hundred-mile trip in thirty-six hours. Here and there he stopped at some pioneer's shack for a cup of coffee and to change to a new horse, but otherwise he galloped steadily on. His ride is an epic of courage and endurance about which Americans would sing ballads, but Edmontonians soon forgot it.

The following Saturday was a bad day, with mounting panic. That afternoon a rumour circulated to the effect that fifteen hundred Indians had attacked the Mounted Police at Fort Saskatchewan. Everyone knew that, if the rumour was correct, the remnant of police left there would stand no chance at all. It was unfounded, however, and at Fort Saskatchewan they were sheltering eighty-four women and children from the surrounding area. When they heard it, the local families stampeded into Fort Edmonton, although some of them left the settlement and went to the St. Albert mission, where they felt the influence of the priests would protect them. At the height of the scare Fort Edmonton took care of seventy-five women and children. Throughout all the trouble, at least four families never sought the security of the fort: the Olivers, McCauleys, Camerons and Robertsons.

Oliver, reporting his feelings on Saturday, April 18, said: "That an unmistakable panic existed in Edmonton town and district on Saturday afternoon and Sunday last must be universally admitted as well as the fact now apparent that it was groundless . . . The movement on Saturday and Sunday was a stampede into the fort and to St. Albert . . . It is 15 days since we last heard from Battleford and the same since we heard from Saddle Lake . . . Ten days have elapsed since our messenger went to Calgary and we have not heard . . ."

Meanwhile, Mowatt delivered his message to General Strange, the commander of the hastily organized Alberta Field Force. On April 22, W. B. Young arrived from Calgary with a despatch from the general, advising that his troops planned to set out from that town on April 20. Then on May 1, Strange's first echelon, Steele's Scouts, crossed the river on John Walter's ferry. The siege, if such it could be called, was over. Strange's troops had many weeks' work to do, but Edmonton was in the clear.

Finally, on May 12, General Middleton defeated the rebel forces at Batoche, and three days later took Louis Riel prisoner. His futile uprising had been squashed. When, two weeks later, Frank Oliver heard of Riel's capture, he rubbed his editorial hands and said: "If Riel is really caught Sir John is in as bad a fix as the man who had a tiger by the tail — he couldn't decide whether to hold on or to let go."

Uppermost in his mind, however, was the fact that the trouble was over. Though for a long period the utmost anxiety — well founded anxiety — prevailed at Edmonton, no shots were fired there in anger and no one's hair was actually raised by anything but fright. The state of war which began March 27 ended on May 1, but there had been no local bloodshed.

A Group of N.W.M.P. at their Edmonton Bunkhouse 1891.

Edmonton Incorporated 1885-1895

chapter 8

THE REBELLION drew Eastern Canada's attention to the Edmonton area, and it poured out government money which gave the hamlet a shot in the arm. Once the army pulled out, it slumped back into the doldrums. But to Edmonton's chagrin, as fast as its prospects waned, Calgary's waxed fat.

In spite of that, an occasional pioneer came to throw in his lot with the northern part of the province. W. Johnstone Walker, for instance, a man with money to invest, came to Edmonton during the summer of 1885. After spending some months looking around, he sent east for a supply of merchandise and set to work building a store on Fraser Avenue (98 Street). When in the spring his goods were freighted in from Calgary by a train of ox-carts, he went into business.

Traffic over the Calgary Trail increased yearly, and in 1886 George Roy was commissioned to survey it. Commenting on it, he said: "In view of the great traffic and immense travel which some day may be done this way my intention was to make the road as straight as the actual direction of the trail between the two extreme points would allow. A little ditching, a small culvert, a slight cut or a few branches thrown on a soft spot will be all that will be needed to keep the trail open."

Though Johnstone Walker was pleased with the location of his store, it suffered the drawback of being some ten blocks away from Alex Taylor's telegraph office, so he broached the subject of a telephone line between the two points. Taylor agreed, and soon all the other merchants between these extreme ends of the city had hooked up to it. Before long Alex was running an extensive system.

In the election of 1885, H. C. Wilson defeated Frank Oliver in his bid for re-election to the Northwest Council. Following that, although the publisher of the *Bulletin* kept his nose thrust into matters political, for a year or so it remained out of joint. Then, for the first time, with the Dominion election of 1887 the Northwest Territories were allowed to elect federal members of parliament. In that election, which gave Albertans one seat in the House of Commons, Frank Oliver held back, preferring to wait for the 1888 territorial election, when once more he made the grade and represented the Edmonton area at Regina.

In June 1887, one of Edmonton's outstanding citizens, the Rev. G. D. McQueen, came to take charge of his pioneer parish. Long afterwards, in recalling his first impressions of Edmonton, he said:

". . . There were six mercantile establishments whose stocks consisted of every imaginable thing from sides of bacon to ostrich plumes. There was also a butcher-shop, a baker's, a blacksmith shop, a land office, the *Edmonton Bulletin* printing establishment, a boat-building establishment, and a carriage-maker's shop, four churches, two schools, four hotels, a post office, telegraph office, grist-mill, saw-mill, and a brick-yard. Small settlements of homesteaders at Namao, Belmont, Stony Plain, Clover Bar, and eastward at Beaver Lake, gave to the little village its promise of a widening agricultural industry to take the place of a receding fur-trade . . ."

Yet Edmonton seemed unable to grow, and in 1887 had a population of but 350. Up to this time, the small influx of Alberta settlers had been to the lands adjacent to the CPR — to the drier lands of the southern prairies. Immigrants had not yet discovered the rich farming lands of the Edmonton area with their greater rainfall, but that discovery would be just a matter of a short time. Moreover, like so many of Alberta's resources which had lain dormant for centuries, its rich soils were not to be used till two conditions were met. The first was a market for their production, and the second was the knowledge of how to farm them.

Just at this point, however, great changes were sweeping Europe and turning it, as well as the eastern United States, into an industrial society. Both there and in Europe these changes were increasing the population and concentrating it into the cities, which necessitated the importation of food. A market for Canadian wheat was now assured, and the recently built CPR could transport Alberta's grain to this market. The first condition had been met.

The second condition, acquiring the knowledge of how to farm these lands came slowly. Part of it had been the development of Red Fife wheat, but even with it, frosts claimed most of the wheat crop. The steel roller-milling process was also part of this knowledge along with the invention of new ploughs, binders, and other machinery which enabled farmers to cope with the problems of large scale farms. The combination of all these factors, and of other developments unknown in 1887, provided the know-how to permit Alberta's vast soil resources to yield their riches.

In the little hamlet of the late 1880's, several men were betting their future on this new resource of soil, which they knew must soon be utilized. When it was, Edmonton, in the very heart of it, would take fire and flare up into a large city. Amongst these men were a few individuals to whom, because of their foresight, integrity, and constancy of purpose, the rest turned for guidance.

Frank Oliver with his newspaper and his wide interest in the political sphere was one. Colourful Matt McCauley, ever ready to lead the throng in any cause of the moment, was another. Then rounding out the trio was John McDougall the successful merchant, calm, logical, and far-sighted. Such men were not content to let Edmonton languish in its primitive fur-trade pattern, and in 1889 they established the Board of Trade — the first one west of Winnipeg.

In 1890 the Calgary and Edmonton Railroad Company started surveying a line towards the little hamlet two hundred miles to the north. By Christmas that year the rails had reached Red Deer. Eventually Edmontonians could hear the very whistle of the construction locomotive. Still the track-layers kept on, till they reached the little frame station building in the railway town south of the river, when all construction ceased.

Then Edmontonians tumbled and realized that the railway officials had never intended to build across the river to Edmonton. Instead, they had bought land on the south side and there they began to create a rival railroad-owned town of South Edmonton, confident that Edmontonians would swallow their pride and come creeping over to buy their lots. But constitutionally Edmontonians were poor creepers, and instead of moving to the south side they stayed put in the old settlement, where, swearing mighty oaths, they set the stage for decades of rivalry between the two towns.

South Edmonton spurted ahead. There, before the first train pulled in on August 10, 1891, Tom Anderson and Joe McDonald sold parts of their river lots to Osler, Hammond and Nanton for a townsite, and donated other parts, and in almost no time at all, the upstart town had a population nearly equal to Edmonton's.

Edmontonians, however, were not alone in their belief in their town's future. Amongst others in Canada who shared it were the directors of the Imperial Bank, who sent G. R. F. Kirkpatrick to start a branch of their institution. He came on the second regular train to reach South Edmonton, but he kept on the move until he had crossed on Walter's ferry and could bask in the welcome Edmontonians were ready to accord him. None of them, of course, could be sure how the bank would do or what manner of man its new manager might turn out to be. They were soon to learn that in G. R. F. Kirkpatrick they had a leading citizen. Though they could not have guessed it, he was to serve them for the next forty-five years.

It soon began to appear that in spite of the new settlement across the river, Edmonton was going to hold its own. One indication of this came in 1891 when Alex Taylor began operating a new marvel of the times, the first local electric lighting plant. He built it on the flats immediately upstream from the present Low Level Bridge. Poles and wires straggled up the hill and three days before Christmas the power was turned on and Edmontonians began paying the following monthly rates:

For a customer's first 16 candlepower lamp—$1.00.
If a customer had two lamps, then each was to be at 85¢; if three lamps—70¢; if four—60¢, and if any number exceeding four, 50¢ per lamp.

About this time, the members of the Board of Trade decided that Edmonton should be incorporated. So in February, 1892, the hamlet with its population of seven hundred assumed town status. The new town embraced 2,160 acres, including the southern half of the Hudson's Bay Company Reserve. By unanimous consent, one of the most progressive citizens, who for eleven years had lived along the trail, Matt McCauley, was chosen mayor. For the time being, the town council met in a room over the butchershop operated by his son-in-law, Bill Howey. There too the volunteer fire brigade kept its equipment.

But no matter how interested Edmontonians were in their new town council, or how envious they were of South Edmonton, they still kept the ear of opportunity to the ground. Through it in June 1892 they heard some of the first rumblings of excitement over oil, for the *Bulletin* reported the existence of "a most peculiar spring north of St. Albert . . . Whether or not the tar is a sure indication of a profitable petroleum field, there is no doubt of the genuineness of the find, and as little doubt that it is not confined to that single locality."

It turned out to be a false alarm. So Edmontonians turned their minds back to the other resource that surrounded the town. This, the rich soil, which from time immemorial had supported the great forests, needed merely the stewardship of the pioneer and the sweat of the ploughman to pour its fertility into overflowing granaries and well-stocked stables.

Rev. D. G. McQueen, first
resident Presbyterian Minister.

Matt McCauley,
Edmonton's first Mayor.

The first townships to be surveyed in the area were naturally those within about twenty miles of the hamlet. These had been divided up in 1882, but, except for a few within two or three miles of Edmonton, a decade went by before settlers came to claim them. While Edmonton had a Dominion government land office at which settlers could file on whichever quarter-section they chose, so far it had led a quiet existence. In January 1891, however, this office received instructions from Ottawa to reserve one hundred quarter-sections in the Horse Hills for a settlement of Germans who were abandoning their homesteads near Medicine Hat and moving north to start over again. Here indeed was good news, one hundred settlers all at once to take up land fifteen miles north-east.

In May, some fifty-three families arrived. They had come by train as far as the end of steel at Red Deer and continued from there by wagons. Some settled in the Horse Hills, but others went to Stony Plain or to Riviere Qui Barre, or out near Rabbit Hill.

The Germans, however, were not Edmonton's only expectant settlers that spring, for at the end of March 1891 the first contingent of Father Morin's French colony from Quebec passed through Edmonton. It consisted of twelve wagons carrying sixty-five immigrants of all ages. This little group, of course, was only the advance guard of a much larger migration which took place during the next few years, nearly all of whom settled in an area radiating north from St. Albert.

According to Frank Oliver's *Edmonton Bulletin,* which was gleefully keeping a tally of increasing homestead entries, prospects were looking up. The paper also recorded further evidence of the settlement's growth by publishing a list showing the total votes cast at each of the polling places in the March 5, 1891, federal election. After listing the number of voters in all of the few polls tributary to Edmonton, Oliver's pen took a dig at one of the election practices of the times, when abuses were common, and singled out the results at the Woodpecker poll near Lethbridge;

"Edmonton	291	Victoria	50
St. Albert	273	Sturgeon	70
Fort Saskatchewan	132	Clover Bar	67
Beaver Lake	22	Lac Ste. Anne	38

"Woodpecker had 13 votes on the list and cast 51 Davis Votes. None for Reilly."

During the year ending October 31, 1891, as a result of a speeded up settlement policy, there had been 429 entries for homesteads at the Edmonton land office, and twenty homesteads patented. During the first ten days of April 1891 there were thirty-four entries and twenty-eight more during the next week. There were sixty in May, seventy-eight in June, and sixty-four in July, so that finally by October 1, 328 settlers had filed on land since the previous April.

When, in 1891, Frank Oliver was elected to the Northwest Territories Assembly, the increase in the number of people in the Edmonton district caused the creation of two new polls, Blackmud and Stony Plain.

The influx of immigrants, small as it had been, was nevertheless vastly encouraging to Edmonton and South Edmonton merchants. In the beginning it probably did less good to Edmonton than to its rival across the river, which was basking in the business the railway had brought it. To increase its prosperity, South Edmontonians set their hearts on having the land office, so, after conniving with Ottawa officials, they set about the task of having it moved, and thereby they set in motion one of the most colorful episodes in Edmonton's history.

As usual, it was Frank Oliver and his *Bulletin* that let us in on the secret machinations of the south-siders, for on June 20, 1892, in blazing headlines he proclaimed:

ROBBERS ATTEMPT TO STEAL THE LAND OFFICE
BUT DON'T GET AWAY WITH IT
Then in the June 23 issue the headlines declared:
DIRTY DEWDNEY IS IN THE STEAL
HE SHOWS HIS HAND—IT IS NOT CLEAN

The previous Saturday, pursuant to his orders, "Timber Tom" Anderson, who a few months earlier had been appointed the Dominion government land agent, called a dray and began loading it with the land office books and records so as to transfer them to South Edmonton. Within minutes, an angry crowd of two hundred surrounded the wagon, took off its wheels and unhitched the horses. Matt McCauley and Frank Oliver sent blistering telegrams off to Ottawa. Anderson, however, trying to carry out his orders, sent to South Edmonton for four more teams. As each of these stepped ashore off Walter's ferry, the crowd took them in charge and sent them back across the river. To restore order, Inspector Piercy of the local detachment of the Mounted Police undertook to guard the wagon and the records over the week-end until Ottawa had a chance to consider Edmonton's objections.

Then on Monday, Superintendent Griesbach brought twenty more police in from Fort Saskatchewan. As soon as word of their arrival got around, Edmontonians concluded that they intended to carry out the move. *The Bulletin,* reporting the next step, said:

". . . To meet this possibility Mayor McCauley, councillor Cameron and J. A. McDougall, J.P.'s, issued an order calling out the home guards organized in 1885 by General Strange, to keep the peace — that is, the land office. At 1 p.m. nearly every able bodied man in town — most of them armed — appeared at the town clerk's office, ready for any event . . ."

For a day or so, Superintendent Griesbach, a wise policeman, marked time while he advised Ottawa of the gravity of the situation. Before blood was spilled, he received a reply indicating that the land office was to stay in Edmonton and that a branch would be opened across the river. The NWMP rode away gladly, and Matt McCauley, at the head of his forty men, all armed with long Snider rifles, retired victoriously. But it had been a near miss which demonstrated that there was a limit beyond which the folly of far-off governments could push loyal men like Matt McCauley.

Having disposed of the land office issue, McCauley and his town council turned their minds to other land problems. Edmonton had grown like Topsy and its growth had been without too much reference to survey lines, which in many cases had been superimposed over an earlier pattern of trails and holdings. As a result, some of its oldest and best citizens found their buildings sitting smack in the middle of the new-fangled streets. For instance, McDougall, the Methodist missionary, who had erected the first building outside the fort, had placed his church on 101 Street. Originally he had located it so as to be clear of the east side of the Hudson's Bay Company's Reserve, oblivious of the fact that in the future that strip of land might be a street. John McDougall, the merchant, too, was trespassing, for his store was sticking out into the street, and others were in a similar fix.

To remedy this situation, the council passed a by-law forcing owners to move their buildings off the streets. The Methodists built a new church and skidded the old one back to the end of its lot, while John McDougall moved his building to Jasper Avenue, west of 101 Street.

John Brown, who had arrived in Edmonton in 1869 and then about thirteen years later had built a store along the old trail between modern 97 and 98 Streets, now found his building to be in the centre of the new Jasper Avenue. Unlike the other old timers, however, he refused to move. The fact that McCauley and his associates had successfully confronted Ottawa's power, made no impression upon John Brown, one-time partner in the firm of Brown and Curry. He just sat tight.

On July 18, 1892, the town council took his case to law, and when in October, Judge Rouleau of the Supreme Court of the Northwest Territories heard the case, he reserved judgment and went home to Regina. In February 1893, the mail brought his written decision that Brown had to move. But Brown appealed. Finally in the spring after he and his lawyers and the town's lawyers had all journeyed to Regina for the appeal, he lost for good, and, moreover, had to pay all the costs. On top of this he had to move his store.

By this time Edmontonians had re-elected Matt McCauley as mayor. As their chief magistrate, he decided that his bailiwick should have a civic hall worthy of its prospects. Accordingly, in 1893, facing the Alberta Hotel across 98 Street, masons and carpenters vied with each other in the speed with which each erected his part of the city hall. The two-storey structure provided space for council meetings, the town's clerical staff, the police force, and the volunteer fire department.

Within sight of the town hall and crammed into the narrow space between Jasper Avenue and the steep cliff, Sheriff Scott Robertson built his hall. Its first floor was occupied by business premises, but its upper storey, reached by the narrow staircase, became Edmonton's actual community centre. It was a combination dance hall and opera house which could seat five hundred people. Across the back was a small gallery, and for the use of Edmonton's more exclusive society, Robertson provided one box. For many years, Robertson's Hall saw most of the town's festive life.

For festivities, however, nothing of that decade could hold a candle to Edmonton's first fireworks display. For the July 1, 1893, sports day, Edmontonians collected $950 for this purpose. The sports ground and race track were north of modern 102 Avenue and the grandstand stood about 103 Street and faced north across what is now 102 Avenue.

When the big show came off, smoke from some forty Indian tepees rose into the quiet air from amongst the sparse poplar trees to the south-west of the track. As darkness came on, the Indians, along with hundreds of other spectators in the grandstand and scores of young folk on the open-air dance floor waited expectantly. Tommy Lauder of the fire department and Bill Ibbotson were charged with the duty of thrilling Edmontonians with the fireworks. In this they exceeded everyone's expectations, because as the first rocket went up it shot its sparks directly into the box containing its fellows, and in a trice they all set out to follow it.

Flames and sparks and whizbangs and Roman candles all went off at once and every which way. Several shot high into the air and curved gracefully before falling to set fire to a tepee here and there. Some, avoiding heights, took off horizontally to sweep the young folk off the dance floor, while others bobbed and ricocheted along the ground to speed the parting grandstand guests on their way. By some miracle, no one was seriously hurt, and when the last red or green spark had sputtered out, all except the Indians agreed that, while the show had not gone off as planned, it had nevertheless gone off, and had been worth the $950 expended on it.

While to Edmonton's citizens the fireworks fiasco had been a pleasant diversion, their main preoccupation was with the new settlers who had begun to look longingly at the lands bordering the town. In the spring of 1892, the first major group of English-speaking homesteaders from Ontario arrived — the 298 Parry Sound Colonists. They were led by Tom Pearce, who, in his enthusiasm, wrote a booklet entitled "Sunny Alberta," and is credited with being the creator of this happy phrase. Most of them settled in the area between Bremner and Fort Saskatchewan and then on east towards Lamont.

Nearly everything they needed had to be produced from their lands and processed by their own hands. Once they reaped their first crops, they could take their wheat to one of the two or three mills in operation at the time. The March 26, 1892, *Bulletin* listed some of these flour mills by saying that Edmonton's wheat "was first ground in a mill run by horse power in the Hudson's Bay Fort. This was succeeded by water mills on the Mill Creek on the south side of the river; on Smoking Lake Creek near Victoria and later by one on the Sturgeon. These again were succeeded by the steam mill owned by Fraser & Company, by a steam mill built by the H.B. Co., since burned down, and by a steam mill at St. Albert owned by Geo. Hutton. These are the only mills west of Regina."

The people over in South Edmonton, however, were soon to improve on the mill situation, for early in March, 1893, the Edmonton Milling Company's south side, steam-powered roller-type, flour mill started to operate. It was erected at the very edge of the high bank just south of Saskatchewan Drive where the Calgary-Edmonton Railway had its two-engine roundhouse. Within a couple of years another mill, the Brackman-Ker Oatmill, was also erected at the end of the trackage on top of the bank and began operating in the fall of 1895.

In May 1892, the *Bulletin* reported William Bird, who had been one of Edmonton's early millers, as having some interesting visitors, for it said: "Thomas Bird of Macleod and his father, James Bird, came to visit William Bird. James "Jimmy Jock" has lived nearly all his life with the Blackfeet and is now 100 years old."

"Jimmy Jock," who had indeed spent most of his life with the Blackfeet in southern Alberta and Montana, formed a link that spanned all of Edmonton's history. In 1795, when the first fort had been built, he had been a little child. When from 1799 to 1816 his father had been in charge of the Hudson's Bay Company's Edmonton House, he had grown up on the banks of the mighty Saskatchewan River. Then by the time doughty John Rowand had started his long reign at Edmonton, Jimmy Jock had gone to seek adventure with the Blackfeet. And all the while, from time to time for the next three-quarters of a century he had kept dropping in at the fort. He had seen the building and finally, decades later, the dismantling of John Rowand's "Folly," the first Big House. When in 1874 Richard Hardisty had built his Big House, he had come to visit it, and now towards the end of its useful life, Jimmy Jock, an extremely old man, had come back for another visit.

For even this Big House was getting old. Hardisty had been succeeded as factor by Harrison S. Young, who had decided to move out of it and to rent it to someone.

Less than a month later, the Hudson's Bay Company had other news for Edmontonians. In September the company started building its new store at the corner of Jasper Avenue and 103 Street. This two-storey brick building, thirty-two feet by sixty, was soon to take its place as one of the major buildings in Edmonton's growing commercial area.

Then, on January 9, 1893, the *Bulletin* recorded the death of another fascinating old timer, Hugh Munro, at Two Medicine Creek, near Choteau, Montana. Munro had been born near Montreal on May 4, 1784, 108 years earlier. In 1802 he had come west to Fort Edmonton, and in 1806 had married a Blackfoot woman and then had gone to live with the Kootenay Indians.

He had lived long enough to enter the era when the Dominion government was taking its first halting steps towards helping the rapidly increasing number of immigrants, for in May 1892, the first official immigration shed was put up. Though of one storey only and forty feet by twenty-five, with a twelve-foot square kitchen in the rear, it was a start towards attending to the needs of some of the newly arrived and sometimes bewildered settlers. That summer too, Ottawa announced that it would build a new land titles office on 100 Avenue at the corner of 106 Street.

Through the bitter winter of 1892-1893, one of the worst on record, one of Edmonton's early immigrants, Chung Yan, a laundryman, had trouble keeping warm, and then on top of that, bore the brunt of intolerant neighbours. During March he inadvertently caused a minor fire by throwing his ashes out on the back of the lot. For a while he was in grave danger of mob action. As the *Bulletin* editor said, echoing popular sentiment, Albertans could do without Jews, Mormons and Chinese.

The same year that Chung Yan came to grief, the first Jew, who had come to stay, put in his lonely and venturesome appearance. This was Abe Cristall, who came to Canada from Bessarabia, and as a recently married man reached Edmonton in 1893. Even though the *Bulletin* editor had been inclined to eschew Jews, it did not take Abe long to find favour with Frank Oliver, and indeed, with most Edmontonians. From the beginning he made his mark in the town's life. Before long the paper began to take a kindly pride in Abe's accomplishments, and from time to time published a line or so referring to him, such as: "Edmonton's Jewish businesses closed for Yom Kippur," or, "Edmonton's Jewish community observing the Passover." But there was no community, only Abe Cristall.

Abe Cristall had chosen just the right time to come to Edmonton, for in the spring of 1893 Edmonton received a new influx of immigrants coming in at the rate of a train-load nearly every day. During one week six trains came in with new settlers and seventeen cars of their effects. The immigration authorities had to procure two large tents to try to accommodate as many as they could. Many of the new arrivals were Swedes who took up land around modern Camrose.

With all these arrivals, traffic congestion on Edmonton's Jasper Avenue reached a new high. On April 27 a serious accident took place at the corner of Jasper and 101 Street. Dad Osborne, letting his horse have its head, sped south in his buggy, while H. A. Finch galloped his road cart west on Jasper. In the resulting collision, three men, all more or less injured, were thrown into the mud. Both rigs were smashed to smithereens and both horses badly cut up. Edmonton's traffic problems were commencing.

To ease these problems somewhat, the town council authorized the grading of 103 Street for a block south from Jasper Avenue. As well as that, the aldermen decided to lay a sidewalk for that distance. The town was spreading out and ungraded streets and bare footpaths would no longer do.

That same month, the civic census-taker counted 1,331 souls in Edmonton, a population which, if correct, augured well. In the eight years since the rebellion, even despite the doldrum years immediately after it, the town had more than doubled in size. That fall too, Kirkpatrick's Imperial Bank reported that, during the first nine months of the year, at $15 an ounce, it had bought $5,200 of Saskatchewan River gold. Some settlers augmented their income by panning gold whenever the stage of the river was favourable.

Meanwhile, the Northwest Legislative Assembly, of which Frank Oliver had been a member since 1888, continued to press for responsible government and fought an epic battle with Ottawa. Then in 1891 the Federal government passed a new act granting most of the things the Legislative Assembly wanted. This act was modified in 1893, when responsible government was achieved as a practical reality even though Ottawa did not concede it formally until 1897.

Most of the settlers in the community were more interested in local problems than in responsible government on a provincial scale, and here and there they established a new post office or school district. Like farmers everywhere, however, the settlers grumbled about the price paid them for their produce. For meat they were paid on an ascending scale per pound, beef 5¢, pork 8¢, mutton and chicken 10¢, and turkeys 15¢. The economy of the area, however, was in an elementary state, for in spite of its productive land and its willing farmers, the Hudson's Bay Company had to import two thousand pounds of butter from Manitoba, while from Ontario C. Gallagher, a butcher, brought in 2,300 pounds of geese and turkeys to supply his Christmas trade.

In 1894, Matt McCauley, who had been re-elected mayor, working with the school board, bought a piece of the Methodist Church property and let a contract for $6,257 to K. A. McLeod for erecting a new school. The structure was called the College Avenue School and faced on today's Macdonald Drive where the Memorial Hall bowling green is now. As its first principal, the board chose K. W. MacKenzie.

In every respect Edmonton was as enterprising as any town anywhere. Lawyers were beginning to see a demand for their services. One of the early firms was S. S. and H. C. Taylor, whose progressing practice enabled them to add a phonograph as office equipment. It was said to take down sounds and reproduce them slowly so that the words could be typed.

In May 1894 the *Bulletin* took note of the plight of one of the recently arrived Ukrainian settlers, when it said:

"Ivan Philipow's dwelling in the Josephburg German settlement in the Beaver Hills, east of Fort Saskatchewan, was burned down on Sunday last. Everything including a cow and calf and $15 in cash. The parents were absent from home at the time and the fire is supposed to have been started by one of the children who tried to light a fire in the stove. The people are Russians and are left practically destitute . . ."

In this manner the *Bulletin* first noted the appearance of Iwan Pylypow in Alberta. Since of the two men, Wasyl Eleniak and Iwan Pylypow, who took the lead in starting the emigration of Ukrainians from Galicia and Bukowina to Alberta, Pylypow was the foremost and the first one to actually reach Alberta, the *Bulletin,* had it realized the importance of the epic story it was overlooking, might well have given him more attention. For Iwan Pylypow and a few associates were the advance guard of the great Ukrainian migration which over the years has meant so much to Alberta and to Canada.

While Edmontonians were considerate of Iwan Pylypow after his home burned down, they were far from kind to their rival city. When Calgary had three thousand people it was granted a resident judge, and Frank Oliver was glad to reprint an item from the Medicine Hat *News* declaring that: "It is undeniable that there is a growing feeling in the territories that Calgary is a pig that wants all the swill in the community trough, and disturbs everyone in its vicinity by its incessant squeals for more."

Calgary, however, was not hogging everything, for more and more settlers were passing it by and coming on to Edmonton. In the spring of 1894, for instance,

Galician immigrants on their arrival in Canada during 1890's.

several families in seven covered wagons completed the 1,600-mile trek from Minnesota to Edmonton. That week too, nine wagons loaded with an oil drilling rig, which was destined to be erected near Pelican Rapids on the Athabasca River, set out from Edmonton to Athabasca Landing. About the same time Ochsner's Brewery started on the south side where Bohemian Maid Beer is brewed today. Within weeks, Tom Cairns set up a similar institution on the flats east of Ross's hotel, and Gibson and Ball got their vats working on the site of the present Royal Glenora Club. All their products were reported as finding a ready sale.

The brewery industry seems to have gotten away to a good start. Putting up a good race for the consumer's dollars, however, was Dr. A. H. Goodwin, Edmonton's earliest dentist, who as a sideline had started a bicycle shop. Actually, the bicycle craze was just beginning to capture Edmonton. For the next two or three years, owning a bicycle was the thing to do.

The mainstay of most Edmonton travellers, however, was the horse, but horses were not always the staid old dobbins about which modern safety councils emote nostalgically. At times they were both skittish and stupid, and not a week passed in any community without having its tally of accidents, broken buggies, broken limbs, or even deaths. Horses were accident-prone. Considering the miles

Col. O'Brien's Klondike party with Hardisty's Big House in background.

travelled, the accident toll was terrific. Typical of equine antics is the story related in the *Edmonton Bulletin* of August 30, 1894:

"A boy mounting a bay cayuse in front of J. Cameron's store yesterday afternoon used a short whip to start the bronco off. This started H. Long's team, which was standing near the crossing and before Mr. Long could get out of the store they were off. Mr. Cameron's horse was standing in a single rig near the store. The team ran into it and upset it, causing the horse to drag the up-turned rig as far as it could in the direction of the Cliff. About the same moment they dashed into J. Edmiston's team which was tied to a post opposite J. Gibbon's, ran the shaft into the shoulder of one of Edmiston's horses severing one of the arteries, at the same time breaking the tie rein and causing the team to run away. Cameron's horse was stopped at the hill and Edmiston's team were stopped at the back of Sutter & Dunlop's; but Long's team ran to the 4 ft. fence enclosing Larue & Picard's yard. This, they both jumped over but the wagon following, broke the fence down and here they were stopped. Some horses in Larue & Picard's yard took fright at the unexpected appearance of the team and they scampered off. Fortunately the damage sustained was not serious. Dr. McInnis was on hand to sew up the artery of Edmiston's horse in time to save its life. Mr. Cameron's rig was slightly damaged and the tongue of Edmiston's rig was smashed. Otherwise no damage was done."

With October 1894 came another election for the Northwest Territories Legislative Assembly, and, of course, Frank Oliver was re-elected. Whereas in the previous election there had been the constituencies of Edmonton and St. Albert, now a third, called Victoria, was added to take care of the new settlers out east of Fort Saskatchewan. As an indication of the growth of the Edmonton area, the following were the polling divisions for the three ridings.

Edmonton	*St. Albert*	*Victoria*
Edmonton	St. Albert	Fort Saskatchewan
Stony Plain	Morinville	Partridge Hill
Whitemud	Glengarry	Josephsburg
Leduc	Poplar Lake	Beaver Creek
Pipestone	Sturgeon River	The Pines
Sandy Lake	Fort Saskatchewan West	Egg Lake
South Edmonton	Lac Ste. Anne	Beaver Lake East
Clover Bar	Athabasca Landing	Victoria
Belmont	Lac La Biche	Saddle Lake
		Whitefish Lake
		Battle River

In December that year the NWMP census counted the population in most of the surrounding area:

Clover Bar 287
Sturgeon settlement 759
St. Albert & Morinville 1,465
Limestone Lake & German settlement 436
Beaver Lake district 428

Fort Saskatchewan 140
Stony Plain 626
Leduc district 678
Egg Lake 98
Victoria 77

In total, the acres the settlers had sown were: wheat, 3,708, oats 12,205, barley 6,647 and potatoes 770.

In the Edmonton area there were: horses 6,549, cattle 10,246, sheep 3,733, swine 8,504.

Early in 1895 J. B. Spurr brought out a remarkably fine directory of the Edmonton district. As well as listing everyone in the town, South Edmonton, Fort Saskatchewan and St. Albert, it gave a list of the fifty telephone subscribers and of the farmers in the various districts. After describing the resources of the area and telling what a rich agricultural region lay all about the town, it hit a sour note, for it said:

"Fruit-growing has not been a success as yet. The few trees planted have grown so rapidly and spindled that they either died from weakness after a year or two's growth or came to unfortunate ends. The only apple grown in this district was grown in the garden of Frank Oliver, Edmonton, in 1893, on a tree two years old, untrimmed and of rank growth. Rabbits settled its fate during the following winter and many other promising trees shared a like fate."

Moreover, indicative of Edmonton's interest in the North, the directory gave a schedule of fares and freight rates on the Hudson's Bay Company's steamboats from Athabasca Landing to Peel River, 1,854 miles downstream on the Mackenzie.

This then was the Edmonton of early 1895, with settlers piling off the trains at South Edmonton, with scows and steamboats plying the river, with Edmonton mines south of the river shipping coal to Innisfail and Calgary, with log booms catching the timber from the vast forests to the west and mills cutting it into lumber. This was the Edmonton into which butter had to be imported and to which turkeys were shipped from the East. This was the Edmonton which, even though it had an inkling of what the future might hold, had not yet found itself.

Steamer "Northwest" at Edmonton. Saw service on Saskatchewan from 1882 to 1897. Played an active part in North West Rebellion.

Edmonton A City
Alberta A Province
1896-1905

chapter **9**

U NDER SUCH MEN as McCauley, Oliver, McDougall and Kirkpatrick, Edmonton made rapid progress. According to the police census of 1895, its population was 1,165, while South Edmonton had 505 people. Calgary, of course, with its population of 3,207, was away ahead of it. But even so Edmonton had established itself as the foremost town of north Alberta and had formed the nucleus about which a city would grow as rapidly as the agricultural population came in to occupy the rich lands adjoining it. And that movement towards homesteads, even if it was taking place slowly, had started, and was bound to speed up as soon as conditions improved.

For the time being, Canada and the continent were in the grip of a depression. Until it lifted, both the West and Edmonton would have to mark time. There was little possibility of exporting any agricultural produce; only furs and gold could be shipped out, and only they brought cash to the town.

The year 1895 slipped by uneventfully while Dr. H. C. Wilson assumed the mayor's chair, but little of interest enlivened the civic sphere. As spring came on all the young bloods unlimbered their bicycles, and on April 22, J. C. C. Bremner of Clover Bar had a serious accident because a boy on a bicycle frightened his horses. As a result, the editor of the *Bulletin* let forth with a blast. "This accident brings up in forcible fashion the bicycle question, which has become serious in many large towns. The number of bicycles in Edmonton this season is very large, and is steadily increasing. That they frighten horses is unquestionable."

On June 13 the editor was of a nostalgic turn of mind, for he looked back wistfully at the old *Bulletin* building which was being torn down. It was built, he said, in December 1878 and used as a store until 1884. From April 1884 to October 1894 the *Bulletin* was printed in it. It was the first building in the country to have 10" x 12" glass in its windows. Prior to that all glass was 7½" x 8½".

The balance of the year saw a few more settlers coming in and an occasional school and post office set up within a radius of thirty miles of Edmonton. The most newsworthy event was the opening of the new $30,000 General Hospital.

During April 1896 the Edmonton Golf and Country Club was founded. Its five-hole course was laid out on what is now the Parliament Building grounds, and for a clubhouse it rented Hardisty's old home. The Big House had indeed fallen from grace.

In May, to help counter-balance this softness that was creeping over Edmonton, twenty-two families of Ukrainians reached the town. The *Bulletin* described them as: "Austrian Poles and naturalized Germans from Galicia. They are described as Ruthenian settlers . . . they use spindles and hand looms to weave their own cloth . . . four of the party have gone out under the guidance of John Borwick . . ." These were relatively well-to-do settlers for they are reported to have brought $17,000 with them, and with this, each of them bought "a couple of cows, a team of oxen or horses, plough, wagon and supplies mainly second hand."

Frank Oliver, who was inclined to judge these Ukrainians harshly, kept hammering away at Ottawa to speed up its campaign to settle the West. By now he was a man of some stature in the West, and when the Federal election of 1896 approached, he resigned his seat in the Northwest Assembly and ran for the single Federal seat allotted to the District of Alberta. He polled more votes than his opponents and set out to make his mark on the Federal stage. In the ensuing Northwest Territories by-election caused by his resignation, the redoubtable Matt McCauley defeated A. C. Rutherford, a young lawyer who a year before had started to practise in South Edmonton.

That year John A. McDougall, who by now was a wealthy man, felt that the time had come to develop his lot on the north-west corner of the intersection of 101 Street and Jasper Avenue. It was an important corner, and his properties in the same block would be enhanced in value if by erecting an imposing building he could fix the corner for all time as the centre of Edmonton's business district. So he let a contract to Kenny McLeod to build of local brick a three-storey block at a contract price of $17,000. Many of the wise ones wagged their heads, but McDougall went ahead to put up Edmonton's most imposing building.

McDougall, however, was more than a shrewd businessman; he was also a devout and contributing Presbyterian. It is not surprising then that in August a tea was held at his house to collect money for more missionaries. The money was to go into a fund for the purpose of sending a missionary to convert the Mormons who had recently come to southern Alberta.

In October the party drilling for oil at Athabasca Landing gave up in disgust when their well, having penetrated to 1,770 feet, was still dry. As their next move, they took their rig downstream to Pelican Rapids to try again. Alberta was having little luck with its search for petroleum products.

Albertans, however, were beginning to nibble at one of their other energy resources. Some ten small gopher-hole mines on either side of the river or along Whitemud Creek were increasing their output of coal to supply the two towns and to export south along the Calgary-Edmonton Railway.

In December, by acclamation, Edmontonians elected John A. McDougall as mayor. During his term Edmonton took a long step in the matter of a railway connection with the south side. For years the town council and the Board of Trade had been urging the Dominion government to build a bridge across the river. Finally, to quote McDougall's memoirs, Ottawa "put up what we considered a bluff and wired us that if we would contribute $25,000 towards the cost of a bridge they would build one. Our population then was only about 1500 and $25,000 in those days was a large sum. But we called the bluff by clubbing together and raising the amount on a joint note through the Imperial Bank and we wired the money to Ottawa the same day their wire was received by us . . ."

When he spoke of "we," he meant himself, Kirkpatrick, Heiminck, Dick Secord and one or two others. These men put up the money, and in due course the ratepayers endorsed their action and assumed their indebtedness for the Low Level Bridge. In spite of the speed with which Edmontonians acted, the completion of the bridge was still five years away.

Then on April 15, 1897, the *Bulletin* published an interesting report:

GOLD

"Already the rush has commenced, and impatient miners and prospectors, local experts, wandering fortune seekers and businessmen not waiting for the ice to leave the river, have staked claims all along the banks from high to low water mark, all seeking to secure a share of the precious metal whose very name is a magnet to attract the millions. From the high river bank directly back of the business portion of the town can be seen far up and down the river innumerable stakes and pins set up there as soon as the frost had left the ground, staking off the newly located claims."

Gold is where you find it, and at the moment, Edmontonians were busy looking for it in their back yard. On May 6, however, the paper began reporting the amazing finds in the Klondike and telling of the rush that was under way to that far-off goldfield. Immediately, many Edmontonians set off to join it. All their lives such men as Norris, Carey, Cust, Dan Noyes, Ed Brosseau of St. Albert, and many others, had been quite used to loading up a string of pack horses and setting out to remote destinations far into the north. Jim Gibbons, the old Forty-niner, was asked what he thought. He averred that there was no particular difficulty in taking horses and making such a trip. To them, a jaunt of some 1,500 miles to the Yukon was more or less routine. At that time at least, half of Edmonton's male population were men of the stamp who could face such a trip without batting an eye. Within weeks, various Edmontonians pulled out for the North.

The bulk of Edmontonians, however, saw a better bet than riding a horse through hundreds of miles of mosquito-infested muskeg. It was to stay at home and act as suppliers to greenhorns who might pass this way with the glitter of gold in their eyes. So, by means of all the advertising at their command, the merchants and the Board of Trade let it be known that Edmonton was the poor man's route to the Yukon and that they stood fast by their resolve to help poor men on their way, so long as they left what little cash they had in Edmonton's tills. Amongst others, McDougall and Secord, the largest competitors the Hudson's Bay Company had, printed a folder indicating what supplies Yukon-bound hopefuls would need and containing a map showing the possible routes they could take. For after all, Edmonton was the most northerly end of steel on the continent.

Every train brought gold seekers — not many, but a valiant few; from Fresno, California, from Pennsylvania, Duluth, and from all over. The August 16 issue of the *Bulletin* stated that: "Nineteen from Fresno, California, including a Mrs. Garner are going to go over land and they brought 80 horses. Another group is sending material to Athabasca Landing to build boats. By last Monday's train there arrived a party of 27 prospectors from California. They are going to go down the river."

Then Kirkpatrick's Board of Trade took another step and hired P. D. Campbell and J. R. Brenton to go to Pelly River in the Yukon. They explained that

"The idea is to get a definite report on the all-land route. The men will keep a diary and send back information."

Two months later they were back with their tails between their legs. No, they had not reached the Pelly River. They had not even been to Fort St. John. Some hitch in their line of supplies had turned them back at Dunvegan. But they were most optimistic and brought back a full report of the excellence of the part of the route they had taken. They brought other information, news not too optimistic. Many of the overland parties were not making very good time. The Fresno party was strung out between Sturgeon Lake and the Smoky River. Others were settling down for the winter at Spirit River or along the Little Smoky, or somewhere in the Grande Prairie, and their prospects for food were shaky. Some indeed were beginning to dribble back.

Looking back over 1897 the *Bulletin* listed the number of Klondikers who had left from Edmonton:

By the Mackenzie River	130
Overland to Peace River	40
By Water to Peace River	5
On snow to Peace River	94
	269

In February 1898 Edmonton's town council sent another man, W. P. Taylor of Lac Ste. Anne, to blaze a trail from Peace River Crossing to the Pelly River. He was to select the best route with the hope that Ottawa could be induced to build a road along it.

Meanwhile, the woods surrounding the town were full of Klondikers and their tents, tepees and flat-sleds. Others camped along the St. Albert Trail and on Ross's Flats. Since most of them were amateurs, they fell for all sorts of queer contrivances and conveyances, such as steam-driven sleighs and a vehicle made by stringing three or four wine barrels on an axle.

Though the bulk of the venturesome set off with orthodox pack horses and supplies, few of them got very far. As old timers from the far north came in to Edmonton on routine business that spring, they reported the failure of many a party of Klondikers. The contrast between these old timers, who knew the conditions of travel in the north, and the hopeful tenderfeet setting out from Edmonton underlined the cause of their failure — inexperience. Actually the route was not unusually difficult for hardened packers, trappers, or traders. For the tenderfeet, however, it was impossible.

Those who chose the water route from Athabasca Landing down the river by way of Fort Smith, Great Slave Lake and the Mackenzie River, fared much better, and many set out along it. A report from Athabasca indicated that some six or seven hundred men were waiting there for the ice to go out. Then when it broke on April 22, 1898, there was a wild stampede down the river. In all, that spring thirteen steamboats had left for the North, all taking their quota of Klondikers. Up to July, one hundred and thirty craft of all sizes had negotiated Grand Rapids. The small police detachment there had its hands full rescuing the unfortunate and burying the reckless. Six hundred men were reported as having passed Fort Smith before June 24.

Of the many who started along the water route, a few were drowned at Grand Rapids and a few more died from various causes farther downstream. The vast majority turned back as the difficulties of the way or disagreements in the parties made their positions untenable, and the remainder, a very few indeed, got through. The experienced leaders of the Segers-Hardisty party carried it through by this route.

Of those who set out overland, perhaps a dozen in all reached the diggings. A few of the rest died enroute, and the remainder turned back. Few got past Fort St. John.

By the early summer of 1898, when many a weary Klondiker had returned to Edmonton, the bloom had rubbed off "the poor man's route" and the rush through Edmonton had slowed to a trickle. By mid-summer Edmonton's leading merchants had dropped the Klondike motif from their advertising.

Then, when everyone was beginning to be touchy at the mere mention of the route from Edmonton, the town's explorer, W. P. Taylor, returned. Leaving Edmonton February 25, he had reached the Pelly River with ease, and on May 23 he set out for home. Ten weeks later still, he and his pack horses turned up hale and hearty, saying that the route was eminently practical and easy to travel. But no one wanted to hear his report. No one was interested any more in the poor man's route. That boom had bust.

Nevertheless, the Klondikers had done well by Edmonton. In all, some 1,500 had set out from there, and if each had spent $300 to outfit, half a million dollars of new money, much of it in gold pieces, had tinkled into Edmonton's tills. Much of this remained in South Edmonton too, but because of the age-old urge that impels travellers who have reached the edge of civilization to feel that they have not really started until they have crossed the first hurdle, the Klondikers first crossed the Saskatchewan River and then stopped to outfit. Edmonton's merchants, watching, rubbed their hands.

But aside from the money, which really was not much even for those days, the Edmonton area received publicity such as mere advertising could not have brought. The Klondike Rush put it on the map. Moreover, with their own eyes, hundreds of newcomers had seen how arable this far northern soil was. Even Klondikers returning disappointed remembered Edmonton and spread its fame. Many fell back upon the town or took a nearby homestead.

About this time, after the glitter of gold had faded, men with the smell of oil in their nostrils took a look at Edmonton. Although the actual year is uncertain, A. W. Dingman, of whom the world was to hear later on, tried his luck with Edmonton's first oil well. While he spudded it in near the Low Level Bridge, close to the Brewery and in sight of Donald Ross's Hotel, none of these factors helped. After a good attempt, he was forced to give up and to move to other parts of Alberta to continue his search.

In the fall of 1898, South Edmonton's leading citizens decided that, like Edmonton, it should be incorporated. When they applied to Regina, the capital of the Northwest Territories, someone there, probably with his tongue in his cheek, wrote back agreeing to the idea, but suggesting that the community should be set up as a village. With unanimity hitherto rare, South Edmontonians scorned the suggestion and sent off post-haste to express their displeasure at the prospect of village status.

The Klondike Rush, however, did more than trigger a demand for South Edmonton's incorporation. It set all Canada afire. For 1897, the magical year of the gold rush, was the fourth year of the depression that had clamped down on North America. By this time banks were going broke, credit was non-existent, and even the free lands of western Canada failed to arouse the spirits of the unemployed or to tickle the fancy of the financially well-off. Then came the injection of a new gold supply, and it triggered a new boom.

Laurier's relatively new government felt its reawakening tingle. Of much more importance to the West, however, was the fact that as Minister of the Interior in his cabinet Sir Wilfrid Laurier now had a man who could get things done, a sometime westerner, Clifford Sifton. Just as he was beginning to get nicely adjusted to the seat of his office chair, the fever of the depression began to fade before the flush of the new gold supply and the new boom was in bud. Just at that time too, by a rare coincidence the rapidly expanding United States found that at last its rush of immigrants had overtaken all the free lands of its west, and that its young folk or any newcomers seeking farm lands would have to look elsewhere. At this point, Sifton, determined to settle western Canada, provided the elsewhere.

Overhauling the homestead regulations, straightening the kinks in his department, and advertising extensively for settlers, he quickly set the tide of immigration rising. A year before, some 16,000 immigrants had come to Canada. During 1897, twice that many answered Sifton's call, and every year thereafter the tide rose higher. Sifton sought settlers everywhere; some from the British Isles, some from Ontario and Quebec, and many from the United States. His call reached mainland Europe, and Scandinavians and Germans poured in. Even the Low Countries and France sent a few, but most colourful and strange of all were the Slavs, who on their arrival in Canada were dubbed Sifton's Sheepskins. These, Poles and Russians, but mainly the people we know as Ukrainians, usually penniless and seeking new land and freedom, began to fill the steerage of ship after ship.

Sifton's policy was a single-minded drive to fill the West with immigrants from any country whence he could draw them. All the West, and especially Alberta, benefited by this policy, and before long its cities and towns were feeling the pleasant push of this new impetus. Of this push, northern Alberta got more than its share, and within a few years, Edmonton began to grow at a rate it had hitherto never experienced.

At long last, Alberta's greatest resource, its soil, was on the point of being used. In the past its furs had been exploited, and a pittance of gold had been picked from its rivers, and to house and heat its few people who lived by furs or gold, some of its timber had been cut and its coal mined. Largely because its time had not come, land, its main resource, had been left relatively untouched.

Once its time came, once the iron was hot, Sifton struck, and his settlers came pouring in. In 1891 Alberta's population had been 25,277. By 1901, two or three years after he got his forge heated, it had trebled to 73,022. In 1891 Edmonton's population had been less than 700, by 1895 it had nearly doubled to 1,165, and by 1901 it had more than doubled again, to 2,626. A small part of this increase had been due to the Klondike Rush, but most of it had come after Sifton's hammer began to hit. And this startling growth in Alberta and in Edmonton was only a tide compared to the torrent of the next decade.

One of the citizens Edmonton gained at this time was Dr. W. M. Mackay, a very old timer of the West, who in 1898 came to the town to retire. Having come to Canada in 1864 as a physician employed by the Hudson's Bay Company, he had spent a third of a century practising at such places as Fort Simpson, Fort Resolution, and Chipewyan. For thirty-four years he was the only medical man in almost half a continent of wide open prairies, vast icefields, mountains, rivers, lakes, and forests. Once, during an epidemic, he made a record trip of two hundred miles from Grouard to Edmonton to supply medical care. The condition of the ice of Lesser Slave Lake and on the rivers was just right, and he skated most of the way to Edmonton.

Dr. Mackay reached Edmonton just in time to see the very first, very crude attempt at moving pictures shown in the town. These were a set of pictures portraying Queen Victoria's Diamond Jubilee which had been celebrated the year before. The operator of the show turned a crank and kept up a patter of comment.

But observing costumes of the women who came to see the show was nearly as entertaining as the pictures themselves. Small hats, sporting an array of feathers, perched on their highly piled masses of long hair. Their dresses, with lace frills at the throat and descending through an hour-glass waist which accentuated their bosoms and hips, reached the floor. Leg-of-mutton sleeves ending in elaborate long cuffs completed a picture undoubtedly beautiful but strange to look back upon.

Except for the bustle as scores of settlers passed through Edmonton on their way to homesteads within some forty miles of the town, 1898 slipped away quietly. Perhaps the town's most exciting times were whenever a blaze called out the fire department. It consisted of about forty volunteers, with a chief on a part-time salary, and a permanently employed driver for the team that pulled the steam fire-engine, which was always kept fired up and was mounted on the hose wagon. The chemical engine and the remainder of the hose, rigged on reels, was pulled by hand. For fire department use, three underground tanks were buried in the streets, one at the Alberta Hotel, one at the corner of 101A Street and Jasper, and another on Jasper Avenue at 103 Street. After each fire, the volunteers took the engine down to the river, stretched the hose up the hill to each of the tanks in turn, and pumped them full again.

On April 29, 1899, the citizens living across the river succeeded in their incorporation project. By June, when Strathcona's mayor, Thomas Bennett, and the new town officials got their feet under them, their census-taker counted a population of 1,156.

Even though it was the terminus of the Calgary-Edmonton Railway, Strathcona could not overtake its rival across the river. By that time Edmontonians were hearing the first rumours of another railway, a competitor of the CPR which operated the Calgary-Edmonton line. Two vigorous and hard-headed promoters named Mackenzie and Mann were wondering if they could pull the magic strings that would induce the Dominion of Canada to virtually finance another trans-continental, which they hoped to build across the prairies and up the North Saskatchewan River. Edmontonians pricked up their ears.

That summer, after many days of rain, the river, usually so benign, rose in one of its record floods, which Malcolm Groat, who had been in the town since 1861, declared was the highest he had seen. By August 21, it had overflowed both Walter's and Ross's flats. Even the cable of Walter's ferry, which, as it sagged over the centre of the river, was never very high at the best of times, was submerged. The water rose around the power house, which was then located near the end of today's Low Level Bridge, and when it started flowing into windows the staff left. According to A. W. Ormsby, who in those days was in charge of the plant, it was out of business for three weeks before all the equipment could be dried out.

The sternwheeler, the "Northwest," provided another of the incidents of the flood. A year or so previously she had been hauled up the bank and left ignominiously stranded high and dry on timbers on Walter's flat. When the river

Edmonton's Business Section 1903. (Jasper Avenue looking east from 102 Street.)

Top: *First locomotive to reach Edmonton in 1902 when E.Y. & P. Railway crossed Low Level Bridge to the station below McDougall Hill.*

Bottom: *Edmonton's first motor car in foreground driven by J. H. Morris. Photo taken about 1905 on Jasper Avenue near 124th Street.*

rose, it picked her up and away she went downstream until she smashed into the newly built centre pier of the not yet completed Low Level Bridge. For ten minutes she hung there, and then ever so slowly, her sides smashed in and her back broken, she swung free and set out on her last run down the river she had known so well. Three days later, one hundred miles downstream, she was still recognizable as she passed the mouth of Saddle Creek, thenceforth to be seen no more. But rust and rot had not claimed her tied up to a stake like a cow in a field. Afloat, as she should have been, she met her end.

But her nemesis, the pier, was disgraced. For it and its fellows proved inadequate for the bridge they were to bear, and as the water rose it submerged them. Fortunately, this gave the engineers another chance, and when the piers once more emerged from the water, they added eight feet to their height.

After the flood Edmonton settled back into fairly routine existence for the remainder of 1899. In October the South African War broke out and old soldiers and veterans of the Riel Rebellion hurried to get into the adventure. As a result, Ottawa decided to organize the 2nd Canadian Mounted Rifles and to base this unit on the pattern set by the NWMP. In December, Major A. H. Griesbach at Fort Saskatchewan got instructions to recruit an Edmonton troop of the Canadian Mounted Rifles. Many young Edmontonians, including his son W. A. Griesbach, Fred Jamieson and one of Matt McCauley's sons joined up. The troop sailed from Halifax towards the end of January 1900, and thirty days later landed in Cape Town, South Africa. Edmontonians eagerly awaited news of their activities and adventures there.

That fall marked Bob Edwards' departure from Strathcona. After a sojourn of a few months, this great character of the West's settlement days, who eventually found in Calgary the environment in which his talents and his *Eye Opener* flourished, brushed Edmonton's dust off his clothes and left.

At Strathcona he had started by putting out the *Strathcolic,* a name he soon changed to the *Alberta Sun.* The Edmonton environment proved a disappointment, and occasionally Bob returned to visit his more congenial friends in Wetaskiwin where "those who were not passing through the folding doors, were coming out, wiping off their chins." He liked Wetaskiwin, but to him "Edmonton is but a snide place which gives everyone the blues." His addiction to liquor and particularly his pungent satire made him unwelcome in the homes of Edmontonians, whom he called "cliff dwellers." In any event, he found their homes uninteresting. "They contain nothing but enlarged pictures of deceased Ontario relatives," he declared. So, after a few months in its unbending atmosphere, Bob Edwards left the Edmonton area to add his talents and his fame to the more congenial Calgary.

Being a Conservative and publishing a paper competing with the *Bulletin* for subscribers, and often puncturing political bombast, Bob Edwards was no friend of Frank Oliver. But in any event, Frank was too busy with his own affairs to feel the prick of Edwards' pen. When in 1900 he ran for re-election he easily out-manoeuvred his tall, polished opponent, R. B. Bennett, to hold Alberta's one Federal seat for the Liberals.

While Edmonton's troop of the CMR's had come home early in 1901 and troopers Griesbach and Fred Jamieson resumed their civilian roles, the South African War did not end until May 1902. Edmontonians, ever ready for a bit of celebration, especially on a day late in May, rejoiced in a manner appropriate to the end of the war. A couple of blacksmiths provided the salute by hauling their anvils across Jasper Avenue to the top of the cliff, placing powder between them and touching it off. The resulting "bang" repeated twenty-one times rolled up and down the great valley, and when the last echoes had died down, the blacksmiths, Jack Kelly and Colin Beals, retired to the shadows of their shop to counteract the ringing of their ears with appropriate liquids.

A few days later, Edmontonians were in a different mood, for on June 2, 1902, after half a century of hardship and great and effective labours in building up the West, Bishop Vital Grandin died. Coming from France as an ailing young volunteer and then being posted to the West after three years' service, at the age of twenty-eight he found himslf Co-adjutor, Bishop of Western Canada. In 1871 he became the first titular Bishop of St. Albert, and during his long and arduous regime he had watched the nearby hamlet of Edmonton grow until it surpassed St. Albert in population and in effect till it approached city status.

In 1902, over on 102 Street and north of 102 Avenue, a huge hip-roofed, barn-like rink was opened. This, Secord's covered Thistle Rink, dominated all the other buildings as for some years it was to dominate at all community affairs.

That fall the Low Level Bridge was completed, and at last Edmontonians could cross the river at will. By that time too, the Edmonton, Yukon and Pacific Railway, conceived during the Klondike Gold Rush, had also become a reality, although a much shorter one than had been planned. Originally thought of as extending from Strathcona to some point in the Yukon, it had shrunk during the delay. In 1902, however, it crossed the Low Level Bridge and ended not 1,400 miles away but four thousand yards as the crow flies from its starting place. The rails wriggled and wound down Mill Creek, straightened out for the Low Level Bridge and dead-ended at the station Mackenzie and Mann had built near Ross's Hotel. Even at that, however, there had been some anxious moments when it had looked as if it might fall through, because the hated CPR had tried to prevent it from making a connection with that company's line and thus to the outside world.

Over twenty years earlier the two-thousand-mile transcontinental CPR had been expected daily. When that fell through, ten more years had elapsed before the two-hundred-mile C & E Railway crept north. Somehow that, too, never reached Edmonton, and again the old timers were disappointed. At last, however, an actual locomotive stood panting on Edmonton's soil after having traversed the full four thousand yards of its track.

In 1903, Del Grierson and Fred Jackson built their revised version of the old Alberta Hotel — the one which, with its round brick tower ending in a spire, is still an important landmark on Jasper Avenue. When it was opened, it was the last word in opulence, even having a shower bath and the first elevator in Edmonton.

In 1903 also, the first Conservative paper to give the *Bulletin* a run for its money got out its first issue in November when the *Edmonton Journal* appeared on the streets.

Hard on the heels of the *Journal* came Edmonton's first car. The *Bulletin* of May 26, 1904, said: "The credit of bringing the first horseless carriage to Edmonton belongs to Mr. J. H. Morris, who, on his return from Winnipeg last evening, brought a two-cylinder autocar. The new carriage created quite an excitement on Jasper Avenue last evening, especially among the horses and small boys."

Fortunately for posterity, Ernest Brown, a young English photographer, arrived in the town about this time. He immediately saw that someone should record and preserve the strange and fascinating history of this new and developing community, and with his camera started to do just that. One of his pictures, for instance, shows Joe Morris's car. For the next forty-six years, through good times and bad, he persevered, and as a result we have been left one of the best photographic records extant.

For weeks Morris's car was the talk of Edmonton, till a new Federal election came to turn everyone's mind to matters of state and mutterings over graft. By this time Alberta, still a part of the Northwest Territories, was entitled to four seats, called Alberta, Calgary, Edmonton and Strathcona. In the Edmonton riding Dick Secord was bold enough to challenge Frank Oliver, but came off a poor second-best.

After the election, Edmonton, with a population of 8,350 as compared to the 2,626 people it had contained three years earlier, applied to the legislature in Regina for incorporation as a city. When on October 8, 1904, its charter was approved, and later, on November 7, it was proclaimed, the city took in 2,400 additional acres. Now Edmonton was away to the races.

The act creating the city specified that until elections could be held, the existing council should hold office. In this way, Mayor William Short continued in office, along with the following aldermen; D. R. Fraser and A. T. Cushing, proprietors of rival lumber companies, James Ross of Ross Brothers Hardware Store, J. H. Picard of the well known old firm of Larue and Picard, E. D. Grierson, owner of the new Alberta Hotel, and Charles May, partner in the contracting firm of May and Copp. When, early in 1905, the new council was elected, K. W. MacKenzie, one of the town's early school principals, became mayor. Associated with him were eight aldermen; W. H. Clark, Thomas Bellamy, J. R. Boyle, D. R. Fraser, J. H. Picard, Charles May, K. A. McLeod and W. A. Griesbach.

On November 7, to celebrate its incorporation, the city entertained several hundred people in the Thistle Rink. As the *Edmonton Journal* said: "The decoration of the hall was not only very appropriate but very elaborate and done in excellent taste. The stage represented a settler's or trapper's cabin, with its outer walls hung with trophies of the chase. A wigwam beside told of the ancient inhabitants. Nearby was an automobile and other marks of modern civilization.

"The walls of the rink were hung with thousands of dollars worth of furs to represent the foundations of Edmonton's prosperity and bunting of all colours gave a comfortable effect to the interior."

While not mentioned in the *Journal* account, the small city police force was present in strength, and here and there the scarlet coats of the Mounties added further colour. The Mounties had just completed changing their badges to take account of their new status. To recognize the valiant work they had performed for the last thirty years and their efforts in the South African War, the Queen had graciously approved the change in their name from North West Mounted Police to Royal North West Mounted Police.

Amongst the distinguished guests in the rink, of course, Frank Oliver sat rejoicing that his little hamlet of Edmonton had fulfilled his dreams and was now on the point of the expansion which for so many years he had foreseen. As he closed his ears to the interminable speeches, he must have wondered about the next steps to be taken in the West. The Northwest Legislative Assembly on which he had served till he moved on to the Federal political arena had finally made its point, and now the government was on the verge of granting autonomy to the West. Prime Minister Laurier, however, was finding autonomy a knobby problem, bedevilled by the rift between French and English and between Catholic and

1905 City Council. In the front row, left to right, are K. A. McLeod, Charles May, K. W. MacKenzie (Mayor), J. R. Boyle and J. H. Hargreaves, Public Works Commissioner. In the back row, left to right, are Ald. W. A. Griesbach, Thomas Bellamy, G. J. Kinnaird, Commissioner, W. H. Clark, J. H. Picard and D. R. Fraser.

Protestant, a split in which as a trouble-maker the question of Roman Catholic separate schools loomed large.

In February 1905, over this vexing question one of his strongest men, his minister in charge of settling the West, Clifford Sifton, resigned. To take his place, the aging Laurier chose Frank Oliver as Minister of the Interior.

As suddenly as that, Frank Oliver inherited Sifton's mantle, and now he was faced with the worries of immigration and the problem of the thousands of Ukrainians who were pouring into the West and against whom he had so often spoken. He was to find that policy-making, no matter how simple it looks when viewed from below, and how stupid, is a different breed of cat when one has to assume its tasks.

No matter what grave debate went on in Oliver's mind after February 1905, Edmontonians, wholehearted in their rejoicing that their member of parliament was now a cabinet minister, acclaimed him as a hero. Even though he had been promoted, it was still necessary for his constituents to confirm him in that office by re-electing him, and this northern Albertans did by acclamation in April 1905. And of all the electors, those in Edmonton had the most to gain for they had eggs to hatch, and with Frank Oliver on the nest, they were already counting their chickens.

Nevertheless, Calgary, the upstart rival barely twenty years old, and its aggressive R. B. Bennett, would bear watching. With its population of some eleven thousand it was the largest city in Alberta, and moreover, it was on the CPR. In any move towards autonomy, Calgary would be certain to be working hard to become the capital of the new province.

But Frank Oliver was the trump card. Edmontonians had stuck by him when three times they had elected him to the Northwest Legislature at Regina and when for nine years they had kept him in Ottawa as Alberta's Federal member. He had eaten of their bread and now he would butter it for them. Had he not written: "While the Saskatchewan runs downhill, while coal will burn or timber grow, or the seed produce after its kind, they [the people of Edmonton] ask no favors of anyone, but with their own hands will build up this country into the best province of the Dominion of Canada."

That was the idea. With their own hands, Edmontonians would seize any opportunity while by skilful manoeuvering they would see that they would always be within grasping distance of anything worth grabbing.

And in Ottawa when the chips were down, Edmonton's Frank Oliver, Minister of the Interior, aided with the grabbing. Ever at Laurier's elbow, he saw that Clause 9 of the Federal Alberta Act declared: "Unless and until the Lieutenant Governor in Council of the said province otherwise directs, by proclamation under the Great Seal, the seat of government of the said province shall be at Edmonton."

Once the act was through, all Edmontonians had to do was sweep in the pot. When they did so on September 1, 1905, the day Alberta became a province, they staged a show of which they can always be proud.

Calgary came to lend its hand to ensure the success of the celebration, and both cities combined to produce the grand concert held the evening before on the ample stage and ballroom of Secord's Thistle Rink.

On the great day, the weather was perfect, and mellow autumn sunshine lighted up Edmonton's magnificent valley. Down on the flats below McDougall Hill lay the half-mile race track, the grandstand, and other buildings of the then new fair grounds. Among the poplars south of it shone the rows of white tents of more than two hundred officers and men of the RNWMP. Surrounded by the oval race track stood the white and blue ceremonial platform bedecked in red, white and blue bunting, with its purple crown. In the bright sunlight and the light breeze, flags and pennants fluttered gayly. On the stand sat many of Canada's dignitaries, while thousands of Albertans, jostling good naturedly, stood and applauded.

For two days and nights, long special trains filled with visitors, including a large delegation of American editors, had been rumbling into the Strathcona station. On the north side the big Revillon Freres warehouse had been fitted up as sleeping quarters for hundreds who came, and Alberta College on 101 Street was a reception centre for one and all.

Along the trails and the few graded roads radiating from the city, freshly-groomed teams jogged past grain fields pulling buggies, buckboards, democrats or lumber wagons. Seated in these, men, women and children, dressed in their best, looked forward eagerly to the history-making fête ahead.

EDMONTON A CITY — ALBERTA A PROVINCE — 1896-1905

The street parade with its marshalls, William Ibbotson and Thomas Lines, started near the Alberta Hotel along a Jasper Avenue alive with bunting and fluttering flags and through great arches covered with grain sheaves, spruce boughs and more bunting. Magnificent horses in their burnished trappings, pulling shining carriages, drew the various personages decked out in military uniform, or, like Mayor MacKenzie and his aldermen, in their high hats and Prince Alberts. In the procession, besides the floats of the lumber mills and the breweries, marched the Old Timers' Association, the Jean-Baptiste Society, and the Boer War veterans, interspersed with contingents of Crees and Stony Indians, while lining the route, two thousand school children shouted and sang. The streets resounded as the Fort Saskatchewan squadron of the recently-organized 19th Dragoons paced by, and the bands struck up; one each from St. Albert, Fort Saskatchewan and Edmonton, as well as the 15th Light Horse Band from Calgary.

At 11 A.M., after this parade had reached the fair grounds and dispersed, Governor-General Earl Grey and his party arrived in their glittering carriages and the military march past began. The Governor-General inspected the three squadrons of the RNWMP, consisting of 211 cavalrymen and their four-gun battery, all commanded by Commissioner Perry. When the platform party took their places they were an imposing group, led by the Earl and Countess, Sir Wilfrid and Lady Laurier, Honourable William Patterson, Sir Gilbert Parker, the distinguished author who was also a Canadian-born member of the British Parliament, Father Lacombe, and many others.

At a quarter to twelve, while the Mounted Police battery galloped up to the high ground where today's Legislative Building stands, and set up its guns, Mayor MacKenzie read an address to the Governor-General, who replied in a suitable speech. Then came Canada's great Prime Minister, Sir Wilfrid Laurier. Courtly of manner, with a finely chiselled face and an Einstein-like aureole of fluffy white hair framing his head, he rose to speak. All was hushed as he recalled his visit to the town eleven years previously. Noting the subsequent development and holding out radiant promise for the future, he said: "I see everywhere hope. I see everywhere calm resolution, courage, enthusiasm to face all difficulties, to settle all problems." He spoke to this people of many nations, urging them to be British subjects, to take their share in the life of this country, whether on the municipal, provincial or national level. "We do not anticipate, and we do not want, that any individuals should forget the land of their origin or their ancestors. Let them look to the past, but let them also look to the future; let them look to the land of their ancestors, but let them look also to the land of their children."

The commission appointing George Hedley Vicars Bulyea as Lieutenant-Governor was read. Then, promptly at high noon, to the accompaniment of gun-fire from up the hill, and in the presence of twelve thousand people, the oath was read to Bulyea, he kissed the Bible, and Alberta had become a province.

Sir Wilfrid Laurier, Prime Minister, and Lord Strathcona speaking at the Inauguration of the Province September 1st, 1905 while seated to his left centre is Hon. G. H. V. Bulyea, first Lieutenant Governor. Nearby His Excellency, Earl Grey, Governor General and Lady Grey.

A Horse Drawn City
1905

chapter *10*

MANY EDMONTONIANS spent Saturday, the second of September, sobering up. Others, feeling that no good could come out of a ceremony held on Friday, decided to have another drink and to forget about it. But there were others who did not care what day had been picked for the celebration so long as the place that had been picked was Edmonton. Now, as the temporary capital of the new province, it held nine thousand people. Moreover, the second transcontinental railway, the CNR, was on the point of reaching this northern city. Edmonton was on the make; Frank Oliver favoured it, and the future smiled on it. With this combination, Edmontonians hoped to pull many a trick out of the hat of the next few years.

The hub of the city extended west from about today's 94 Street to 106 Street, and from the river bank to 103 Avenue. At the corner of Jasper and 98 Street, stood the new Alberta Hotel, while the General Hospital formed the focus of an extension west from the main town. The intersection of 101 Street and Jasper was the heart of the shopping area, holding this distinction by virtue of McDougall & Secord's brick buildings on two corners, and the Windsor Hotel on another. Along the four streets radiating from this point occasional three-storey brick buildings or two- or three-storey frame buildings towered over the smaller, false-fronted stores and the intervening lots still covered with their original trees. Some of the small shops were shacks no bigger than a modern kitchen, and the space taken out of their front by a normal sized door left room for only a narrow window. Cheek by jowl along the few main streets were banks and livery stables, saloons and stores, poolrooms and office buildings, Chinese restaurants and laundries. At the corner of Jasper and 103 Street stood the Hudson's Bay Company's store built in 1892, while across from it was the Presbyterian Church of 1902 vintage, and overlooking the river bank on the east side of 101 Street was George McDougall's whip-sawed lumber church dating back thirty years.

To separate these buildings, many of them still smelling of freshly-sawn lumber, and all of them raw in their newness, from the street, a wooden sidewalk rose and fell as it followed the surface of the ground. Here and there, at intervals of one wagon width, hitching posts stood like sentinels. On some sections of sidewalk iron tethering rings had been bolted into the planks, and along others rails extended the width of a store-front. Much of the time these became precarious perches for idlers retailing the latest gossip. Staggering along in erratic sagging lines, the telephone and electric power lines, taking little pride in their dressing, ran hither and yon.

This vigorous, recently enlarged young city, where the number of new-comers vastly exceeded old timers of five-years' standing, where nearly everybody was less than forty years old, and where men far outnumbered women, got its motive power from horses. Most of the stores, and many of the houses, used electricity for lighting only. In other residences coal oil supplied the lights. Hardware stores handled any petroleum products sold, but, except for a gallon or two of gasoline used by the few dry cleaning establishments, and a few jars of vaseline, coal oil for lighting and axle grease for wagon wheels formed the major contribution made by the oil industry. In the many small mines and the four sawmills negligible quantities of lubricating oil were used, but as yet the oil age had not threatened the oats era.

Since the early days of the original Edmonton House, pack and saddle horses had been used for transportation. Now that the surrounding country was opening up and being surveyed, strings of pack horses entering or leaving Edmonton for far-off places had increased and were a regular feature of everyday life. For half a century, Red River carts, drawn by oxen or ponies, had also been major factors in Edmonton's life, but after the CPR had reached Strathcona their numbers had dwindled, and now in 1905 they were relatively rare. During the previous fifteen years buggies, democrats and wagons had superseded them. Then the previous year Joe Morris had unloaded his Ford, and the first car made its way along what a visitor had described as "that dog-leg of a street that used to be the only thoroughfare in Edmonton." By 1905 there were half a dozen of these monsters with their rotating flywheels and their detonating cylinders, but as everybody knew, these cars were mere passing fancies. Both the light tripping and the heavy hauling had to be done by good old reliable horses.

But within the limits imposed by almost total absence of internal combustion engines, what the traffic lacked in density it made up in diversity. Strings of twenty or thirty pack horses trotted or frisked about, hazed along by two or three hollering packers. Smart surreys flashed by pulled by well-groomed check-reined horses, curried and combed to within an inch of their lives. Indians' democrats, with one or more wheels wobbling perilously, dragged by derelict raw-shouldered skeletons, crept along. Buggies, ox-carts and carriages wound their way in and out of the traffic. Depending upon whether the previous week had enjoyed a dearth or a down-pour of rain, cabbies whisking a fare along raised a cloud of dust or splattered pedestrians with mud or slush. Covered wagons ending their sixteen hundred mile trip from Minnesota brought new settlers to stare at Jasper Avenue. Now and then a fire-engine with its galloping team lurched and swayed around corners, or a Mountie walked his sleek horse along, and later, perhaps, Sergeant McCallum of the city police, returning from a patrol of the outlying residential areas, stopped to let his horse drink at some convenient trough.

Huge black Percherons, proudly displaying their brass ornaments, arched their great necks to drag drays piled high with pyramiding beer kegs. Loads of shiny black coal, drawn by fringed footed Clydesdales, or wagons piled high with new smelling lumber fresh from the mills in the valley, made their way to and fro, dodging teams drawing bricks to one of the many building sites. Ox-teams, slobbering and slow, not yoked as in older communities but pulling by means of collars and traces, plodded along. Half-breeds rode by on their ponies or be-laboured their despondent, half-starved horses, while a dozen mongrel dogs ran alongside or, with their tails pressed down tightly, ran along under the vehicle. Nearby farmers fetched great billowing loads of hay from their meadows to livery barns or markets, and outgoing settlers with their all on one rickety wagon and with a cow tied behind, crawled along towards whatever destiny might hold for them thirty, or sixty, or ninety miles out in the bush. Occasionally a car chugged by, scaring the daylights out of many a country-bred nag and touching off at least one run-away team, whose wildly careening wagon soon spilled its contents and passengers and went swaying and bouncing down the street, till a collision with another vehicle, a pole, or a store, reduced it to a battered wreck. In short, all the traffic of a burgeoning civilization, all drawn by beasts, gave action, colour and variety to Jasper Avenue.

But all these were merely the horses that were in motion. Others, either saddled or hitched to vehicles, were tied to sidewalk rings, posts, or rails. Any vacant lot beside or behind any of the bigger stores was full of horses munching hay or merely waiting for their drivers to return. The market square was full of other teams and wagons, and in front of the many livery barns a constant pro-cession of teams stood to be hitched or unhitched. Then too, when in town between trips along the main roads that led to different sectors of the newly opened country-side, the livery stages stopped at these stables. These stages, drawn by four horses, made scheduled trips along the Athabasca Trail, the North Victoria Trail, and between the city and many another embryo town not served by a railroad.

Livery stables, built wide enough for a row of double stalls, along each side and a broad aisle down the middle, and long enough to hold maybe fifty teams, dominated every second block. Their haylofts filled the great cavern under the high hip roofs. At the front on one side of the passageway was a large room for the storage of oats. In the office, alongside other horse medicines reposed bottles of iodine and creolin, and these lent a distinctive odour to the place, which, mingled with the ammonia smell from the stalls, steeped the stable in a pleasant, if distinctive, aroma.

Within a horseshoe's pitch of any livery barn stood an unpretentious black-smith's shop. There, with his bare, sweaty torso covered with grime and bulging with muscles, a cheerful smith repaired farm machinery, fixed vehicles, and shod horses. Closely related to the stable spacially and spiritually were the offices of the veterinarians, who found much to do in this horse-drawn world. Allied to the blacksmith's shop also, and usually close by, were harness shops, for much of Edmonton's industry centered around its mode of locomotion. Moreover, many a shoemaker's shop catered to the needs of the town folk for smart shoes, and to lumbermen, miners, farmers or teamsters for heavier, thick-soled footwear.

A stroll along any of Edmonton's close-in side streets took one past a repetition of shops all devoted to these important industries or services; livery stables, blacksmiths' shops, veterinarians' offices, harness makers and shoemakers. But in the same vicinity were other businesses catering to the comfort, or at least the service, of this pioneer agricultural frontier. There were hotels of all grades, from clean, well-run establishments, to flop houses crawling with bed bugs. Each had its saloon with its brass rail, long mirror, brass spitoons and sawdust-strewn floor. Not far to seek were other houses run by madams.

Beside any of these varied business places great piles of sawn wood, brought in by farmers to trade to grocers or householders stood stacked in their yards.

Some places burned coal mined in the valley, and this was stored in a shed behind, or else discharged through a chute to the basement.

On the main streets, on Jasper Avenue, 101 Street and 97 Street, the leading hotels, the Alberta, Pendennis, Imperial, Grand View, Queens and Windsor, catered to the public. Along these streets too stood the stores of the leading merchants:

J. H. Harris & Co.—women's clothing. McIntosh & Campbell—furniture.
The Mays Coal Co. Crystal Palace Clothing Emporium.
Kelly & Moore—men's clothing. John I. Mills—men's clothing.
McDougall & Secord. Hudson's Bay Company.
Gariepy & Lessard. Johnstone-Walker.
MacKenzie's Book Store.

These establishments, and several others, crowded with customers and merchandise, carried all the groceries, including plugs of smoking and chewing tobacco, and snoose, as well as the hardware and the rough, sturdy clothing needed at mine, mill, or farm, and also displayed a surprising array of the latest fashions in hats, dresses, and suits.

No less varied were the stores' patrons and the crowds that milled along the wooden sidewalks and stopped to watch the many buildings going up, sometimes two or three to a block. For Edmonton's builders were busy, some erecting steel frameworks, some building with brick, and dozens throwing up wooden stores with false fronts. The ra-tat-tatting of the riveters, the rasping of hand saws, and the banging of hammers, kept up a continuous commotion, while the redolence of newly-sawn spruce lumber filled the air.

To any newcomer freshly arrived from New York, London, or Lisbon, the crowds were a never failing interest. From the sidewalks rose a babble of languages. These varied all the way from the soft accents of negroes coming in to take up land, to the sing-song of passing Chinese, and the soft sibilants of Cree-speaking half-breeds. Broad Scotch brogues competed with the idiom of Yorkshire and Lancashire, Cockney voices challenged the dialects of western, central or southern United States, while on every hand, scores of other immigrants conversed in Scandinavian, Slavic or Germanic tongues.

Clothing, too, varied from the homespun of various Europeans to the more uniform high-bibbed overalls, blue work shirts, and buckskin jackets which old timers and newcomers alike found so practical on the frontier. Here and there a mounted policeman in his service uniform and stetson stood out smartly. But the crowds were composed mainly of women. A few were nicely dressed women whose husbands were already established in the city. On them the hour-glass figure had appeared as their waists went higher to give greater length to their hobble skirts, which partially revealed their high buttoned shoes. Their crowning glories were ridiculously large and ornate hats. Most of the women, however, were newcomers wearing plain, serviceable clothes. The bright plaid scarves and blouses of the squaws and half-breed women, some with papooses on their backs and most with one or more black-haired, button-eyed cherubs in tow, enlivened the scene. The Galician women wore their shawls, white, yellow, or a subdued red.

Men sported moustaches, great sprawling, saggy, untended growths, for here on the frontier everyone and everything had to fend for itself. Most men wore beards. Some were grey, some black, and others red, but one and all showed streaks of rich brown. For tobacco in many forms comforted these hirsute men of the frontier. The scent of cigars permeated sidewalks and shops. On every hand men pulled out plugs of tobacco, and before handing them on to their neighbours, cut off a slice or two, pulverized them, and, filling a pipe, struck a match on the seats of their pants, then exhaled a great cloud of blue and generally rank smoke. Anyone who did not smoke gnawed off a chunk of sweet black chewing tobacco or stuffed his upper lip with snoose. At vantage points in stores and saloons, but never quite in the right spot, brass spitoons waited to receive the overflowing juices generated by these delectable morsels. Too often, to the discomfort and discolouration of floors and stoves, they failed sadly. Cigarettes were rare, but cigars, pipes, chewing tobacco and snoose, were the hallmarks of the age.

The best residential area lay south of Jasper Avenue between 101 and 107 Streets. There Frank Oliver had built his house (south-east corner of 103 Street and 100 Avenue), while Dick Secord was working on his (south-west corner 99 Avenue and 105 Street). In the same vicinity, many another splendid brick or wooden house attested to the owner's pride and his confidence in this growing city.

Farther out north-east or west, the homes, though much less pretentious, were nevertheless solid and comfortable. Beyond them, of course, the houses became smaller and had more tree-clothed vacant lots between them, until out at the edge, around 116 Street, many a tent-sized shack sided with lumber or tarpaper housed newcomers. Many of these, though tiny and primitive, were nevertheless clean and comfortable, with yards kept tidy by owners looking to the day when, as fortune rewarded their efforts, a room or two could be added and some paint applied. Interspersed all along were tents sheltering those who, having recently rushed in, either could not find, or could not afford, accommodation to rent. Many of these were clustered down on Ross's Flats below McDougall Hill, or in one or two other locations in Edmonton or Strathcona, where most of their owners were camping until they could locate homesteads in the country.

By the end of 1905 Edmonton had six miles of sewers and some fifteen miles of water mains serving 405 customers. Most of the citizens on the outlying streets and many even adjacent to the mains had their water delivered in tank wagons. Outdoor toilets, like twin rows of staggering sentinels, flanked the rutted lanes. On the back of most lots, with a wisp of hay curling out of its loft and a pile of manure behind it, stood a stable big enough for two or four horses, and sometimes a cow. During the day, the children took her a few blocks north or west to pasture on some favoured small meadow or on other vacant land. Gardens, which supplied vegetables all summer and potatoes for the whole winter, filled the rest of the back yard. In many cases, potatoes decorated the front yard, but here and there some grass or flowers added a touch of home to a street otherwise strictly utilitarian. Far uptown, of course, in the area containing the better homes, lawns, flowers and even fruit trees, lent an air of permanency and beauty to the streets.

The majority of the outlying homes had neither water nor electricity. But in spite of having to hold the weekly bath night ceremony around a washtub half way between a wood or coal-fired kitchen stove and the wash stand with its pails of water, everyone kept clean. Clothes washing was done by bending over a tub, and ironing by the light of a coal oil lamp and by means of sadirons heated on the stove. Fortunate indeed was the home which owned one of the new-fangled Edison phonographs.

In the better homes down towards town, of course, maids, the daughters of German or Ukrainian immigrants, did the housework. Many a chatelaine was delighted with these obedient, hard-working servants. To their parents who laboured in the city or were out trying to clear up their homesteads, these girls' earnings went a long way to secure the immigrants' success in this new land. At the same time, they learned English and the customs and dress of the city.

In many cases, their fathers worked at the jobs made available because of the city's rapid growth. Some laboured in lumber mills, some in the mines, and others by supplying all the manpower that went into digging basements with shovels and wheelbarrows and building new stores and homes. Many of them worked far underground, driving through the big sewers, which, maybe fifty feet below the street, were to serve the city that was to be. Most obvious were the gangs working on the waterworks ditches dug down eight or nine feet to escape the frost. For in those days no mechanical monsters went clanging along the street, clawing away at the ground and leaving a neat, clean ditch in their wake. These 1905 ditches were dug by hand with picks, shovels, and crow-bars, wielded by scores of men working elbow to elbow all along the excavation. Another gang looking for work stood close by, hoping to step into the place of anyone too tired or too lazy to keep up the steady stooping and shovelling.

Not all this activity was concentrated into what we now know as the centre of the city a few blocks from the corner of Jasper and 101 Street. Much of the city's industry was down on the river flats: Ross's Flat, on which the new steam power plant had been built in 1902 where it is today; Walter's Flats, across the modern 105 Street bridge; and Fraser's Flats, on the left bank of the river east of 95 Street. For on these flats spread out handy to the river were the great lumber mills; Walter's, one on the south bank and another on the north side of the river on the point of land now occupied by the city waterworks; and Fraser's mill at the river's edge on modern 100 Avenue and 92 Street. Close to it, tearing the terrain into heaps and gouges, was Little's Brick Yard. Jack Pollard's Brick Yard was west of Walter's mill where later on the footings of the High Level Bridge sank deep into its workings. On the north side of the river, west of the bridge site, was Sandison's Brick Plant, and another similar venture was trying its luck with the clays that now underlie the Municipal Golf Course. Most of the coal mines scattered along the river bank for miles and generally small ventures, dug their coal out by driving in horizontally more or less from the water's edge.

In season, from the thick stands of spruce timber upstream for eighty miles, to each of these lumber mills drivers brought great log booms down the river. These log drives, long since gone from the river, brought many a lumberman out of the woods each spring to ride herd on the logs, anchor them to the pilings driven deep into the river's mud, and then head for the nearest saloon. Of these pilings, the only set visible now, when the water level recedes, is that off-shore from Walter's old mill.

From these mills and brick yards on the flats came the lumber and bricks of which the Edmonton of the 1905 era was built. From these mines along the river's edge came the coal that kept Edmontonians warm. And all this lumber and brick and coal had to be lugged up the steep hills on the Edmonton or the Strathcona side. It took trained teamsters applying brake and check-block and line, and sturdy horses putting their whole heart into the exhausting climb up these hills, but somehow, day after day and month after month, they did it.

Like all the building material, all the thousands of persons entering Edmonton had to climb or be carried up the river hills. Each one, businessman or butcher, prima donna or prostitute, had to come up McDougall Hill. And each was carried up the long slope by horses. For the Edmonton of 1905 was a city made possible by pony or cayuse, Percheron or Clydesdale. And whether on the flats, climbing the long hill, or taking a breather on top, everyone was shrouded in the haze of wood smoke that rose from the industries down by the river or was wafted in from the great forest fires burning ten, fifty or a hundred miles back in

John Walter — Boat Builder and Lumberman.

the bush. Week after week, the afternoon sun descended as a red ball in the west as over the growing city hung the aromatic pall of wood smoke, tinctured at times by the acidy fumes of eoal fires. If at times the exhaust fumes from one or more of Edmonton's half-dozen cars fouled the air, they were quickly diluted by the pervading pleasantness of wood smoke, or cut by the spicy savour of ammonia wafted from the piles behind every stable.

This, then, was the Edmonton of 1905; bursting at the seams, bubbling with energy; rejoicing in its horse drawn might, rightly assured of its future; touched with the magic of a new land awakening, and tinctured by a kindly medicinal mixture of mill smoke and manure.

On the political scene, the leading men had accomplished much, and had their eyes on further goals. When on September 1 he had been named Premier of Alberta and had been called upon to form a government, the Honourable A. C. Rutherford, Strathcona's sitting member in the Legislative Assembly of the Northwest Territories and a Liberal from away back, knew which men to ask to fill the cabinet posts. Assigning himself the posts of Provincial Treasurer and Minister of Education, he appointed C. W. Cross of Edmonton as Attorney General. To W. H. Cushing of Calgary went the post of Minister of Public Works, while W. T. Finlay of Medicine Hat assumed the duties of Provincial Secretary and Minister of Agriculture. Finally, to round out his cabinet, Rutherford appointed L. G. DeVeber of Lethbridge as Minister without Portfolio. In this way, Calgary and Edmonton and the other two cities in the new province were represented.

Premier A. C. Rutherford had been born in 1857 in Carlton County, Ontario, and for the decade ending 1895, after graduating from McGill University with a BA and BCL, had engaged in law practice in Ottawa. Then he came to Strathcona and started an office there. In 1902 he had been elected to the Northwest Territories Legislative Assembly.

Having set up his temporary cabinet and taken steps to get some office space in Edmonton, and to begin transferring documents pertaining to Alberta affairs from Regina to Edmonton, Rutherford had to look to the task of dividing

Alberta into constituencies. Out of these constituencies would come the MLA's who would have to make many decisions during the next four years. One of these decisions, Rutherford hoped, would ensure that Edmonton would remain the provincial capital. To him it was obvious that Edmonton, being near the geographical centre of the province, and having been the headquarters of this region for a century, should continue to be the capital of the area. But there were other opinions, and some advocated placing the capital at Red Deer, Calgary, and even Banff. Setting constituencies then was a job requiring care.

Rutherford, however, was a careful man, and Charlie Cross a cunning one, and each lived in sight of old Fort Edmonton. Primarily, the constituencies had to bear some relation to population, but because the sparsely settled area north of Edmonton was so far flung, the element of geography had to be taken into account. Due to the fact that for the previous decade the area between Red Deer and a line across the province some fifty miles north of Edmonton had received the bulk of the new settlement, it was natural that a majority of the twenty-five constituencies should lie north of Red Deer. Settlers in this area looked to Edmonton as their trading centre. And looking to Edmonton, perhaps it would be natural for them to want it to continue to be the capital city.

But the constituency makers had another string to their bow. If many of the northern areas radiated out from Edmonton as spokes from a hub, why not make their constituencies radiate similarly? As a result, as well as an Edmonton constituency, eight of the twenty-five electoral divisions did just that, and a man could live in Edmonton and be close enough to his electors that, given a hearty enough breakfast, he could jump from his porch to his bailiwick; St. Albert, Stony Plain, Sturgeon, Strathcona, Victoria, Vermilion, Leduc, and Wetaskiwin.

Having tidied up that situation, Rutherford called Alberta's first provincial election for November 9, 1905. In elections, Albertans rarely do things by halves, and this first one was no exception. When the results came in, Rutherford's Liberals had won twenty-three of the twenty-five seats. In Calgary, R. B. Bennett, the most capable and certainly the most vocal of the government's opponents, had been nosed out by twenty-five votes. Matt McCauley, Edmonton's first mayor, had been elected in the Vermilion constituency. In Edmonton, though opposed by W. A. Griesbach, Cross won decisively. On one occasion during the election, Frank Oliver spoke on behalf of Charlie Cross. At this meeting Griesbach was given a chance to state his case, and, noting that Oliver was going to give the main address in favour of Cross, compared himself to Oliver in the relation of Little David confronting the giant Goliath. When Oliver rose in rebuttal, he said that he was surprised that instead of Griesbach using the weapon which David had used so successfully on Goliath, he preferred to use the weapon Samson had used so destructively on the Philistines — the jaw-bone of an ass. Although undoubtedly that political joke was far from new at that time, the audience, much to Griesbach's discomfiture, howled with laughter.

Following the election, provincial politics bubbled away quietly under the surface, awaiting the sitting of the legislature which was to come in the spring.

While September 1, 1905, had been a great day for Edmontonians generally, it was a sad day for W. G. Tretheway, the street railway promoter. Well over a year earlier he had promised to have the first two miles of the transit system in operation by that day. When it dawned, however, the only sign of any railway was a wagonload of gravel that had been dumped on a corner of Jasper Avenue. While at the ceremonies bands played, soldiers saluted, and orators forecast great things for the future, up at the city hall the treasurer pocketed the $10,000 "good faith" deposit Tretheway had made. For the time being, although the city treasury was somewhat richer, any city transit system was still an unresolved problem.

Some seven weeks later, however, Edmonton's own transcontinental railway, Mackenzie and Mann's CNR, became a reality. At 10:30 on the morning of November 24 the track layer completed the line to the Edmonton station, and Mayor MacKenzie declared the afternoon a public holiday. That day "In the presence of thousands of citizens of Edmonton and visitors from all parts of Central Alberta, Hon. G. H. V. Bulyea . . . drove home with unerring blow the silver spike which held in place the first rail of the Canadian Northern Railway to reach the station in Edmonton." In the Queen's Hotel that evening at a banquet attended by two hundred guests, the city tendered its thanks to Donald Mann and to some of the visiting Mackenzies.

At long last Edmonton was on a transcontinental railroad, and now passengers going direct to Winnipeg could reach there after a trip of twenty-five hours. While, of course, the CNR did not follow the exact course of the old Winnipeg Trail, it did cut across the parklands along the same general route, crossing the river at North Battleford, going on to Saskatoon, and thence south and east to Winnipeg. Though for the moment this railway stopped at Edmonton and was thus not yet a true transcontinental, it was destined to go on west to Jasper and the Coast. The CPR, which twenty years earlier had spurned Edmonton and created Calgary, and eight years later had not faced up to the task of crossing the Saskatchewan River and had thereby set up Strathcona, had better watch out.

For now Edmonton's opinion was one to be considered. Now, out of Alberta's 160,000 people, fifty thousand of them were urban dwellers, and of these, according to the Edmonton papers, fourteen thousand were said to live in Greater Edmonton, which, of course, included Strathcona. The seeds of greatness were taking root, and now both people and press were beginning to think in the new term Greater Edmonton.

Under Mayor K. W. MacKenzie, the city administration was expanding. At the beginning of the year the new Department of Public Works had come into being, with R. R. Kealy as City Engineer. In his report to council in December, he explained how the expenses of his branch had totalled $10,243 and pointed to the streets he had graded and the wooden sidewalks he had laid for the $50,000 capital budget he had been allowed. At the same time, S. Evans, the Chief of Police, accounted for the $4,424 he and his constables had received, while the city Medical Officer, Dr. E. A. Braithwaite, explained how he had spent $1,958 on health matters, including $493 for relief and welfare. The Telephone Department, which had recently purchased Alex Taylor's Edmonton District Telephone Company for $17,000, reported five hundred customers and showed a profit of $4,150. The city power plant and distribution system, stating that it had 650 customers and fifty-three street lights, reported a profit.

During the year, several small industries had started up. Of most interest were the new mines, which, in response to a limited export market and to a large increase in the local population, had opened. Three of them, J. Baldwin's, Bush & Son, and the City Coal Company, started in Edmonton. In Strathcona, John Walter added to his growing holdings and to the industries in what we know as Walterdale by starting, in association with W. Ross, the Walter & Ross Coal Mine. Its pit entrance was at the shoulder of the hill directly across the river from today's Legislative Building. When it got into operation and sank its hundred-foot shaft, it provided work for 125 men. Other new mines were opened at Namao and on Big Island.

As a whole, except that the transit system situation was still up in the air, 1905 had been a good year and the aldermen were in a friendly frame of mind. In the election that winter, Charles May became mayor, and young Griesbach, who had received the most votes as an aldermanic candidate, continued to serve on the council. Early in January 1906 he married Janet Lauder, whose parents had settled just north of Edmonton a quarter of a century earlier and later had come to town to operate a bakery.

Weather-wise, too, to the disappointment of Edmonton's many coal mines, 1905 ended well, with exceptionally mild weather to Christmas and a mere trace of snow, for this was the beginning of one of the mildest winters on record. Except for some moderate cold in January and early February 1906, the whole winter was most unusual. According to the report of the recently set up Provincial Department of Agriculture;

"February — The month which was cold in the beginning ended in a thaw. Prairies are well bare of snow but there is still a little in the bush; poplar buds are bursting; sap running in soft maple and pansies are in bloom in gardens.

"March — Wheat being sown on the 10th, and general by the 24th. Geese seen on 2nd., ducks on 4th. and a blue jay on 10th."

With such a mild winter, it had been difficult to keep the ice in the closed Thistle Rink in good enough shape for the final hockey game, March 12, 1906, between Strathcona and the Edmonton Thistles for the Calgary Brewing Cup. The minute that Strathcona went down to defeat and the teams skated off the ice, a gang of workmen set to in the rink. They had two days and a bit in which to prepare it for a momentous occasion, because on Thursday, March 15, at 3 PM, Lieutenant-Governor Bulyea would arrive to open the first session of Alberta's first legislature.

Teams dragging heavy loads up McDougall Hill.

*Edmonton Lumber Co. with Anderson's
Brickyard in background, 1907.*

Confirmed As Capital

190[

chapter *II*

VISITORS ANXIOUS TO SEE the opening of the session poured into Edmonton. Ever since February 16 when Lieutenant-Governor Bulyea had held the first official government house reception, excitement had been building up. Since as a federal cabinet minister Frank Oliver had to live in Ottawa, the Lieutenant-Governor had rented his house on the corner of 103 Street and 100 Avenue, so that for the time being it was Alberta's Government House. As the opening of the session neared, visitors jammed Edmonton. In the middle of March the farmers surrounding the city could do little on their homesteads, so many of them drove to town. During the Monday, Tuesday and Wednesday preceding the great day, even the aisles of all trains arriving at Strathcona were crowded with those who from pleasure or business motives came along to see the spectacle. At the same time, all the MLA's who did not already live in Edmonton or Strathcona made their way thence.

On March 14, leaving matters till almost the last minute, the city council, under the new Mayor Charles May, voted $1,500 to pay for an "At Home" to be held two days later for Members of the Legislative Assembly, and presented them with 1,400 invitations which they could issue to their friends.

Next day, at 3 o'clock, Lieutenant-Governor Bulyea arrived at the Thistle Rink on 102 Street to open the session. During the interval since the hockey game, the rink had been transformed with flags, streamers and bunting. The legislators sat around in conventional fashion facing the dais, while behind them and on both sides four thousand visitors took up every available inch. After the election of the member from Cochrane, C. W. Fisher, as Speaker, Governor Bulyea delivered the Speech from the Throne, which had been worded so as not to touch upon the subject that was in everybody's mind — Was Edmonton to remain the capital of Alberta?

Having set itself in motion, the legislature adjourned while everyone went over to the McKay Avenue School to the Premier's reception. It too was a gala affair. The following night the City of Edmonton's "conversazione" took everyone back to the Thistle Rink to "introduce the members to the social life of the city." It lasted from nine o'clock till midnight, and the "gayly dressed throng promenaded or conversed in groups along the sides and about the tables. At twelve the

Lieutenant-Governor's party retired and dancing was indulged in for a couple of hours."

Bob Edwards of the *Calgary Eye Opener,* aware of the coming tussle over the capital and naturally jealous of Calgary's interest, commented: "At this function we met many charming ladies prominent in Edmonton's society, and they certainly were most attentive and cordial to the visitors. We shall always think kindly of them for this.

"The rest of the stay in Edmonton was made up of private luncheons and dinners, the intervals being taken up by refusing drinks . . . believe us they are a whole-souled people. Of course their motto is, 'What he have, we hold,' but that is their business.

"They take it for granted up in Edmonton that they are going to get the capital. This is not to be wondered at, since Calgary has not made the slightest effort in that direction. The citizens of Calgary are not a unit, the same as they are in Edmonton. Up there, there is constant evidence of union and community of interest. There are no inter-knocking societies. The business and professional men seem to be on excellent terms of camaraderie and the women are all on speaking terms and seldom snub each other. This is a wonderful showing."

Nothing that could be done to impress Edmonton on the members was left undone.

Then, having cleared the social air, the new government, holding all subsequent sessions in the McKay Avenue School, got down to business. For a while the members indulged in the usual long-winded, resounding speeches given with an eye to their effect back in their own constituencies but which impressed nobody as much as they impressed their deliverers. On March 21, J. T. Moore from Red Deer patted his party on the back by saying: "We are fortunate that the sceptre of power has been placed in the hands of the Liberal party." Though the twenty-three Liberals already knew that they were lucky, and smugly patted their pocketbooks, and though the two Conservative members were not listening anyway, everybody greeted his effort with applause. The speech and the handclapping were the things to do.

Then, according to the *Edmonton Bulletin,* A. Puffer, member for Lacombe, with a name most appropriate for an MLA, "in rising complimented Mr. Moore on the able address and on the multiplicity of subjects which he had covered." Multiplicity of subjects perhaps was a polite term for wandering all over the map and talking through his hat, but it served and drew fresh applause.

In the same speech, however, Moore had averred that "if these walls could crumble so that we could look abroad and see the vast army that is headed for Alberta, the multitude of people for whom we will have to legislate, we would be able to appreciate the task that is before us here."

And there he had something. That was why Edmonton was growing, why the province had been created, and why these members held the sceptre of power. Alberta's agricultural hour had struck. Its almost unlimited soil lay waiting, machinery to work it was ready, suitable wheat was at hand, trains were ready to transport its progeny, and markets were clamouring for it. All that was needed was farmers, and by paddle-wheeler, train, covered wagon and ox-cart, they came rolling in.

How they came rolling in is shown by the statistics. In 1901 Alberta's population had been 73,022; by 1906 it had more than doubled to 185,412, and nearly half the newcomers came to farm, while the others helped to swell Edmonton and Calgary's population. And indeed the rush to the province had only started.

For in Alberta there was land for thousands and resources for everybody. In the area tributary to Edmonton alone, there were 50,000 square miles of it, and that meant 200,000 quarter-sections. That in turn, once these quarter-sections were settled up, meant 200,000 families, and that meant one million people all trading in Edmonton. As well as all these farmers, of course, there would be all the small towns that would spring up in these farming communities; and they would all be tributary to Edmonton. This then, was the land that would make Albertans and Edmonton rich. By 1906 most of the quarters within forty miles of Edmonton had been taken. All those near the Calgary and Edmonton Railroad, of course, had been filed on shortly after the railroad came through in 1891. Most of the area immediately adjacent to the Canadian Northern Railway from Lloydminster to Edmonton was also homesteaded. A few miles back from that, north or south, however, the land was open.

And settlers came not only from Europe, but from Eastern Canada and the United States. In the spring of 1906, according to Charles Sutter, Dominion Immigration Agent at Edmonton, daily arrivals had averaged between three hundred and five hundred. Newcomers overflowed the immigration building and filled the hotels. The authorities opened new quarters at the Exhibition Grounds, and a new immigration hall north of the CNR tracks. The agent spoke of a contingent of nine train loads of United States settlers all bound for the prairies that had recently started from Chicago, and it was only one of scores. Mr. Harrison of the Land Office had difficulty keeping up with prospective settlers; some mornings a long line-up stood waiting outside his 100 Avenue office.

Since settlers were opening up the country, many promoters proposed to run railways out to serve them. But, since by way of land grants given to railroad builders by various governments, many an astute businessman stood to make an immense profit, nearly everybody tried to secure a railway franchise. Securing it did no harm, and if, as sometimes happened, the promoter could follow through and build it, he obtained title to hundreds of thousands of acres. If he failed to build, there was a chance that he could sell the franchise at a profitable price to someone else. In any event, there was no harm in trying.

Throughout all the prairie provinces at that time, no one liked the CPR. Its freight rates appeared exorbitant, and the fact that the Canadian government had given it large grants of land rankled in the farmers' minds. While on both these counts the railway, with its attitude of "the public be damned," may have been riding rough-shod over everyone, and therefore, was deserving of criticism, few of its critics stopped to realize that without the railway their farms would still have been virgin wilderness and the farmers would not have found a way to transport their products. They never allowed to enter their heads the fact that without the railway nearly all of them could never have become prairie farmers but instead would still be labourers in Europe or Eastern Canada. The CPR was a big corporation; in contradistinction to farmers, utterly unselfish all of them, all big corporations were soulless monsters; consequently, by legislation and regardless of its rights, the CPR must have its wings clipped.

Alberta's first legislators, therefore, passed an act taxing the railways' rights-of-way and thus made themselves highly popular with the people, who regarded the act as a measure aimed at the CPR and one which could be used in a vengeful manner. The CPR took this to the courts, and with respect to taxing its main line, the act was found to be *ultra vires,* although its branch lines could be taxed.

And yet almost in the same breath and certainly in the same session, the legislators who had voted vindictively against one railway opened their arms wide to several other proposed railways. On the one hand they wanted railways to run everywhere, but on the other, felt that railways should carry freight for practically nothing. On April 9 the legislature approved applications for five Alberta railway charters.

So far, although it was pressing heavily on each Member's mind, everyone had shied away from raising the momentous question of which city should become the permanent capital. On April 17 the town of Red Deer put on a reception and dinner for the MLAs, plying them with good things and bombarding them with speeches pointing out Red Deer's merits as a site for the capital. Premier Rutherford stated that, under the Alberta Act, Edmonton was to be the capital until the legislature decided otherwise, and promised that he would see that the House would have a chance to decide the issue during this session.

Finally, in the House, the Hon. Mr. Cushing rose and at the close of a long and a good speech, during which he said: "Calgary has been and is now the largest business centre in the province and will continue to be," he moved that the capital be transferred to Calgary. Once his motion was seconded, Moore moved an amendment, stating that the capital certainly should be moved, but only for half the distance which the Hon. Mr. Cushing advocated, and should therefore come to rest in Red Deer. No one rose to second his amendment, so Hiebert tried his luck with an amendment advocating that Banff be the capital. But he too could find no seconder.

By this time the afternoon and much of the evening had slipped by before Cushing's motion was put to a vote. The members representing the eight constituencies from Red Deer south voted in favour, but that left the sixteen members north of that point to vote against it. That also left Edmonton as the capital of the province. Cushing had done the best he could, and now the tension was over.

One of the next matters to be considered by the legislature covered the field of transportation. Cars were becoming numerous, and cars could conceivably become a source of provincial revenue. Cars, therefore, became the subject of an act. All the evidence pointed to the fact that it was needed, for besides the half a dozen cars already in Edmonton, the *Journal* of January 17 announced the arrival of a shipment of Buicks in the city. These were said to be capable of speeds up to 40 MPH, had a 22-29 HP engine, and cost $1,800. Then on March 24, the *Edmonton Bulletin* said: "Carriveau and Manuel, who are doing a large business with their benzine buggies, have ordered another carload of automobiles from Chicago — they are ordering Fords this time, all high-potential machines, capable of making great time on the good roads which converge on Edmonton." Moreover, a Toronto firm dealing in used cars had been advertising that: "A modern car is as easy to run as it is to drive a horse—and actually safer than most horses and actually less expensive to keep."

Accordingly, on April 23, 1906, Mr. J. R. Boyle, the member for Sturgeon, moved "an Act to Regulate the Speed and Operation of Motor Vehicles on Highways." This act provided that the owner of a vehicle must "register with the Provincial Secretary and take out a permit. He is given a number and a license and is requested at all times to carry the number exposed and to carry lights at night, bearing the number on the glass . . ."

Proper legal speeds varied. They were to be "twenty miles per hour in the country, except when passing from the rear vehicles drawn by horses, when it is required that the speed be cut down to ten miles an hour. When meeting a rig, the speed limit is five miles an hour." If, however, the animal was frightened or got out of control, the car driver was to stop. In a city, town or incorporated village, the speed was to be 10 MPH, and everywhere, unless he could prove that he had taken all reasonable precautions, a motorist was liable for damages if he frightened a horse.

From this point on, the House rushed through the rest of its business, and, on May 9, before proroguing, passed an act to enable the creation of an Alberta university, as well as acts incorporating the cities of Medicine Hat, Lethbridge, and Wetaskiwin.

On the municipal level, Edmonton's council was having problems coping with the thirty percent increase in population experienced during 1906. The fact that as Alberta's capital city Edmonton's place in the sun was assured was all very well. Every Edmontonian could rejoice that at last the city was to take its rightful place in Canadian affairs. All the members of the Board of Trade could pat themselves on the back that their hopes were being confirmed, that their efforts were being rewarded, and that Edmonton was indeed destined to be a great city. All the real estate vendors ran around rejoicing, unrolling maps of new building lots and pocketing folding money. The city council, however, faced with the task of coping with this rapid expansion and of finding the dollars to finance new streets and waterworks, and to pay for expanding fire and police forces, not to mention worrying about health conditions and a thousand and one lesser problems, was kept busy.

One problem was the possibility of the CPR extending across the river from Strathcona, and the council set up a committee to discuss the matter of a high level bridge. The CPR promised to start such a bridge immediately, and also to start building freight sheds in Edmonton. Now that the other transcontinental, the CNR, was serving the city, the CPR was suddenly quite friendly.

But the CNR was not the only other transcontinental, because the Grand Trunk Pacific was also on its way west and Edmontonians hoped that it too would come through the city. They were so anxious that they fell for the bait dangled before all cities and towns in Canada by all railways — for a substantial subsidy the railway would enter the city. Edmonton's council under Mayor May contracted to put up $100,000 and pile on top of that benign tax exemptions providing the GTP would do three things. The railway was to establish its main divisional point between Winnipeg and the Coast at Edmonton; it was to run its main line through the city limits, and, after crossing the Clover Bar bridge, it was to loop a line south into the city so as to bring its trains into the existing CNR station.

On many fronts Edmonton was busy. Ever since his return from the South African War, young W. A. Griesbach, who was becoming a citizen to be reckoned with, had been talking about the need for a militia. Early in 1906, the Federal government decided to establish a cavalry regiment in the Edmonton district, and selected squadron commanders with the rank of major from Edmonton, Strathcona and Fort Saskatchewan. Some of these appointments, of course, were political, but much to the chagrin of all local Liberals, Griesbach, a heretic Conservative, immediately became a lieutenant in this body.

About the same time, to cope with increased garbage and a rapidly expanding network of back alleys, the city fathers brought into being another horse-carried department when it organized the city scavenging system. New subdivisions sprang into being, and lots were being sold in Westmount and Glenwood. New houses sprang up everywhere. So much work was going on that in April 1906 the Carpenters and Joiners Union threatened to strike unless their staggering demands were met. They wanted, and finally got, an eight-hour day, with a minimum daily wage of $3. At that time the city was paying 65¢ an hour for top quality stone cutters and 25¢ an hour for common labourers.

In spite of the progress being made on all fronts, however, meetings of the mayor and aldermen were not all sweetness and light. Many a vexing problem stemming from political affiliation or sheer human pettiness arose to dispel the tranquillity of council meetings. Most jobs which carried any prestige or salary with them, whether in the federal, provincial or civic service, were allotted because the applicant was a good party worker. While this system produced an occasional outstanding employee, such as Fire Chief Lauder and several others, it left a lot to be desired and led to frequent crises in the city staff. In March 1906, for some reason, council fired the fire chief. When they heard this, his staff, undoubtedly good friends all, and probably of the same political persuasion, resigned in a body. Next day while Edmonton was without a fire-fighting force, a blaze broke out. To the credit of chief and staff, however, they rallied around, extinguished it and then once more declared themselves unemployed. The council had a knotty problem on its hands, but it solved it by reinstating everybody.

Then too, there was the outcry caused by a council meeting held in camera. The *Edmonton Journal* jumped in to lead the pack, saying: "Secretary-Treasurer Kinnaird Defies the City Charter, Declines to Furnish Copies of Minutes of Last Meeting of City Council." Even in the face of that, Kinnaird refused to divulge the minutes of the meeting, and for days his stubbornness was the talk of the town. The council, which had put him in this position, supported him in his loyalty to them, but eventually they had to back down and let the people know what their elected representatives had been up to. Still believing that their action had been right, the council appealed to the legislature and sought an amendment to the city charter making it legal to hold meetings in secret. This, of course, the government very wisely turned down.

If some of the doings of council were kept secret, however, the state of the isolation hospital was open for all to see. In spite of having some waterworks and sewers, sanitary conditions in the city were bad, and amongst other diseases, typhoid was prevalent. The previous December the council decided to set up what it called a temporary isolation hospital in a building which the city owned in the nuisance ground, then located near Rat Creek in the vicinity of present day Clarke Stadium. Council directed that this building be "improved and made comfortable for patients," and by and by a tent with a leaky roof was added. This place, usually called the pest house, was considered to be the last port of call for bad cases of contagious diseases. Few returned from it.

Not far away was a slaughter house and Rat Creek School. A year or so earlier, according to the city council minutes, residents of the district north of Sutherland Street (106 Avenue) refused to send their children to Rat Creek School because there was no sidewalk and because the school was close to the nuisance ground, the slaughter house and houses of ill-fame.

But a temporary hospital was not enough and the newspapers made an issue of the problem. While they undoubtedly exaggerated the terrible conditions prevailing there, they stirred up enough outcry to bring on a civic enquiry. According to the papers, doctors charged with looking after the patients were rarely to be found there, the attendants were usually drunk, while the nurses, unable to use the overflowing sanitary trenches, had to resort to the nearby creek. The investigation went a long way to improve the patients' chances of recovery and resulted in a new $19,000 isolation hospital being started a few months later.

The *Edmonton Journal* also complained of other nuisances and published letters pointing out that of late automobiles on Jasper Avenue were "showing bursts of speed crowding 15 MPH." These cars were getting out of hand.

About the same time, the council faced up to the fire fighting problem and took steps leading to the organization of a full time professional fire department.

The council's next move was to look into the financial standing of its city-owned electric light department and to decide that the time had come to reduce power rates. All in one motion the rates were slashed from 16¢ per KWH on the top step to 13¢, while the low step of the rate was cut from 5¢ to 4¢.

On the utility front, Strathcona also announced a step forward, when, on April 21, 1906, its new waterworks system went into operation. Strathcona was going ahead and was planning to seek incorporation as a city. Though its population was less than Edmonton's, it had the advantage of being much more compact, so that any taxes it had to spend could be used on works concentrated into a smaller compass. During 1906 Strathcona built a new town hall and laid a few hundred feet of concrete sidewalk along Whyte Avenue.

All Edmonton-bound passengers had to detrain at Strathcona, and were taken across the river by a variety of horse-drawn buses. In 1906 one enterprising Edmonton hotel installed a heater in its bus. The arrival of a train was always an event, and daily, many citizens wandered down to watch one come in. Some of them, of course, came to meet passengers, but most of them were merely gregarious and curious, watching the locomotive shudder to a stop and seeing if anyone they knew might be getting off. Debarking passengers had to make their way through this friendly mob and along the platform to where a line-up of some twenty buses waited. All of these, of course, were horse-drawn and each of them was in charge of a hotel employee who did his best to see that he had a full load of guests to take back to his hotel whether it was merely in Strathcona or across the river in Edmonton. Until all the passengers were accounted for, the yard was a noisy, bustling place, as each driver tried to secure all the business he could. "Alberta Hotel — Alberta Hotel — Windsor — Cecil — Castle — King Edward Hotel" — the soliciting cries went on and on.

Many of these Edmonton hotels had just been opened during the last few months, for the years 1906 to 1908 were boom years for hotel construction. In 1906, for instance, the Cecil, Castle and King Edward opened their doors for the first time. With the rapid interest in burgeoning Edmonton, hosts of visitors came to see what this new pioneering city might hold for them, and the hotels were full. So were their saloons, for these were the great meeting places where in an hour a stranger could take the measure of this new frontier, or else find, when he came to next morning minus his wallet and papers, that the frontier had taken his. In either case, he was caught; either he liked what he saw and stayed, or he had no money to take him away. As an eastern paper reported about this time, "Edmonton always has a long hook for suckers."

The spate of new hotels threw many an older hostelry into decline. Prior to the opening of the King Edward, the Alberta had been the city's top accommodation. Because of the personality of Bob McDonald, the manager of the Windsor, that establishment had come to be recognized as the sportsmen's hotel. The new King Edward drew patrons from both. Then even as the Cecil Hotel was opening its doors, wreckers were tearing out the doors and windows of Edmonton's oldest stopping place. For Donald Ross's hotel, which had been opened in 1876, had come to the end of its rope and was being replaced by a new Edmonton Hotel.

The summer of 1906 saw the end of another landmark, the Hardisty house, outside the old fort, when, after using it as a pest house for the victims of the recent smallpox plague, the city fumigated it by burning it down. Since the destruction of Rowand's Big House shortly after 1874, the Hardisty house had been the home of Fort Edmonton's chief factor. More than any other building, it had seen all the details of the thirty-years' expansion which had bridged the gap from the days when fur was Alberta's only resource to the influx of 30,000 farmers. Though its end was inglorious, fate had decided to honour its commanding site overlooking the magnificent river valley, for plans were already afoot to build Alberta's new Legislative Building there.

Another of the big events of 1906 was the fire which destroyed Robertson's Hall, which for so many years in the old part of the town had been Edmonton's lively social centre.

During 1906 the city council set in motion a paving program, embarked on a street railway venture, voted funds for an incinerator and for a new exhibition grounds. The isolation hospital had been built, the old Hardisty house burned down, $200,000 had been spent on sewers, $65,000 had been voted for the telephone system, and Strathcona had agreed to take service from it. All this had been done on a mill rate of 10½¢, which had brought in $109,724.19 in taxes, and from a voters' list which by 1906 had jumped to 2,875 from the 935 listed the year before.

With all this in mind, the mayor and aldermen went to the electors in December to ascertain their wishes. Out of this election, W. A. Griesbach emerged as the new mayor, and set about to cope with the city's growing pains.

About this time, applying their goodwill to housewives' problems, the ladies of the Beaver Chapter of the IODE took up the matter of the scarcity of Anglo-Saxon maids. They worked out an arrangement whereby they would provide $56.40 fare from Liverpool for any girls who wished to try their luck in Edmonton. Under this scheme they expected the first applicants to arrive in May 1907, whereupon they would be employed in Edmonton's better homes at $12 per month. By instalments, to be withheld from their first six months' wages, the maids were to repay their passage money.

During the closing months of 1906 the weather smote Edmontonians harshly. In the middle of October all of Edmonton's dozen or so cars were jacked up on blocks and abandoned for the winter, because heavy rains preceded still heavier snows. November, with severe storms and an all-time record of snowfall, stopped all construction work, and December with its record-breaking cold weather and with snow falling continuously from the 4th to the 10th, again on the 13th and 14th, and from the 28th to the 31st, brought nearly everything to a standstill. The terrible winter of 1906-1907, such a marked contrast to the previous one, was at hand.

That was the first Canadian winter for some thousands of European immigrants who had homesteaded here and there all over Alberta, and it made them sit up and take notice. Some of the many still housed in tents in the bush fell back upon Edmonton for the winter. Many others came in looking for work, but due to the weather, it was hard to find. In spite of that, remarkably little was paid out in what was called Charity and Relief. Considering all the thousands of immigrants who had come to the province and to Edmonton during the preceding two or three years, it would have been unnatural if some had not needed help. During 1905, the Provincial Department of Agriculture, which had charge of that phase of the province's business, reported: "At the formation of the Province assistance was being given to two females. These have been continued as a charge upon the fund at the disposal of the province." A year later its report said: "In all, during the year relief was afforded in whole or in part to some ten families. The Department is exercising the greatest care with regard to this work so as not to give assistance other than where it is absolutely necessary and then only for as short a time as possible . . . During the year six paupers were buried at the public expense."

The only businesses which profited by the severe season were the coal mines, and their increased output provided some work. In the Edmonton vicinity twenty-three coal mines were going full blast; nine at Edmonton, four at Strathcona, five at Clover Bar, and five at Namao. In the fall of 1906 Humberston's new mine far downstream started operating, and the hamlet of Beverly began to grow around it.

Reporting on Edmonton's mines, the Provincial Public Works Department noted a change in their method of operating, for it said: "In several cases the industry has passed the stage where the mineral can be economically worked from small tunnels driven in at the outcrop of the seams, and several companies have signified their intention of sinking shafts to catch the seams at such points where their mining operations will be close at hand to the railway. Already two shafts have been sunk, one of them to a depth of 200 feet, while a third shaft has been started on the Belmont property which bids fair to be the largest mining concern in this district."

As well as these twenty-three mines in the Edmonton area, another thirty-six were operating in the rest of the province at places such as Canmore, Bankhead, Lethbridge, and in the Crowsnest Pass. Alberta, which a quarter of a century earlier had utilized only one of its resources — furs — was coming into its own. Now five of its resources had been recognized and were being used; furs, land, timber, coal, and at Medicine Hat, natural gas. Resources, of course, are no good in themselves; they must be used, and they can only be used when people want them, and not only are willing to develop them, but know how. Word of Alberta's resources had got abroad, and already people came flocking in to use them. A few little mills nibbled away at the edge of Alberta's tremendous timber stands, but the extent of good timber was virtually unlimited. In the mills at Edmonton alone, 22½ million feet of lumber were cut in 1906. Alberta's seams of coal also began to be developed. The geologists, still unaware of all the beds there might be, reported Alberta as having at least half of all the coal in Canada. By that year some thirty thousand farmers had acquired about ten million acres of land. The rush of homesteaders, however, had only begun, for it had come to be realized that there were at least an additional thirty million acres to be had for the asking.

With all these resources suddenly laid before the world's hungry maw, all that was needed to make Alberta a rich and populous province was for people to come to work them and capitalists to supply the money to make that possible. And in 1906 both capitalist and cultivator were clamouring to come in.

A band of settlement sixty miles wide extended from Red Deer to Edmonton. For a radius of fifty miles around Edmonton, taking in today's towns of

Entwistle, Barrhead and Westlock, homesteaders were living in temporary shacks. East to Lloydminster a strip of land forty miles wide and nearly two hundred miles long, bounded on the north by the North Saskatchewan River, had been claimed. Wherever the recent railways penetrated; along the CNR to Lloydminster, north to Morinville, and west to Stony Plain, new towns were springing up. During 1905 in the Edmonton Land Office alone, 3,099 homesteaders had filed on land, and during 1906, 5,122 more had filed. By 1906 in the territory tributary to Edmonton the villages of Lloydminster and Lavoy, Vermilion and Vegreville, and Mannville and Mundare had been incorporated. So had Stony Plain. Because many stores had started in these places and in the new hamlets in the country, many wholesale businesses had located in Edmonton.

Whether one's outlook embraced the province or merely the city of Edmonton, prospects were rosy. Optimism was a-wing. With a connection south to the CPR, with the whistles of one transcontinental railroad echoing through its new subdivisions, and with those of another emitting anguished toots as a few miles to the east it scrambled to overtake its rival in reaching the city, Edmonton was on the mark. With its coal under foot and timber and rich farm land all around it, Edmonton was on the march. Everyone was sure of the future, and ready to face any of the problems it might bring. In such a mood, Edmonton, the Capital of Alberta, ended the year 1906.

The old Bush Coal Mine.

Henry Marshall Tory, first president of the University of Alberta.

John A. McDougall, pioneer merchant, prominent citizen and mayor of the city, who arrived in 1877.

Years Of
Rapid Growth
1907-1908

chapter *12*

DURING 1907 AND 1908 Edmonton's population continued to increase about thirty percent a year. New industries started up, and along Jasper Avenue for about ten blocks, as well as in the older sections of the city east of 101 Street, new brick hotels and business blocks sprouted. The Board of Trade boasted of the city's growth, but the city council and its treasurer worried about it. Some fifteen thousand people barely established themselves were called upon to provide streets, sewers, sidewalks and telephones, and a host of other services for the thousands who were coming in or would be living in Edmonton three or four years hence. Financing posed a difficult problem, especially when in April a wave of panic swept the New York stock market, and thenceforth the rest of the continent suffered a recession.

Perhaps it is little wonder that this 1907 problem swirled the twenty-seven year old "Boy Mayor" W. A. Griesbach a bit beyond his depth. The first two or three tasks he undertook were minor matters, and he got results. On taking office, he was distressed by the littered condition of the town hall, which at the time was on Fraser Avenue and Rice Street (98 Street and 101A Avenue), and, finding that sweeping and tidying up fell to the police department, he called Evans, the Police Chief. Evans, an old soldier, listened gravely, agreed that the city hall was in a mess, and promised to have it cleared up.

At this time, amongst other more or less harmless characters who, due to indolence or inebriety, were constantly falling into the clutches of the police, was Billy Childs. As Griesbach was leaving after his talk with the Police Chief, Evans called a constable and said: "Go out and arrest Billy Childs." The new mayor thought little of the remark until a few hours later when, on coming out of the town hall, he found it cleaner than it had ever been and Billy Childs still sweeping up.

Since Griesbach's discussion with the Chief of Police had brought such quick results, he loaded him with another job. This time Evans was instructed to clean up parts of the city, and to do so was told to order the houses of prostitution, which were more or less interspersed amongst other residences, to move farther out of town. This salutory measure Evans also carried out to the mayor's satisfaction.

The next problem fell into the hands of the plumbing department, because in some manner it found itself saddled with a baby, whose father had died of typhoid and whose mother was at death's door. There being no proper organization to deal with a case of this kind, the men in that department saw to it that the child was cared for and then discussed the matter with the city commissioners. These worthies did what they could, but also, in the presence of someone in the *Edmonton Journal,* expressed the opinion that, if the boy turned out to be dull, "he might do for the council, but if he is bright, we can make a commissioner of him."

The councillors evidently let that remark go by because they were up to their ears getting the transit system started. It was to be financed by a debenture issue, so they took steps to raise the money and to try to get the street railway rolling.

Street cars, however, were only one item in the long list of services. Edmonton citizens, envious of Medicine Hat's natural gas supply, began casting about for some means of heating with gas. They did not have to cast far, for soon all sorts of propositions turned up. For the next sixteen years Edmontonians entered upon their long game of hide and seek with promoters, during which, by plebiscites, votes of the council, rejecting votes by the burgesses, propaganda, barrages of criticism, and a host of charges of corruption and calumny, they enjoyed a heart-warming though coal-stoking time.

First of all, in April a corporation calling itself the North West Oil and Gas Company, entered the picture. This was the company which, according to the reports of the Geological Survey of Canada, drilled a well to a depth of 1,150 feet near the south end of 101 Street and another on the north side of Jasper Avenue which reached 1,800 feet before it too was abandoned. Immediately someone raised an outcry charging that the mayor was one of the company's inside men (probably untrue), that some of the senior employees of the city hall were company stockholders (possibly true), and that some of the council were company shareholders (probably true). A couple of weeks later, in spite of this rumour, the council, by the casting vote of the mayor, approved a franchise with this company. Three weeks later, because of the outcry, the council agreed to submit the gas franchise to a vote of the citizens. By this time someone else seems to have entered the picture by proposing an artificial gas scheme. In the ensuing June election, the North West Oil and Gas Company lost out and a coal gas plant was approved.

Then towards the end of September, Cyrus S. Eaton, (today's multi-millionaire), arrived in Edmonton with the proposition of making producer gas out of straw. He asked for a franchise, promising to lay thirty-six miles of mains at a cost of $300,000 to his company. As the months went by, Cyrus Eaton found that the straw, which generally rotted away in the farmers' piles, suddenly assumed tremendous value when he offered a market for it. Thus another scheme went overboard. Then H. L. Williams, who was boring for gas out Morinville way, sought a franchise for his employers, the American-Canadian Company. He too got turned down.

These, of course, were the days when big corporations earned the reputation of high-handedness and crookedness which they have been trying to live down ever since. This was the era of unbridled competition, of wasteful duplication of facilities and of governments not grown up enough to regulate properly. This was an age when nearly all politicians at nearly all levels expected to be bribed in one form or another, and usually were.

In any event, after Williams was turned down, the question of a gas utility for Edmonton was left open to anyone else with nerve enough to propound another scheme. For a long interval no one came forward. The burgesses had voted themselves into a corner. They wanted gas, but on the one hand they were afraid that someone might make money out of supplying it, and on the other, that, if the city did so, it might lose money. That left everyone sitting on the fence, some facing one way and some the other. But for a long time, no matter which way they faced, they could see no other promoter who would entrust his proposition to their vacillating votes.

Meanwhile, Strathcona was also looking for a way to get gas, and it entered into a franchise agreement with a Cleveland firm called International Heating & Lighting. After a lot of scurrying around, Strathcona found itself in the same position as Edmonton — without gas.

Although Strathcona, with its 1907 population of 3,500, was being far outdistanced by Edmonton, nevertheless its prospects looked so good that on March 15, 1907, it was incorporated as a city and had its boundaries enlarged to take in 5.98 square miles. Despite the fact that much of the land taken in was still in uncleared farms, and despite the fact that for nearly fifty years into the future much of it was to remain in this condition, the extension of Strathcona's boundaries was a wise move. It gave room for expansion, provided the real estate boys with something to subdivide, and if by chance any institution requiring a large space should just happen along and wish to locate in Strathcona, there would be room for it.

Then, by the merest coincidence, less than three weeks after the new boundaries had been established, just such an institution came looking for a place to come to rest. On April 6, 1907, Premier A. C. Rutherford announced that the site of the provincial university was to be in Strathcona. Calgary, having lost out as the capital city, assumed rather naturally that the other political plum, the university, would fall to its lot. Red Deer also hoped that this fruit would drop into its basket. Edmontonians, of course, were strictly neutral — even generous — let some other city have it. How about Calgary, Lethbridge, or Medicine Hat — any place other than Edmonton? Then someone thought of Strathcona, Edmonton's old rival, which to some extent had been left out of everything. In a sudden burst of generosity, the provincial government officials, all based in Edmonton but eminently impartial and definite in their opinion that it would not be fair to put it in Edmonton, handed the university to the City of Strathcona. Calgary howled, but that just went to prove how obviously self-seeking Calgarians were. Against a decision so patently impartial, how could any fair-minded man object?

A few days after that announcement, the real estate boys, ever ready to cash in on every opportunity, advertised a sale of lots in a new Strathcona subdivision which they called University Park. About the same time, someone with an eye for good residential property, even though it lay outside Strathcona's boundaries, offered lots for sale in Grandview Heights.

Then, attracted by the prospects of the new city, another of the many optimistic newspapermen ventured to establish the Strathcona *Journal*. Like many other papers in the early west, its life was short. It operated long enough, however, to record a tragic mine accident.

On the night of June 8, six men died in Walter's Mine. A brush fire sweeping up the hillside from the direction of today's High Level Bridge set the pit-head ablaze. The noise of the roaring flames awakened pit-boss George Lamb, who batched alone in a nearby shack. Worrying about the five men working ninety feet below, he hurried down the airshaft to warn them and then tried to lead them to the surface and safety. By this time the wooden ladder was aflame, but Lamb climbed through the fire, only to die as he reached the surface. The other men never got out of the mine but were found dead at the foot of the shaft.

To Strathcona and Edmonton people came flocking. Many came to invest in business of one sort or another and to buy houses or have them built, but early in June the *Journal* estimated that about two thousand people were living in tents. By fall it expected to see five thousand tent dwellings.

To alleviate that situation, the real estate agents, actually having the time of their lives, were doing all they could. Out of some two hundred businesses in Edmonton, eighty-two or nearly half of them were real estate agents, and many of the other businessmen were not averse to taking a turn at buying and selling lots. During the year many new areas were subdivided, including Earnscliff, Ellerman, Lynwood, Richmond, Santa Rosa, Cromdale, Belvedere, North Jasper Place, and Dwyer. The last one was out near Dwyer's Packing Plant in what later came to be called North Edmonton.

A quick look at the businesses themselves is instructive in so far as it shows perhaps more clearly than by any other means what life was like in the embryo city. Henderson's Directory for 1907 gives us such a look, which, while it may not have included every establishment, does present a good cross-section.

Leaving out the gold dredge, which was turning over the river's gravels, and the fourteen churches which were busily mining in their medium, the rest of the heavy industry consisted of two flour mills and three grain elevators, four lumber and two brick yards, with a cement brick manufacturer, a pork packing plant, and a woollen mill.

There were eight printers in addition to the following five newspapers: The Edmonton Bulletin and the Edmonton Journal, both dailies; the Alberta Herold, printed in German, and Le Courier de L'Ouest (French), both weeklies; and the Alberta Monthly.

The Edmonton Opera House, the Edmonton Theatre, and the Bijou Theatre provided entertainment to suit every taste. Even movies of a sort were shown, for the Bijou usually included at least one "Comedy Cartoon" in its weekly fare.

There were thirty-four retail stores and nine retail tobacconists, thirty-five physicians, nine dentists, nine music teachers, two taxidermists, and one typewriter dealer. Assisting the eighty-two real estate agents were seventeen loan companies and eleven banks. The horse-drawn Edmonton-Strathcona bus line, twenty hotels and eighteen restaurants catered to bachelors and travellers, while two steam laundries competed with an unknown number of Chinese wash-tubs. One brewery and one aerated water manufacturer provided sustenance for the thirsty, while one cigar-maker offered his wares to bewhiskered frontiersmen. Thirteen livery and feed stables supplied board and lodging to a large horse population. Closely related to them were one wagon-maker, one carriage manufacturer, several carriage dealers and carriage painters. For those who set their ventures afloat, one boat-builder offered his services, while for those of a more sedentary nature, bedsteads — iron and brass, were offered, as well as baths — folding.

Truly Edmonton was a business community catering to pioneers, whether of city or country. In this community, however, one pioneer business stood out by itself. This was the firm of Manuel-Corriveau, which, marking time at the moment but looking to the future, advertised gasoline engines.

Several of the merchants stocked a small assortment of sports equipment, because golf, soccer, curling and hockey were starting to play a more active part in community life. Though golf had been played for over ten years, the burning of the old Hardisty house set the golfers searching for a new clubhouse and a place to play. Since early Edmontonians seemed bound to have the taxpayers participate in various business enterprises such as the power plant and the street railway, they also induced the city council to start the first municipal golf course in Canada. It was laid out on the flats west of today's High Level Bridge and has since developed into our Victoria Municipal course. To also utilize the same links, the Golf and Country Club built its clubhouse at its eastern edge.

Of perhaps greater general interest than the golf course was Diamond Park stadium which was completed during 1907. For many years this was to be the centre of much of Edmonton's sporting activity, including baseball and soccer, and there the famous Deacon White aroused the fans' fervour with his rugby football teams' excellent performance.

Other signs that easier times had arrived came with the opening of two more theatres, the Kevin and the Lyric. While they were being readied for patrons and players, the eight-year-old Edmonton Club, having purchased a piece of property from ex-mayor Matt McCauley, was erecting the brick structure at the corner of 100 Street and Macdonald Drive.

A block away, Edmonton's wonderful Incline Railway began to take shape. Since the Edmonton, Yukon & Pacific Railway station was down on the flat and more or less in line with the steps descending McDougall Hill, Donald Ross, Joseph Hastyn, and one or two other citizens, decided to put an inclined lift beside them. Eventually this was rigged up with rails and cables and pulleys, so that a team drawing a wagon of coal, for instance, could drive on to the deck of the cable-car and be whisked up to the level of Macdonald Drive and go on about its business. There were two such decks or cages, so that as one ascended, the other descended and to some extent helped to pull the first one up. From top to bottom, measured along the incline, its rails were 230 feet long with a rise of 88 feet in that distance. The trip up took one minute, with a maximum load of 12 tons. Unlike the Edmonton Club, however, the Incline Railway was not financially successful. After the novelty wore off, its owners found it unprofitable, so that its active life spanned only two or three years of Edmonton's history.

Before the Incline Railway's shiny new paint had time to get scuffed up, the new brick Terrace Building was completed immediately east of where the hole for the basement of the new Legislative Building was being dug. The Terrace Building became the main provincial government office, and for the next few years it accommodated the sittings of the Legislature.

About the same time, Edmonton suffered one of its most spectacular fires when the post office, which had only been built a year or so, caught fire. Getting in the way of the fire brigade, thousands of people crowded around to gasp as the sheets of flame spread along the roof and roared upward, to applaud when the several well directed streams from the fire department's pumps centred in on the blaze, and generally to enjoy themselves or to shout commands or advice to the hard-pressed firemen. Almost coincident with the destruction of the post office came an announcement that the post office department was putting on its first eight mail carriers.

The increasing population of both city and province presenting additional markets for Alberta's coal encouraged several venturesome businessmen to open new mines. Seven of these were started in Edmonton or the nearby district, including the Rosedale Coal Company, the United Collieries Ltd., and the Dawson Coal Company. At Morinville the industry was groping towards mechanization, for in 1907 one of the mines there put in a compressed air coal cutter.

Adopting new inventions, however, was not confined to the West, for in October Marconi opened up stations in Ireland and at Glace Bay, Nova Scotia, and started wireless communication with Europe. Both the world and the West, though still in the horse and buggy age, were at the door of a new era.

That fall too, out of perhaps a thousand buffalo which were left alive in the whole continent, 475 bruised and bedraggled beasts were shipped up from Montana and unloaded at the newly established Elk Island Park. There they were held over the winter until the Wainwright Buffalo Park was fenced and ready to receive them. In the spring, while a few were left to live in Elk Island Park, the rest were shipped to Wainwright.

Out of all the millions of these shaggy beasts which in their wild freedom had once blackened Alberta's grassy hillsides, these few, cooped in box cars, returned to be penned in a park. Traversing by train the old Winnipeg Trail to Lamont, the trail along which in the past Paul Kane and so many other travellers had shouldered their way through dense herds numbered in thousands, these imported animals attracted scores of curious or sentimental onlookers. Most of them were seeing buffalo for the first time, but many of the spectators were men still in their sixties who thirty-five years previously, as young pioneers threading their way over the prairies, had often wandered in sight of huge herds for days on end. To these old timers, white, Indian or Métis, these caged creatures evoked nostalgic memories. To them too they were a reminder of how, about 1880, when the buffalo were vanishing a half-breed by the name of Pablo had caught a few calves and in a sheltered Montana valley had protected them and their progeny until after the lapse of some twenty years he had built up the only significant herd in existence. To Michel Pablo, the half-breed, Alberta and America owe the miracle of their preservation.

While the buffalo were arriving, however, Edmontonians were beginning to worry about their runaway boom times. The call for funds to finance new utilities was rapidly catching up with the city treasurer. In July he announced that the city had used up all the money it had and that Kirkpatrick of the Imperial Bank would not lend it any more. The ratepayers had done all they could, for their assessment, keeping up with the city's growth, had risen from some $17½ million the year before to nearly $23 million. Everyone applauded the increased assessment but bemoaned the increase in tax rate from 10½ to 13½ mills. As the *Edmonton Journal* remarked: "The increase of the total tax rate indicates a tendency which if continued, must be attended in the future by undesirable results." A sage remark indeed.

Meanwhile, all the civic capital ventures were at a standstill until more cash came to cover pay cheques. While Alberta as a whole had the confidence of Canadian investors, the city of Edmonton had temporarily overexpanded itself. Then, at the end of September, the *Journal* reported that "Edmonton's head is again above water in the financial stringency slough." In other words, the city sold $679,000 of five percent debentures. It did so at a price, however, for they brought only ninety-three cents on the dollar.

Rumblings of discontent echoed along Jasper Avenue, and even invaded the council chamber. Accusations of incompetency were levelled at Griesbach, Edmonton's boy mayor, and his council. The year opened on a high note, finances had been no foreseeable problem, a new telephone system and a street railway had been forecast, but as the year wore along, financial stringency stalked Jasper Avenue, and Edmontonians, looking up and down that dog-leg street, failed to see either automatic telephones or street car conductors. As a result, John A. McDougall, the capable businessman, whose acumen, as well as making him rich, had often aided Edmonton, was practically drafted for the office of mayor.

In spite of some uneasy moments about its finances, however, the year 1907 was good to Edmonton. Scores of new buildings were put up, new mines opened, new industries were getting a foothold, and the sawmills turned out a record cut of lumber. Even with the massive influx of newcomers to the city and to the surrounding homestead areas, Edmonton ended the year with only eighteen families on relief. Many a family spent the winter in one of the hundreds of tents that fringed the built-up areas, but, except for these eighteen, they looked to their own efforts for support. Offsetting the loss of money paid out in relief, however, was that which had been spent on cars. In the whole of Alberta ninety-five automobiles were licensed, and of these, Edmonton had twenty-nine, Calgary twenty-eight, Lethbridge nine, Medicine Hat eight, and Strathcona six. Prosperity sat on Edmonton's doorstep.

At the beginning of 1908 Mayor McDougall had his hands full. Taxes were sadly in arrears. The two school boards had not received their money from the city which was heavily in debt to the bank. The telephone system was in a mess, the proposed street railway, long delayed, was in a fuddle, and what was Edmonton to do about the proposed High Level Bridge? One by one, McDougall untangled these problems and set the new ventures on the proper rails.

As a start, he bore down on the company which had contracted to install twelve hundred automatic telephones. Visiting Toronto, he found the company still in the promotion stage. Cancelling their contract, he went on to Chicago and arranged with another firm to get busy. By April, under his driving hand, what was claimed to be the first automatic dialing system in use in North America, was operating in Edmonton.

Then, turning his attention to the street railway, the problem which had once been given to a contractor to solve and when he failed had been taken on as a civic venture, McDougall appointed Charles E. Taylor as superintendent. Between these two, and much to everyone's relief, ties began to be laid and rails to be spiked to them.

Once the actual construction of the street railway got under way, it made remarkable progress, and the first street car to rumble along the new tracks on a trial basis did so on October 30. A little over a week later, the system's two cars were in operation. One end of the tracks was at 95 Street and 111 Avenue, and from there they ran south to 106 Avenue, whence they jogged west to 97 Street. Then going south, they turned west on Jasper Avenue as far as 116 Street. At last the Edmonton Transit System was a reality, and by the end of the week Superintendent Taylor advised the council that the receipts averaged $4 per car per hour run. When a month or so later all the accounts were in, the street railway had cost $323,505.75, a figure a little above the estimate.

The people of Strathcona, who a year earlier had entered into a franchise with the Strathcona Radial Company, which so far at least had not made any move to lay tracks, watched enviously. When the Edmonton city council took steps to buy out the Strathcona franchise, none of the south-siders objected to the fact that by way of the Low Level Bridge the Edmonton Transit System would some day run street cars to Strathcona.

The ease with which that transaction was accomplished encouraged McDougall and his council to approach Strathcona with the idea of amalgamating the two cities. Accordingly, in September 1908, he wrote the mayor of Strathcona, making the suggestion, and asking if the rival city might consider appointing a committee to confer with a similar Edmonton body. Two weeks later McDougall received an answer, saying that any amalgamation "plans were premature."

For the time being, that was that, but the Edmonton city council had many other matters to occupy its time. On the whole, however, during McDougall's administration, the city advanced on many fronts. Besides the street railway, the automatic telephones, and the move towards the High Level Bridge, the city had completed its new incinerator in the nuisance grounds on Rat Creek. The new fire hall on 104 Street, "equal to any fire hall in America," was finished and operating in July.

Meanwhile, Strathcona was also growing and not the least cause of its expansion was the fact that at its west end a new university was to come into being. Like many another great institution, it grew from very small beginnings. Even then most Albertans thought that its creation was a foolish waste of money. For, on the whole, Albertans were men of muscle — with much of it in their heads. Frank Oliver, for instance, prescient in many other matters, could see no necessity for it. He is reported to have said: "We don't need any college here at all; if we did, it would be to turn out horsedoctors."

Hard on the heels of the passage of the University Act of 1906, Premier Rutherford, a McGill graduate, who was such a major force in promoting education in the province, began casting about for someone — naturally a McGill man — to assume the task of bringing the university into being. Fortunately, he hit upon Dr. Henry Marshall Tory, who originally had come west to found a McGill college in British Columbia. On January 1, 1908, the premier gave him a clear hand to get the job under way.

Starting with forty-five students and a staff of four professors: W. H. Alexander, Classics; E. K. Broadus, English; L. H. Alexander, French and German, and no relation to his namesake, and professor Muir Edwards, an engineer, the first classes were held on September 24, 1908, in the top floor of Queen Alexandra School. Dr. Tory proved his worth by gathering distinguished scholars to start his university, and soon brought from McGill, Toronto, Harvard, Oxford and the Sorbonne, the yeast that was to raise Alberta's university by its own bootstraps.

Dr. Tory called his first Convocation, a body of 364 resident graduates of British and Canadian universities, to meet in the Strathcona Opera House (later on the Princess Theatre on Whyte Avenue) on October 1908. For the next two years the classes were held in Strathcona Collegiate Institute, while steps were being taken to erect the first university building in the 250 acres of bush on River Lot 5, which twenty-five years earlier had been homesteaded by A. Patton.

In the spring of 1908 the university published its schedule of fees, as follows:

	Arts	Applied Science
Material fee	$ 5.00	$ 5.00
Insurance per term	10.00	20.00
For degree	5.00	10.00

Having set the university on its proper path, Premier Rutherford turned to some of the province's other business. Railways, roads, telephones and schools all had to be provided, and not gradually, but all at once. Blessed with its rich resources, Alberta had little difficulty attracting capital either to be invested in industry or to be borrowed by municipal, city, or provincial governments.

On the federal scene, Sir Wilfrid Laurier called another election for the fall of 1908. Edmontonians, loyal as ever, re-elected Frank Oliver, and he continued to represent them as Minister of the Interior. After the ballots were counted, charges and counter-charges of bribery and corruption echoed back and forth, but since neither Liberals nor Conservatives had kept their fingers out of the pot, no one dared to press the charges too far.

By the end of 1908 Edmonton's population had increased to 18,500, all its civic utilities and services had expanded, and many of the social amenities usually associated with larger cities had come its way. New ideas and new inventions were on the way. All the newspapers and periodicals noted advances being made in the scientific world, and these were common topics of conversation. Aviation, for instance, and news of what was being done in that line in England, France and the eastern United States, was read eagerly. Many held that the new heavier-than-air flying machines would be developed to the point where they might become useful. Others, agreeing on what a boon some form of flying could be to Alberta with its great distances and with the vast untapped riches of the Far North, felt that airships were the only answer. Even when the airship being shown at the Fair in Calgary in July caught fire and in moments was destroyed, fortunately without any casualties, this faction refused to be daunted. In any event, whichever way time would decide the airship versus heavier-than-air flight, all Edmontonians agreed that some day flying would be practical.

Perhaps as significant in its own way as experiments in flying and other scientific advances was the 1908 decision of the city council that distribution and sales of milk from bulk containers would have to stop. From that point on, all milk delivered in the city had to be in bottles. Typhoid and other contagious diseases were all too prevalent, and this advance in hygienic milk delivery was a welcome step forward.

But other advances were made on the social as opposed to the scientific front. Almost immediately, the university, small as it was, became the nucleus around which other cultural activities revolved. Since Edmonton's beginnings, good music and excellent musicians had filled a large place in its life. Some four years earlier the Edmonton Operatic Society, directed by Vernon Barford, had presented its first production in Robertson's Hall. Towards the festivities surrounding the inauguration of the province, Barford made a major contribution, conducting the official mass concert in the Thistle Rink. Then, when in 1907, Governor-General Earl Grey had proposed a national drama and music festival, Edmonton's many outstanding musicians, Barford, Howard Stutchbury, W. J. Hendra, and others, talked the matter over and wondered why Alberta should not have a music festival of its own. From talk, they quickly moved to performance, and on May 5, 1908, in the first Provincial Musical Festival, using two halls, one hundred musicians competed in eleven different classes. The outstanding feature of the whole festival was the chorus of two hundred voices and an orchestra of forty pieces, directed by Mr. Barford. Of the festival, the *Bulletin* said: "This has been the greatest musical event that Western Canada has yet known, drawing talent from various points in the province, between Edmonton and Cardston."

Perhaps of no less portent, even if on a different plane, was the conversion of the Bijou Theatre to operate as a full-time movie house. For a few years, two or three theatres, such as the Kevin, the Lyric, and the Bijou, had shown short movies as part of their entertainment, but the Bijou, at what is now 10166 - 100 Street, was the first to take the rather risky plunge to full-time movies. It could hold 240 patrons, and admitted these at ten cents each, and, as it turned out, made a good profit. Indeed, shortly after King Edward's death in May 1910, the twenty-minute reel showing his funeral attracted nearly ten thousand during its two-day run.

Sitting in pitch darkness, the patrons watched as A. R. Lawrence cranked the projector. Usually the show consisted of a comedy or an educational film, followed by the feature, which often included Maurice Costello and Wallace Reid, the romantic idols of the time. Serials became a permanent part of the performance, and week after week the movie-going audience came back to see another drama-packed instalment.

Since this was long before the invention of sound tracks and even before the days of sub-titles or dialogue flashed on the screen, the audience had to follow the story by the actors' unaided antics. To make up for this deficiency, the movies were uncomplicated but action-packed affairs. By their gestures, facial expressions, and even the way they were dressed, the audience always knew which were the heroes and which the dark villains. To aid in audience interpretation, Mr. Lawrence, busily cranking the projector with one hand while with the other he re-rolled the film, commented as the show went along. Once the Bijou Theatre got into its stride, it offered stiff competition to the various sports activities which had previously provided much of Edmonton's entertainment.

On hockey nights, however, its crowds dwindled, for just at this time in Edmonton's sports history the Thistles were working themselves into a frenzy over the Stanley Cup. As citizens of a coming metropolis, the city's businessmen, led by J. H. Morris, the department store man, did all they could to advertise Edmonton and to make a mark which Eastern Canada would never forget. Far and wide they searched for players, even luring Lester Patrick and Tom Phillips, two of the biggest names in hockey, from Montreal.

Alas, while the telegraph at the CNR station ticked out the news of the two Stanley Cup games, the Montreal Wanderers won. The great effort to win the Stanley Cup had failed by a narrow margin, but nevertheless it had failed, and because Edmonton had over-expanded itself financially, it was many a long year before it was to repeat its try for this cup.

While Edmonton's combative spirit was at an all-time high over hockey, another new organization sprang into being and began practising for its role in a much grimmer world. For that summer the Edmonton Fusiliers was formed, the first militia infantry regiment west of Winnipeg. Now, with both a cavalry and an infantry battalion, Edmontonians were being initiated into some of the practices of war and enmeshed in some of the red-tape always associated with peacetime armies.

So, at the close of 1908, with many and varied activities, Edmonton did not lack for entertainment and excitement. Perhaps as exciting as anything else was the city's rapid growth, as indicated by the many brick buildings under construction and the new businesses starting up. Then too, on each of the street railway and the light and power plant, over $300,000 had been spent. The new automatic telephone system had come into operation at a cost of nearly $200,000, and already there were over eight hundred subscribers.

The police department, with its headquarters in the city hall, consisted of Chief Major W. Beale, four sergeants, and six constables. The fire department at its headquarters on Fraser Avenue had twelve men under Chief R. G. Davidson. Stationed there too were the chief's buggy, a chemical engine, a horse wagon, a ladder truck, a steam fire-engine, and seven horses. At the other station, in the hands of Captain T. G. Lauder and his six men, were five horses, a chemical engine and a hose wagon.

The waterworks department had a pumping capacity of 5,500,000 gallons per day, while the elevated steel tank in the west side of the city held sixty thousand gallons. There were thirty-two miles of water mains and twenty-five miles of sewers. The telephone system included four miles of underground cables and some thirty miles of overhead wire. Forty-one miles of wooden and six miles of granolithic sidewalk kept Edmontonians out of the mud. About one mile of Jasper Avenue was paved with bitulithic material, another mile of side streets was macadamized, and still another mile was covered with carbolithic wood block pavement on a concrete foundation.

As well as one high school, there were seven public schools, one separate school, two colleges and five hospitals. The city was well supplied with churches; five Baptist, four Methodist, three Anglican, two each of the Roman Catholic, Lutheran and Presbyterian faiths, and one each of the following persuasions: Christian Science, Greek Catholic, Ruthenian, Salvation Army, and Seventh Day Adventist. Finally, the Exhibition Ground was still on Ross Flats, the Royal North West Mounted Police headquarters was where it is at present, and Edmonton's two-year-old federal penitentiary, under Warden Matt McCauley, cared for its customers, who, as a diversion, mined coal under its site.

The total number of business ventures had grown amazingly, and as well as all the older types of business, some new ones were offering their services. Amongst these were four artists, one commercial artist, one detective agency, eight dyers and cleaners (often called pantoriums), a manicurist, two orchestras, two undertakers, one Turkish bath, and one dealer in Olds automobiles and supplies. As an indication of the boom in real estate and construction, Edmonton had forty building contractors and seventy-four real estate agents.

The most timely of these businesses was Dwyers' new packing plant which had been made feasible by an expanding farming community and by the fact that the new railway provided a direct connection to the east. Before it was finished it was taken over and finally opened by the J. Y. Griffin Company. Not only had it cost a million dollars, so that it was said to be the largest such plant in Canada, but it brought with it Edmonton's first big industrial payroll. Such a payroll, relatively exempt from seasonal fluctuations, helped to stabilize the city's economy.

Across the river, Strathcona operated its own light, water and sewer systems. Its telephone service was on the point of being taken over by the Alberta Government Telephones. While it could boast of having the University of Alberta, it met its other educational requirements with one separate and two public schools. The Adventists, Anglicans, Baptists, Lutherans, Methodists, Moravians, Presbyterians and Roman Catholics each had one church. Dashing hither and yon with their maps and plans to handle affairs more mundane, Strathcona kept twenty real estate agents busy.

Back in Edmonton, Mayor McDougall, satisfied with a successful year, refused to run in the December elections. In his stead, the citizens elected Robert E. Lee with a large majority.

EDMONTON a history

By the end of 1908 Edmonton's course was set. Although its population was only 18,500 and its total area was only 7.17 square miles, while across the river Strathcona had 4,500 people and an area of 7.54, the city's pattern had been moulded. Provided with all the utility services and social amenities usually found in larger, older cities, it had made a good start. The first major hurdles of a city getting itself under way had been cleared. No matter what growth lay in store for it, its essential character had been set. It was served by two transcontinentals, and the end of the CPR steel was just across the river waiting the construction of the High Level Bridge before advancing into Edmonton. Its main streets, Jasper Avenue, 101 Street, Kinistino Avenue (96 Street), and Fraser Avenue (98 Street), were busy with all the cosmopolitan trade of a city. From here on, regardless of what growth Edmonton might experience, any changes would be filling in empty spaces on the grid of streets and avenues that were Edmonton. Thousands more people might come in. Larger buildings might be erected. New and finer churches might be conceived, but they would be additions to the city of Edmonton that in all essentials was here now.

The Incline Railway looking up 101st Street, 1907.

The Imperial Bank, 1907.

The King Edward Hotel.

Continuing Expansion

1909-1911

chapter *13*

AS NEW HUNDREDS flocked to town, new subdivisions proliferated, and hobble skirts flared out to a walking width, Edmonton grew at an amazing pace. As higher and higher the brick buildings rose till they were three and even four storeys — and higher and higher the women's skirts went till they were eight inches from the floor, Edmonton began to take on a new look.

While its growth was based on the rapid development of Alberta's soil, nevertheless by a bit of luck it had three advantages over any other city in the province. It was the only city in the whole of northern Alberta, whereas, there were three in the southern half. Already some of the advantages of this fact were obvious.

Its flourishing packing plant industry, for instance, which served all of northern Alberta, had a payroll much greater than its counterpart in Calgary, which had to share the southern cattle with Lethbridge or Medicine Hat. Time and time again as the years went by, Edmonton's isolation as the only city in the north counted heavily in its favour.

Then too, it was the capital of the province, and the eternally expanding civil service payroll meant much. Moreover, the university, still in its infancy, was certain to attract more dollars, many of them from Calgary, to be spent for supplies and for student board and room.

Although these three items were aces in the hole, it was the support Edmonton received from the surrounding rural areas that counted most. While the number of livestock increased all over the province, the average Alberta farmer's mainstay was wheat, and Marquis wheat was just coming into its own.

In 1909 the better farmers watched the results Charles Saunders of the Dominion Experimental Farm at Ottawa was having with his new wheat which ripened several days earlier than Red Fife. By 1906 he had produced about a bushel of it; in 1907 and again the next year it was tested at Indian Head; in the spring of 1909, four hundred samples were distributed to western farmers to be tried. During the next couple of years prairie wheat growers clamoured for it because at long last Saunders had developed a wheat which could be grown successfully in the West.

Each year farmers concentrated on breaking more land. While the figures for the northern half of the province are difficult to determine, the picture can be obtained by considering the number of acres seeded to wheat in Alberta and by assuming that the share of these acres tributary to Edmonton was nearly half of the whole. In 1908 the Alberta wheat acreage was 271,000. In 1909 it grew to 385,000, and by the spring of 1910 it had vaulted to 879,800. At the same time, since these crops were sown on new land, the yield of some twenty-five bushels to the acre was high.

The farmers' selling price per bushel of wheat remained around 70¢, a figure which may appear low, but, when considered in terms of the purchasing power of the dollar in those days, was fairly good. The farmers were at least making a living, were optimistic, and were looking forward to the years when they would double or treble their acreage. As a result, both city and country had every hope of witnessing a series of good years. And on this hope Edmonton businessmen were capitalizing.

Keenly aware of the importance of agriculture and determined to further cement the ties between town and country, these men took steps to bring the new Exhibition Grounds into being. Much of James Kirkness' old River Lot No. 26 was occupied by a swampy lake, and because land there could be bought relatively cheaply, that area was chosen for the new grounds. Purchasing the land during 1910, the city authorities put it in shape so as to open it the next year in time for the usual fair.

The city's growth, pleasing as it was to everyone else, was a headache to the power plant superintendent, for he found himself continually running short of power. No matter how fast he installed new machinery, the load grew faster. Then he had to go to council for more money for new installations, and dealing with the city fathers can often be a slow and disheartening process. At the end of January, 1909, however, he got their consent to put in a new set of 1800 HP boilers with engines to go with them. For the time, these were large, and the last word in modern machinery.

On the score of new mechanical developments, on February 24, 1909, the *Journal* reported the first aeroplane flight ever to be made in Canada. That day, in Nova Scotia, John McCurdy flew his Silver Dart half a mile. Edmontonians were properly impressed, and for a few days everyone talked of this curious feat.

Edmonton, however, was not to be far behind Nova Scotia in seeing one of the earliest plane flights, for on September 7, 1909, Reginald Hunt, a carpenter who had built his own plane, flew it for thirty-five minutes. It had taken him three years to assemble the parts and to build his machine and fashion its four-bladed propeller, of which he said: "I based my design on the fans that keep flies from sleeping in restaurants." The very next day, far away in England, Captain S. F. Cody, although not the first to fly there, achieved fame by staying aloft for sixty-three minutes in a factory-built plane. Reginald Hunt, however, had won through all by himself, but bad luck turned him to other interests. Next year his hopes in the aeronautical line ended when, in preparing to perform at the Exhibition, he crumpled his hard won plane against a fence.

Harking back to old times, however, came a reminder that old Fort Edmonton had fallen on evil days. The provincial government had decided to use part of it as a poultry station and set men to clean it out and alter it. Amongst other gear which had to be cleared out were ten 25-pound kegs of black powder. The men rolled nine of these into the river, but the tenth set out on an independent career. Billy Lund, the fireman at the Terrace Building, thinking it would make good fuel for his boilers, trundled it over to them, but his plans were thwarted and he was ordered to clear out with his keg.

Dejected but not despairing, he carried it over to his tent. There, as he sat thinking about the powder, he poured some of it into a pan and set it on the stove to test it. It was good. When it exploded, it flashed over to the keg, which reacted with what the *Bulletin* described as a "deafening detonation which shook buildings for blocks." Poor curious Lund was badly burned and battered. His dog was in the tent at the time, but thereafter this companion of happier hours was neither seen or heard again.

About this time many fine homes were being erected near the edge of the high bank between the old McDougall Mission Church and the site of the Parliament Building. In that area real estate was selling at high prices, and downtown property on Jasper Avenue near 101 Street was changing hands at $10,000 per front foot. During that summer, workmen erected several three and even two four-storey buildings in the business section which was extending along Jasper Avenue as far west as 107 Street. All this building activity and particularly the transactions in real estate put many a venturesome man on easy street.

The Hudson's Bay Company, of course, with its great three thousand acre Reserve was the biggest landowner. It had subdivided that portion of it from 107 Avenue south to the river and had sold most of those lots. It still owned the bulk of the old Reserve, however, and was hanging on to it — a piece extending generally from 107 Avenue north to 122 Avenue and from 101 Street west to near 122 Street. By 1909, this large empty area of some 2½ square miles had become a stumbling block in the city's orderly expansion. Around its western, eastern and northern fringes promoters had opened up some small subdivisions and sold lots. City services had to be extended to these remote sections and thus stretched out for miles, circumventing this bothersome empty land which the company hung on to, hoping to make a killing out of it later on.

Passing well clear of this Reserve and on its northern side, the new raw grade of the Grand Trunk Pacific Railway not yet covered by a kindly growth of weeds had entered the city. That company, however, had fulfilled its contract with the city and had looped a line south so as to draw its trains into the CNR station on 101 Street, which was soon to be rebuilt as a union station.

That summer, too, the rivalry between Edmonton and Strathcona, championed by the South Side's new *Strathcona Chronicle* and the *Edmonton Journal*, broke out afresh. For some weeks, the *Journal* had teamed up with the Simmons Soap Company in a campaign which gave away free soap to *Journal* subscribers. In Edmonton and in the surrounding country their efforts had met with such success that they decided to invade the *Strathcona Chronicle's* bailiwick. Since the only report we have of this affair has come to us from the *Chronicle,* we should perhaps view it with a certain amount of caution, but for what it is worth, the following is that paper's version of the affair. "The Journal-Simmons Soap Campaign canvassers appeared in Strathcona yesterday and began their campaign here. They met, however, with very little success since they discovered that the Strathcona people who read the Journal do not use soap and the Strathcona people who use soap do not read the Journal."

Blithely unaware of this bickering, Lord Strathcona arrived about this time to accept an honourary degree which the university, ever mindful of its empty coffers, wished to confer on him. By now, this man, who had risen in the Hudson's Bay Company service until by long-headed financing he had obtained wealth —

which he used to finance the CPR when it was in desperate straits — was well along in years. But the old man still showed the keenness that had made him so outstanding and the same alertness which, while other Canadians had stood around dithering, had made him millions, and at the same time had immeasurably improved Canada by far more than the millions he amassed.

While in Edmonton, Lord Strathcona and the aging Father Lacombe got together and spent a few happy hours reminiscing at Government House. Then three weeks later, on October 1, 1909, while some of the magnificence of the river valley's mellow fall beauty still remained, Governor-General Earl Grey laid the cornerstone of the new Legislative Building.

That December, Edmontonians, well pleased with Mayor Robert Lee, re-elected him. It had been a good year. Even the two huge gold dredges operating in the river and reminiscent of Edmonton's past, had closed the season with a profit. Scores of new homes had been built. The number of churches had grown, with the building of two more Roman Catholic and one new Presbyterian houses of worship, as well as the meeting places of two denominations described rather quaintly by Henderson's Directory as undenominational, The Church of God and the West End Gospel Hall. Looking to the future, two automobile garages and three oil companies appeared in the list of businesses.

The cost of living was not a vexing problem. Men's imported tweeds and worsteds were selling at "Regular Price $15.00 to $18.00 per suit. On Saturday $10.50." Food too was cheap, as will be seen by the following list of groceries and meats appearing in one of the Capitol Mercantile Company's ads for March 1909.

Tea per lb. 50¢	Dates per lb. 10¢
Coffee per lb. 40¢	Prunes per lb. 12½¢
Rice 4 lb./25¢	Raisins per lb. 10¢
Tapioca 3½ lb./25¢	Molasses—3-lb. tin 20¢
Raspberries—2-lb. tins 20¢ tin	Syrup—2 lb. tin 20¢
Pineapple—1½-lb. tin 15¢	Round Steak 10¢ lb.
Canned apples, per gal. tin 35¢	Boiling Beef 6¢ lb.
Clams—1-lb. tin 25¢	Pork Shoulder 8¢ lb.
Oysters—1-lb. tin 25¢	Pork Chops 10¢ lb.
Bird's egg custard powder 15¢ tin	Sausages 10¢ lb.

Business kept up its brisk pace all through the winter, and by mid-summer 1910 many new amenities had begun to take shape. Over in the woods on the university property the new Arts Building had been started. Although its construction dragged along for two or three years, it was a sign that the new institution of higher learning was forging forward.

In April when the first faint wash of green began to suffuse the vast valley below the site of Rev. George McDougall's first church, his daughter Eliza, Mrs. R. Hardisty, laid the cornerstone for a new brick McDougall Church. Two weeks later, King Edward VII died. When in June the city fathers turned the sod for the new $225,000 city hospital, they named the Royal Alexandra after his highly respected widow. Downtown business was as brisk as ever, and that spring D. J. McNamara purchased the property on the south-east corner of Jasper and 105 Street for $80,000.

In March 1910 Dr. Whitelaw, the city's Medical Health Officer, ran afoul of the law and was fined $10 for speeding. The police had clocked him on Jasper

*Lieutenant-Governor, G. H. V. Bulyea, Lord Strathcona and Premier
A. C. Rutherford in grounds of temporary government house — where
Oliver Building stands today.*

Avenue at 17 MPH. In court, the doctor expressed doubt about the speed, averring that since his car had a broken differential, he doubted if he could have induced it to tear along at that terrific rate. For that very reason, the day before the case came up he had sold the car. "If," he said, "I had believed it would go that fast I'd have added another $100 to the price for which I sold it. If this goes on," he added, "we will all have to get speedometers installed." To which the magistrate replied: "I have taken that precaution."

In spite of this and other excitement in the city, Edmontonians, realizing whence much of their bread and butter came, kept an eye on the north. That spring the *Bulletin* noted some northern activity when it reported that the mail for the north had left by horse and sleigh for Lac La Biche. From there, it reminded its readers, that Alex Loutit, a famous half-breed, would take it in hand and mush his dog-team to Fort Resolution and then bring out the south-bound mail to Lac La Biche — a 3,500-mile round trip. Having done that, he would rest up for a while or take on some other shorter jaunt before he set out again to complete his routine of two trips a year to Fort Resolution.

Much nearer the city, March found everybody talking about the hydro plant which was to be started near the mouth of the Sturgeon River to supply Fort Saskatchewan with unlimited, cheap power. The idea must have been catching, for in June a company calling itself the Edmonton Heat & Power Co. Ltd. proposed to build a 30,000 HP plant on the Saskatchewan River at Rocky Rapids, a hundred miles above the city, and thereby to make a major reduction in Edmonton's power costs. Though discussed in council and talked of for some time, this project was temporarily shelved.

If, however, the attempt to use the Saskatchewan to produce power was unsuccessful, nevertheless, the river still found a vital place in the field of transportation. In 1909, as evidence of this, John Walter felt it would be profitable to build his new steamboat "The City of Edmonton." From then on, when the water in the river was deep enough, it supplemented other river transportation by plying back and forth downstream as far as Hewlett's Landing north of Lloydminster. For the next eight years, pulling up to little wharves here and there along the 200-mile stretch of the river to unload commodities for the settlers in the north-east corner of the province, or to load up with grain or other farm produce, the City of Edmonton filled an important role.

The council, of course, had many other things to occupy its attention. Becoming alarmed over the citizens' back-sliding, it closed down a private miniature park called Happy Land, where rumours said deep and mysterious evils were encouraged. A few days later, with similar paternal interest in its citizens' well-being, the council banned the sale of ice-cream on Sunday.

Then, turning to matters more physical, it announced with pride that the paving of Jasper Avenue from 111 Street to 116 Street had been finished. Moreover, since the CPR was going to come in over the High Level Bridge, and since its proposed station would be at 109 Street on the north side of Jasper Avenue, arrangements had to be made to create an underpass adjacent to it. This was the city's first underpass. At the same time, the council announced that finally a contract had been let for the High Level Bridge at an estimated cost of $1,428,793. Since this bridge was to have a traffic deck to permit easy access to and from Strathcona for all the heavy team traffic of the day, it was reported that its cost would be shared. Edmonton and Strathcona were to pay $238,000 and $50,000 respectively, and the provincial and dominion governments $175,000 and $125,000, with the rest coming from the CPR coffers. These payments were only a minor worry to Edmonton, because it still lay in prosperity's lap. Its mill rate was 17 and its assessment had risen $5 million over the previous year's $25 million, and each month during the summer of 1910 its bank clearings showed a growth of about fifty percent over the year before.

In July 1910, to cope with its expanding population, the city council took final steps to annex a large area — 4,800 acres, or 7.50 square miles. When it was through, Edmonton occupied 14.67 square miles, more than double its former area. Out near the new north-west corner of the city lay the railway hamlet of Calder, while the new north-east corner butted against that of North Edmonton, which had been incorporated as a village in February 1910.

New subdivisions proliferated. Some of them, such as the Groat Estate, Norwood and Parkdale, were within the former city limits. Most of the new ones, however, were in the area annexed that summer. Many of these subdivision names have become lost during the intervening years, but typical ones within the new area and still in existence are the following:

West of the Hudson's Bay Reserve; Inglewood, Hempriggs, Woodcroft and Sherbrooke.

East of the Hudson's Bay Reserve; Northcote, Woodland, Fairview, Westwood and Eastwood.

Then, really reaching out and even going beyond the new city limits and beyond the north boundary of the Hudson's Bay Company Reserve to stretch out north and east of Calder, were the new areas of: Wellington, Kensington, Rosslyn and Lauderdale. The lot peddlers had a real jag on.

Still reaching for more land, the Edmonton city council once more approached Strathcona, resurrecting the idea of amalgamation. That fall, on both sides of the silvery river, the merits and demerits of such a union came in for lively discussion. By the end of November, it appeared that the issue might be put to a vote of the burgesses in each of the cities. Strathcona's council, perhaps not unduly suspicious of being tricked by its northern neighbour, tried to cover all loopholes. It asked the legislature to amend its charter by adding a clause that would prevent any Edmontonians who owned property in Strathcona from voting on the amalgamation issue. It was well to watch these people north of the river.

That fall, taking advantage of one of the views overlooking the city's magnificent valley, the province purchased a large piece of property immediately west of the Groat Ravine for the government house it intended to build. Then too, on November 23, promoters of the GTP, equally cognizant of the attraction of a beautiful setting, bought a site overlooking the silvery river far below for their Macdonald Hotel.

One day earlier, the rival railway, the CPR, which for so long had avoided Edmonton and now was hurrying to make amends, announced the purchase of property on Jasper Avenue for its proposed six-storey CPR building. Then in December, Abraham Cristall, who in 1893 had been the first Jew to come and to remain at Edmonton, showed that he too could build hotels, and hotels higher than any other building in the city at that time. Just before Christmas, well before the CPR Building was started, he opened his $100,000, five-storey Royal George Hotel. Like so many other enterprising Edmonton pioneers, his seventeen years in the city had raised him from a poor boy to a man of substance. For many years his hotel was to be the hub around which much of 101 Street's activity revolved.

By 1910, of course, Edmonton had many merchants of Jewish stock, who, seeing opportunities, came to apply their energy and ability to developing the city. By that time, Edmonton had indeed become cosmopolitan in the sense that a variety of ethnic groups had come to rejoice in its freedom and partake of its opportunities, if perhaps scarcely so in the sense of ultra-sophistication. Edmonton's population, including those people born in Canada or the United States, or coming from the British Isles, was about 70% Anglo-Saxon. Some 3% were French-speaking. People from Germany or the Scandinavian countries, many of them after a stay in the States, made up about 8%. Over 15% were of Slavic stock, including some Poles, but mainly those we know now as Ukrainians. The remainder of the population came mainly from Belgium, Holland, Hungary, Greece and Italy, with a sprinkling of Chinese and a few Negroes from the United States.

Many of the Greeks quickly found an outlet for their talents in the restaurant business or in small grocery stores. They met brisk competition from the Chinese, a clever, hard-working, long-suffering folk, who, starting with every handicap against them, soon established themselves in these fields and in little laundries and market gardens. Due to their colour, their difficulties with the language and to the quite unwarranted hatred they aroused in the breasts of immigrants from the Western States, they were invariably the butt of jibes and jokes often far from funny, but by turning the other cheek they hung on and prospered. The Scandinavians, great-hearted, good humoured, adventurous folk, who throughout hundreds of years of roaming had left their Viking mark in a quarter of the place-names of eastern England and had passed their Norse red hair down to their Scottish and Irish descendants, found it easy to adjust in any English-speaking city. Those of Germanic stock, similar to the Scandinavians in most ways, exhibited more of a tendency to congregate in certain areas of the city, such as near the packing plant, where they formed a reliable labour source.

Partly by choice and partly because they had no choice, the Ukrainians, who had many strikes against them, tended to keep to themselves. In their homelands the majority of Edmonton's other immigrants had enjoyed a large measure of democracy. To the Ukrainians, democracy was a welcome but wholly untried way of life, and towards it, over a difficult language barrier and against the seething intolerance of the Canadian West, they had to grope their way. Since in a great measure the English language is made up from Norman, Norse and Teutonic components, the French, Scandinavian and Germanic tongues and names fell not too strangely on Anglo-Saxon ears, but to them, Slavic in any form was foreign. Though a large percentage of the Ukrainian men were often proficient in two or three languages, none of them had ever encountered English before. For many years they were a race apart. Throughout their early years in Canada they carried much of the burden of heavy construction labour, and still form a major part of Edmonton's labour supply.

Though the Ukrainians, when they arrived, had had little opportunity for schooling, and though an overwhelming percentage of them were illiterate, they brought with them a deep piety and an intense respect for learning. By 1912 they were publishing their own newspaper, "The New Society," edited by Thomas Tomashewsky. No matter how great a sacrifice parents might have to make, they insisted that their children attend school. Moreover, at every opportunity they tried to partake of the life of this new city in this new and strange world. It is then no surprise to find them playing what part they could in the 1910 civic elections, and to find that eight of the candidates held a special meeting for them, in which Paul Rudyck, one of their intelligentsia, acted as interpreter.

In this election G. S. Armstrong was chosen mayor by acclamation, while over in Strathcona, Arthur Davies, who had been the town's mayor in 1905, was put back into that office. As it turned out, these men who were so popular with both electorates carried the load that brought about the two cities' amalgamation.

Perhaps because during the previous two years the builders had over extended themselves, little commercial building took place in Edmonton in 1911. Most of the construction going on was financed by the province, which had the Parliament Building and a new Land Titles Office under way, or by the city, which was erecting the McCauley School and the Royal Alexandra Hospital addition.

If, however, the slackening of the building boom tended to subdue Edmontonians' excitement, the fight between the council and Commissioner Bouillon sent it soaring again. He appears to have been a competent, forthright individual as brimful of talent as he was bereft of tact. At this time when many a candidate ran for office with an eye to the graft he could pick up, such a man as Bouillon who would not compromise with cupidity was undoubtedly needed. During the ensuing uproar, it was shown that Bouillon at times had stepped on the toes of many a councillor's get-rich-quick scheme or barred the gate against an ex-alderman's graft.

But Bouillon did not stop at criticizing aldermen who in council voted lucrative contracts to each other; he turned his icy stare on sticky-fingered or incompetent department superintendents. In practically no time at all the battle lines were drawn. On the one side stood Bouillon, supported by his rectitude, by those of his religious faith and by the faint but fickle echo of interest of the large part of the populace whose members saw no opportunity of getting in on the graft. On the other side stood many a civic leader or employee all raring to fight but all handicapped somewhat by having one fist in the community pork barrel. Trying to calm the combatants came Mayor Armstrong, neutral and untouched by the scandals but anxious to get on with the city's business.

Week after week Edmontonians talked of little else while the Gilbert and Sullivan comedy played itself out. The attacks, sallies and counter attacks, the forced marches, retreats and ambuscades which ended seven months later would make an interesting book of their own.

While the histrionics of the Bouillon affair were strutting across the stage, someone turned the spotlight on R. W. Ensor, the strict chief of police, who had found many ways to draw down everyone's wrath. He began to enforce the law, an unforgivable foolishness; he caught some of the mighty, an incredible folly. Such a law officer could not be tolerated, and soon Ensor was at loggerheads with everyone. For once, all three newspapers found themselves making common cause and making it against the stubborn chief of police.

His dismissal was a foregone conclusion, but before it came the *Journal* found another opportunity to ridicule him. He had requested the city to provide him with a summer helmet upon which should be emblazoned the word "Chief." This gave the paper another chance to needle him, and it rose to the occasion by saying: "However, if the city feels it cannot stand the expense of luxuries the Chief might be induced to go without a hat — as there is a vacant spot on the top of his head where his title could be inscribed."

By that time, however, Edmontonians were caught up in another excitement, another Dominion election. Once more the great Sir Wilfrid Laurier led his

Liberals, this time on a policy of reciprocity with the United States. Frank Oliver, Minister of the Interior, and his *Edmonton Bulletin* forecast that the Liberals would sweep the country, but instead, the Conservatives swept them out of office. Frank himself was safe enough, and when the election results were flashed on the front of the *Bulletin* office by slides, they revealed that he had defeated Griesbach by a handsome majority. From then on, however, he was to be merely a private member on the opposition side of the House.

With the change in government, heads began to roll in the Dominion civil service. Many a patient Conservative supporter was rewarded for his faithfulness, but, amongst other Liberals, the postmaster went looking for a job, while Matt McCauley was fired as warden of the penitentiary. Leaving Edmonton he went out to Penticton to become a fruit grower. One more of Edmonton's early colourful figures had fallen before the march of politics.

Aside from the tempest in the Bouillon teapot and the excitement of the election that virtually ended Laurier's career, little of moment occupied Edmontonians' time. For a few days in February, on paper at least, the city experienced a brief oil boom. Ever since 1892 when oil seepages had been noted in the vicinity of Morinville, that area had tempted the venturesome. Dry holes had been drilled out that way, but hope of oil riches dies hard, and when the Dominion government offered to lease oil rights on one hundred sections of land near Morinville, on the basis of only one section to any individual, speculators were ready to give them a whirl. As a result, when on February 10, 1911, these rights were sold, sixty-one oil companies were incorporated, while others followed in a day or so. All of the incorporation papers were drawn up in the law offices of Short, Biggar and Cross. All of them had interlocking directors, who each had the right to one section and who in various combinations floated companies which it was hoped would entice the unwary into putting up money for the risk involved, while those on the inside hoped to garner any profit that just might accrue. In all, the one hundred companies were to have $100 million of capital stock.

Oil with its fascination made another play for the McMurray Tar Sands, when on April 6, Peace River Jim Cornwall and A. Violette offered to bring five or six tons of asphalt from the sands to pave Edmonton's streets. To this the council agreed, but there is no further record of any subsequent development of the sands or of the extension of Edmonton's pavement.

Over at the university, however, the wells of knowledge had started producing, for on May 17 the university awarded its first earned degrees. That spring too, over in the trees, Athabasca Hall was opened. In due course it became a residence, but it had the honour of being the first of the university buildings to come into operation.

While over in Strathcona the university was beginning to show results, Edmontonians kept herding the guileless folk across the river towards amalgamation. For months the talks and negotiations had gone on, and on September 27 they culminated in a plebiscite in each city. On that day Edmontonians voted 667 for and 96 against amalgamation, while on the other side of the river the South Siders, not quite so eager, voted 518 for and 178 against. At last the feud which had lasted for twenty years, since the CPR had dead-ended at Strathcona, was officially over. All that was left to do now was to tidy up the official papers and that could wait till next year.

In both cities, business, while scarcely booming, was nevertheless bustling, although indeed the influx of new homemakers had fallen off slightly. Everybody realized this, but the only man who was really concerned was Mayor Armstrong, and even he did not get excited until the Dominion census figures were released in October. When he saw them, he blew up, swearing that he would have the police department make another count. For the Edmonton figures showed only 24,882, and if the tally for Strathcona were added to that, the total for the combined city was only 31,064. But then Federal census takers were well known for their tendency to deflate mayors and boards of trade.

Except for its anger at the Dominion census people, the city of Edmonton closed the year 1911 on a quiet note. It had been a fair year, but with any luck 1912 would be better.

Jasper Avenue looking West, about 1911.

Boom Years 1912-1914

chapter *14*

THE YEAR 1912 was indeed better. It turned out to be Edmonton's all-time boom year. Before it was over, the combined cities' population had jumped over sixty percent, from 31,000 to 50,000, new subdivisions sprayed out, new street car lines fanned out, new buildings raised the city's skyline, and new civic scandals trod on each other's heels. Before it was over, Edmontonians had tied a millstone of debt around their necks that it took thirty-five years to shed. And yet as the year ended it appeared that such a spree could go on forever. Headaches were to come in 1913, and remorse after that, but in 1912 the sky was the limit. Luck, disguised as merit, piped, and all unaware that it was to take them thirty-five years to pay off the piper, deluded Edmontonians danced.

Early in the new year, with mutual bowing and scraping, the councils of the two cities pranced through their nuptial dance and sang their valedictory songs. The consummation of the wedding came on February 1, 1912, when the provincial legislature passed the Edmonton-Strathcona Amalgamation Act. By its terms, the one-time rivals coalesced under the name of Edmonton and were governed for a month by Edmonton's existing mayor and council. Then new elections were held. So that the South Siders would always be certain of representation on the council, the Act provided that in any election the three South Side candidates with the highest votes would be declared elected. After that, the rest of the city's council was to be filled by those who had the highest overall number of votes.

One of the other clauses provided that within eighteen months the new city must construct a bridge at 105 Street capable of bearing a railway as well as other traffic. Still another compelled the new city to extend the street car tracks here and there in Strathcona. Amongst others, an extension was to run from the corner of Whyte Avenue and 104 Street south to 76 Avenue. Still another was to be a line west along 76 Avenue to 111 Street. From there it was either to turn north till it reached University Avenue and follow it west and finally circle back to Whyte Avenue, or it was to continue straight west from 111 Street for a distance of 2,960 feet (practically to Saskatchewan Drive). In providing for this extension west along 76 Avenue, the legislators brought into being the famous McKernan Lake street car line.

Throughout the months of negotiation which led to the Amalgamation Act, Edmonton was the assiduous suiter, Strathcona the coy coquette. On the evening of January 31 the Strathcona council met for the last time, cleaning up odds and ends of business. Rumour has falsely accused it of working late that night signing contracts for new paving right and left, because then the combined city would have to implement and pay them, and thus with respect to paved streets Strathcona would be put in preferred position. This rumour appears to be untrue. What did happen is that during the previous year the councils of both Edmonton and Strathcona signed several contracts for paving, knowing that the enlarged city would eventually have to foot the bill. As it turned out, Strathcona's aldermen were more daring, and for decades the South Side could boast of much more paving in proportion to its population than the North Side.

A week after the legislature validated the amalgamation, it amended the cities' charters with respect to votes. In 1910 it had dealt with this question and had made it legal for tenants or for those whose wives were tenants to vote in city elections. Now in 1912 it went a step farther and extended the vote to all persons paying rent. Although Mayor Armstrong, ex-Mayor J. A. McDougall and Alderman MacInnis, foreseeing trouble, objected to this change, the legislature passed it anyway. In less than a year it was to lead to an interesting situation.

Because amalgamation had been pending, Edmonton's usual 1911 civic elections were postponed till the united city could vote. On February 17, G. S. Armstrong was re-elected mayor with a large majority, along with three aldermen from the South Side and seven from the North Side. One of these was the battler Joe Clarke. For the first time, a woman, Miss Bessie Nichols, found herself sitting on the school board.

As usual, the aftermath of these elections was a clamour that voters had been bribed, ballot boxes stuffed, and some candidates were crooked, and as usual the clamour was correct. Proving that, however, was another matter. In the thick of the uproar stood Joe Clarke, who successfully defended an action aimed at unseating him. Boom times and the ordinary citizen's conviction that a man was not smart unless he could rake in some graft led to other episodes during 1912 and started some of the heartiest rows ever to shake city hall.

To begin with, there was the business of extending 102 Avenue, which at the time ended at 99 Street. In 1912, 97 Street, a flourishing business thoroughfare, was seeing its glory fade before the competition of 101 Street. Alderman Dr. MacInnis, who along with four others owned property on 97 Street, advocated extending 102 Avenue through to 97th. To this the other aldermen agreed, because nearly all of them were good friends of Dr. MacInnis and nearly all of them followed the precept of "I'll scratch your back if you'll scratch mine." So, in secret they instructed MacInnis to go around in equal secrecy to purchase the twenty-six lots that were needed to permit the street to be extended. Of these twenty-six, Dr. MacInnis owned three. Part of the secret too was to be that, while he was to use city money to buy them, he was to do so in his own name and finally transfer them to the city. All of this he did. But complications set in, and one of them was fighting Joe Clarke. The uproar he set off ended in judicial investigation at which all of the aldermen disclaimed authorizing the doctor's irregular proceedings, so poor MacInnis was left out in the cold. In the end, in a long, written judgment, Justice Harvey found that neither MacInnis nor anyone at city hall had been guilty of any wrong-doing. It had been a near miss, however, and in ensuing years MacInnis's name was not on the roll of aldermen.

Not only streets but street car lines too kept the aldermen from getting bored. When in 1911 W. J. Magrath, who built the stately mansion in the Highlands, which is now Bishop Savaryn's Palace, started selling lots out there, he paid the city $20,000 to extend the car lines to them. The best way of accomplishing the same end, however, was to be on the council. For instance, to serve the Calder area, the original idea had been to route the rails along the St. Albert Trail. When these were laid down, however, they headed straight north along 124 Street, because some of the city fathers were busy promoting the Inglewood area.

As we have seen, however, there was nothing underhanded about the McKernan Lake street car line which, rocking and swaying west through bush and marshes and passing nearly a mile of empty lots on 76 Avenue, ambled along till at Saskatchewan Drive it reached a group of three or four houses belonging to university professors. In good years its operating loss was a mere $5,000. No matter what it cost, however, no matter how often it went off the track, no matter how far its rails sank into the ooze around McKernan Lake, the city was stuck with it.

An entirely different breed of cat was the St. Albert inter-urban car line. An enterprising individual — and scores of trusting adventurers to whom he sold shares — were stuck with it. And yet on paper it had looked so rosy. Edmonton was expanding and subdivisions out north-west were overleaping each other and would go on doing so until surely Father Lacombe's old mission some eight miles out of Edmonton would find itself part of the city. As one owner of a quarter of land, which he decided to subdivide, put it: "Yup—I'm going to split her up into lots but I haven't made up my mind whether to call her a suburb of St. Albert or of Edmonton — but I'm going to parcel her up and peddle her."

But all that was during the long-forgotten days of the boom. For forty years cows drowsed away the heat of summer on this man's quarter. The less durable St. Albert inter-urban passed into oblivion when on a black day in 1915 its car-barn and its sole street car, one borrowed from the city of Edmonton, burned up. For decades, however, until modern bulldozers overwhelmed it, the line's old grade formed a conversation piece for wayfarers along the St. Albert Trail who could look west and see it as a grass-covered ridge heading into the spruce timber on its lonesome way out towards Big Lake and St. Albert. Sic transit inter-urban transit.

Fate likewise overwhelmed many of the carefully plotted and peddled subdivisions which extended out to areas encircling the city for a radius of perhaps two miles beyond any lots which sported homes. Dream subdivisions they may have been, bought by dreamy-eyed buyers, but their vendors were wide awake. The 145-acre Hagmann estate, which now forms a westerly part of the municipal airport, is a good example of the sort of money involved. In 1898 Hagmann bought it from the Hudson's Bay Company for $10 an acre. When he sold it in 1912 for $850,000, that is, $5,862 per acre, he realized a tidy profit. While this may have been an exceptionally high price even for 1912, and while the figures reported may even have been an exaggeration, many other similar pieces of land were changing hands at similar fabulous prices.

These, however, were paper prices. Hagmann never disclosed how much actual cash he folded up and put in his pocket, but it is doubtful if he got more than ten percent down. The trick in getting rich by dealing in real estate was to start out with a few dollars and then play the game on a margin basis. In that way one could soon become a paper millionaire without increasing one's actual cash.

McKernan Lake street car at Whyte Avenue
and 104th Street.

Crowd on 103rd Street near 103rd Avenue
and H.B.Co. land sale 1912.

Provincial Legislative Building with Fort Edmonton in foreground, 1914.

And therein lurked the snake. It was all very well to sell a piece of land for $850,000 and let the purchaser subdivide it and sell it as lots at ten percent down, with the rest in installments, but when the day of reckoning came and the installments never materialized, the purchaser had nothing to pay his debt to Hagmann, or whoever it was, and it was only a matter of time and legal process before the land reverted to Hagmann. Nevertheless, ten percent cash on $850,000 for a piece of land that had cost $1,450 was not to be sneezed at.

In 1912, however, the day of reckoning was somewhere away over the horizon, somewhere out amongst the surveyors, who took in cash for the lines they cut and the stakes they hammered into the new subdivisions. Much nearer at hand lay the large remnant of the unspoiled Hudson's Bay Reserve. Edmontonians hungered for lots, and by merely marking them off and advertising them, the Hudson's Bay Company could sell them in a flash. Before putting them up for sale the company paved a magnificent broad thoroughfare about two miles long diagonally through its reserve, laid in it the rails for street cars and called it Portage Avenue. As it turned out, street cars never ran on those rails, and for at least thirty years few indeed were the buildings that fronted on it. For these decades, during the daylight its lonesome reach became a speedway for youthful car drivers, and after dark, a quiet parking area for couples. When its day came, however, a day that found street cars obsolete, and after its name had been changed to Kingsway Avenue, it became a built-up street, and what is perhaps more important, a major throughway for today's heavy traffic.

But we are anticipating. After paving Portage Avenue and subdividing its property, the Hudson's Bay Company advertised that it would hold a public sale on May 13 and let it be known that on the day before that it would hold a public lottery by means of which 1,500 investors would obtain tickets entitling each of them to buy four lots. The time of the lottery was advertised, but where it was to be held was a secret to be divulged later. The prospective buyers, however, finally ferreted out the location, and to quote Tony Cashman in *The Edmonton Story:*

"In a flash, there was a lineup of thirty people. Inside an hour they were lined up down to 102nd Avenue. And through the night the rumor flew and the line grew. It grew right around the block and back to the church again. And as we said, the most unobservant of men could not be unaware on that night of May 11, that all the gentlemen rushing along with boxes and campstools and chairs were up to something important. It was a gay, good-natured crowd. People who feel they've put something over are generally gay and good-natured. When the official announcement of the location appeared in the *Bulletin* at six o'clock that morning, there were twelve hundred and eighty-five men in line. By that time, some were cooking breakfast over open bonfires. One party had played cards all night by the light of their car headlamps. By nine o'clock there were fifteen hundred in the line . . ."

The lots were snapped up. Five hundred and forty-five Edmonton purchasers bought 1,431 of them and paid $3,683,000 cash, while far away in London, England, eager buyers paid $660,000 for 112 lots. On paper, the company realized $4,343,000, and at that, it had put only forty-seven percent of its reserve on the market.

By the time of the land sale three notable buildings were at some stage of construction; the eight-storey Tegler Building, the nine-storey McLeod Building, Edmonton's tallest structure, as well as the Civic Block. This was Edmonton's third city hall, and whatever it may have lacked in style it was built commodious enough to be a credit to the city as it was in 1912 and for forty years to come.

For when the council authorized its construction, the year's civic census had revealed an outstanding jump in the population. According to it, Edmontonians now numbered 53,383, and, therefore, the city had grown far more than anyone had dared to hope. All would have been well with this amazing population if this census had not also been the basis upon which Edmonton's voters' list was to be compiled.

Under the recent amendments to the city's charter, all those people paying rent were allowed to vote on civic matters. The exact interpretation of this amendment was hard to determine. In hundreds of cases the census taker had interpreted it generously and listed many as having the right to vote, whereas, Tom Walker, the city assessor, taking a narrower view, declared that they did not have that right. Then the fat was in the fire. Except for that, the total figure of 53,383 would never have been questioned.

Walker, scrutinizing the list, struck off hundreds of names, and later his opinion was corroborated by Chief Justice Harvey, before whom, largely because of the uproar raised by Joe Clarke, the matter was laid. Clarke, a politician who on every occasion boasted of his concern for the "honest working man" as opposed to "certain interests" whom he never named, pretended to scent all sorts of injustices in the city's assessor's revision of the list.

As Tom Walker had said: "Every visitor, domestic servant, hotel porter, bellboy and potboy" was shown as a voter. Some of the cases brought to light are described by Tony Cashman in his inimitable manner in *More Edmonton Stories* as follows:

". . . He found that in five small cottages on 97th Street there were alleged to be 172 Chinese gentlemen living. All were said to be 'naturalized British subjects, entitled to vote.' Tom also found the names of eleven Japanese gentlemen, all naturalized British subjects, all residents of the Alberta Hotel. Investigation showed no Japanese gentlemen living there. The list showed still another 115 citizens residing in the Alberta. The patriotic census taker had copied out the hotel guest book for a period of several weeks and entered all the travelling salesmen, vaudeville comedians, and visiting firemen of all trades, as bona fide residents of Edmonton. The Presbyterian General Assembly had met in Edmonton during the time of the census. The visiting ministers were also listed as bona fide residents of Edmonton the Magnificent . . . And while the city had been divided into 27 districts for the census, Tom reported that some enterprising booster had rung in a 28th district. North Edmonton was still a separate village, but someone had added 905 residents of North Edmonton into the population of the city. 905 North Edmontonians, all entitled to vote in Edmonton. When Tom did a little further checking on the cards, he found only 855, not 905. At the tail end of the list, the enumerator had written: 'Fifty residents who refused to give their names.' And that's the stuff of which Edmonton's population for 1912 was made up . . ."

When Chief Justice Harvey, in whose lap the problem had been laid, rendered a decision, it backed up what Tom Walker had said. The learned Justice's decision did not please Joe Clarke, who, as he was leaving the courtroom, got into a row with city solicitor Walt Bown and is reported to have declared "I'll see you with a rope around your neck — you and the rest of the grafters, crooks and thieves may have one more year to work, but . . ." Had it not been for all the fuss raised by the census taker's list, no one would ever have questioned Edmonton's 1912 population of 53,383.

Regardless of which side anyone took in that battle, everyone agreed that Edmonton was enjoying an unprecedented influx of immigrants. On August 30, when the *Bulletin* made a count, it found that despite the fact that the city council had thrown open the Granite Curling Club and some temporary school buildings as sleeping quarters for newcomers, 2,671 people were camped in tents on the river flats or around the fringes of the city. Some of these indeed had spilled over into the areas annexed that summer.

The Act of Amalgamation had not only included all the lands that Edmonton and Strathcona had occupied previously but added even more land to the north side so that now the city contained 23.21 square miles. But even that was not enough. Annexation was in the air, and the people of North Edmonton put their heads together with those of Edmonton's city council and on July 22, 1912, the city absorbed the small town. Then a little later, on October 14, the growing city annexed another 380 acres lying mainly east of what had been North Edmonton. Once these acquisitions were legalized Edmonton occupied an area of 24.80 square miles.

While the annexations were in progress, on August 1, 1912, to be exact, what Edmontonians of that time called the East End bridge (Dawson Bridge) was opened to give access to the Dawson Mine and to make it somewhat easier for the Clover Bar farmers to reach the city's downtown area. For a few years after it was built, huge horses drew their heavy coal wagons over it, now and then meeting a rustic democrat. Then when coal mining ceased, its deck planks lay warping in the summer sun, to be rattled occasionally by a farmer's wagon or a milkman's van. And yet, fifty years later, it came into its own as one of the few bridges trying manfully to cope with modern traffic.

The bridge and the annexation lent leverage to the real estate promoters' arms. During this, the land speculators' golden age, real estate offices reached a peak never dreamed of in earlier years. Along Jasper Avenue, 97 Street, 101 Street and Whyte Avenue, and in fact in nearly every hole or corner, these offices sprouted till by the end of 1912 Henderson's Directory counted thirty-two real estate brokers, 135 financial agencies, and 336 real estate agents. The city swarmed with them. And then there were runners. As Tony Cashman said:

"The runners, like all the real estate crowd, had a phenomenal knack with a map. Their control of a map is an art now lost forever. They could unroll it without tearing it, hold it steady in a high wind, point out a choice lot with a deft wave of a thumb, and never break stride. They acquired their art through constant practice. The length of Jasper Avenue, on a good business day, you could see maps opening and closing with the precision of window blinds.

"The runners would often make immediate sales on the street, but most of their work consisted in getting the customer into the net and luring him to the office, where the promoters would gaff him.

"Runners were not to be confused with curbstone brokers, who also worked in the open. The curbstone brokers were the pet peeves of orthodox real estate men. Curbstone brokers were the sort of gentlemen who commonly seek a livelihood following racehorses from city to city and whispering sure-fire tips to bettors. Most of them operated around First and Jasper, or around the railroad stations. They were skilled at picking out a stranger just arrived in Edmonton. They would engage the stranger in conversation, get the conversation around to real estate, and then usually sell the stranger a lot. Their operating expenses were practically nil. They'd take an option on a lot, for maybe a dollar, then transfer the option to the stranger for a hundred dollars. It was perfectly legal, but orthodox operators felt that curbstone brokering lacked tone, and caused them unfair competition."

Though much of the real estate promotion was a mirage, the clatter of hammers and the whine of hand-saws was real enough as everywhere carpenters and bricklayers built the new city. All the while too, riveters, balancing precariously on the end of the great steel girders of the High Level Bridge, waited there while other sections were swung into place and until they could insert the white-hot rivets and whack good sturdy heads on them. Day after day the river valley rang with the rata-ta-tat of riveting hammers. Day after day too, masons had been scrambling along scaffolds high in the air as layer after layer they closed in the dome of the nearly complete Parliament Building. Then on September 3, the Governor-General, the Duke of Connaught, assisted by the Duchess and a host of dominion and provincial dignitaries, officially opened the majestic edifice.

A day or so earlier another milestone in Edmonton's history was declared complete. On August 30, the Canadian Northern Railway line to Athabasca Landing was finally opened for traffic all the way through. At last civilization was reaching out towards Edmonton's Far North. This railway, which replaced the thirty-year-old wagon trail that the Hudson's Bay Company had opened up, gave Edmontonians rapid connection with the steamboats which, even if interrupted by various portages, carried merchandise down the Athabasca, the Slave and Mackenzie rivers to the Arctic Ocean. Edmontonians had always looked to the north, and this tangible evidence of their interest in it helped to cinch even tighter the long-standing bond between the two.

In September 1912 the city council had another round with the recurring problem of obtaining gas and referred it to the people. This time the proposal was to build a gas producer plant which would have cost about three-quarters of a million dollars, but by a decisive majority, the voters rejected it. At the same time, they were asked what they thought of bridging the river in the vicinity of 142 Street, and this they endorsed by a large majority.

As a reminder that even in the midst of its abounding prosperity and its splendid isolation in western Canada Edmonton was part of a wicked world, the *Bulletin* of October 14 reported that one hundred of the city's Serbians, Bulgarians and Greeks had been recalled to the Balkans to prepare for war with Turkey. Few read the news item with more than casual interest, for they had many other things on their minds and the weeks were wearing away towards the annual civic election.

G. S. Armstrong, who had served so well, had decided not to run for mayor and new men scrambled eagerly for the job. On December 10, William Short won with a clear majority over both Magrath, the rich man, and Joe Clarke, the contentious one. As the year closed, Edmontonians looked back upon it as the most notable in the city's history.

Quite apart from matters of material prosperity and boom times, one or two developments marked the beginning of a new trend in social affairs. In January 1912 a group of the most prominent women in the city, including Mesdames Bulyea, Sifton, Rutherford and McQueen, as well as Emily Murphy, organized the Women's Canadian Club, pictured on page 199. More and more, women were reaching for the spotlight.

This was evident when a year earlier, for the first time, a woman, Miss Nichols, was elected to the school board. Then, when in May 1912 the first class of students who had received all their university training at the new Strathcona institution graduated, five out of the eighteen were women.

In matters more mundane, however, 1912 had been a year of unprecedented growth. For one thing, the Hudson's Bay Company had paid $193,172.50 in taxes. For another, the city's budget for 1913 had been set at $12 million. Moreover, the voters' list had jumped from 10,769 individuals in 1911, of whom 8,336 had been on the north side and 2,433 across the river, to some 17,000.

In Alberta 15,000 more farm families had come in to push the fringe of cultivation still farther back and to reap riches to pour into the cities. Edmonton's true population ended the year at 50,740, an increase of sixty-three percent in one year, while during the twelve months, building permits had soared to $14,447,000, four times the figure for the previous year. It had been a record-breaking year, one of great expansion, great accomplishments and great scandals. But best of all, Edmonton had generated a head of steam such that undoubtedly 1912 would be merely a prelude to what lay ahead.

An epidemic of fires marked the early months of 1913. On January 13 the *Bulletin* reported that over the week-end the loss was estimated to be between $50,000 and $100,000. Then, three days later, a quarter of a million dollar blaze destroyed the five-storey Canadian Consolidated Rubber Company's Ker Block.

Except for the fires, the first quarter of the year was quiet. Though there were hundreds of unfinished houses, and though the Tegler and the McLeod buildings and the Macdonald Hotel were still not finished, little work could be done on them during the depth of the winter. It was a slack period and was expected to be. Many men, well heeled from their summers' work, took it easy, enjoying the city's bright lights. Many others could not find work to do. From time to time, to add to these unemployed, came gangs of men reporting that the CNR contractors had laid them off. Far out west, beyond Jasper, that railway, creaking its weary way through canyon and coulee, was slowing up, and it was rumoured that Mackenzie and Mann were in financial trouble. To the thoughtful waiting for the boom to begin again in the spring, the large number of unemployed, Mackenzie and Mann's shaky position, and the epidemic of fires, were disturbing straws in the economic wind.

In the middle of May a *Bulletin* editorial commented confidently that although the Canadian financial position was tight, Edmonton was still growing and optimistic. In fact, it said Edmonton was the only city in Canada to show an increase in bank clearings over the corresponding week the previous year.

And yet the winds of depression were rising.

Nevertheless, civic business and civic planning had to go on, and late in February 1913 the council sat down to consider another of the expanding city's needs. Jasper Avenue, 97 Street and 101 Street were busy, built-up thoroughfares, but north of Jasper and between these other two streets lay a languid backwater. The council decided that that area would tie in with its new civic block and would make an ideal civic centre. Many an alderman rubbed his hands. In all that area the city owned only two lots, whereas, between them the aldermen owned many and could buy others. Immediately the prices put on property there skyrocketed, but some aldermen paid these prices, secure in the knowledge that they could resell to the city at a purse-pleasing profit. Then the council passed a by-law preventing anyone selling property there to any purchaser other than the city, and on March 18, 1913, the council announced that "The municipal council of the city of Edmonton deem it advisable to establish a civic center, being a park or

Edmonton branch Women's Canadian Club 1912. Back row, left to right, Mme. Cauchon, Mrs. F. C. Jamieson, Mrs. J. H. Riddell, Mrs. A. F. Ewing, Mrs. Duncan Marshall, Mrs. H. M. Tory, Mrs. G. S. Armstrong and Mrs. W. A. Greisbach. Front row, left to right, Mrs. D. G. McQueen. Mrs. G. H. V. Bulyea, Mrs. Murphy, Mrs. A. L. Sifton and Mrs. Gray.

open space for the purpose of building thereon various buildings of a public or semi-public nature, and laying out the said lands in an ornamental manner."

When the purchase offers for these lots, which hitherto had been by-passed by the business section, were added up, it appeared that the city would need over $2,700,000 to buy them. Realizing that even in Edmonton that was a tidy sum of money, the city solicitor insisted that the burgesses express an opinion on this purchase, and so towards the end of March they voted on a by-law to cover this expenditure — voted on it and voted it down. The expensive lots which the wise men had cornered were left in the backwater, and — although this is anticipating a little — they were left till tax sales gathered them in.

If, however, the aldermen were frustrated in their concern over the city's dying downtown area, they had room to manoeuvre on its outskirts. On March 25 they annexed 9,620 acres, just over fifteen square miles. Speaking generally, they took a strip a mile wide on the north side of the city, half a mile wide on the west, as well as sundry quarters of land in the south-west, and a strip a mile wide east of what had been Strathcona. After this annexation, the city's area was 39.88 square miles.

All this new area and all the new subdivisions, as well as confusion between streets bearing similar names on both the north and south sides, brought the question of street numbering to a head. The council received so many proposed solutions to the problem, both from serious citizens and crackpots, that they deferred the matter until the next year.

During that otherwise dull winter and spring, Edmontonians enjoyed some first class entertainment. As an indication of Edmonton's new status and of its underlying vein of culture, the *Bulletin* of January 14 reported that Sarah Bernhardt had enthralled a large and deeply appreciative audience, saying that "the Divine Sarah added Edmonton audiences to countless thousands under her sway." In a similar manner, on April 18, John McCormack exercised his mastery over a packed auditorium.

In May, to cater to the thirst for vaudeville entertainment, the new Pantages Theatre (now the Strand) opened. Built on the south-west corner of the intersection of 102 Street and Jasper, with boxes and balconies, it was the last word in posh plushness. Giving an afternoon and an evening performance, acrobats and comedians, singers, dancers and magicians, trained seals, and girls, beautiful girls, all took their turns to the audiences' unfailing delight. Over the years many famous and well remembered performers came to Edmonton's Pantages to say, do, or sing their parts — Will Rogers, Buster Keaton, Stan Laurel, Joan Blondell and Sophie Tucker. Over the years Edmontonians came to cherish the gold paint and the glitter of the well-patronized theatre.

Tucked away in the cellar of the Pantages was the never to be forgotten American Dairy Lunch. It was a cafeteria operated by two Greek experts, George Spillios and Harry Lingas. Whetting the appetite for its wholesome food, its long counter spread with pieces of pie, cakes and puddings and baked apples, was a sight to behold. Then too, near the counter, with grass growing on its rocks and a school of gold fish swimming in it, was the fountain. Sitting at the white tables tucked into corners and alcoves, sometimes under the very sidewalk, a hungry boy could eat his fill, while people went tripping and clumping along over the glass that was set into the pavement. Overhead, done out in outlandish costumes and holding up the ceiling, little Czech wine gods, some wearing only a barrel, pushed away with all their strength. Never was there a place like the American Dairy Lunch.

But then, the city of 1913 with its hundreds of horse-drawn vehicles and its frequent cars was such a marvellous place anyway. Along the streets, the signs advertising the owners' business stuck out all over, some painted on boards like the one over the combined shoe-shine stand and hat cleaning establishment, which sported a picture of the long-nosed Dr. Chapeau, LD, (lid doctor). Other signs were composed of groups of electric lights. The king of them all, however, the sign over Bob McDonald's Selkirk Hotel, only blossomed into full glory after dark when the lights came on and the streets blazed. This one, rigged high on the hotel roof, showed by the successive combinations of light bulbs a man pouring a glass of beer, lifting it to his lips, then quaffing the liquor.

Then too, the city of 1913 had another marvel, the newly-opened High Level Bridge. On June 2, the first train crossed it, and the *Edmonton Journal* gushed: "With the blowing and shrieking of many whistles and sirens, cheers from the scores of workmen employed on the bridge, and the hurrahs of the 200 or more passengers, the first passenger train to cross the Saskatchewan River between Edmonton South and Edmonton North over the new High Level Bridge was heralded this morning.

"Prompt to scheduled time train No. 33, consisting of seven cars, including one baggage car, an express car, one second-class car, two first-class cars, and dining and parlor cars, left the Edmonton South depot at 11 a.m."

Later on, in an eight-column headline the *Journal* proclaimed:
"STUPENDOUSNESS OF HIGH LEVEL BRIDGE IS AMAZING"
Going on, the article explained that it had taken three years to build at a cost of about $1 a rivet. Three men had lost their lives by falling from the bridge, while another had been killed in a cave-in. The bridge was said to be only fifty-two yards short of half a mile in length, and was the only one of its kind in the world, having a railroad and a double street car track on the upper level, and a roadway and dual sidewalks on the lower. The length of superstructure was 2,555 feet, the total height to top of piers 100 feet, while from ice level to base of rails it was 157 feet. The south end of the bridge was 10.34 feet higher than the north end.

In 1911, when Sir Robert Borden's new Conservative government took office, small clouds on the horizon began to point their warning. Aside from these dots, scarcely visible to any but the most perceptive, Canada, and especially the West, was booming. Railway gangs dug and carried and wheeled barrows, sweating all over the prairies as they threaded a network of railways through millions of acres of ripening wheat. As far as the eye could reach, these rich fields spread, and every year saw more land ploughed. Every year too saw more people flocking in, eager to enlarge the cultivated fields and to push ploughs farther back into the fringe areas, until in 1913 immigration to Canada reached an all-time high of 402,000.

By then, however, the storm signals were up. The era which had opened up the West was not only over, but the West was vastly over-expanded. Speculation piled upon speculation had counted too heavily on the vast wealth it was capable of contributing. By mid-summer 1913, the money markets were collapsing, and one of the major tremors that toppled them was the imminent bankruptcy of Mackenzie and Mann's CNR empire.

Although Edmonton was probably the last area to be hit by the hard times, they were beginning to show in less construction, in more men looking for work, and in real estate salesmen wondering where all their clients had gone. The city council also began to feel the chill of the cool financial climate. Enmeshed in the obligations contained in the new fifteen square miles it had so recently annexed on the one hand and finding on the other that its tax collections were failing badly, it was in a difficult spot.

In keeping with the city's amazing growth, the council had launched a major program of public works. When it was finished in 1914, the mileage of paved streets had increased from five in 1912 to thirty-five, while that of graded streets had grown from twenty-six to 181. The miles of sidewalk had doubled, to reach 140, while the length of watermain had likewise doubled, to 128 miles.

Of trifling concern compared to that was one of the health department's problems. The city's inspector, looking into dairies, reported that out of a total of 159 which pastured their cows hither and yon all over the city's far-flung sub-divisions, twenty-six were very sanitary, eighty-six were fairly clean, but forty-seven were a hazard to health.

One of the year's fires burned down a well-loved landmark, the Thistle Rink on 102 Street. The loss of this institution, which had been the centre of so much community activity, brought many a nostalgic pang. Though the rink's life had been a mere decade, it had witnessed the city's transition from a town of some four thousand to this city of 63,000.

Meanwhile another institution was rapidly gaining ground, for 1913 did much to raise the university in status and in structure. Alberta College (now St. Stephens) had been built in 1912, and this was followed by Athabasca Hall in 1913, and the contractors had made a start on the Arts Building. As well as these physical evidences of growing up, the young university increased in academic stature by opening a Faculty of Law in 1912 and one of Medicine the next year, and by planning to start an Applied Science Faculty in 1914. In 1913 also but on the other side of the river, the civic library accepted Andrew Carnegie's grant of $65,000.

Even though times were a bit depressed, not even that could dispel Edmontonians' interest in getting a supply of natural gas. For twenty-three years the people of Medicine Hat, straddling a large gas field, had toasted their toes before gas radiants. Lethbridge and Calgary, too, along with the intervening towns, had enjoyed this perfect fuel since 1912 when Eugene Coste's company had piped it in from the Bow Island field. Then, right at their doorstep, Calgarians had stumbled over the Turner Valley field. Far to the north, down the Athabasca River at Pelican Rapids, gas bubbled out of an old well, and farther north still, along the Peace River, voyageurs since Alexander Mackenzie's days had cooked their moose steaks over gas seepages. Why then, since Alberta was one vast sedimentary basin, except for a few mountains along its west edge — why could not somebody find gas near Edmonton?

To try to bring matters to a head, a group of Edmontonians banded together and each put up $100 and organized what they called the Industrial Association, which was to go to work and find a gas field large enough to supply the city. They hired Clapp and Huntley, a pair of English geologists, and sent them afield.

In the late fall the *Bulletin* declared that "Oil fever hits Edmonton." It went on to explain that four townships about ten miles north and west of Athabasca Landing had caught the public's fancy. On November 26, speculators filed on 70,000 acres there. Next day, according to the paper, "Oil excitement continues:

Turning sod for the first university building, Athabasca Hall 1909, Premier A. C. Rutherford holding plough, Dr. W. D. Ferris holding reins.

Starting on September 24, 1908, on the top floor of the Queen Alexandra School, with Dr. H. M. Tory as president, four professors and 45 students, the university erected and moved into its first building, Athabasca Hall, in 1911. Its enrolment had risen to 613 by 1918, and to 2,372 by the fall of 1939. By 1966 the full time staff numbered 850 teaching 11,515 full time day students. By 1965 the university's investment amounted to $62 million and during 1966 $22 million more was put into buildings and equipment.

100 Claims filed yesterday." By November 29 it was all over, for the *Bulletin* said: "Rush to oil subsides," and concluded laconically "No actual boring has been done yet."

A week later the Edmonton papers were off on another tangent. In Europe, the United States and Eastern Canada, the tango had arrived. It appeared that even though this terrible dance had been banned by the Vatican, Buckingham Palace and Ottawa's Rideau Hall, all the forces for good could not prevail and it was spreading.

About this time, the Medical Health Officer issued his report covering the past year. He had dealt with twenty cases of smallpox, 198 cases of diphtheria, fifty-six of tuberculosis, and commented: "During the year smallpox though not nearly so common as in 1912 when there were 71 cases, broke out at intervals and required a great deal of attention to keep it under control."

On top of the tango and smallpox came unemployment. Stories of what a soft life Edmonton's unemployed led drew hundreds of workless men to the city. On January 9, 1914, five hundred men were reported to have come in on the CPR from the south and a further influx was feared now that Foley, Welsh and Stewart, the CNR contractors, had quit work on the nearly defunct railroad to Vancouver. The civic relief department reporting in mid-February advised that it was doing all it could for some four thousand unemployed, and amongst other assistance was finding work for some of them on city relief projects.

To complicate matters further, a number of Industrial Workers of the World (IWW) organizers arrived in Edmonton, and by marches and other agitation started to foment trouble. Dubbed "The I Won't Works," this group was a militant labour faction which had incited riots and bloodshed and had become a serious menace to law and order in the northwestern States. Usually led by Anglo-Saxons or Irishmen, it recruited a large following from the recent non-English-speaking immigrants. On Sunday, February 1, three hundred unemployed, headed by IWW leaders, paraded to two city churches and the group in the McDougall Methodist Church threatened to camp there if their leaders were not allowed to hold forth from the pulpit. Coming at a time when graft and inefficiency had undermined the morale of the Edmonton police department, the IWW inspired troubles had an ominous ring.

While Edmonton was plagued with unemployment, the city council began to come to grips with another problem. Revenue from taxation was falling off. In March the treasurer reported that a million dollars of 1913 taxes had not been paid, and $250,000 was still outstanding from previous years. The city was skating on very thin ice and these tax arrears were not only embarrassing but a portent of what was to come. The council considered a by-law by which any land on which taxes had not been paid for three years could be claimed by the city for the amount of the arrears.

In spite of worries over unpaid taxes, the city was still growing, for the civic census completed June 4, 1914 reported Edmonton's population to be 72,516, of which 56,229 were on the north side and 16,287 across the river. These figures undoubtedly included many unemployed, for the number of males over twenty-one was stated to be 29,723, while the females in the same age group numbered only 17,881.

During April 1914 the geologists, Clapp and Huntley, reported that the Viking area looked like a good gas field. They had found good strata, but, of course, no wells had been drilled.

Then three weeks later, Calgarians, always unpalatable, became insufferable. For in Turner Valley, at five o'clock, May 14, the Dingman well came in. "At 2 A.M. there was 1000' of high grade oil in the well, rising rapidly with prospects of overflowing before morning." On May 16 the *Bulletin* said: "Calgary people have gone oil mad," "Oil shares jumped from $12.50 to $200 each." Forty new oil companies were floated in a week, and down-at-the-heels real estate salesmen switched from town lots to oil stocks.

Without bothering to lock their doors, a host of Edmonton's lot peddlers hurried off to Calgary. Others remained, however, and within three days of Dingman's discovery, one hundred new oil brokers' offices opened in Edmonton. Mayor McNamara caught the first train to Calgary, bought property in the oilfield, and announced that he would start drilling within six weeks. On May 21 the *Bulletin,* after a careful survey, estimated that $100,000 of good Edmonton money had been spent on oil stocks the day before. On May 22 it declared that oil brokerage offices had opened all down Jasper Avenue between McDougall Avenue (100 Street) and 101 Street. One company had rented a stand in a Jasper Avenue lunch counter, and another had a temporary office in the front of an ice-cream parlour. Edmontonians, alas, were casting their money into these to buy worthless paper, and, whereas Calgarians actually had oil, Edmonton's citizens had only Clapp and Huntley's drawings of oil strata printed in its *Gazette*. Edmonton's land boom had long since burst; so had Calgary's, but Calgarians, vexatious though they were, were blessed with an oil boom.

During 1914 Edmonton adopted its present system of numbering its streets and houses. As the city grew, the problem of finding one's way around became increasingly complex. The streets in the older areas of town had either been named after outstanding pioneers or bore geographical names, such as Winnipeg, Calgary and Peace River, and in passing from one to another did not follow any logical sequence. That situation was not too bad, but whenever someone subdivided a new part of town there were no restrictions upon what he might name the streets in his area. His streets linked up with those in adjoining areas but· they usually bore different names or different numbers.

For example, a person who lived on what is now 111 Avenue was on Muskoka Avenue if he was west of 121 Street; Norwood Boulevard if he was east of 101 Street; Shand Avenue if he was between the Grand Trunk Pacific tracks and 82 Street; and Gibson Avenue if he was east of Fraser's Lane (74 Street).

Amalgamation with Strathcona further complicated the problem. So did the annexation of another square mile on the southern outskirts, when on June 19, 1914, the city took in land which is now in the Allendale, Coronet, Duggan and Speedway subdivisions. The system in force in Strathcona was to number the streets and avenues as north-east, north-west, south-east or south-west of the intersection of our 82 Avenue and 104 Street.

The amalgamation, however, brought the whole business to a head, and after a plebiscite the council instituted our present numerical system, under which the point of reference became the corner of Jasper and First Street, although the latter was now renumbered 101 Street. Thoroughfares running generally north and south took their cue from it. The numbers of the streets decreased as they went east from 101 to 100 to 99, and so on, and increased as they went west from 101. The east and west thoroughfares were called avenues, although the name Jasper Avenue was retained, and the numbers of the avenues north of it began marching off as 102, 103, etc., while those south became 100 Avenue, 99 Avenue, and so on. Since from time to time some reference to one of the old street names comes up, we have included a table showing old and new names in the Appendix.

Not long after Strathcona disappeared as a city, Lord Strathcona, after whom it was called, died on January 21, 1914. The death of the old man, who long ago had been an Hudson's Bay Company employee and after rising in the company's service had played a major role in settling the Riel Rebellion, and who had finally gone on to organizing the CPR, marked the end of an era. His death came at the transitional point where pioneering had ended and was being succeeded by cultivation and where the rapid changes which were soon to overtake farming and to revolutionize life in the western cities that had grown up around his company's old trading posts were underway.

For during the previous decade the inventors and scientists had been coming up with new machines and processes at a rate never equalled previously. New farming machinery was appearing every year or so and the new-fangled automobile, which for nearly a decade had appeared on Jasper Avenue as a freak contrivance, was being remodelled year after year and had been improved to the point where everyone coveted one. Airplanes too were a new contraption which might just possibly have some application in the future. Then too, the Germans had brought out lighter-than-air craft and the word Zeppelin was known to everyone. It had some ominous aspects such as hovering overhead and seeing everything that was going on below, but the big powers, France, Germany and Britain, by some sort of high level agreement, had pulled its teeth, for they had made it illegal to drop things from it. Then too, Germany had built some very successful submarines, new and interesting devices, but here too the great powers had declared them illegal for war use.

Although in 1914 the West and Edmonton were not aware of how rapidly the era of change could overtake them, nevertheless forces in remote Europe had reached a point where they were soon to boil over. As soon as they should do so, Canada and even the innocent Far West were also to be scalded. The world which for so many decades had been in a state of relative peace was ready to explode.

Then on June 27, 1914, far away in a place called Sarajevo, capital of Bosnia in the remote Balkans, someone shot and killed Archduke Ferdinand, heir to the throne of Austro-Hungary. To Edmontonians this was a titillating bit of information to be stored away in their minds for the next time someone mentioned Vienna or waltzes or beer gardens.

To the German war lords, however, who had long been waiting for Der Tag when they would break out their banners, that was the day — an assassination that might be fanned into the war they awaited so eagerly. All during July, Germany, blowing on the coals, alarmed the rest of Europe.

Edmontonians, busy with civic scandal, new power plant schemes, the possibility of getting a supply of natural gas, and the fact that at last an E.D. & B.C. train had crossed the Athabasca, and fretting over the bursted land boom on the one hand and Calgary's newly found oil boom on the other, were too busy to even watch. Only on July 30, 1914, did the *Edmonton Journal* make any front page comment on the possibility of war.

On that day Germany delivered an ultimatum which France could not take. Hours later German armies, pointed at Paris, marched through Belgium. As suddenly as that, as surprisingly as that, World War One had started.

The 1912 U of A Graduating Class (The first class receiving all their university training in Alberta).

The Great War
1914-1918

chapter *15*

THE WAR WAS ON. Canada was involved in it, and Edmonton, hitherto shielded by the calm isolation of the agrarian West, was startled to find that it too was part of the world which included even remote Europe. A significant part of the settlers who had homesteaded during the last fifteen years had been Americans. With their pioneering background and the fact that of all settlers they had come with the most capital, they made a specially significant contribution to Alberta. Many of them came in to partake of any opportunities the city of Edmonton might hold, and by their aggressiveness and enterprise added much to its progress. Some generations previously, however, they had turned their backs on Europe, and with their eyes only on this pioneer land found it hard to see why that decadent continent should give them any concern. Moreover, few of them were any too kindly disposed to England, and, as far as they were concerned, if Germany conquered Britain, little would be lost. Feeling only slightly less indifferent towards England were most Canadians of two or three generations' standing.

To all but the more recent immigrants from the British Isles, the war in Europe was far away. Nevertheless, suddenly on the night of August 4, Edmontonians became thoroughly aroused. Crowds of several hundreds assembled outside the newspaper offices and sang "Rule Britannia," "The Navy Lads in Blue," and "The Maple Leaf Forever." The next evening was described as the wildest in Edmonton's history, when British, French and Russians, marching shoulder to shoulder through the streets, sang "God Save The King," "The Marseillaise," and "God The All Terrible," (the Russian National Anthem). Led by the Citizens' Band and the Edmonton Scottish Pipe Band, one thousand volunteers and reservists marched from the CPR station through the heart of the city to the east end. The patriotic demonstration continued far into the night.

Anxious for action, veterans of the South African War and former British regulars clamoured to enlist. Foremost amongst these were F. C. Jamieson and his Alberta Mounted Rifles' comrade, W. A. Griesbach. Within a few days they were off to war as Officer Commanding and Major, respectively, of the cavalry unit, which, since 1911 had been called the 19th Alberta Dragoons. In less than three weeks, this unit, 240 strong, entrained for Valcartier Camp. Equally prompt were the Legion of Frontiersmen and the Edmonton Scottish Pipe Band. Both left for Eastern Canada, where they were absorbed by the Princess Patricia's Canadian Light Infantry. On August 7 the Department of Militia authorized the 9th Battalion. Its quota was filled from the ranks of the peace-time group, the 101st Regiment (Edmonton Fusiliers), commanded by Lieut.-Colonel E. B. Edwards, and it hurried off to a training camp in the east.

Suddenly Edmonton was at war.

During three weeks, when each day's news bulletins were worse than yesterday's, Edmontonians were jerked from a world where only profits, oil shares and land titles had counted, to an unreal world where armed might with its brutality and barbarity, brushing aside all resistance and putting aside all humanity, swept across the benign Belgian countryside. During these three weeks, the Germans, a million strong, crumpled the Belgian forts and swaggered on into France. Even as Edmonton's 19th Dragoons and its 9th Battalion were recruiting, 90,000 men of the British Expeditionary Forces with their 15,000 horses and 400 cannon, in a desperate effort to help their allies to stay the invincible Germans, were landing in France. Even as the 9th Battalion was entraining at Edmonton, the flower of the British regiments was mowed down by the thousands at Mons. Fighting magnificently, countering cannon with raw courage and discipline, they hung on, backing to the Aisne River and then to the Marne, and there they stopped the Germans. Every day's news was more bitter than the last. And each day more iron entered each Albertan's soul. By the time the Battle of the Marne quietened down, Edmontonians were swarming to enlist.

As Lieut.-Colonel G. R. Stevens so well expressed it in his *A City Goes to War*.

"Men were no problem. From time to time the heart cries out, rejecting the routine, seeking the crusade. So it was in August 1914. Seldom has there been a greater outpouring of the spirit of generosity and of sacrifice. In the cities men formed long queues at the armouries; in the countryside they handed over their uncut crops and livestocks to their neighbours, locked the door and headed for the nearest railway station. When the momentous tidings filtered into the northland a complete survey party on the Slave River downed tools and walked out 400 miles to enlist. There was dedication in the air; . . ."

Speaking of the scores of men who on one occasion lined up in front of the little armoury on 100 Avenue (the former Land Titles Office) waiting for its doors to open so that they might enlist, the *Edmonton Bulletin* said:

"The temper of the men who kept vigil for hours outside the door to be sure of their places when recruiting commenced was indicative of the sentiment of the country. There were big men and little men, men clad in overalls shoulder to shoulder with men in furs, artisans and office workers, men of idleness, men of leisure and men who had leave of absence for the day to make their applications. There were men who carried active service medals from many campaigns beside lads who had never handled a musket, old men and young men — every kind of man — but all with a single purpose and determination; the defence of Empire and of honour.

"It was at three o'clock in the morning when the first man had stepped up to the door of the armoury. He was a robust fellow with frost-laden clothing. When the first call for men had reached the far north he left his home in the Peace River country and journeyed to Edmonton and had been waiting here ever since his arrival for the chance to enlist. Every few minutes his line was augmented and by nine o'clock the waiting men numbered over a hundred."

Events moved quickly. Just over two months after war was declared, the 19th Dragoons and the 9th Infantry Battalion sailed for England. For what morale-building effect it might have, each man carried one of Sam Hughes' booklets assuring its owner that, because of the speed with which they had been transformed from civilian clothes to uniforms, Canadians were the wonder warriors of the world, an opinion which, without batting an eye, all of us have believed ever since. About the same time, another cavalry unit, the 3rd Regiment Canadian Mounted Rifles, began recruiting in Calgary, Medicine Hat and Edmonton, and more Edmonton boys joined it. Then, as soon as Lieut.-Colonel F. C. Jamieson and his Dragoons landed in England, his second-in-command, Major Griesbach was called back to Canada, promoted to the rank of Lieut.-Colonel and charged with the task of raising the 49th Battalion. On December 26, he set to work, and before long this unit, recruited from Edmonton and the surrounding country, was marching up and down the city's streets. The 49th, which included such officers as Major C. Y. Weaver, an Edmonton lawyer, Major Justus Willson, Captain R. G. Hardisty and Captain R. H. Palmer, all of whom had seen previous war experience and all of whom were to rise to greater prominence, became Edmonton's favourite regiment.

While hundreds of Edmonton men fought for four years in various battalions and groupings, the 49th was the only Edmonton infantry regiment which went through the war as a unit and returned to the city as such. While men who had enlisted in other battalions saw service equally devastating, the experiences of the 49th are symbolic of the sacrifice and service of all Edmonton's soldiers.

Recruiting for that battalion started at the armoury on January 4, 1915. By now, all Anglo-Saxon Canadians came rolling up to join up beside the British, French and Belgians. To them too the war had become a reality. Still sitting on the fence were the neutral nationalists, the Swedes, Italians and the Americans, while pulled two ways between loyalty to their fatherland and to this new land were the Germanic peoples who found themselves in a most unenviable position. Their newspaper, the *Alberta Herold,* printed in German in Edmonton, was taking a strong pro-German stand. For instance, even in November 1914, it came out with gleeful articles and headlines as follows: "1st britischer Super-Dreadnought gesunken?" "Germans march again upon Warsaw," "Russians Entered into Trap and 23,000 Captured," and many others. Early in 1915, just in time to avoid being forced to do so, the *Herold* ceased publication.

Edmontonians could not do too much for their soldiers. On August 6 the city council discussed the case of civic employees who were enlisting, and voted to continue to pay half the man's salary to his dependants during his absence. Shortly afterwards it decided that, if the families of enlisted men could not keep up their payments for water, power and telephone, they should nevertheless continue to enjoy these civic services. Over and above this, the council continued free street railway tickets to soldiers. As well, a transfer company offered free storage for twelve months for soldiers' personal effects. The period would have been longer, but everyone felt that the war would be over before another year rolled around.

In October, as well as voting $5,000 to the Canadian Patriotic Fund and to the Edmonton Board of Welfare for assistance to soldiers' dependants, the council placed the Exhibition Grounds at the disposal of the military authorities. Thanks to Sam Hughes, the erratic Minister of Militia, these headquarters were prevented from having a "wet canteen". The local Red Cross, the St. John's Ambulance Association, the IODE, and the Women's Canadian Club, all stepped up their activities. Other ladies' clubs, lodges and union brotherhoods chipped in for comforts, entertainment and amusement for the troops. No city, nor its people, entered more wholeheartedly into the war effort and to the service of its soldiers and their dependants.

On February 11, 1915, Lieut.-Colonel Jamieson's 19th Dragoons went into action in France. Now Edmonton was really at war, hanging breathlessly on the news bulletins and the telegrams that started spelling out the names of dear ones wounded or killed. North of Ypres on April 22, 1915, they witnessed the first infamous gas attack, when the Canadian Division made a glorious name for itself.

On April 29, Edmonton's 49th Battalion entrained for the East and a week later sailed from Montreal. On June 14 the battalion marched into the lines of its confreres, the 9th Battalion Canadian Expeditionary Force, which was now a base formation at Shorncliff Camp. There they remained, training and marking time till the fall.

But Edmontonians, in sending the 49th Battalion overseas, had only started to raise battalions. Three more units were recruited early in 1915, and the fact that from all points of the countryside men came flocking in to join up alongside their city cousins increased the bond that bound Edmonton to the large area tributary to it. In April 1916 the 51st Infantry Battalion and the 63rd, under Lieut.-Colonel George B. Macleod, sailed for England. Hard on their heels, the 66th Battalion sailed in May 1916. None of these three regiments went to France as a unit, but all of their men saw bitter service there as reinforcements in other battalions. While they were recruiting and getting preliminary training, Edmonton swarmed with young soldiers and some not so young, who, by falsifying their ages, got past the recruiting medical officers.

Then, early in October 1915 came word that the 49th, which had been chafing under training in England, had finally succeeded in getting itself into the war. Of all the units raised in Alberta, it and the 31st and the 50th Battalions were the only ones to maintain their identity as they went through the struggle. For some months only small parties of the battalion had occasional contact with the actual front line, for they were kept back doing menial chores in the rain, muck and mud. It was January 1916 before the 49th took over a sector of the front line, and that month received its first casualties, three killed and eight wounded.

By June 1916 the battalion was in the thick of the Battle of Mount Sorrel, where it distinguished itself and where it endured its first heavy toll of casualties—52 killed, 265 wounded, and 69 missing. Once more, in September, the 49th showed its mettle at the Battle of Flers-Courcelette, losing 43 killed, 191 wounded and 19 missing. It was there, however, that the battalion gathered in its first Victoria Cross, for young Private John Chipman Kerr manifested some of the spirit that had led him to homestead in the Peace River country and to walk out to enlist.

Back in Edmonton, as the months went by and the casualty lists came out, the war began to come into focus. This was no lark which would soon be over, no shining crusade, but a bitter reality of death, crippling wounds and muddy trench warfare such as the world had never seen and actually was never to see again. So far, except for the sheer guts and the grim resistance of the British, French, Belgian, Canadian and Australian troops, the allies had nothing to exult over.

The defence the French put up at Verdun had seriously weakened that nation. The British fronts at Ypres and on the Somme ended in costly stalemates. Italy too had made little progress. And so it went on other fronts, in the Middle East, and at sea. Only the massive Russian forces seem to have made any headway. In the United States, President Wilson, still indecisive and apparently still unwilling to try to swing his people to the allied side, listened while millions of United States mothers sang "I did not raise my boy to be a soldier."

But in Edmonton, Americans, beginning to see the other side of the picture, began enlisting. For this there was plenty of opportunity, because as fast as one battalion was recruited, another began calling for volunteers. The 138th Battalion sailed in August 1916; the 194th Highlanders and the 202nd sailed in November. Finally, Lieut.-Colonel Jim Cornwall's 218th Battalion went overseas in February 1917.

Out of Alberta's relatively small population, some 25,000 men had enlisted, while their mothers, wives, widows, sisters and sweethearts knitted socks, rolled bandages, made pyjamas, or packed parcels with chocolate and other dainties for their men overseas. Employees in many fields assigned contributions to the Canadian Patriotic Fund. To provide well merited assistance on the home front in 1916, the legislature passed the Act for the Relief of Volunteers and Reservists, which provided a moratorium for all who had enlisted. Over at the university where the war had choked the enrollment down to three-quarters of what it had been, 222 men had enlisted by mid-summer 1916, and even that early in the war eleven of them had been killed.

The year 1914 had started in a depression and that year, moreover, the farmers' crops were poor, but the war's needs quickly put money into circulation. The ideal, or indeed heavy rainfall of 1915, ensured a heavy harvest. Wheat yielded 31.1 bushels to the acre, a phenomenal return never exceeded before or since. Moreover, the acreage seeded to wheat increased amazingly and doubled from 1,371,100 acres in the spring of 1914 to 2,605,000 in 1916. During that two-year period the average prices paid all farmers rose from 91¢ per bushel to $1.33. Here and there even an occasional farmer began to own a car, and Henry Ford's Model T's, durable yet simple in design and operation, began to bounce and chortle along country trails. The rich resources of land tributary to Edmonton were beginning to pay off.

Coal mines all over the province became busier than ever as their production, which in 1911 had been 1,694,564 tons, rose to 4,648,604 in 1916. All of Edmonton's local mines were hoisting coal as never before, and since the CNR and the GTP had opened up the mountain coals, mines at Pocohontas, Brule, Entwhistle and the Coal Branch all began to contribute wealth and to provide payrolls which found their way to Edmonton. As money from farm and mine began to pour into Edmonton, to be added to that gained from increased manufacturing and merchandising and to mingle with the private soldier's pay of $1.10 per day, Edmonton, in spite of a declining population, presented an active scene.

For one thing, on Christmas Day 1914, the new arena saw its first hockey game and was opened in a burst of glory. This game started an era in sport which was to make the barn-like arena — later re-christened The Gardens — the centre of civic interest for half a century.

Then during 1915 the Macdonald Hotel opened with a brilliant celebration, which was one of the few bright spots in an otherwise drab year. With the

Macdonald Edmonton had come a long way from the days of forty years previously when Donald Ross's "pioneer house of accommodation" had been the only hotel in Alberta, to this splendid new chateau-type edifice which in all its appointments was the equal of anything in Canada. During this interval the Alberta Hotel, which had installed the first elevator in the city, had become the leading hostelry (a claim sometimes disputed by the Windsor) and finally had been superseded by the King Edward. Now the new "Mac" became the centre for civic and social entertainment, a position it was to maintain for decades.

Despite the fact that the arena and the Mac had been opened and the fact that everyone was busy, the face of Edmonton did not change. A few other buildings which had been under construction were completed, including Grandin Separate School and Kenny McLeod's marvellous nine-storey building. Aside from finishing up these structures, very little other building took place.

For at last the truth was out; the Edmonton of 1912 and 1913 was badly overexpanded and overextended, and years must elapse before the development of even Alberta's rich resources would warrant a city of the size or area to which Edmonton had grown. The optimism of the boom days, assuming that Alberta's remarkable expansion during the decade ending 1911 would go on and on — a growth that had quadrupled Alberta's population and one which during the five years ending in 1911 had more than doubled — that optimism was over. For the depression of 1913 had slowed the growth to a crawl, and the war had throttled back the influx of immigrants to a trickle. No longer was money poured out to build branch railway lines all over the place. The rosy-tinted money that had poured in from outside had given a false but temporary blush to Alberta's economy and now it was money on which its investors were looking for a return.

Edmonton's great boom was now but a memory. Practically the only railway construction capital still coming in was balancing itself precariously on the E.D. & B.C. Railway's muskeg-ballasted right-of-way, winding its way through black spruce forest towards the Peace River country. The much touted CNR and GTP, which Edmontonians had welcomed so warmly, had blasted their separate lines through mountains and canyons to the Pacific and had become transcontinentals, only to find that very few people had really wanted them after all, and that fewer still were willing to ride on the trains or to load their box-cars with paying freight. By 1916 both of them were bankrupt. Their promoters, having enjoyed years of interesting work and having put by fortunes for a rainy day, sat back to enjoy their wealth. Their investors who had put money into their securities found that the rainy days were here indeed, and stood by helplessly while their lithographically perfect bonds dissolved into worthless paper. The politicians who had pocketed all the loot that came their way and in return had granted the promoters millions of acres of the country's finest lands, kept their mouths shut and looked away. The government, which had been guided by the politicians' greed and the promoters' guile, had to conduct salvage operations, assume debts and defunct roadbeds and rolling stock, and out of the mess disgorged the Canadian National Railway.

As a result of all the slackening in the pace of actual economic expansion from that conjured up a few years previously, Edmonton's population, which in 1914 had been 72,516, dropped off to 53,846 by 1916. Some of this falling off was due to men enlisting, but the rest was caused by individuals adjusting themselves to the city's inability to provide economic livelihood for them and moving away.

In a similar manner, Edmonton's tax rolls came in for readjustment. In the scores of boom-time subdivisions titles to lots were acquired by paying down a very small margin in the hope that next day some other softy would take them off one's hands. When next day that happened, all was well with the world and the venturesome gambler plunged his augmented paper profit into still another venture. But a day came when the boom bust, and no one wanted to take any more lots off anyone's hands. Before that it had been like a game of musical chairs, with more chairs than players, so that when the music stopped everyone landed safely and then the music set off again. But one day, by some malign mischance, somehow, somebody shifted the chairs and took all but one or two away, and when the music stopped, one or two lucky ones were found sitting, while all the rest of the gaily dancing mob found themselves standing up laden with titles to lots. And then the stern faced city assessor came demanding to know who owned each lot and gleefully handing out tax notices. This was a rule of the game that no one had remembered, and when confronted with it many slipped down to Calgary. For the southern city had invented a similar game played with oil stocks in which, when the player got mowed down, no aftermath of a spoil-sport came along to thrust tax notices into empty purses.

Those who stayed with Edmonton, the valiant 53,846 still stuck with their lots, stretched their credit to the limit and hoped that by some miracle they could break even. But it was no good. After dunning them politely but persistently for three or four years, the city tax man took title to their lots. Not that the city wanted them, but because the law said that was the thing to do. So, from time to time, the Edmonton newspapers carried multi-page spreads listing the lots to be sold at the next auction. As a result, Roland Sladden, the city clerk, filled his every idle moment during 1915 and 1916 and many a subsequent year auctioning tax sale lots in public sales. In all, tens of thousands of lots went under the hammer in the quiet room where no one ever bid and where day after day Sladden pronounced the formula "Sold to the City of Edmonton," until for nearly every man, woman and child left in the city, one lot was taken off the tax rolls and transferred to a city which did not need them, and, as it turned out, was not to sell them for three decades.

Not only were the war years a time of reckoning for real estate hopefuls, but they brought everyone else down to earth. To all those who had unthinkingly believed that the new world, and particularly the free West, was somehow removed from the realm of human frailty and that somehow or other it had developed a breed of superior beings, the war came as an eye-opener. Neither the new world nor the new West could live in monastic seclusion. Moreover, none of its saintliness had rubbed off on the mass of mankind. After all, the world was a sinful place and a theatre where the full play of human emotions of love, hatred, suspicion, greed and ambition, went on regardless of wishful thinking, and from it not even quiet little backwaters such as Edmonton could remain insulated. Having tasted all this disillusionment, Americans, Canadians, and Edmontonians had to recast their thinking. The world of the previous decades of the great open spaces was indeed a thing of the past. From here on, even Edmonton would have to live in a changing world and to learn to become part of it.

So far, aside from creating some minor commodity shortages, the war had scarcely affected business. One activity that it could not quench was the incurable itch that goads men into searching for oil or gas. Acting upon the recommendation the geologists Clapp and Huntley had made, the Industrial Association drilled a well at Viking, eighty miles south-east. At last luck was with Edmontonians, for on November 4, 1914, the discovery well roared wide open. So did the people of Viking. According to the Extra issued by the local paper next day:

"Viking sprang into gas fame early Wednesday morning November 4, 1914, when the drillers at the Viking gas well struck a flow of gas that exceeds the expectation of the experts who located the well.

"C. M. Flickinger, one of the crew rode with lightning speed on his motor cycle into town and got the telegraph and telephone wires busy at sunrise."

For all the good his rapid ride did, Flickinger might as well have walked into Viking, or not even bothered. Between civic turmoil which unhorsed Edmonton's Mayor Billy McNamara, squabbling over whether a company or the city should undertake the venture of supplying gas, and the electors voting themselves into a stalemate, a year and a half elapsed before, late in 1915, the Northern Natural Gas Development Company obtained a franchise. Even then eight years were to go by before gas reached Edmonton!

Natural gas was not the only new resource Edmontonians had their eyes on. In 1915 their electrical power situation was unsatisfactory, and their plant would soon need enlarging. So despite the pleas of the coal mine operators, the city entered into a contract with a company which proposed to build a hydro plant at Rocky Rapids, some one hundred miles up the Saskatchewan River and to sell power to the city. Unfortunately, due to the difficulty of raising large sums of money in wartime, which the Viking Gas Company also encountered, the scheme fell through. It left two souvenirs of its passing; one in a rural post office established near the Rapids, which was called Power House, and the other, the good faith deposit of $50,000, which fell into the city treasury.

It was a fall of another sort, a rainfall, which kept Edmontonians hopping that summer. For by raising the level of the river four feet higher than it had been in 1899, it did damage at Edmonton estimated at $750,000. This estimate, which was probably conservative, was due to flooding Fraser's, Ross's and Gallagher's flats, parts of them to a depth of ten feet and washing away the Edmonton Lumber Company's mill and Walter's mill, as well as their log booms. The city electric light and pumping plants had to be shut down because the water put out the fires in the boilers. Many houses were destroyed, and the damage to others was very great, while for varying periods eight hundred families were rendered homeless. The only death, however, was that of an infant which its mother dropped into the swirling waters when trying to make her way along a floating sidewalk.

That year too old Fort Edmonton was torn down. As the October 13 *Journal* said:

"Something resembling panic reigned among citizens who value the historic, when the news spread abroad this morning that the fort was 'taken' by sacrilegious workmen. This fear was allayed by the statement . . . that Edmonton was still to retain its fort . . .

"Removal operations commenced Monday afternoon (Oct. 11) on the main building of the group and by noon today it was practically razed to the ground. It is intended to pull the buildings down, remove them to a permanent site, and rebuild them. The buildings have become somewhat dilapidated through lack of care. They will be rebuilt and renovated without interfering with their historic characteristics and adapted to museum purposes."

But someone in authority lied. He is reported to have told his foreman to hurry up and get "that thing" torn down. "Once it's out of the way everybody will forget."

All in all, 1915 had been an eventful year, with the war in progress, with votes for a hydro scheme and for and against natural gas, and with a once-in-a lifetime flood. Even that, however, did not end the excitement, for no sooner had these issues faded into the past than a new one raised its head. That was prohibition. Across nearly all of Canada, eager reformers, lacking in understanding of human nature but overflowing with zeal, had gradually pressed their case until during the war years most provinces clamped down various laws prohibiting the manufacture and sale of spirituous liquors. Alberta, caught in the tide raised by emerging women's organizations, including the recently convened farm women, the temperance, and other Protestant church groups, fell into the trap. In 1916, in response to their catchy campaign theme song "Prohibition, Prohibition,/ To the polls away/ Vote for Prohibition/ On election day./" Alberta became dry. The actual voting on the question was held on July 21, 1915, with the drys winning over the wets by 58,295 to 37,509.

Experience proved the law to be a mistake. Although the ardent admonitions of crusaders, aided by the somewhat doubtful temperance hopes of the ordinary citizens had shut the saloons, legislation alone could not remove the age-old thirst from parched throats, and succeeded only in replacing the sociability of a friendly drink with furtive trips to the "blind pig". Laws could stop legal sale of liquor, but chemistry and the act of producing alcohol from fermented grain allied to human demand, all aided by nefarious business enterprises, proved too elementary and elemental to be suppressed by laws. In the country, "stills" operated

The great flood of 1915

in the safety of the bush. In the cities, including Edmonton, a vast network of blind pigs, usually in the poorer sections of town and often associated with brothels, sprang up to set the law at naught and to vex loyal policemen, who should have been put to more useful tasks.

Against this gloomy background, Katherine Stinson, the amazing twenty-year-old aviatrix, astounded Edmonton's exhibition crowds with her incredible daring as she looped and dived, spiralled and plummeted her Curtiss biplane. She flew up from Texas to perform in the city, and her visits in 1916 and in two subsequent years let thousands of gaping Albertans see their very first aeroplane. Even though the war news recorded the progress the Royal Air Force was making with its new reconnaissance planes, and even though letters began to tell of sons or friends switching from the army to the air force to fly these flimsy machines, few Albertans had ever seen one.

Amongst the thousands watching this famous woman and gasping at her performances were a group of high school girls, who, although totally unaware of it, were shortly to go on to a fame equal to Katherine Stinson's. This group, all from the recently opened McDougall Commercial High School, coached by one of their teachers, J. Percy Page, had already achieved local fame. In 1914, after winning the Alberta Provincial Basketball Championship, they formed the Commercial Graduates' Basketball Club—soon to be known world-wide as the "Grads". In 1915 and 1916 they retained their provincial championship, and thereafter for a total of twenty-five years were to bring more fame to Edmonton than any other individual organization or event.

The war years to the end of 1916, while they drastically changed the world outlook and brought bereavement to many an Edmonton mother and wife, made little economic impression on the city. Still suffering from the indigestion induced by the boom, the war's economic uplift may have kept Edmonton from collapsing, but it did not send it surging ahead. One small annexation was under consideration, and when it came about in 1917 the city took in the quarter of a square mile that had been the hamlet of Calder. No noticeable change altered Edmonton's skyline or its byways. Though everyone was employed, the population, still adjusting itself, had continued to drop. Thus far the war's effect on the food supply was negligible. Grocers were asked to try to prevent hoarding and told to try to ration out their supply of sugar and one or two other commodities, but there were no other clamps on consumer spending. Since the war had started, the cost of living had gone up ten percent, but since it had been depressed to start with, the effect was scarcely noticeable.

The provincial scene in which the economy was perhaps seventy-five percent agrarian was optimistic. The two new railways giving access to millions of new acres were wobbling their way north over muskegs and making good progress. By the fall of 1916 the E.D. & B.C. had reached Spirit River and was heading for Grande Prairie and Peace River Crossing. The Alberta Great Waterways had reached Lac La Biche, where a rejuvenated hamlet a hundred years old was stretching itself to fill up its magnificent setting on the shores of its majestic lake. Throughout all the province, wheat and cattle were the farmers' standby, and since the start of the war the wheat acreage had doubled and its selling price was good.

Horses, still holding the agricultural front, were no strangers when they drew farmers' wagons to Edmonton's market square, for in spite of several smelly cars, the city was still in the horse era. The gasoline barrel, however, was beginning its battle with the oat bucket. In 1913, in all of Alberta, there had been only 3,773 cars, and now three years later, 9,707 of them were putting around getting in the horses' way and cluttering up streets and trails. Civilians had begun to realize their value. And they were real values too, especially the Model T Fords, the Tin Lizzies. Now and then they broke down, but when they did an axle shaft cost $1.90, a front axle, installed, $12. Any fender cost $4. A whole new radiator, however, was expensive at $15, while a complete engine block set one back $25. On farms and in cities, cars were challenging the old lumber wagon.

Canada's and Britain's armies, however, still bewildered by the German's mechanization and air force, sent charging cavalry to be mowed down by machine-guns, and still lumbered along supported by horse-drawn wagons. In the summer of 1916, at Sarcee Camp outside Calgary, where many Edmonton soldiers were training, the Governor-General, the Duke of Connaught, came to review the troops. Midst pirouetting equestrian staff officers, the Duke received the salutes. Leading the march past, a troop of cavalry preceded the score of foot-slogging battalions, and finally when the band struck up the old tune, the tune already obsolete, "Wait For The Wagons — Wait For The Wagons," the Army Service Corps, the army's supporting troops, trundled their horse-drawn vehicles past the saluting point. Even as they did so, however, everyone from Duke to drummer boy already knew that modern warfare would no longer wait for the wagons.

For that matter, all civilian life was changing too, and at a rate never witnessed before. For one thing, movies, still silent but with a printed dialogue, had risen to dominate the entertainment world. With them came a new set of heroes; Charlie Chaplin with his droll humour, Mack Sennett with his speedy comics, Fatty Arbuckle, the Keystone Cops, and pie throwing. For the first time, actresses became continent-wide celebrities; Mary Pickford, Mabel Normand, Mae Marsh and Theda Bara, the vamp. For relief from the realities of war hundreds flocked to the movies.

Ordinary women too began to share in the changed era when the war released them from the rigidities of the nineteenth century traditions. From slope-shouldered, shapeless dresses, women began to puff out their skirts and to shorten them. To their collars, wrapped high up to the ear tips, and their small hats perched tall, they began to add monkey fur and silver fox and flared coats.

For women were on the march. In April 1916 the Alberta legislature gave them the right to vote in municipal and civic elections. Later that year in Edmonton, Mrs. Emily Murphy, the author, was made a police magistrate.

Meanwhile, the Americans entered the war on the allied side. This action immediately gave direction to a large number of Albertans of Anglo-Saxon stock who had emigrated from the isolationist mid-continental United States and to many immigrants of Germanic extraction, all of whom felt that they could now aid in the war effort with a clear conscience.

Mounting casualties at the front stirred friends and relatives in Canada to resent those who had not enlisted, the "slackers", or those who hung back in the effort entailed by the "War to Make the World Safe for Democracy." In this spirit, in June 1917, the Canadian government introduced compulsory military service.

On February 12, 1917, the 49th Battalion lost its first commander when W. A. Griesbach was promoted to brigadier and given the command of the 1st Canadian Brigade. He was succeeded by Lieut:-Colonel R. H. Palmer.

Then in April the 49th was in the thick of the Battle of Vimy Ridge. August found them slugging it out at Hill 70 and by November they were in the midst of the major engagement at Passchendaele. During this battle the battalion earned its

*Major-General the Honourable
W. A. Griesbach*

second Victoria Cross, when young Private C. J. Kinross, from down Sedgewick way, attacked a machine-gun. Alone and in broad daylight, he rushed it against point-blank fire, killing its crew of six men and wrecking the gun.

Even though the Germans were throwing in everything they had in an effort to break through, crumple and separate the allies, by mid-summer 1918 everyone knew that they had failed. Then once more at the Battle of Amiens, hundreds of Edmonton's soldiers in various fighting units, including the 49th Battalion, took a leading part as the allied armies began pressing the enemy back. The next major engagements were the Battle of the Scarpe at the end of August, and a month later at Canal du Nord.

Then a month later still, after moving quickly over the fields of France, mopping up small groups of Germans and pursuing others, Canada's armies came to the end of hostilities. November 11, 1918, had arrived. With it came emotional exhaustion, memories of four years of hell and horror, hardihood and heroism, and the prospects of a peaceful return to Edmonton.

Edmonton's Exhibition Grounds in action.

The 49th Battalion returns, March, 1919.

The Roaring Twenties
1919-1929

chapter *16*

I N THE FALL OF 1918, however, when everyone, realizing that victory was near, looked forward to the day of rejoicing, a strange malady, the Spanish Flu, stalked the world. The first Alberta cases occurred when six infected train passengers alighted in Calgary on October 4. By October 18, although no Edmontonian as yet had caught the disease, all city schools, churches and theatres were closed, and public meetings banned. Next day forty-one cases were reported in Edmonton, and three days later that figure had risen to 127. The provincial Board of Health ordered everyone to wear gauze face masks in public.

By October 26, when 695 cases had been reported, the authorities had divided Edmonton into districts, each in charge of a graduate nurse, and had allotted to each as many volunteer helpers as were available. Pembina Hall at the university had been set aside as a temporary hospital, capable of caring for 150 cases. By October 30, 2,000 cases had been reported, and the city's death toll had risen to forty-four.

For this dread disease killed swiftly. Many it spared. Some it smote lightly and they lived. Others, mainly the young adults, the vigorous providers and the young mothers, it cut off. One day the victim complained of lassitude and a headache. Next morning he was delirious, and, if he had been marked by the 'flu for one of its victims, he died before another sunrise. Whole families came down with it, and though it was rarely fatal to all of them, in some cases it did claim mother, father and children.

Many were stricken in hotels, but there was no place to take them. To November 4, Edmonton's death toll was 120, and 29 more died next day. On November 6, 54 more died, the highest mortality in any one day. By November 11 —Armistice Day—the toll stood at 262, but the number of new cases was falling off. The province ordered all large stores and businesses to remain closed until 12:30 each day, in order to free more people for volunteer work.

News of the Armistice reached Edmonton at 2 P.M. All over town alert citizens, waiting for the word, set off a shrieking chorus of factory whistles, bells, and the fire department's sirens. Work stopped. As if by magic, and heedless of the 'flu, crowds gathered in the streets. That night impromptu parades, shouting and whooping, passed and repassed along Jasper Avenue. At the corner of Jasper and 101 Street the frolic focused around a big bonfire.

Next day an incessant stream of decorated automobiles paraded back and forth past sidewalks lined with flag-waving pedestrians. That evening the Great War Veterans organized a torch-light parade which converted Jasper Avenue into a river of lights and packed humanity. The war to make the world safe for democracy was over and we had won.

Simultaneously, we were winning the battle with the Spanish Flu. As November wore on, the situation eased slightly. On November 20, the total deaths in the city stood at 354, and during the next four days rose to 362, 363, 369 and 377. Up to that time, at the emergency hospital in Pembina Hall, 301 patients had been admitted, 174 had been discharged, and 72 had died. By the end of November, however, the city lifted the ban on church and theatre assemblies, but proposed to keep public schools closed till January 2. Then November 27 set a welcome record. For the first day since the scourge had struck, no deaths were reported. Several new cases continued to be reported for another month, however, but they were less deadly. During the first two weeks of December, 507 cases were noted, accompanied by 43 fatalities, but the epidemic was almost over.

Over the whole province some 30,000 had caught the disease, and before the end of the year one in every ten of them had died, a total of 3,259, of which Calgary accounted for 341 and Edmonton 445. As the New Year came in, a chastened and a prayerful Edmonton bowed its head in thankfulness that the affliction had passed on.

Then in the forenoon of March 22, four years less one month since the battalion had left Edmonton, 30,000 citizens lined Jasper Avenue and crowded down to the CPR station to watch the 49th come home. Admission to the station and the platform had been restricted to the Next-of-Kin Association, while along the approaches to the station a thousand veterans were drawn up. Waiting to welcome the warriors were Lieutenant-Governor Brett, Premier Charles Stewart, Mayor Joe Clarke, Bishop Gray, and many other clerics and dignitaries. As the first train, rumbling over the High Level Bridge came in sight, clacked over the Jasper Avenue overpass and hissed to a stop, the 49th returned. The Edmonton Journal News Boys' Band struck up to add its welcome to the cheers. Never had there been such a day in Edmonton's history.

Eventually, with the crowd falling in behind it, the battalion marched east through the crowds lining Jasper Avenue, turned onto 101 Street, then west again to the armouries. There, for the last time, the 49th Battalion forming up, heard its last "Dismiss," and the war was over.

That evening, at a citizens' reception at the armouries, Lieutenant-Governor Brett presented Brigadier Griesbach with an illuminated address. At the same time, the city of Edmonton gave him the dress sword which has become a memento of the war, during which Edmonton and its tributary territory raised eleven battalions and contributed some 20,000 men — the war to end all wars.

During the ensuing weeks the returned men, trying to get their ideas back into a peacetime focus, had a difficult time. Between them and those who had not gone to war a wide gulf of comprehension yawned. Bridging it called for many readjustments, and these depended on the character of the individual. After a reasonable interval, though still and forever marked with the mauling of four years' nightmare, most of the returned men forced themselves back into their old pattern of civilian endeavour. These were the great majority, those of essentially stable mould. A small minority, those whose inherent instability had inevitably been augmented by the war's fearful emotions, felt that peace owed them everything. On the whole, to their credit, the returned men, overcoming odds never comprehended by their civilian cousins, soon filled their old niches and went on to successes that the war had merely interrupted.

Their adjustment was made more difficult because they had returned to a hornet's nest of labour unrest. For this there was some cause, as the workers, never too well paid, watched the bare-faced graft practised by the war profiteers. Behind the unrest too stood the old IWW organization which became that sinister progenitor of the OBU, the One Big Union, which, when it was launched in Calgary in March 1919, brought with it fear of a Canada-wide revolution. The celebrated Winnipeg strike of 1919 was but one of its manifestations, while in Edmonton the publication of the "Soviet" and a general strike were others. The strike commenced on May 26 and while it lasted, though bread and milk deliveries were maintained, power to industries was cut off and the street car service stopped. By May 31 the barbers had returned to their chairs, the electric and dairy workers were back, the movie houses reopened, and teamsters and taxi drivers resumed work. The general strike, which for a time threatened to get out of hand, had petered out, but it had an unsettling impact upon the returned men.

It was such a period of unrest that might have been expected to produce a mayor like Joe Clarke. A colorful character, he was expert at fabricating causes for the underdog — causes of great sentient if of little economic sense. On such causes he rode to power during 1919 and 1920 to produce a stirring if unproductive era in civic politics.

During the first few weeks, as the ex-soldiers passed back and forth along Edmonton's streets, they realized that only in the matter of traffic had the city really changed. Cars were not only common now, but plentiful. By 1919 there were ten times as many cars driving up and down Jasper Avenue as there had been in 1913. In 1916 Alberta had 9,707 cars, while 1917 had 20,624, and now in 1919 there was 34,000. These cars, Buicks, Hupmobiles, Hudson Sixes, Chevrolet 490's and Dodges, imparted a new busyness to the streets.

Actually, it was good to walk about Edmonton, which, with its wide, straight streets and its frequent open spaces, was such a far cry from the cramped crookedness of English or French towns with their miles of stone buildings cemented together. For, as the legacy of the boom days, Edmonton was like a vast crossword puzzle on which a few words only had been filled. Along Jasper Avenue, from 102 Street west to 109 Street, one or two three-storey brick buildings on each side of the street and usually on corners, indicated where the side streets took off. Between these brick bastions, wooden false-fronted stores, sometimes with a second storey, were sprinkled at random, while weeds bloomed or trash blew about over half the lots in each block. Here and there, usually on a corner lot, stood a small frame building; a shoemaker's shop, a smoke-shop, a popcorn stand, or a grocery store. Even Jasper Avenue left plenty of room for fresh air to circulate.

A block or so off it and a few blocks north along 101 Street, all paving stopped, to be succeeded for some blocks by gravelled streets and then by mud or rutted dust. Rocking their way along some of the streets and main avenues, streetcars, swaying and plunging and tearing their trolleys free from the wires, rolled and lurched along precariously on rails elevated on ties hidden by weeds and rose bushes. Usually through residential streets but frequently over marshes or through blocks still sporting their undisturbed forest, the dauntless motormen guided their streetcars to varied destinations.

If downtown Edmonton was a crossword puzzle half filled in, its outlying suburbs were a puzzle barely started. There were, for instance, the little settlements out Jasper Place way and the railroad colony of Calder. Five miles east of it, across the meadows, was the packing plant community of North Edmonton, and far around to the right, along the river bank, four or five miles from downtown, was the posh Highlands district. Across the river from the Macdonald Hotel and far beyond the modest homes dotted along Strathcona Road lay Strathcona, ending near Gainer's Packing Plant in King Edward and Bonnie Doon. Then, heading west along a sketchy forest-wrapped trail and skirting McKernan Lake, the haunt of nesting ducks, 76 Avenue led to the little settlement high above the silvery Saskatchewan, near where the Whitemud Creek road started down the hill. While over the years estimates of the population of this hamlet varied from a pessimistic fourteen to a wildly inflated thirty — not houses, but people — it was nevertheless served by a streetcar line. The trip by trolley to any of these outlying retreats, McKernan Lake, North Edmonton, Calder or the Highlands, was usually an interesting, invariably a leisurely, and at times a lonely achievement. For the Edmonton of 1919, with tens of thousands of empty lots, had plenty of room to grow. Interloping Calgarians scoffed, saying that Edmonton, with its far-flung boundaries, was the largest city in Canada with the least population. In silence but not in humility, Edmontonians bided their time.

But in 1919, when after an absence of five years the soldiers returned, the city's appearance had not improved. It was true that the tents, which in the boom days had formed a fringe between town and country, were gone. So were some 18,000 people who had been here in 1914, for now the population was down to the 54,000 mark. So were the transient, map-bedecked real estate offices. So were the saloons, but their functions were being filled officially by drug stores dispensing liquor by prescription and unofficially by furtive bootleg joints concentrated mainly, though far from wholly, in the downtown area east of 101 Street and north of Jasper Avenue. Prohibition had driven liquor underground.

As well as the price of liquor, the cost of living had risen — some 58% since 1914. But if it cost more to live, everybody had more money to jingle, and 1919 was a far contrast from the depression five years earlier. Everyone was prosperous, and everyone expressed that affluence by a desire to live more abundantly. The spirit of change was in the air.

In the farming areas where the price of wheat had risen from 61¢ per bushel in the spring of 1914 to $2.31 by the spring of 1920, and where in general good yields had prevailed, the farmers had tripled the acres sown to wheat from 1,371,100 in 1914 to 4,074,500 in 1920.

By this time Marquis wheat, which had made its modest appearance in the West in 1909, had come into its own as the great wheat ideally suited to Alberta's harsh climate. Without it, the farming picture would have been vastly different and the farm economy vastly poorer. Moreover, in all of Alberta in 1911 some 17 million acres had been settled and ten years later that had risen to 27 million. During the same period, the acres under cultivation had nearly trebled. Then too, while most of the land in the south of the province had been taken, millions of acres north of Edmonton were still unclaimed. As more farmers came in to till it, Edmonton had to grow.

It began to look as if the optimists of 1913 had been right after all when they had over-built and over-expanded Edmonton. It began to look as if the straggly skeleton formed by the city's sparsely garbed streets radiating out through empty spaces to remote suburbs such as Calder and Bonnie Doon might some day be clothed with houses, stores, and maybe even an occasional garage. Though there had been little change in Edmonton for several years surely renewed growth was not far away.

But Edmonton's growth did not hinge on farmers alone. The city fell heir to all the business emanating in the Far North — Lake Athabasca, Great Slave Lake and the Mackenzie Basin. Now that the E.D. & B.C. had reached the Peace River and the AGW had nearly reached Fort McMurray, Edmonton had further consolidated its position as the Gateway to the North. In that direction lay a great future. For it would only be a matter of time till more farmers moved into the north and settled all the way to Keg River and to Fort Vermilion, and till Canada's North really opened up. For a century Edmonton had been the handmaiden to the North; soon the city would be its beneficiary.

In 1920, with the release of millions of young men from the daily shadow of death, the world entered one of its fastest moving decades. So did Edmonton when its thousands of young men came back all bent on remaking the world, on having a good time, or at least better times, and all bent on utilizing some of the scientific know-how that the war had uncovered. They were in a mood to put to pleasant use the relatively new inventions of the motor car, motion pictures, jazz, radio, and aeroplanes.

Amongst the hundreds of brilliant, daring young men with the larger vision was a remarkable group of youths who, having joined the army, were snapped up by the Royal Air Force and became pilots or air engineers. Every Canadian city had its share of them, but none was in a better position to profit by them than Edmonton, for beyond its vast farming areas lay a thinly populated hinterland, and beyond that extended a remote resource-filled north. Of these war pilots, Edmonton could boast of "Wop" May, George Gorman, Roy Brown, Keith Tailyour, "Punch" Dickins, and Jimmy Bell, who, before the war, had worked for the city engineer's department. In that group, although Edmontonians were slow to realize it, the city had an asset beyond measure.

Every Edmontonian, and indeed every Canadian, knew Wop May and Roy Brown. Between the two they made headlines when they had shot down Germany's apparently invincible Great Red Knight, Baron Richtofen, the most famous and the most feared enemy ace. On his first combat mission, Wop May had been attacked by Richtofen, and then from out of the dogfight Brown had swooped and shot down the Red Knight. Both Brown, who stayed in the east after the war, and May went on to become fighters as deadly as the Baron had been, and when Wop returned to Edmonton wearing the ribbon of the Distinguished Flying Cross he had thirteen enemy planes to his credit. Surely if anyone could lift Edmonton into the air age, May could.

During the war, with her exhibition performances Katherine Stinson had thrilled Edmontonians. About that time they had subscribed a fund to help the RAF buy more planes, and in recognition of their generosity the air force had named one of their "Jennys," a Curtiss JN4, the "EDMONTON". When the war was over, the air force donated this particular plane to the city, which stored it away in the Manufacturers' Building at the Exhibition Grounds. Between Katherine

Wop May — First War Ace and a leader in Edmonton's civilian flying.

Stinson, the "EDMONTON", Wop May and Roy Brown, Edmontonians were becoming air-minded.

In May 1919, Wop May and his brother Court organized the May Airplanes Ltd. with a capital of $20,000, and the *Edmonton Journal* announced that "Commercial aviation on a big scale will be carried out by well known city businessmen." Elaborating on this, Court May said: "Photography and aerial map-making will be one of the main objects of the company. We have also secured the agency for a reliable make of plane which should retail in Edmonton at $3000."

That month the May brothers rented the "EDMONTON" from the city for $25 a month, and they were in business. For an airport, they arranged with farmer Walter Sporle to use his pasture northwest of the city as a landing field, and put up a rough shed for a hangar. Operating from there, they began stunting, delivering token shipments of newspapers to nearby towns, taking passengers aloft for a spin and giving flying exhibitions at Western Canada "B" Circuit Fairs. Before long, as the *Bulletin* said: "Already thirty-five passengers have ridden in the EDMONTON. The plane has gone up to 3,500 feet, the highest yet in western Canada." Now and then to stir Edmontonians up, May flew under the High Level Bridge, and once, swooping low over the Ross Flats Field, he piloted Mayor Joe Clarke when he threw the first ball in an inter-city baseball game.

Other returned fliers had the same idea as Wop May, and in 1919 Captain Keith Tailyour induced Jock McNeill, the key figure in Edmonton's taxi and moving business, to set up another company. He and Tailyour, associated with E. Owens, R. L. Green and Peter McArthur, incorporated the *Edmonton Airplane Company* and proposed to start daily flights, "two to four trips a day as the demand warrants," and to start a service to Peace River. For this they bought an Avro Plane. For an air harbour they leased a corner of the Hagmann farm, which some years previously during the real estate boom had figured so prominently.

On it, near the end of Portage Avenue, where the Edmonton Industrial Airport is, they put up a rough hangar.

In the fall of 1919, the Edmonton Air Force Association came into being. About this time, Ottawa set up the Canadian Air Board to keep an eye on flying activities, and it began to make rules designed to prevent hazardous low flying and stunting. As well, it began licensing pilots and aircraft. The old Jenny, the EDMONTON, was registered as C-AA1. Wop May and George Gorman received Commercial licenses Nos. 7 and 8, and Peter Derbyshire, their mechanic, got Air Engineer's Certificate No. 6. Though Edmonton was certainly not behind any other city in its air-mindedness, nevertheless, those venturesome enough to put their money into planes and flying facilities, like those who ventured into oil exploration, had little assurance of success.

Late in 1920, however, the news of Imperial Oil Limited's discovery at Fort Norman electrified Edmontonians. Oil! A new oilfield, a phenomenon as rare in Canada as a breathless politician. All Canadians pricked up their ears, but Edmontonians talked of nothing else. Though the new field was down the great Mackenzie River, nearly a thousand miles away, Edmontonians had a prior claim to pride in it, because it was in their bailiwick — in Edmonton's Northland. The Imperial Oil Company, vitally concerned with following up its find, bought two old German all-metal Junkers, and, hiring George Gorman and Elmer Fullerton, sent them north. At Fort Simpson, three hundred miles short of Fort Norman, the propellers on each of the planes were smashed.

Then northern ingenuity went to work, and with hand tools and some oak sleigh boards, fashioned a propeller, fastening it together with glue made on the spot from moose hides. The plane crews, the Hudson's Bay men and the mission staff all pitched in while the mechanics overhauled one plane's engine. When they tried the new propeller it stood the stress and the crew returned to Edmonton without incident.

By this time, however, the Imperial Oil had had enough of aeroplanes. Moreover, the excitement of the new oilfield had died down. The neat little package that Edmontonians had envisaged, combining oil age and air age, had cracked up. And with it, for the time being, went the hopes of Edmonton's frustrated airmen. Gorman left for California, Fullerton went back east to the Air Force, Punch Dickins got a job flying with the forestry patrol, Jimmy Bell continued to work for the Soldier Settlement Board, Wop Map went to work as a salesman, and weeds covered the air-strips.

Edmontonians, however, were having more luck with another group of young men. During the war, organized football had languished, but at its end Deacon White started to assemble another Eskimo team. During 1921 the team vanquished Calgary and beat Winnipeg. Then, looking farther afield, the Eskimos challenged the Toronto Argonauts. The game was played in the east. Loyal Edmonton fans flocked to the Empire and Monarch Theatres, because each of these had arranged to receive a running summary of the game by telegram. Two or three hours later, gloomy crowds emerged, for the score ended at Toronto 23, Eskimos 0.

Once more, during the 1922 season, Edmonton players, now called the Elks because they were under the banner of that lodge, made a laughing-stock of all teams in the west. That year, however, for the first time, they became official contenders for the Grey Cup, but when the final came off, Queen's University turned them back to the tune of 13 to 1. After that, Edmonton's interest in football waned.

Edmontonians, however, did not confine their interests to football because the Eskimo Hockey team with Duke Keats, Art Gagne and Joe Simpson, were Edmonton's idols when in 1923 they played against Ottawa for the Stanley Cup. For three or four more years before the team was sold to the National Hockey League, Edmontonians witnessed splendid hockey.

One team of athletes, however, the Commercial Grads Girls Basketball team, consistently kept Edmonton's name before the public. Welded into a remarkable organization by the discipline and scientific coaching of Percy Page, their even more remarkable coach, the Grads could always be relied upon to uphold Edmonton in the world of sport. Year after year, from 1914 to 1920, though its members changed, the team thrilled Edmontonians with its sportsmanship, its perfect co-ordination and its unfailing record of winning the provincial championship. The pitcher that goes off to the well, however, gets broken at last, and in 1921, by the narrowest margin, the Grads lost to the University of Alberta girls. Though, as the years went by, the world was to hear much more of them, for the time being they too had been beaten.

On every front the good old standbys were disappearing or being put on the shelf. The army battalions which had served so valiantly had been disbanded. Even the glorious 49th Battalion was a thing of the past. It had lost its identity when in March 1920 Ottawa revamped Canada's military machinery. Under the new régime, an Edmonton Regiment was gazetted, made up of two active militia and three reserve battalions. The first battalion was to perpetuate the old 49th. Then in September 1921, Edmonton's greatest soldier, Brigadier Griesbach, retired with the rank of General.

In 1921, then, everybody was in difficulty. The Edmonton Grads had lost their championship. The Eskimos had gone down to defeat. The barnstorming aeroplane companies had apparently come to the end of their runways. Griesbach had dropped out of the public eye, the price of wheat was dropping rapidly, and the sixteen-year-old Liberal government had been swept out of the Legislative Building. Then, rubbing salt into the sores, the census revealed that Calgary with its 63,305 people was still significantly ahead of Edmonton with 58,821, and still growing.

Economic conditions, however, were by no means disastrous, because even in the midst of what was after all a minor recession, everyone felt reasonably secure. It was the let-down that bothered everybody — the disappointment. At the war's end everything had seemed so rosy. Civilian activity had been revived, everyone had been re-dedicated to peace, men were back working, and wonderful new advances in living promised so much for the future; and then a continent-wide slump set in.

In spite of it, the city saw a few minor buildings put up. To accommodate the hundreds of cars, one-storey but roomy brick garages were built here and there along Jasper Avenue from 103 Street west for a few blocks and along the side streets north of these. Except for them, and the magnificent new Library erected on Macdonald Drive in 1923, the only other material change was the fact that finally, nearly a dozen years after Calgarians had been heating with gas, the Viking gas reached Edmonton.

The Northern Alberta Gas Development Corporation, which had been given a franchise in 1915, had proved up the Viking field, but even then it could

Commercial Grads — Canadian and International Champions, 1924, Back row: Eleanor Mountifield, Connie Smith, Percy Page, Abbie Scott, Daisy Johnson. Front Row: Nellie Perry, Mary Dunn, Winnie Martin, Dorothy Johnson.

not raise money during the war. Edmonton's exasperated city council saw a glimmer of hope of breaking the jinx, and in 1921 made an arrangement with a new outfit, the Great West Natural Gas Corporation, but the burgesses turned this down. There the matter rested until International Utilities of New York came along with enough financial strength to get things done. After buying out the old Northern Alberta Gas Development Corporation, which still had a valid franchise with the city, and setting up a new company called Northwestern Utilities Limited, they went to work.

Putting some $4 million into the venture and setting scores of men to work, they laid a gas line through the Beaver Hills, past Cooking Lake, and into Edmonton — some eighty miles of it in eighty-eight working days. Northwestern meant business. By the night of November 9, 1923, nine years and five days after the Viking discovery well had blown in, they were ready to turn on the gas. Then, in pitch darkness, at the north end of the 105 Street Bridge, Mayor D. M. Duggan lit the flare, which, as it shot up, showed thousands of up-turned faces, all rejoicing that at long last gas was here.

Many Edmontonians, however, did not rejoice, for they lived by mining coal and they could foresee a rapid decline in that industry. Over the next few years mine after mine shut down. By 1929 the Federal government, which still owned the Penitentiary site where Clarke Stadium is now, finally shut down the coal operation, and residents of that area who had worried about soil subsidence breathed a sigh of relief.

In spite of the fact that by 1924 wheat had fallen to 65¢ per bushel, the same price it had been before the war, and in spite of the fact that air activity around Edmonton had fallen to a low of absolute zero, Edmonton still made progress. For one thing, recognizing the tremendous output of wheat in the region tributary to Edmonton, the Dominion government erected its imposing terminal elevator in the northwest corner of the city. For another, the gas had been turned on. For still another, some new railway lines had come into being. In 1920, the CNR line along the north side of the Saskatchewan River to St. Paul and on towards Cold Lake had given easier access to more farming country. In 1922 the AGW, which had taken such a long time to wind through the sand hills north of Lac La Biche and to wiggle over the moose wallows beyond that, finally reached the top of the hill above the Athabasca River near Fort McMurray. By 1924 it extended down the long grade to river level at Waterways. The AGW helped Edmonton's northerly oriented businessmen to cut their costs and to increase their trade with the Far North.

About the same time, other Edmonton businessmen engaged in a new enterprise which was to be a boon to all isolated farmers and a godsend to Edmonton's customers in the Far North. This was Alberta's very first radio broadcasting station, CJCA. In the spring of 1922, on top of the Journal Building, a spidery network of masts and stays and braces traced against the soft spring sky, arose to support the new station's antenna. On May 1, in a mere corner of the *Journal* newsroom, Mayor D. M. Duggan, MLA, spoke into a fantastic horn-shaped microphone and declared CJCA to be officially opened, and here and there in the city, eager amateurs with "cat's whiskers" and crystal sets and with ear-phones clamped to their heads, actually heard him talking. As they sat hunched over and tense, and passed the ear-phones to other members of the family gathered in a tight knot around the crystal set, each in turn heard snatches of music and singing, which by this new magic jumped the miles of empty air from the newsroom to their very own kitchen table. They listened to Beatrice Crawford, the talented Edmonton pianist, and David Jones, James Kerr and Mortimer Johnston, all playing or singing for their benefit. A new miracle had reached Edmonton.

Born in the heads of experimenters and scientists, nurtured carefully by the exigencies of the war, and now made available by the enterprise of venturesome businessmen, this miracle of radio ushered in a new era. Far out in the country, a farm family in each community listened, and next day over the rural telephone called up the neighbours to declare proudly that they had heard the broadcast. Away in the north, at Fort Vermilion, Fort Simpson and Fort Resolution, with bated breath, fur traders tickling their crystal sets with the whiskers listened to this new magic leaping over the leagues to bring them into instant contact with Edmonton — the first rent that was to cleave their ages-old curtain of isolation.

The *Journal* ran a series of articles showing how to build a radio set for $3. Radio had recently passed from the experimental stage to becoming a marketable product, but the supply could not keep up with the demand, so it was necessary to build your own set. Each issue of the newspaper carried brief items on set construction and how to improve reception.

Three days after the first broadcast, a group of singers from McDougall Church became the first choir in Edmonton to sing for radio. The fall of 1922 saw the "Igloo Hut" radio club originated by CJCA, followed later by the "Night Fliers" and the "Radio Ramblers". It soon became obvious that radio was to play a vital part in providing a life-line for lonely pioneers far removed from Edmonton.

Soon, crystal sets became common, and from farmers, prospectors and trappers came letters expressing their thanks for news and entertainment. Edmonton's radio station CJCA had gone a long way towards welding farm and city into a unit and tightening the bond that had always linked the city and the Far North. Before long, with its regular program of "Calling the North," traders, policemen and priests, received news and business instructions from Edmonton.

On a different plane, the University of Alberta grew physically and in stature. Since the war, a university farm had been started, the nucleus of a hospital had been set up revolving about a Soldiers' Civil Re-establishment Hospital and a new and architecturally interesting Medical Building adorned the growing campus. As returned men, impressed with their need for more education, flocked to the university, its enrolment, which had been 613 in the fall of 1918, rose to 1,106 the next autumn.

Ever since 1916 when by some 58,000 votes for it, and only 37,000 against, Albertans had brought prohibition upon themselves, many had regretted it. Bootlegging and its associated ills had become so rampant by 1923 that, by a major turnabout in sentiment, liquor was voted back to the tune of 94,000 to 62,000. This time, however, "hard liquor" was to be sold only by government vendors, while beer could be obtained by the glass in rooms associated only with hotels, and for some reason called "Beer Parlours".

These beer parlours, clean enough physically, legally and morally policed, and serving their purpose as troughs for the thirsty, were crude, bleak, noisy and ill-ventilated. Reflecting some of the crudeness and the harshness of pioneer life on the prairies, indicating how much was lost when civilized men were transplanted to the frontier, these parlours, usually large rooms, provided a means of mass transfer of beer from kegs to customers. Their walls rocked with the shouts to which neighbours, sitting knee to knee at a table, were forced to resort in order to communicate above the resounding bedlam rising from gesticulating guzzlers. Rarely was it possible to indulge in a drink sipped reflectively or in the balm of quiet discussion. Even at that, beer in beer parlours was better than no beer at all. Although some bootlegging was still necessary because the liquor stores closed at six P.M., so that after that time of day taxi drivers had to take on the task of supplying thirsty wayfarers, nearly all the "blind pigs" closed up. In the cities at least, fearful that women might contaminate men weakened by beer, the law decreed that each sex be served in a separate room.

For even though during the war women had started to assert themselves by obtaining the franchise and shortening their skirts, they were still shackled by ancient male taboos. In the matter of dress, however, they were rapidly unshackling themselves. The layer after layer of the old cotton undergarments had given way to the much more convenient and sexier silk. The long black stockings had beat a retreat before sheer hose, while low pumps had replaced the high laced shoe. Bobbed hair too had arrived — and the cloche hat. While the change in dress from a few years back was dramatic, and while it expressed women's demands to look like and be treated like human beings, the current unmoulded shapeless sheath, with the hips dropped nearly to the knees and the skirt ending at them, was scarcely beautiful.

Co-incident with women's emancipation came jazz, powder puffs, rouge, lipstick, flappers, and a new sport named "petting" and a new game called parking. To aid and abet this activity, a variety of new cars—closed ones—became familiar on Jasper Avenue; the Essex coach, Chrysler, Willys Knight, Overland and Pontiac —cars with self starters. In many ways they set everyone free; country folk found it easy to get to town, not once or twice a year but every week; Edmontonians began touring.

For indoor amusement, the movies, developing all the time, offered Charlie Chaplin, Buster Keaton, and the be-spectacled, eager, fresh-faced Harold Lloyd. Along with much vulgarity and sexual glamour and Rudolph Valentino in *The Shiek,* came Clara Bow, the "It" Girl.

The movies, however, needed background music, and from the musicians employed, the early Twenties saw the formation of The Edmonton Symphony Orchestra. About this time too, Edmonton's Art Gallery got its start when in 1923 The Art and Historical Museum Association started displaying pictures. Heading up this activity, Mrs. David Bowman was supported by Dr. R. B. Wells and William Johnstone.

Though the movies were making great technical progress, and though they provided increasingly interesting entertainment, they still could not compare to Edmonton's own basketball team, the Grads, both in playing perfection and their hold over Edmontonians. For the Grads were a phenomenon beyond comparison. Ever since they had started playing back in 1914, they had been in the public eye, winning championships year by year, until in 1921 by a very narrow margin they had been defeated once. After that, they rallied, and for the next few years went on to unprecedented successes. By 1926 they had become world famous.

In 1924 they attended the Olympic Games in Paris, and although girls' basketball was never an official event, they played exhibition games against teams from Paris, Strasbourg, and other cities, and won them all. Through the Grads, the whole world came to know of Edmonton. The girls, all one-time students of McDougall Commercial High School and all devoted amateurs, changed from year to year. While it is impractical here to name all of them who played so brilliantly down through the years, the Grads of 1922 had been: Daisy and Dorothy Johnson, Nellie Perry, Eleanor Mountifield, Winnie Martin and Connie Smith. By 1924, when the girls went to the Paris Olympics, Connie Smith had dropped out, and little Mary Dunn and lithe Abbie Scott formed valuable additions to the team. So it went, some girls going off to other ventures and new ones stepping into their smart uniforms. And trained and disciplined by Page's genius, they won and won and won, and, following his strict code, none but girls of the highest moral character entered the Grads' ranks. No wonder Edmontonians, Albertans and Canadians loved them and basked in their reflected glory.

As year after year the Grads ran up their amazing record, the years rolled around to 1926, when the census takers visited Alberta and Edmonton. Their figures showed that for the previous five years the number of people in the province had remained almost static. Its population was 607,599, a gain of a mere 19,000, or 3.3%, as compared to gains of over 100,000 and over 100% ten and fifteen years earlier. The proportion that was rural had shrunk slightly, however, and now stood at 61%. Most of the gain had gone into the cities. Edmonton had accounted for a third of the increase, and now, with 65,163 people, it had almost caught up to Calgary's population of 65,291. Edmonton was still about 7,000 short of its record established in 1914, but was edging back up there. Its post-war growth had come about through an increase in the service industries, such as movies, primitive radio shops, gasoline vending stations, and garages. No new large industries had heard Edmonton's call, and very few new buildings had been erected. Its streets were practically the same as they had remained since 1913, with two or three of the main ones paved, many gravelled, and the rest au naturel. With the passage of years, some of the freshness had worn off the buildings. This was especially so in some downtown portions of 95 and 97 Streets, to which the footloose element of many races and colours had gravitated.

But even though downtown Edmonton was drab, its citizens, and especially its young folk, found much to like in it and many places where convivial company added greatly to the gaiety and the joy of living. The American Dairy Lunch, with its marvellous arrays of pies, puddings, baked apples and other succulent snacks, as well as sturdy meals, was a favourite gathering place for old and young — city folk or country friends. Similarly, the White Lunch Cafe with its spotless interior, its white marble-like table tops, and its wholesome and tasty fare, was another rendezvous. Then too, on warm summer nights the soda fountain at the Owl Drug Store on the corner of Jasper Avenue and 101 Street was a blaze of lights. As its soda water dispenser sizzled and hissed and as ever so many people, boys, girls and old people too, enjoyed themselves, it was a centre of good fellowship.

In winter, Edmontonians turned to another common meeting place, the Central Skating Rink on 112 Street and Jasper Avenue, where today's Devonian Building rises almost as high into the air as the rink was long. There, from 1922 till after the Second War, Dad Barnes provided skating for all and the cheerful camaraderie of open air exercise.

During its earlier years, during the early twenties, to keep pace with the rapidly increasing popularity of automobiles, garages had multiplied. At the close of the war, Alberta had a total of 29,250 cars. By 1926, the number had more than doubled to 65,101. Included in this provincial total were 4,362 trucks and 646 taxis, and their presence on city streets put a dint in the horse population to such an extent that here and there some of the old-time livery barns had either been torn down or remodelled into garages.

With all its new cars and its increased population, Edmonton was optimistic. The war had been over for several years, the recession that followed in its wake had been mild, and now it too was over. Alberta, however, was only exploiting four of its main resources — soil, minerals, lumber and furs. Since the wealth garnered and spent by farmers so far out-classed that of the other resource industries, Alberta's cities depended almost wholly on the farming areas. In the rest of the world times might be good or bad, but what counted in Edmonton was how times were with the farmers.

For the farmers, the turning point had been the 1925 crop. That year they had seeded over five million acres of wheat, which had yielded well. Its price of $1.19 per bushel was fairly good, and, as a result, they had money to jingle. On country trails cars became common. The trend to farm mechanization had also started. A very few combines made trial runs in the wheat fields, and that year 11,311 tractors were doing many horses out of work, and in the country too the horse population had begun its long and inevitable decline.

These trends were to continue. By the fall of 1929 the area in farms in Alberta increased from 28 million acres three years earlier to 35 million acres, and much of the increase was in the north. The area under cultivation likewise rose from 13 million to over 16 million acres, while the acreage seeded to wheat rose rapidly year by year to 7,451,000 in the spring of 1929. The years 1927 and 1928, however, were the halcyon years, with each producing yields of 171 million bushels, records which were only to be equalled or exceeded in two subsequent years. Even though the price per bushel had dropped to 98¢ in 1927, the farmers' income from wheat stood at $168 million, a figure not to be exceeded for eighteen years. With such relative prosperity, mechanization of farms continued apace. The number of combines increased to 2,523, the number of tractors doubled, while the number of horses declined further. By this time, most farmers had a car or a light delivery truck.

During the same period, the total number of farmers in Alberta reached a record high of some 95,000, and since most new farmers were in the north of the province, Edmonton could claim some 58% of them as customers. As a result, Edmonton, which had been over-built with an eye on its resource of soil was now beginning to experience the satisfaction of having the resources developed to the stage where they were catching up with her.

While Alberta farmers were enjoying some of their rare years of prosperity, and while Edmontonians were egging them on, Canada and the world were revelling in one of the greatest binges in history. Everything was rosy; the world was at peace, the Empire had never been more solid, Charles Lindbergh had flown the Atlantic, and in New York, Chicago, Toronto and Montreal, the stock exchanges were buzzing with buyers. In Canada, factories worked overtime. In Alberta, a few barrels of oil were rewarding two or three of the hundreds of hopefuls who drilled wells.

In May 1926, Edmonton's city council, urged on by Mayor Blatchford, voted $400 as an estimated cost of preliminary work on the airfield. By coincidence, that same day, far away in the rest of the world, Commander Richard Byrd made his first aeroplane crossing of the North Pole. A month later, by a certificate issued at Ottawa and bearing the number One, Edmonton's Hagmann estate, the old McNeill airstrip, became the first officially designated "Public Air Harbour". At a subsequent meeting, after Kenny Blatchford's term of office had expired, the city council declared that this field, which had already cost them $600, should have a name, and fittingly called it after one of the men who had tried so hard to raise Edmontonians' sights to the skies — Blatchford Field. Finally, on January 8, 1927, up from High River, Punch Dickins and another pilot brought their Siskins, which could fly 145 MPH, to assist Mayor Bury to open Edmonton's Air Harbour No. 1.

In 1927, basking in the Creator's blessing, Canada, approaching its 60th birthday, celebrated its Diamond Jubilee. The Peace Tower carillon at Ottawa was dedicated. The first Canada-wide radio hook-up came into play. The great

Blatchford Field—forerunner of Industrial Airport.

Charles Lindbergh visited Ottawa. Across Canada gala celebrations made the great day memorable. From coast to coast the country buzzed with ice cream and strawberry festivals, chicken suppers, baseball games, three-legged races, egg-and-spoon races, historical pageants and floats. In Edmonton, watching a procession two miles long, everyone rejoiced. In it, as well as Ford and Chevrolet cars, many other makes showed off their styling; Star, Falcon-Knight, Whippet, Chandler, Hupmobile, Auburn and Velie. Unfortunately Frank Oliver could not be present when the Old Timers' Association unveiled a statue in his honour.

The Edmonton Diamond Jubilee celebration, if it did little else, revived everyone's interest in aeroplanes. Lindbergh had flown to Ottawa, and Paul Calder, an Edmonton boy who had flown during the war, brought his Siskin up from High River to perform for the occasion. When he took off to do his stunting, Kenny Blatchford, now the federal member for East Edmonton and a long-time advocate of more aid in making Edmonton a flying centre, had climbed into Calder's plane. Blatchford, when he had been mayor, had done all he could to further Edmontonians' air-mindedness. Though he worked hard, he had met with many disappointments. Edmontonians were just not interested.

During 1927 word got about that the British government planned to donate a pair of light planes to each of three Canadian cities, and suggested that these be Montreal, Winnipeg and Vancouver. Edmontonians got up on their ears, but cooled down when they realized that the city had no organization able to accept one even if it had been held out to them. Once more, Kenny Blatchford called a meeting, and out of it came the Edmonton and Northern Alberta Aero

Club, with Wop May as its president, and S. A. Yorke, Punch Dickins, John Sydie, Jimmy Bell and Enoch Loveseth as directors. In due course, it received two Moth planes. Before long it had eighty-five members attending its ground school.

In 1928 Wop May, Cy Becker and Vic Horner set up Commercial Airways Limited. That summer saw the first class of Edmonton-trained pilots receive their certificates. They were R. P. Owen, Art Rankin, Alex Clarke and R. F. Brinkman.

On December 10, 1928, a western Canada mail, express and passenger service got under way with a Western Canada Airways' plane leaving for Calgary and Regina and another arriving in Edmonton. That day too, Edmonton citizens were called upon to vote for a by-law covering an expenditure of $23,860 to develop the airport. They turned out in force to cast 14,971 ballots, the biggest vote up to that time in the city's history, but the by-law failed to carry. Edmontonians, who had dilly-dallied along for so long before getting a transit system and who had shilly-shallied about for years trying to make up their minds over gas, had vetoed expanding the airport. That evening as Mayor Bury thanked Edmontonians for his re-election, he also rebuked them. "Approval had meant so much to Edmonton," he said.

Then fate and Wop May and Vic Horner took a hand, and by a great feat of heroism stirred Edmontonians into an ashamed consciousness of their lethargy. On December 31, some five hundred miles away in the northern wilderness, at Little Red River, near Fort Vermilion, diphtheria broke out. The doctor at Fort Vermilion wired to Edmonton, asking that antitoxin be flown in.

Dr. Bow, the deputy minister of health, turned to the Aero Club, and almost immediately, in 33° below zero weather, Wop May and Vic Horner set forth upon their dangerous mission. Radio station CJCA broadcast to all the north, to the Hudson's Bay men, the Revillon Frères men and to all villages, farmers and trappers, asking them to watch for the plane and report its progress.

Next day, after spending the night at McLennan, the two fliers, nearly frozen from hours of exposure in the cramped seats of their open cockpit, reached Fort Vermilion alive. Due to poor fuel taken on at the remote northern post, their engine kept cutting out and made their return trip even more hazardous. After landing at Peace River, they spent a day tinkering with their engine, and then set out for Edmonton.

In spite of the cold and falling snow, 10,000 Edmontonians awaited their arrival at the primitive, penny-pinched Blatchford field. Someone estimated that the number of cars parked nearby and along Portage Avenue was the greatest ever to be seen at one event. As the nearly frozen pair taxied to a stop, they were engulfed, lifted out of the cockpit and carried about. Edmontonians, skimpy with the cash to make the airport fit for planes, were long on sentiment. And well they might be, for the exploit they had followed by radio and newspaper reports in their easy chairs at home, was a rare act of heroism and a foretaste of what Edmonton boys could do and would do when they began flying to the North.

That spring, Wop and Vic made a business trip to California and surprised Edmontonians when they brought their Commercial Airways' new Lockheed Vega into Blatchford field. It was huge, it could carry four passengers and a payload of 600 pounds. Perhaps too, with the memories of their blizzard-bucking trip to Fort Vermilion still stinging in their frostbites, it was no surprise to find that Wop and Vic's new plane had the first enclosed, heated cabin to reach Edmonton.

To compete with them, however, James Richardson's Western Canada Airways of Winnipeg announced that that spring, with pilot Punch Dickins based at Fort McMurray, it was to start a regular air service between that point and Chipewyan, Fort Smith, Fort Resolution, Hay River and Forts Providence and Simpson. Extending his territory on July 1, 1929, Dickins set his plane down on the Mackenzie River at Aklavik. It was no wonder that that year he became the second winner of the McKee Award.

Meanwhile, during the summer of 1929, the city council, feeling that in spite of the fact that the by-law had been turned down, they had better take matters into their own hands without waiting for another vote, authorized $35,000 to be spent on the airfield. In part, they hoped that enough of the sentiment engendered by May and Horner's December mercy flight remained amongst Edmontonians that they would surely pass the by-law the next time it was submitted. Soon, the money expended produced four smooth runways 200 feet wide and 3,500 feet long. Thenceforth, much of the risk of landing and takeoff at Blatchford field disappeared.

Then, as though in answer to Mayor Bury's prayer that Edmontonians would stay air-minded long enough to ratify the council's action, a new excitement gripped everyone. In September, Colonel MacAlpine's party, piloted by Stan Mac-Millan and "Tommy" Thompson, went missing in the Arctic. When, several weeks later, it was found and brought out, all Canada exhaled a sigh of relief for the party and acclaimed the pilots who had searched. Even as they did so, Edmontonians passed the airport by-law overwhelmingly.

Then on February 4, 1930, Jimmy Bell was appointed Master of Blatchford Air Harbour. He had waited long for this airport, and with single-minded devotion, he had worked for it, and now that it was an accomplished fact, he was put in charge of it. Nothing could have been more fitting than his appointment, and as the next thirty-two years were to prove, no one could have served Edmonton's aviation cause better than Jimmy Bell.

Then in 1929 the increasing specialization that was taking place in civilian fields found its way into army organization. That year, Edmonton's militia was stepped up so as to include not only the First Battalion Edmonton Regiment, the 2nd Battalion Edmonton Fusiliers and the 19th Dragoons, but also the 69th and the 92nd Field Battery of Artillery, 13th Divisional Signals, 33rd Field Ambulance, 18th Company Canadian Machine Gun Corps, the University of Alberta COTC and the Royal Canadian Volunteer Reserve.

But to changes in the army the men on the street paid little attention. To them, times were good, the war was long since over, and there would never be another one. Their interests lay elsewhere. For one thing, the movie industry had come out with an innovation. In the fall of 1927 Edmontonians swarmed to see and hear Al Jolson in The Jazz Singer, their first talking picture.

One other lively interest, of course, was the Grads' basketball team. In spite of the fact that by now its victories were taken for granted, Edmontonians always turned out to adore and to cheer the team. The fact that the Grads' fame focused the limelight on Edmonton was secondary. So, indeed, was its record of wins — a record unparalleled in the basketball world. What counted with Edmontonians in what now must seem a remote era was its greater and more endearing record of clean play and good sportsmanship.

Once more in 1928 the girls performed at the Olympic Games, this time in Amsterdam, and, of course, won all the games they played. During the interval from the previous Olympics in 1924, the personnel of the team had changed completely by the process of some dropping out year by year as new girls took their places. But though the players changed, the performance and the masterful coaching continued.

About this time, in a wholly different but equally feminine field, five Albertans, led by Emily Murphy of Edmonton, established the fact that in Canada women were persons and as such could be called to the Senate. Doing so took quite a fight, which went to the Supreme Court of Canada and then on to the Privy Council in England, which on October 16, 1929, decided that women were indeed persons. Aiding Emily Murphy were Mesdames Irène Parlby, Louise McKinney, Nellie McClung and Henrietta Edwards. Some ten years later, in the lobby of the Canadian Senate, Prime Minister Mackenzie King unveiled a bronze tablet honouring these great Canadian women, who, because of their fight, have since been referred to as "The Famous Five".

Important as this step forward may have been to women in their fight for equality, another advance equally important in man's control of his surroundings appeared on Edmonton's streets during the same year when the first neon advertising signs began to brighten Jasper Avenue. Contributing their cheery colour to the city and helping to dispel some of the old-time drabness, they caught on immediately and soon neon signs brightened every business street.

Except for the fact that at initiation time each fall, when for a few hours university students came storming across the High Level Bridge to snake dance and cavort along Jasper Avenue and to annoy everyone with their silly antics, Edmontonians paid little attention to that institution. In spite of that, and of the fact that any university graduates were still scorned by practical men who had acquired their knowledge, however skimpy, "the hard way", and who begrudged the taxes they spent on this educational frill, the university continued to progress. By 1928, the enrolment had reached 1,560 — a good showing for a first generation crop of pioneers. That year the great Dr. Tory retired. For twenty years, battling the odds inherent in a pioneer civilization, he had built up a highly respected centre of learning, and, having seen it well launched, he set forth on a new career to start Carleton University in Ottawa.

Like Dr. Tory, looking back over his accomplishments during twenty years, Edmontonians too could be pleased with the city's progress during the decade following the war. For one thing, over the years since the end of the war, builders had taken out some $2 million of permits each year. Some slowing up in construction had been experienced around 1925 and 1926, but after that matters had straightened out and began to forge ahead. In 1927, building permits had risen to $2,569,000, in 1928 they were $3,375,000, and now in 1929 they were leaping ahead at $5,670,000.

For another, Edmonton's population, which ten years earlier had been about 55,000, had now grown to around 75,000. The only fly in the ointment was that times were even better in Calgary. By 1926, Edmonton and Calgary's population had been neck and neck, but then Calgarians had taken the bit in their teeth and had shot forward till in 1929 they were once more some three thousand ahead. But at least, though it was far from filling the vast framework of suburbs and subdivisions which Edmontonians of 1912 had laid out, Edmonton had finally caught up to and now exceeded the population it had contained in 1914 before reality had overtaken it and deflated it back to the vicinity of 50,000. At last,

Edmonton was beginning to grope towards filling the oversize shoes into which it had stepped so confidently during its youthful boom.

Now that women were persons, now that cars abounded and the pall of prohibition had lifted, now that neon lights imparted a festive glow to Jasper Avenue, now that on every hand prosperity reigned, a new era had dawned.

Corner of Jasper and 101st Street during land boom days prior to 1914. Advertising for Dunvegan and Grouard townsites.

Depression And Doub.
1930-1939

chapter *17*

T HEN ON OCTOBER 29, 1929, something snapped. That day the New York exchange traded over sixteen million shares, to make it the busiest day in all its long history. And the saddest one, for that day the heretofore unsuspicious speculators lost nine billion dollars. The world-wide binge was over.

Looking back, hindsight sadder still could detect many indications that that day was coming — that the great boom had been as artificial as Edmonton's land boom of 1913. By all nations and all governments, by all capitalists and all cultivators, the law of supply and demand had been flouted. Patiently biding its time, it struck back, first a few light taps, and then the knockout of October 1929.

Before long, the bottom had dropped out of everything. The impact of the economic upset was felt as early as Christmas 1929. Farm prices had fallen. Unemployment hit the cities, and a growing "scarcity of money", — something ascribed to malign influences — cut purchasing power and paralyzed everyone's will. By 1933, thousands in the prairie cities and all farmers in the drought areas of southern Alberta were on relief and the governments of the prairie provinces were broke.

With little or no money to buy fuel so their tractors could pull their ploughs, mowers and binders, farmers fell back on horses. With no money to buy gasoline for their cars and trucks, they found themselves in a sorry plight, for during their flush years while they had driven an old Ford or Chevrolet, or even a current model car, the spokes of their democrats, buggies and buckboards had buckled up and rotted. Turning their backs on their broken buggies, they turned their hands to their cars or trucks. Lifting the motor out, attaching a tongue and double-trees to it and dispensing with the windshield, they hitched it behind a team of oat-burners. Their horseless carriages had failed them, but so long as they could grow enough feed for their team, they could get about. Their Chevrolet cars and their Ford Phaetons had been turned into what, in a derisive reference to the one-time Albertan who was now Prime Minister of Canada, they called Bennett Buggies.

These were the years when families in Saskatchewan, piling into a hayrack all that drought and depression had left them, began the long trek to wetter lands in Alberta's north and in the Peace River country. Before setting out, many of them had sold, through a government guaranteed scheme, what poor skeletons of cattle had lived that long for a price of $1.05 — a hundred-weight! As day after day these itinerants from the south and east rolled their wagons into Edmonton, the authorities provided them with hot soup and other food and sped them on their way north, wagon-load after wagon-load of them. Sorry as Edmontonians were for them, they were glad to see them urge their horses out of the city.

Alberta farmers were not hit so hard as those in Saskatchewan, where the drought was worst, and northern Alberta farmers fared better than those in the south of the province, but even they faced years of hardships which tried their souls and seamed their weather-beaten faces. During the good years, with farmers' cheerful optimism, they had bought more land, invested in modern machinery, and in doing so had laid on their shoulders a burden of debt which, given good times, would have been wearying enough, but faced with lean years, was impossible to carry. They had to default on their mortgages, and through poverty, debt and worry, they steered a bitter course. Many a former homesteader, who in good times had been lured by the city's bright lights, returned broke to his few acres in the country, and increased the number of farmers dividing up an already hopelessly low income. By 1936, the number of persons living on farms rose 7%, to bring the total to 99,732 — a record never exceeded before or since. Meanwhile, the consumer price index dropped 22% from 1929 to 1933. The farmers' wheat, however, had dropped 40%. For every bushel of wheat which had gone to buy a pair of boots in 1929, it now took two bushels. In the drought areas a man might spend all the wheat he had reaped off five acres to buy his wife a cheap cotton dress.

Then slowly, ever so slowly, the upturn in farming income began. The rains returned, wheat production picked up, and the price improved, till by 1939 it was 52¢ a bushel. That year the farm value of wheat reached $84 million, nearly double what it had been in 1933, but still only half of what it had been in 1928.

In many respects, Edmontonians, because they could grow very few vegetables and could not produce poultry or eggs, suffered more severely than their country relations. In towns and cities, casual labourers were the first to feel the pinch and to go on relief. Then it spread to the semi-skilled, and then to the skilled carpenters, bricklayers and other workers. Soon they too were living off the weekly dole of food, then clothing, and finally rent money. Many thousands, however, too proud to go on relief, held out through months of unemployment till, having exhausted their last resource, they too gave in. Eventually everyone's reluctance to seek relief was followed by a passive acceptance. In many cases individuals passed on to the third and final phase, that of demanding all they thought they should have.

Hard times and unemployment brought Canada a new social unrest, a dissatisfaction with old political parties and a demand for a new Commonwealth modelled on the mirage of the new Russia. With discouraged farmers looking for some break in their miseries, despondent city folk driven to despair, and many of the young generation riding the rods, the time was ripe for Tim Buck and his Communists.

Buck moved in to bring trouble to a head, and using the freight car transients and hundreds of relief workers who had left their camps in British Columbia, he started a trek to Ottawa. The RCMP stopped it at Regina, where a riot flared and resulted in the death of one policeman and 130 arrests. Even in the depths of depression, however, the country failed to respond to Communism. Canadians, with their grounding in democracy, had enough understanding to steer clear of anarchy — but only enough. Buck failed.

Nevertheless, westerners were searching for new gods. In Alberta, new political brews were seething. The UFA (the United Farmers of Alberta) government, a good one, which for fourteen years had guided the province with integrity, found itself in the same boat as all other governments, adrift and helpless. To stir the new brew came William Aberhart. Discouraged because even his good graduates could not obtain employment, this Calgary religious leader and high school teacher lashed out at the economic system. During a temporary sojourn in Edmonton, Charles Scarborough, a teacher in the capital city's Victoria High School, introduced him to Major Douglas' theories of Social Credit. Overnight he became converted. Striding on from there he imported to Alberta what Stephen Leacock called "certain profundities of British fog, impossible for most people to understand, which in sunny Alberta, by force of prayer, turned into Alberta Social Credit". In leading the movement, Aberhart, a dedicated man, combined the functions of a prophet with an amazing capacity for planning and organization.

In the depths of the depression, one and one-half million Canadians out of ten million were on relief, economic conditions had never been worse; crops had failed, prices had fallen, unemployment was rampant, and every country and city merchant was at or near the end of his tether. Wild rumours spread in Alberta of people wearing gunny sacks, which was true, and to some extent had always been true, and of farmers reduced to eating gophers, which was not true, but the wildest rumours falling on the ear of despair have a ring of truth.

Nevertheless, Edmontonians and all Albertans had endured great suffering and frustration. On top of all their other troubles, their creditors, the banks, mortgage and machine companies, themselves nearly insolvent and blindly unaware of how close they were to touching the match to the explosive of revolution, bore down on them. Conditioned by years of farm-movement-sponsored, but dimly understood, monetary reform propaganda, the disgruntled farmers, looking for some tangible cause for all their misery, focused their hatred on the banks and loan companies. And marching beside them were their city cousins.

Most Albertans, lacking any knowledge of the intricacies of economics and convinced that miracles could be wrought by wishful thinking converted into legislation, felt that they had to strike out at something, and that something became the "system" — Prime Minister Bennett, the UFA government, the banks, and the Big Shots.

Aberhart's exposition of monetary reform — of Social Credit — filled them with a clear conviction. After all his panacea was the final flowering of their long-held monetary views. His theory, made intellectually obtuse by such terms as "Cultural Heritage," "Monetization of National Resources," "Control of Credit," "Fountain-pen Money," "Just Price," and "Basic Dividends," was difficult if not impossible to understand. But one did not need to understand, one had only to believe. Such slogans as "Political Liberty with Economic Security," and "The Struggle of the Powers of Light against the Powers of Darkness," made it easy to believe.

Then too, the announcement that a basic dividend of $25 a month would be paid to everyone, was an immense drawing card. Some — a handful — of Aberhart's followers may not have taken this too seriously, but school teachers, the poorer farmers, the almost bankrupt small businessmen, and the working class generally, were completely sold on the government's ability to pay this money and to pay it more or less immediately after the election. Once the Social Credit government came to power, no one need any longer fear high interest rates, unemployment and mortgages; suffering from crop failure would be a thing of the past, while the standard of living would climb.

No leader exhibited such a divine spark as Aberhart. Albertans followed him, touching the hem of his garments in absolute belief in the righteousness of the cause he espoused so sincerely and so emphatically. Any of the more astute or economically literate who professed doubt about Social Credit theories were immediately classed as enemies to whom the faithful should turn a deaf ear. Albertans were seized by a mass hysteria which has rarely come to the surface of this continent and one which forms a dire warning for the future of what Congo-like depths despair can plunge even those with a long-established democratic tradition. Mob psychology had taken over to an extent almost unbelievable in what everyone hitherto had considered an informed electorate.

On election day in August 1935 a record number turned out. Whereas at the previous election 182,000 had voted, this time 302,000 came out to cast their ballots. That night when the boxes were opened, fifty-six Social Creditors were elected, along with five Liberals and two Conservatives. No UFA men had made the grade. The year before in Saskatchewan the electorate had turned out the Conservatives. Within a year R. B. Bennett and his Ottawa Conservatives were sent packing from the federal scene. No government pursuing orthodox policies could stand the strain of the depression.

The depression was an era of crackpot schemes. The Townsend Plan was afoot in California, Howard Scott and his Technocrats roamed Canada, while burning the fiery cross the cowardly hoods of the Klu Klux Klan set up groups in Alberta. A Canadian crisis of such magnitude had never happened before. Like all Anglo-Saxon leaders, Bennett and Mackenzie King and their advisers were not mentally geared to cope with it and perhaps could not have been expected to do so. For though they never realized it, a new era was dawning. The depression wrought greater changes in Canadian and in Alberta social values than those who endured it could realize. Much of our modern welfare state, with its unemployment insurance, old age pensions and welfare can trace their conception to it. Indeed, many of the results for which Aberhart fought have been realized since his death — but clad in orthodox garb.

As it turned out, and as the next few years were to show, most of Aberhart's theories were impractical. His compassion for the underdog, however, was not. His methods were wrong, but his revolt brought results. A further quotation of Stephen Leacock's remarks is apropos. "Whatever may be in it (Social Credit) in Alberta it led to partial repudiation of public debt, and scaling down of mortgage interest, things done however, under other names, in Saskatchewan . . . We cannot yet tell whether Social Credit was the end of something just ending, or the beginning of something just beginning."

Perhaps in comparison with the suffering in the slum-strewn areas of the large eastern cities, Edmontonians were fortunate. Nevertheless, being so dependent upon agriculture and having that crumple up underneath it, Edmonton had a bad time. Men walked the streets looking for jobs, or stood in long lines at the employment offices, or moved over to lengthen the bread lines or those leading to the soup kitchens. The relief agencies provided food, clothing, fuel and shelter, usually by a voucher system, but necessarily on a meager scale. During 1931, out of a population of 79,197, 14,573 Edmontonians drew direct relief. Out of some 18,000 city families, 2,601 were on relief. During 1932, 17,815 men and 2,785 women signed applications for work. Many of the jobs they found were of a very temporary nature, and some of them were on projects especially created to provide employment. Everyone winked at minimum wage laws.

The city or the province could have taken one year of unemployment and excessive relief costs in their stride, but one bad year followed another, on through 1933, 1934 and 1935. In 1929 Edmonton entered the depression with some 75,000 people; by 1936 an additional 10,000 had flocked in. Even though the city's population grew, however, its assessment dropped from $66,500,000 in 1931 to $53,500,000 in 1938 and the mill rate had to rise. By 1938 it had climbed to 54.0, and once, in 1934, it had sky-rocketed. Year by year, Edmonton was getting further into a financial hole. With some tens of thousands of city-owned empty lots on its hands — a large percentage of the total — its tax structure was askew, and by 1934 the city owed the Imperial Bank 2½ million dollars.

G. R. F. Kirkpatrick, who had been the bank's first manager when in 1891 it became the first such institution to open its doors in Edmonton, was still at its head. During that long span, he had handled the city's account, and many a time he had come to the city's rescue. But, during the depression, when the city's main asset was this vast number of empty lots and when its debt of 2½ million dollars was one of the bank's major assets, Kirkpatrick called upon the city fathers and talked hard sense. They followed his advice that they raise the rate for a year and thus try to liquidate their overdraft. In 1934 the mill rate jumped to 64.0.

Building permits, another indicator of the presence or absence of progress, give another idea of the times. From a high of $5,670,000 in 1929, they dropped to $4,301,000 in 1930, and then plummeted to a low of $428,000 in 1933. From there they rose very slowly to $865,000 in 1937, and then made a spectacular jump to $2,806,000 the next year. During the depths of the depression, when it was needed most, construction virtually stood still.

During the whole decade the few noteworthy buildings constructed could be counted on the fingers. The Birks Building, a holdover from the roaring Twenties, was completed in 1930. In 1936 Canada Packers started their new and modern packing plant. When the *Journal* announced in bold headlines that its construction was about to start and that thereby *three hundred men* could obtain work, the effect was electrifying. Hundreds of men showed up at the site, men who for years had been looking for work. Here at last was some tangible evidence that the depression was losing its frigid grip.

Of somewhat similar psychological value was the expansive new neon sign which that year the gas company erected on the Agency Building. Its animated figures, visible for blocks along Jasper Avenue, provided another much needed symbol of brightness.

As might be expected, movie theatres made some progress with the opening of the Roxy on 124 Street in 1938 and the complete renovation of the downtown Capitol to a plush, modern movie house under Walter Wilson's direction the same year. In a different milieu, the Al Rachid, the first mosque in Canada, was built on 111 Avenue to add a cosmopolitan touch to the city. That year too, the T. Eaton Company built its ultra modern store, and its main rival, the Hudson's Bay Company, started enlarging its premises on Jasper Avenue. Before long, these new stores played their part in brightening up the city by converting to the latest advance in illumination — fluorescent lights.

The construction of Eaton's new store provided work, and not only that, the city took advantage of a timely exchange of property in the vicinity and straightened out much of the jog where 102 Avenue intersected 101 Street. This jog, a result of the river lot system of survey, had already become a traffic hazard, but by angling the portion of 102 Avenue west of 101 Street north a few feet, it was made continuous with that portion east of 101 Street. A year or so later, the old King Edward Hotel expanded toward the north and built an addition which occupies part of what had been the old avenue.

Except for a slight increase in population and a further descent into dowdiness, Edmonton did not change during the Thirties. Building-wise and street-wise, it was still the same city it had been when the 1913 boom-time carpenters took off their aprons. The mileage of streets, water mains and similar utilities gives a good idea of how slowly the city progressed.

	Mileage				
	1914	*1920*	*1925*	*1936*	*1939*
Street paving	46	49	51	58	62
Water mains	155	165	186	246	248
Sewers	141	152	171	206	210

The most noticeable increase was in water and sewer lines, which expanded a block at a time for several years as outlying homes obtained this service.

Throughout the Thirties, however, there were several householders who, to escape the heavier taxes in the city, moved out beyond the city's limits and built small homes in what came to be called Jasper Place. There, taxes were indeed less, but for many years, except for electric light, most of the lots lacked all utility service. At the end of the depression Jasper Place was on the map, but its population was only two or three hundred.

Beverly, on the other hand, which had been incorporated as a town during boom days when the coal mines there kept everybody busy, had grown to a town of about one thousand by 1929, and continued around that mark for the next decade.

Thinking back to the depression, we are apt to remember only the dramatic, the hunger, the bread lines and the Bennett Buggies, and we are apt to paint an excessively black picture. What we are apt to forget is how the grim conditions welded everyone, whether employed or unemployed, into a new camaraderie. Traits of kindliness, helpfulness and neighbourliness, sometimes dulled during prosperous times, shone forth anew during the depression. What we might forget too is that many thousands of people, who were lucky enough or good enough to keep their jobs, hardly felt its sting. It is true that from time to time their wages were cut, but, unlike today when that dare not happen, it had often happened before. While they felt sorry for the less fortunate and contributed to their help, they were scarcely aware that the bottom had fallen out of the world. To these thousands, except for what they heard over the radio or read in the papers about hard times, the world rolled along very much as it had always done.

The newspapers, of course, extracted all the drama they could out of the situation. At first the *Journal* and the *Bulletin,* both amazed at this new Social Credit theory that was sweeping the land, teetered uncertainly, scared to challenge it head-on and yet afraid to be found keeping company with it. After some reversals of policy by each of the papers, the *Journal* challenged the theory and in its fight with Social Credit fairly frothed at the mouth.

Now that he was Premier of Alberta, with a large majority in the legislature, Aberhart was faced with the task of performing what he had promised — implementing Social Credit. Now that he was sitting in the premier's chair, the simple solutions he had so often advocated suddenly appeared much more complex than he had anticipated. And as reality began to confront him, the *Journal* began an "I told you so" campaign. Every move he made, every word he said, and every prayer he uttered, was seized upon in an attempt to make him appear ridiculous.

Trying to spell out Social Credit theory into legislation that would hold water was difficult indeed, and most of the government's economic legislation was as leaky as a well-worn sock. During three or four sessions the legislature passed The Alberta Social Credit Measures Act, the Alberta Credit House Act, the Alberta Social Credit Act, and several more, but they were all *ultra vires* or quite rightly were disallowed by Ottawa.

All the while the *Journal* ridiculed Aberhart and Aberhart vowed to "fix" the *Journal*. Then as tirade followed diatribe, the government fired a salvo at that newspaper and called it THE ACCURATE NEWS AND INFORMATION ACT. The *Journal* exploded. This legislation, an act to gag the press, set off a fresh tantrum. In due course, this act reached the Supreme Court, and it too was turned down.

In April 1936 the province defaulted on bonds totalling $3,200,000, and by legislation cut the interest rate on its outstanding bonds in half. During June and July the government issued what it called Prosperity Certificates, and forced some road contractors and their employees to take these in payment for their services. These were scrip issued in denominations of $1 and $5, and on their back were little squares to which any merchant who deigned to accept them as legal tender and who happened to have them in his hands on any Thursday stuck a stamp purchased from the Alberta government. In theory, these stamps were a tax, and by the time a year was up the various merchants through whose hands they had passed, were supposed to have affixed enough stamps to equal the face value of the scrip. At the end of that year, whoever held them could turn them in, and, if they were properly stamped, could get the original dollar value back from the government. In December that year the government was asking its civil servants, and asking pretty peremptorily, to take half their pay in these Prosperity Certificates. This "funny money" was bound to fail, but a courageous citizen, Charles Grant, hastened its demise by legal action which was carried through to the Supreme Court, where the certificates were adjudged not to be legal tender. Actually, the government only issued some $360,000 of them, and within a short time it redeemed $340,000. The rest were kept as souvenirs.

The *Journal* had a field day vilifying the government and its "funny money", and continued to revert to the fact that all told thirteen of the acts passed by Aberhart's government during its special sessions had been disallowed.

Looking back now, we can see that, while the *Journal* editor was undoubtedly sound enough in his economics, his furor availed nothing. His fight for freedom of the press, however, was not only valid enough, but valiant too. For in due course, the *Edmonton Journal* received the Pulitzer Award for "Leadership in the Defence of the Freedom of the Press in Alberta." This, a signal honour, was the first time this award had ever come to a Canadian newspaper.

Of course Edmontonians had other amusements besides the *Journal*-Aberhart fight. The university students, less apt to take part in public controversy than their modern counterparts and still too close to hod-carrying fathers to rise to bearing placards, occasionally, by their snake dances and other pranks, provided some levity. All throughout the depression their ranks grew — from 1,560 students in the fall of 1929 to 1,790 the next year, and to 2,327 by the fall of 1939. This increase was partly due to the fact that boys leaving high school could not get jobs. It was also partly due to a rising appreciation of the usefulness of university training and an awareness that in a pecuniary way the world is always more kind to a man with a degree.

Nevertheless, the university was in desperate financial straits and even in the scholastic year of 1939-1940, when times had improved considerably, the province's contribution to its one institution of higher learning was a mere $425,000.

Nearly all other cultural activities suffered likewise. Only the movie industry progressed as year by year new developments made the films more and more realistic. Mae West in her direct bawdy roles enjoyed her heyday during the early Thirties. A few years later, Shirley Temple became everybody's sweetheart, and Walt Disney's animated fables swept the land. During 1939, Clark Gable and Vivian Leigh's performance in Gone With The Wind marked an all-time high. But alas, even as early as 1929, the old reliable Pantages vaudeville fell before the motion pictures' increasing technological perfection and was transformed to an orthodox movie house.

In 1932, partly because of the lack of musicians whose livelihood had depended on silent movies and partly because of the general difficulties of the times, the Edmonton Symphony Orchestra disbanded. On the other hand, three years later the Edmonton Civic Opera grew out of the ladies' chorus of the Women's Musical Club. Starting then and destined to carry on for some thirty years, Mrs. J. B. Carmichael thrilled the musically minded by her capable direction of the Opera group. During the depression Mrs. Elizabeth Sterling Haynes began her long and intensely productive reign in the field of drama.

The depression was a time of testing for those dauntless devotees of the arts who carried on despite it. By sheer tenacity they hung on, yielding on this front but holding the line on that one, and ever persisting. The old Empire Theatre, once so elegant, became a symbol of the times when little money could be spent on entertainment. Little by little it got shabby, here and there chairs broke and were not repaired, and when year by year, pieces of the panelling warped and shredded away, they were left to hang in tatters.

Adding a musical comedy touch to the otherwise dreary civic election campaigns of the Thirties, Fred Speed, a wistful carpenter, made five abortive consecutive attempts to gain the mayor's chair. Announcing antipathy for quack politicians, in 1934 he convinced fifty electors to mark their ballots in his favour. Undismayed, he was back in the ring in 1935 with a platform which certainly might have been expected to yield him better results, for he advocated reform of the monetary system. While his views did bring a large percentage increase in his following, he nevertheless polled only seventy-two votes. Next year, trying another tack, he restricted his campaign speeches to recitations from Shakespeare, but the great dramatist's ideas were a poor second to monetary reform, and Speed's total vote slipped back to fifty-four. Again in 1937, on some other platform, his sixty-two voters left him at the bottom of the poll. Then in 1938 his persistence paid off a little better, for 198 citizens, catching some of Speed's unquenchable spirit, voted for him. They were not enough, however, for John Fry was elected with a handsome majority of 13,000.

Another politician whose perennial appearance on the ballot made him the city's mayor during 1919-1920 and during 1935-1937, kept Edmontonians entertained in various ways. That was Joe Clarke, and when he ran, the citizens were either violently for or violently against him. In his younger days he had been to the Klondike, but of equal importance in Edmontonians' eyes was the fact that he had also been a good athlete. As mayor he did all he could to encourage sports of one kind or another. Football was his favourite, and for many years he tried to bring the present stadium into being.

In 1906, in the general area of the modern football field, the federal government had established the penitentiary — abbreviated in popular parlance to "the pen", but curiously enough spelled Penn. Since it was sited over a coal seam, its inmates were put to work mining, and for years Edmontonians boasted that theirs was the only penitentiary in Canada which mined its own coal. Then, although in 1920 the prison was closed, the underground workings, now in the hands of a company called the Penn Mine Company, continued to undermine the surrounding area. Edmontonians, no longer proud of the mine, objected to its continual burrowing hither and yon under the east end, and on many an occasion Mayor Joe Clarke beseeched Ottawa to have it stopped. By 1929 Joe's efforts paid off and the mine was closed.

But Joe was far from through with the Penn site, and before long had it transferred to the city. Then he helped to set up an organization which in 1938 constructed the present stadium and grandstand. That year the Eskimos, revived by the efforts of Nick McPhee and other businessmen, once more aroused Edmontonians. Their spurt was of short duration, because when the war came along they once more fell into the background. When the stadium was finished Joe Clarke was entirely off the council, but that body, casting around for a name for their thriving property, very fittingly called it Clarke Stadium.

While all of these varying activities helped Edmontonians to take their minds off some of their daily problems, their standard antidote was still the Grads, who during the Thirties continued their winning streak and their hold on the citizens' sentiment. In 1932 they won at the Olympic Games at Los Angeles, and when in 1936 the next Olympics were held in Berlin, they repeated the performance. Their unique record is too lengthy to detail here, but part of it is given in the Appendix. Finally in 1940, with the war on and having no more worlds to conquer and after being champions for a quarter of a century, the Grads disbanded.

After any of these varying activities, either football or basketball, or at any other festive moment, Edmontonians flocked to their favourite Rite Spot. For the Rite Spots, five in all, with three of them on Jasper Avenue, were a chain of remarkable hamburger stands. All Edmontonians of those days still recall with mouth-watering memories the excellence of the hamburgers, doughnuts, pie and coffee prepared for them under the watchful eyes of Mr. and Mrs. Clarence Morris.

While the Grads were the city's outstanding genuine amateur athletes, other sports' leaders besides Percy Page were continuing the uphill battle to preserve the old Greek view of sports, "The trophy is worthy of the chase". One of these now honoured in the Canadian AAU Hall of Fame was John Leslie of the police force, who devoted some thirty years of his life in Canada to fostering amateur sports. In doing so, he attended various British Empire Games and some of the same Olympics in which the Grads played a part. For many years he was secretary for Canada of the Amateur Athletic Union. He died suddenly in 1943, the day before he was slated to assume the duties of Edmonton's chief of police.

Joe Clarke . . . Mayor of Edmonton 1919-1920, 1935-1937 and an outstanding sportsman who brought Clarke Stadium into being.

Punch Dickins

Leigh Brintnell

Matt Berry

Grant McConachie

A few of the scores of Edmonton's outstanding "bush pilots" who pioneered in northern flying.

Because Edmontonians worshipped the Grads, it was no wonder that they involved the girls in a parade and a dual celebration which not only showed them off but also gave public recognition to two of the city's flying heroes, Wop May and Punch Dickins. In 1928 Dickins won the McKee Trophy. In the spring of 1930 Wop received word that he was the 1929 winner. On May 12, 1930, the premier, the mayor and many another big-wig, joined in a parade from 98 Street and Jasper Avenue to the Legislative Building. For blocks the 30,000 citizens lining the streets cheered for the central figures — the Grads and their coach, Percy Page, and Wop and Punch. No one realized more clearly than these two aviators that, while they received the crowd's acclaim, it was, after all, a tribute to all of Edmonton's daring bush pilots.

Although the depression did nothing to help the growing airport, nevertheless, its restraining claws could not hold back an industry so pregnant with potentiality. Ever with an eye on the North, Edmonton found that most of its airport business was similarly oriented. On many an occasion when the bush pilots, foreseeing the opportunities of the future, were financially powerless to press their visions forward, Edmonton's businessmen rallied to help them. Though scraping the bottom of their own financial barrels, they advanced capital and helped to launch what must have appeared to be risky air ventures. To these businessmen Edmontonians owe much more than they realize.

Gradually, the bush pilots, as they were beginning to be called, were expanding their knowledge of the North and devising new tricks and new equipment to cope with its rigours. In 1930, for instance, Punch Dickins flew the first northern plane to be equipped with short-wave radio, one of Western Canada Airways' Fokkers. That year too, Punch became involved in the "Copper Rush" to Great Bear Lake. One day that fall, on Dickins' arrival at Jimmy Bell's air harbour, the pilot is reported to have said that he had counted "seven machines at Fitzgerald, two at Fort Rae, six at Hunter Bay, two at Coppermine. And as we flew from Coppermine to Hunter Bay we passed two more machines in the air."

At last the North, with its mineralized pre-Cambrian rocks, was coming into its own, and aeroplanes were the combination to unlock its widely dispersed vaults. True enough the pre-Cambrian regions were far north of Alberta, but Edmonton, the gateway to them, was their beneficiary. Because of the business inherent in its interest in the North, the Edmonton Flying Club was described in eastern papers as the "Outstanding Aviation Centre in Canada". And now the thoroughly airminded Edmonton citizens planned to do all they could to keep it so. In 1930 the Edmonton Aero Club established two Dominion records; it rang up the most flying hours, and it turned out the greatest number of licensed pilots. Among these young pilots was Grant McConachie, who, after a spell in northern flying, was to write his name in large letters in world-wide aviation circles.

By 1931 the Dominion authorities had set up a chain of beacons, which, blinking and flashing all through the nights, guided pilots from Winnipeg to Regina, Saskatoon, Calgary and Edmonton. That year too, the world-famous flyers, Wiley Post and Harold Gatty, in their *Winnie Mae,* made Edmonton one of their refuelling stops. Travelling into the morning sun, they refuelled in Edmonton and went on in one non-stop hop to reach New York. They had circled the globe in nine days, a new record.

They could not have done so, however, if they had not had an assist from one of the reminders of real estate boom days, Portage Avenue, slicing its way straight as an arrow through two miles of weeds on the old Hudson's Bay Company's Reserve. Blatchford Field adjoining it was inadequate to allow the *Winnie Mae,* laden with 540 gallons of gasoline, to lift off, but the long concrete vista of Portage Avenue was perfect.

That year Leigh Brintnell started his Mackenzie Air Service, and two other experienced northern pilots, Matt Berry and Stan McMillan, started flying for him. Before long they were taking in supplies to Labine's Eldorado Mining Company's camp at Great Bear Lake. Later, as more development took place, the Mackenzie Air Service shared with water transportation from McMurray the task of taking material in for the concentrator there.

Assisted by aircraft, more and more prospectors began wandering around the pre-Cambrian Shield, tapping a rock here or sampling a streak there. Though results were slow in materializing, some of the prospectors hit pay-dirt. By 1936, many of them had found gold veins, and Yellowknife, with its Consolidated Mining & Smelting, its Negus and its Giant properties, came into being. Two years later, between them these mines were turning out over $2 million of gold. Other mines, Wray Lake, Snare River, Beaulieu River and several others, began to interest Edmonton's financial men. All this activity found its supply base in Edmonton, and to ensure that the mines were served efficiently, John Michaels was largely instrumental in setting up the Northwest Chamber of Mines, with a well known mining man, L. E. Drummond, in charge of it. This move in itself did much to ensure Edmonton's predominance as the gateway to the Far North.

As the years went by and the northern mines developed, all of Edmonton's pilots began taking a hand at unloading gold and silver ingots at Blatchford Field. Many Edmonton bush pilots won the coveted McKee Trophy. Captain Maurice Burbidge of the Edmonton Flying Club carried it off in 1932. He was followed in 1933 by Walter Gilbert, and in 1934 by Elmer Fullerton. Then, as a change in pace, in 1935 the winner was W. M. Archibald, a pilot himself, who as manager of the Consolidated Mining & Smelting Company had sponsored so much airborne exploration. He was followed the next year by the redoubtable Matt Berry.

In 1937, young Grant McConachie, who had been flying fish and anything else he could get out of the north and generally keeping his financial affairs afloat, pioneered in a new direction toward Whitehorse. He decided that by incorporating Yukon Southern Transport Ltd., he could hold his own by serving the sparse settlements which lay along the old Klondike Trail of '98. To make this feasible he obtained a contract to fly mail to Whitehorse. On July 5, 1937, he took off from the Cooking Lake Seaplane Base on the first flight and made the trip in eleven hours. Little knowing how rapidly fate and world war would follow in his wake, he led the way through canyons and over mountains to the Yukon. By this time, of course, planes were equipped with two-way radio, and the Dominion government established ground radio and weather stations at Fort St. John, Fort Nelson and Lower Post.

By 1937, forty-two planes were working out of the base at Jimmy Bell's Blatchford Field. Mining in the far north was becoming an important industry, with major mines operating at Yellowknife and on Great Bear Lake. A second hangar and then a third were built at Edmonton's municipal airport, while Ottawa, finally aroused from its lethargy, provided money for better runways and more land to make them longer. Within a year or so, Trans-Canada Air Lines came into being, and regular passenger service gave Edmontonians commercial access to the rest of Canada. How far Ottawa was keeping an eye on Europe, and how far it was concerned solely with keeping up with the growing air industry in the United States, is hard to say, but for Edmonton the modern air age had arrived.

In much the same way that men like Mayor Blatchford, Jimmy Bell, Wop May and Grant McConachie, had pulled Edmonton's airport up by its boot-straps, a few local men, struggling against adversity, kept Edmonton's militia regiment alive by their determination. It was quite a struggle too, for in a democracy everyone wants to forget war the moment it is won and has no time for anyone who suggests getting ready for a future one.

In such a situation Edmonton's leading soldiers found themselves during the depression. No one but they gave a thought to the army. Looking to the past, however, the great Vimy pilgrimage of six thousand old soldiers helped most Canadians to remember the last war. So too did the unveiling of Edmonton's cenotaph in 1936. The year after that the former mayor and one-time Major-General, W. A. Griesbach, was put on the shelf of Canada's Senate. Wars were memories only, but a nation should preserve some souvenirs of them.

As a souvenir, however, Griesbach refused to lie down. In 1938, in a much quoted speech, he predicted that war with Italy, Germany and Japan was imminent. Some people pricked up their ears, but many pushed them further into the sand to try to avoid even hearing what was going on.

At that time Mussolini had long since settled matters in Ethiopia, and Japan was putting more pressure into its war with China. In 1938 Hitler took over Austria and the Sudetenland. As a result, the Edmonton newspapers published pictures of Sudeten refugees leaving the city to start new lives on bush homesteads near Pouce Coupe, British Columbia. About this time, General McNaughton, Canada's Chief of Staff, was asked for a report on the state of the military stock-pile. His report said: "Except as regards rifles and rifle ammunition, partial stocks of which were inherited from the Great War — there are none." All of his report was in the same vein and concluded with the wry statement: "About the only article of which stocks are held is horses. The composition of a modern land force will include very little horsed transport."

Then with the thunderheads of war piling high into the sky, Their Majesties King George VI and Queen Elizabeth, toured Canada, and on June 2, 1939, visited Edmonton. Albertans by the thousands flocked to see them, some out of the curiosity that drags crowds to gape at a movie star, but most because of a tightening of the throat muscles inherent in confronting face to face these dutiful symbols of all that was fine in the centuries-old British tradition. From stands erected to hide the emptiness bounding the two-mile stretch of Portage Avenue (that day renamed Kingsway Avenue), 68,000 Albertans watched and cheered. Other scores of thousands congregated along downtown streets. For the occasion, Edmonton's army units added colour and verve.

The *Edmonton Journal* seized the opportunity to point out that "The volunteer militia is starved . . . the appropriation for the militia must be increased."

Some two months later, on August 25, Germany and Russia signed their non-aggression pact. Then on September 1, Hitler's bombers and panzer columns started their quick clean-up of Poland. Two days later Britain was at war, and on Sunday, a week later, Canada declared war on Germany.

Their majesties, King George VI and Queen Elizabeth passing nearly five miles of crowded bleacher seats along Portage Avenue occupied by 68,000 people, June 2, 1939, when avenue was renamed Kingsway.

Jasper Avenue 1931

World War Two And After

1939-1946

chapter 18

EDMONTON WAS AT WAR AGAIN. This time, however, it was with a better understanding of what war was all about and with some readiness, though still woefully inadequate, on Ottawa's part. Moreover, between the wars, the Prince of Wales Armoury had been built and the army now had a headquarters. Furthermore, back in 1923, the navy had opened HMCS Nonsuch in an abandoned Hudson's Bay Company stable. As interest in nautical matters grew, the Nonsuch expanded to become the base for Edmonton's surprising naval contribution to the war. Few Edmontonians, however, called to mind the interesting coincidence that the Nonsuch, started in a Hudson's Bay Company stable, bore the same name as the tiny ship which in 1668 that company had sent out to Hudson Bay to see if trading in Canada would be a profitable venture.

During the First War the Exhibition Grounds and its stables had been taken over by the army. During the Second War they were assigned to the air force and as No. 2 Manning Depot became the principal centre for many of the empire's airmen who arrived in Edmonton for the British Commonwealth Air Training Plan.

Even though World War II had started, an air of unreality prevailed. Edmontonians had become more blasé and the war had not hit the man on the street with the same impact experienced twenty-five years earlier. The centuries-old Hudson's Bay Company made the most noteworthy display of interest when in its windows it exhibited a collection of the recruiting posters used during the previous war. As in that other war, all the various peace-time organizations pitched in to help shoulder the new effort.

On September 1, 1939, Ottawa placed the Loyal Edmonton Regiment on a war footing, and Col. Stillman began signing up men in the city and sent recruiting officers to Peace River, Red Deer, Vegreville and Wetaskiwin. Although it was the successor to the old 49th Battalion and bore Edmonton's name with distinction, the Loyal Edmonton Regiment was only one in a host of units of all three services in which Edmontonians served. Since it maintained its identity throughout the war, perhaps we may consider it as typical of the contribution Edmontonians made in various other branches of the army.

By the beginning of October the battalion was up to strength. On December 8, at a ceremony attended by five thousand Edmontonians, John Michaels, who had a hand in so many ventures, gave the battalion the instruments for a first-class band. From Halifax a few days later, the battalion, 831 strong, sailed into the wintery submarine-infested Atlantic. Amongst its officers were Major E. B. Wilson, Major J. C. Jefferson, Captain K. A. Hamilton, Captain E. W. Day and Lieutenant Alan Macdonald. On the last day of the year the unit sailed into the mouth of the Clyde.

Up to this point, though everyone feared the worst, the war had been surprisingly innocuous. Poland, of course, had been laid waste, but in France and Belgium opposing armies merely watched each other. In Britain the war was still unreal, while in Canada, Mackenzie King, outstanding Prime Minister though he was, bobbed about timidly in a sea of uncertainty, occasionally popping into the security of a curtained room to consult a spiritualist medium. As yet, concerned with holding his ill-matched French and Anglo-Saxon team together and asserting Canada's independence from an undefined and illusory chimera, his heart was not in the war.

Then on May 10 the real war set in, for that morning the *Blitzkrieg* started, and Hitler's armies crashed into Belgium and Holland. That day too, Britain, fed up with the unfortunate Neville Chamberlain, laid itself in Winston Churchill's hands. Immediately a new spirit swept the allied world.

By June 14, Hitler's armies occupied Paris, and France fell out of the war. Invasion stared Britain in the face. Between the hosts of Germany and allied defeat stood Winston Churchill, who a few days later stirred the world with his "Let us brace ourselves to our duties and so bear ourselves that, if the British Empire and its Commonwealth last for a thousand years, men will still say 'This was their finest hour'." The Battle of Britain was about to begin. And the British, bearing its brunt and now in desperate straits, rallied around their inspired leader. Now the war was real — too real.

All summer Edmontonians in many army units traipsed around Britain doing all that was required of them but fretting over inaction. All the while the men acquainted themselves with the new-style weapons and manoeuvres which took advantage of yet mocked the rapid technological progress that a quarter of a century had brought.

Even when nearly a year later, in June 1941, Hitler, by another of those mistakes that often decide the outcome of a war, flung his armies and his air fleet against Russia, Edmonton's soldiers were still in Britain. Though officially the United States remained neutral, it leaned heavily towards the allied side, and during 1941 worked out its Lend-Lease Act, which provided inestimable help against Hitler. Even on December 7, 1941, when the Japanese attacked Pearl Harbour and brought the United States into the war, Edmonton's soldiers were still carrying out exercises and practising new techniques. Moving about, they practised this and perfected that proficiency, and waited, while at Stalingrad the aroused Russians minced up Hitler's 6th Army, and while in Africa the 8th British Army, working with the Australians, New Zealanders and Americans, harried Rommel's armies and captured some 225,000 enemy soldiers.

Finally, to get a crack at the real war, the Edmonton regiment, now under Lieut.-Colonel J. C. Jefferson and Major E. W. Day, sailed down the Clyde on June 29, 1943, on its way to join General Montgomery's 8th Army in Italy. In less than two weeks, it landed along with some 80,000 men of the 8th Army at the southern tip of Italy. Heading inland across the mountainous terrain and travelling in a circle about Sicily for two months, the regiment mopped up units of enemy resistance. It had a tough time at Leonforte and Adrano, and finally crossed the Straits of Messina to mainland Italy.

This spell in Sicily was its first taste of real warfare, and in it Edmontonians proved themselves to be soldiers fit to carry on the proud tradition of the old 49th. An old soldier, sizing them up and remembering how their fathers had fought in the First War, thought them to be less tough, less reckless and less individual than the men of the original battalion. On the other hand, they were better trained, had a wider range of abilities which this new type of warfare demanded, and were better disciplined. This was to be expected. Their fathers had been pioneers in the West, tough, reckless individuals, whose boast, and, to some extent whose loss, was that they loathed discipline. For in spite of Sam Hughes' 1914 booklet assuring everybody that Canadians were the world's wonder soldiers, they were to suffer from a lack of training and discipline.

The Second World War was so vastly different from the first that perhaps its only common denominators were wounds and death. Where for months in the mud of France the old 49th had slogged it out in muddy trench warfare and a month's gains were counted in hundreds of yards, this new warfare was mobile. In four weeks in Sicily the Edmonton Regiment helped drive the Germans two hundred miles. It was a war of tanks, trucks and transportation, of buses, bulldozers and Bailey bridges, of radio, anti-aircraft guns and massive fire power. In such a war the boys from the prairies, to whom machinery was second nature, were in their element. In such a war where electronics was called into play, the new generation, better educated and better technicians, found full scope for their civilian adaptiveness. In such a war which involved extensive manoeuvres, Albertans, accustomed to focusing on vast distances in their daily life, were at home.

During 1944 the allied forces took Rome and Naples, and started pressing north towards Florence. On July 25 Benito Mussolini was captured. The Loyal Edmonton Regiment soon found itself in the thick of the heavy fighting for the Gothic Line and the Rimini Line. At the bitter battle of San Fortunato the Regiment distinguished itself again before reaching Italy's east shore once more. Other battles followed, but finally they spent their sixth Christmas away from home at the seashore near Rimini.

Until the spring of 1945 the Germans, backing up towards the Alps, held on, but then in one day 230,000 of Hitler's troops surrendered. By that time most of Edmonton's soldiers had been transferred to France and Holland and were pursuing broken remnants of the Germans there. On May 1 Hitler committed suicide, and two days later the war with Germany was over.

While it has been easy to deal with the exploits of the Edmonton battalion because it stuck together as a unit, the parts played by Edmontonians in other services, such as the Signals, Ordnance, Engineers, Artillery, and others, were equally as great.

So too was their service at sea. Scores of vigorous young Edmontonians answered the Royal Canadian Navy's call. Canada, hitherto nearly devoid of any naval tradition, started from scratch to do what it could to assemble its navy and its seamen as it went along. The navy built, bought or borrowed hundreds of cruisers and corvettes, destroyers, torpedo boats and mine sweepers, and sent them out into the cruel, wintery Atlantic to escort merchant ships along the life-line to Britain. During the amazing exploit that was the Battle of the Atlantic, Canada's naval ratings, often recruited from the baldheaded prairies but alert in the rumbling bellies of escort vessels, convoyed 25,000 merchant ships to Britain. Then, in other sectors of the far-flung seas, and on the way to Sicily, Africa and Western Europe, Canadian and Edmonton boys faced up to Germany's well-trained navy.

In the same way, Edmonton's contribution to the Air Force was spread over many units which served in so many flying capacities and groupings and on so many fronts that it is impractical to follow the fliers in any detail. Due to the fact that many of the air heroes of the First War were still alive and taking part in the civilian air industry they had created for it, Edmonton may well have been the most air-minded city in Canada. Then on top of that, due to the fact that the Air Force, even if it was the most dangerous of military services, was also the most glamorous, young Edmontonians joined it. Even though official lethargy on the part of Prime Minister Mackenzie King and his colleagues during the early months of the war made it difficult for Edmonton boys to start training as fliers and delayed their entering the Air Force, once they had an opportunity, they leaped at the chance to get into the air. Before the war was over, however, a quarter of a million Canadians were in the Air Force, and of its 18,000 casualties, 17,000 lost their lives!

Even before the war started, the Canadian government was not sold on its RCAF, and for several years in succession more young Canadians crossed the ocean to enlist in Britain's RAF than could get into Canada's Air Force. Mackenzie King's view was that an air force was only needed "sufficient to look after the defence of the Dominion." Feeling that, with the United States on one flank and Britain on another, a direct attack on Canada was most unlikely, he maintained but a token force. For these reasons, many a young Canadian and several young Edmontonians made magnificent contributions to the world's defence as members of the RAF instead of the RCAF.

When Canada got going and began to lavish money on its Air Force, Edmontonians flew and fought in all the far-flung theatres of war. Their courage, capability and initiative exhibited time and time again in the many branches of war-time flying was certainly equal to that of their comrades from America, Australia, Britain or New Zealand. Whether they served in the Battle of Britain as fighter or bomber crews, as intruder squadrons, army co-operation units, reconnaissance, or Coastal Command, or as ground staff on hundreds of airfields liable at a moment's notice to be bombed or machine-gunned, hundreds of Edmonton boys did their bit. In Edmonton's enthusiastic support of the Air Force, the city officially adopted RCAF 418 Squadron, which in its valour and fame amply repaid the gesture.

While its soldiers, sailors and air force men were doing their part all over the world, Edmonton carried on in a supporting role. In 1939 the city had emerged from the depression with 90,000 people. By 1941, in spite of the fact that many of its young men and women were overseas, its population had crept up to 93,817. For those Edmontonians who kept an eye on Calgary, this figure was a noticeable achievement, for at last, after trailing Calgary for many years, the northern city was now the larger by 5,000 people. During the long decade of the Thirties, while the province's population growth had been nearly ten percent, much of the increase had occurred in its northern half, and this was all to the good for Edmonton.

During the closing months of the depression the province's economy had been gradually righting itself; the onslaught of the war had quickly put everyone to work again. As a result of the First War, the Federal government had learned a great deal, and in 1939 began applying war-time controls and financial policies aimed at preventing prices, profits and wages from skyrocketing. Consequently, while everybody found work to do, inflation was held in check. By the end of the war the cost of living had risen only twenty percent. Canada, as well as supplying military personnel, found an invaluable role in manufacturing munitions and equipment. The United States, for a year or so technically neutral but otherwise pitching in on the allied side, assisted Canada in many ways so as to keep the country's financial situation stable. With this assistance, Canada finally emerged from the war as a strong manufacturing nation which had spent $18 billion on the war, had paid its way, and was financially solvent.

In various ways, Edmontonians played a part in the Dominion's manufacturing effort. Moreover, the increasing demand for farm production led to better conditions in the surrounding countryside, and this in turn led to greater business and greater employment in the city. Then, superimposed on all this activity, came a great influx of air force trainees. The RCAF took over the university residences and hundreds of young men trained there. The Exhibition Grounds were commandeered and became a Manning Depot, and through it passed hundreds of other young volunteers. For the air force, the Canadian Pacific Airlines took on the task of operating an Air Observers' School and called upon Wop May with his vast experience to head it up and to staff it with as many of the old bush pilots as he could find. After these various training efforts swung into action, Edmonton swarmed with eager youths in their blue air force uniforms.

The influx of civilians and military personnel was the first noticeable sign of the changes which were coming over the city. Along with it came the virtual transformation of the airport, where by means of Jimmy Bell's air harbour, Edmontonians made a major contribution to the war effort.

One of Canada's greatest offerings to that effort was the magnificent part it played in the Commonwealth Air Training Plan, turning out 130,000 pilots, navigators or bombers. The Edmonton Aero Club, which had established an enviable record during peace-time, added to its laurels. First of all, Blatchford Field was transferred to Dominion jurisdiction. Then, almost overnight, it became the busiest airport on the continent. The Department of National Defence started a tremendous program of building new hangars and barracks and offices for trainees.

On top of the efforts in meeting the combined British and Canadian needs, Edmonton suddenly came into focus as a strategic centre in United States defence plans. Keeping an eye on the Japanese, who were suspected of keeping an eye on Alaska, the United States resolved not to be caught napping. Accordingly, in 1940, Canada and the United States combined forces in the Permanent Joint Defence Board, and that brought a searching look at the old Klondikers' route to the Yukon. The Americans, needing a rapid way of building up Alaska's defences, resorted to a huge airlift operation. Edmonton pilots, who were still available to be diverted to other activities, pitched in to help. Pilot Con Farrell, promoted to Wing Commander, was placed in charge of maintaining the greatly stepped up operation which became known as the Northwest Staging Route. Airfields along Grant McConachie's civilian Yukon Southern route to Whitehorse had to be up-graded, and hundreds of United States servicemen came in to do it. Once the Americans went to work, huge hangars sprouted as if by magic amidst a forest of huts at the east edge of Blatchford Field. As a temporary expedient, some of the existing runways were lengthened by the use of strips of steel mesh hastily shipped in from the United States. New runways were also built and soon began to accommodate the endless stream of freighters, fighters and bombers which were soon making their way to and from Alaska. All of this bustle, added to that of a new aircraft repair branch set up to mend crippled planes shipped over from the Battle of Britain, made Blatchford Field the busiest sector of Edmonton. On top of this, Canadian Pacific Airlines bought out Mackenzie Air Services and McConachie's Yukon Southern Transport, and started to enlarge their operations, all aimed at Yukon and Alaska.

Then on December 7, 1941, far away in the Pacific Ocean at Pearl Harbour, the Japanese caught the Americans napping and destroyed their Pacific fleet. That did it. Now Americans were officially at war, and in a mighty jump they leaped to the defence of Alaska, pausing in Edmonton on the way. But even when Americans are pausing they whiz around, and if Edmontonians had been amazed at their activity on the Northwest Staging Route and on the airlift to Alaska, they now found themselves whirled off their sober old feet. In short order the Americans built most of the institutional accommodation they needed, including a United States army hospital and an army recreation centre. For part of their office space they shipped in lumber from the great forests of California and flung up the Redwood Building on Jasper near 112 Street. They also obtained more space by renting the old Empire Theatre.

No grass had time to grow to hinder the American leap to Alaska. Bombs had rained on Pearl Harbour in December; on February 2, 1942, the United States engineers were called in to discuss the possibility of a road to Alaska; on February 14 they were told to build one. February 16 saw them in Ottawa, and on March 9, five officers and 127 men of a quartermaster detachment detrained at Dawson Creek. For as well as 302 miles in Alaska, the United States had offered to build and maintain 1,221 miles of highway on Canadian soil.

Before long this detachment was followed by 10,000 troops, 7,000 pieces of rolling equipment, forty-one American and thirteen Canadian contractors, and 17,000 civilians. By August 1, 1942, 858 miles of highway had been located. By September 24 clearing crews, working from each end, met at a point 305 miles west of Fort Nelson, and four days later the first truck from Dawson Creek reached Whitehorse — 1,030 miles, at an average speed of around 15 MPH. A month later, the last gap on the road far beyond that was closed by a ceremony at Kluane Lake, 151 miles north of Whitehorse. The first convoy from Dawson Creek arrived at Fairbanks on November 22. Although it still required up-grading and was not considered to be in final shape till October 15, 1943, this Alaska road, previously considered an impossibility, had been pushed through 1,523 miles of the world's worst terrain in nine months. It had cost $139 million, and after the war was destined to be sold to Canada.

Even though the Americans rushed the Alaska Highway through in record time, they had only reached the stage of picking out its right-of-way when on June 3, 1942, the Japanese struck at Alaska by attacking Dutch Harbour. Immediately the United States redoubled its efforts to send aircraft to its isolated northern state, and a day or so after the attack 30 USAF DC-3's came whining in to a landing in Edmonton. Servicing them presented difficulties to the airport authorities and the mere problem of parking them was a major task because they blocked up all the taxi strips on the field. Their arrival, however, was only a beginning, for, as Jimmy Bell recalled when reminiscing after the war: "For reasons of security, the complete story can never be told. But I'll never forget a great day in June of 1942 when five hundred planes passed through here, mostly *en route* to Alaska."

Planes of all sorts, arriving and leaving every minute or so, placed a nearly unbearable load on the airport's facilities, for not only was the United States sending everything it could to Alaska, but it was engaged in another major effort which was hushed up at the time. That was the transfer of hundreds of lend-lease planes to Russia. Amongst them were some fifteen hundred P-39 Bell Airacobras which passed through Edmonton at this critical time. While those in close touch with the airport knew what was going on, this great effort to help Russia was an official secret. It was never mentioned in the newspapers and it was not until late in 1943 that the United States Secretary of Defence made an explanatory announcement.

Bell, busy as a hen with chicks seeing that this heavy volume of traffic landed and took off smoothly and safely, may have thought that handling five hundred planes a day was a major undertaking, but he was to find out that even then Blatchford Field had not reached its limit. On September 23, 1943, the field staff established what was thought to be a North American record when in one day 860 planes passed through their hands.

Because the field was so busy with planes going about their vital defence missions, it became obvious that pilot training should be shifted to other fields such as Penhold, so as to leave Blatchford Field for more pressing duties. About this time too, the American authorities decided to build a satellite field to relieve the pressure. They selected the site at Namao, some ten miles north of Edmonton's post office, and after they had spent $7 million there, that major field took its place in the American scheme of things. Taking in 2,560 acres and having 7,000-foot runways, it was the largest airport on the continent, and as soon as it was ready it slipped into high gear, still ferrying lend-lease planes to Russia.

In conjunction with the Alaska Highway, the Americans decided that they needed oil from the Norman Wells field, so over mountains and muskeg they built the 500-mile-long Canol Pipeline to supply a refinery at Whitehorse. Second in interest only to the highway, this pipeline resurrected all the romance in Edmontonians' souls. Wrapped up in one parcel, it had all the elements that appealed to the hundreds who for so long had looked to the north and dreamed of the day when its riches would come into their own.

Since the pipeline was to cross over the Mackenzie Mountains from Fort Norman on the Mackenzie River to Whitehorse in the Yukon, it revived memories of the days of Edmonton's Klondike rush. Although few realized that the line was to take a route as direct as possible and therefore did not correspond to the way the Klondikers had tried to get through, its construction recalled those Edmontonians who half a century earlier had struck out for the goldfields.

It also recalled the excitement of the days of 1920 when Imperial Oil Limited had discovered oil at Norman Wells. In those days Charlie Taylor, a geologist and a brother of Alex Taylor who in 1886 had installed Edmonton's first telephone system, had been associated with George Gorman and Elmer Fullerton, the fliers who had piloted the two Junkers planes on their accident-ridden trip to the wells.

Then too, whereas the Alaska Highway had been served by one of Edmontonians' railway ventures, the old E.D. & B.C. Railway, which though heavily over-taxed, had performed admirably in getting material through to Dawson Creek, this Canol project had relied heavily on Edmonton's other north-seeking railway, the Alberta Great Waterways. Down it went trainloads of pipe, which at Waterways were taken in hand by river scows and floated for hundreds of miles down the

Athabasca and Mackenzie rivers — the old waterways which, though remote from Edmonton, had for so long been part of the city's route of communication with its great north land.

The Canol pipeline was an indication that at last the resources of the far north were to be developed. The north in which so many Edmontonians had invested money, the north towards which Edmontonians had pushed railways and in which they had developed a major system of water transportation was beginning to vindicate their long held hopes.

During the building of the Alaska Highway, the Northwest Service Command naturally located one of its main engineering offices in Edmonton. The giant consortium of contractors, Bechtel, Price and Callahan, which played such a large part in the highway and in the Canol project, established a headquarters in the city. Before long they built the warehousing facilities which came to be known as the American Railhead out near 142 Street. Somehow it seemed fitting that the railway spur to serve it was a continuation of Edmonton's first railway, the Edmonton, Yukon and Pacific of 1902 vintage.

With all this activity directed towards Alaska, the so-called American invasion hit Edmonton as hundreds of United States personnel made their homes and headquarters in the city and rented every bit of available office and living accommodation. For two or three years, ordinary commercial travellers, still going about their civilian business on a greatly curtailed scale, had the utmost difficulty finding sleeping accommodation in Edmonton. In all the hotels, two or three wayfarers bunked in one bedroom or even in one bed, and many men stretched out to sleep on the floor of hotel lobbies.

The streets swarmed with American personnel. As well as taking all the available accommodation, they were accused, probably with some semblance of truth, of taking over the beer parlours and all available girls, and of stripping the stores by sending shoes, fur coats and English china back home.

Their very presence and the amount of money they had to spend overtaxed but gave a lift to Edmonton's entertainment facilities. During this régime Tony's Steak House, near the Corona Hotel, became well known for the excellence of its cooking. For years the supper dances at the Macdonald Hotel had been the mainstay of the city's smart young set. The influx of various military personnel added to the presence of hundreds of well paid Americans, overloaded the Mac's facilities and before long reservations for the supper dance had to be made three or four weeks ahead. During this era another of the old Hudson's Bay Company's stables was converted to a new use and became a dance hall called The Barn. In it scores of younger Edmontonians, as well as hundreds of military people and Americans who spent some time in the city, enjoyed its camaraderie.

Undoubtedly it was partly responsible for the fact that during their stay in the city several hundred Americans married local girls. Although before being posted to Edmonton many Americans may have had only a vague idea that somewhere far away amidst the snows of northern Canada lay a city called Edmonton, their stay here introduced them to some of the city's merits, and as well as marrying local girls, many of them returned to live in the city after the war.

While many an Edmontonian, annoyed at the crowd and at the sight of American uniforms everywhere, wished they would go home, their behaviour was exemplary. Trained by half a century of service club greeters and imbued with the almost pathological American desire to be friendly, they leaned over backwards to be agreeable. And Edmonton appreciated their attitude and liked them.

On Sunday, November 15, 1942, almost a week before the break-through ceremony at Kluane Lake, nineteen and one half inches of heavy snow fell in one record-breaking short storm on an Edmonton completely without snow removal equipment. By late afternoon Sunday the transit system gave up the fight and streetcars remained stranded at various points along the lines. By Monday morning, when everyone was anxious to go to work, neither automobiles nor trucks could buck the drifts. By Monday evening one or two streetcars were rolling along the heavily populated lines. Bakeries and dairies warned householders that no deliveries could be expected before Tuesday.

Drifts, sometimes fifteen feet deep, halted all movement along roads in the surrounding country. Even Jasper Avenue was waist-deep in drifts, and a few venturesome souls brought their skis and enjoyed the thrill of speeding down Jasper Avenue, dodging the car tops that were visible above the drifts. For three days the Highlands district was completely isolated.

Prior to this time Edmonton had given no more than perfunctory thought to snow removal equipment. In eastern cities, larger and more frequently plagued with crippling storms, snow removal as we know it was just beginning. Fortunately for Edmontonians, the Alaska road organization and the American Airforce were in town. They pitched in with scrapers, loaders and trucks, and before long had cleared enough of the main streets so that traffic could move again.

While, of course, the Alaska Highway and the airports overshadowed all other activity, even without them Edmonton was still a busy and prosperous place. Once more eager hands exploited the resources within its vast tributary area. The mining ventures on Great Slave Lake and Great Bear Lake in the far north progressed steadily. Yellowknife was now a busy town of some 2,000 people, and each year its mines added some millions of dollars of gold to strengthen Canada's financial position. By 1942 the workings at Goldfields on Lake Athabasca, however, had been closed down. In spite of that, the business of supplying the north boomed as many an old timer had hoped it would and kept a great many Edmontonians employed.

Though natural gas had replaced coal in Edmonton's furnaces, and as a result the nearby mines were not operating to capacity, the province's coal production was in high gear. In 1938 Alberta's mines had shipped 5,230,000 tons, and from that point on their output climbed to an all-time record of 8,824,000 tons in 1946. The railways, busily shuttling war material back and forth, still used steam locomotives and took a third of Alberta's coal output. Mines all over the province were operating, but those up the Coal Branch had never been busier, and their wages all found their way to Edmonton's merchants. Throughout the war Alberta's mines employed nearly nine thousand men.

Between its three resources, the metal mines of the north, the coal mines mainly to the west, and farm lands everywhere, all doing their utmost for the war effort, Edmonton was kept busy.

With such activity, the province's financial position improved year by year. As it did, the clamour for Social Credit subsided but remained far from dormant. During 1943 thousands of Social Credit supporters were saddened by the death of Premier William Aberhart, who had led them in two spirited and successful campaigns. His disciple, Ernest Manning, a man sought out by destiny, assumed his mantle.

On January 21, 1945, Edmontonians found themselves lamenting General Griesbach's death. Unfortunately he had not lived to see the war's end. Towards

Canada's ultimate victory he had contributed much. In 1940, as Inspector General of Canadian forces in western Canada, he had managed to get himself back into harness. Turning up everywhere for the next three years, he boosted everyone's morale, until in 1943 illness forced him to resign.

On Tuesday, May 8, 1945, Edmontonians celebrated VE Day (Victory in Europe) in a subdued but typical manner. Joyful crowds gathered downtown with confetti and noise-makers; in the market square one group burned an effigy of Hitler, but on the whole the crowds hung around as if waiting for something to happen. Though they were joyful enough, and certainly immensely relieved, perhaps the fact that war was still raging in the Pacific damped their rejoicing.

When Japan caved in, however, and Edmontonians celebrated VJ Day on August 15, everybody cut loose into what many believe was the city's greatest celebration. It started with a huge victory parade, which was followed by dancing in various areas fenced off for the purpose. A huge old time dance filled the market square, while at the corner of 100A Street and 102 Avenue, the younger folk let themselves go in all the vigour expressed in the dances of those days. Here and there bands played, while the crowds sang "Waltzing Matilda," "Roll Out the Barrel," and many other war songs. For once the serious concentration so typical of Edmonton crowds vanished as spontaneity took over.

One of its expressions was a queue extending two blocks from the door of the government liquor vendor. Another was that displayed in one of Johnstone-Walker's windows where swastikas and other Nazi emblems had been thrown into one ash can and a number of Rising Sun flags had been cast into another. Above them appeared the simple statement, "That's That".

Like so many of Edmonton's soldiers, the Loyal Edmonton Regiment was still in Europe. After Germany's collapse, it carried out a number of cleaning-up operations in Holland and elsewhere, and for a while part of the battalion was stationed in Berlin. It was not until October 6, 1945, that its train pulled into the city.

But when it did, Edmonton went all out. Edmontonians took advantage of the return of the Loyal Edmonton Regiment to symbolize their gratitude for what all the men from the city and the surrounding area had done in one or other of the units of Canada's armies. Gathered at the saluting base at the corner of 101 Street and 102 Avenue were Lieut.-Governor Bowen, Premier Manning, Mayor Fry, and many other figures prominent in the city's life or intimately connected with the regiment. Of all these, the troops responded most wholeheartedly to Mrs. W. A. Griesbach, now a widow. Though it was a raw, windy day, the crowds' welcome and enthusiasm for Edmonton's own regiment, which had been away for over five years, presented an unforgettable and moving experience.

At last the war was really over.

Once more, after five long years, Edmontonians, both soldiers and civilians, turned back to the ways of peace. As one example, the university residences which had been turned over to the RCAF were now available to students of peace-time arts. As early as the fall of 1944 many veterans swelled the university's enrolment to 2,679 and one year later swept it to 3,447.

Everyone longed to pick up civilian life where it had left off five years earlier. But that ideal turned out to be impossible, for radar, atomic energy, electronics and jet engines had catapulted the world into a new era and the leisure and prosperity made possible by automation was just around the corner. In fact, in a small way, it had been showing up even during the war. For instance, before 1941, new movie theatres, the Varscona, the Garneau and the Odeon, had been opened. The movie industry, at its zenith in 1946, was never more prosperous and its box-office returns had swelled to fantastic heights.

Though various indigenous cultural activities had hung on through the long depression and had been throttled back during the war years, nevertheless, due to the untiring efforts of individuals who could not be repressed, the cultural pot was kept simmering. Mrs. J. B. Carmichael had kept her Edmonton Civic Opera alive and interesting. The Edmonton Symphony Orchestra, which had been disbanded in 1932, was revived in 1945, and with Mrs. Frank Mills as president and Abe Fratkin as director, it started upon a new career. In 1946, in the theatre, the Belasco Players, who had suspended operations during the early war years, started again. That year too, an outstanding woman, Mrs. Elizabeth Sterling Haynes, who until her death in 1957 devoted her amazing talents to the theatre, won the Canadian drama award for outstanding contribution to Canadian theatre. Over the years she undoubtedly inspired more people to creative abilities than any other person in the city. In the realm of painting, in 1945 the Edmonton Museum of Arts, under President Dr. Edgerton L. Pope, got a fresh start in the new Market Building, with R. W. Hedley as director. In 1946 the cultural yearning of the Ukrainians burst forth into a Folk Festival, including a parade through the streets in traditional costumes.

Now that the war was over many a businessman, alderman or economist tried anxiously to peer into the future. Mackenzie King had assembled the best Canadian cabinet of all time, and in this group the Hon. C. D. Howe stood out above all the others. That government and its civil service advisors had tried to prepare for the change to a peace-time economy, and on the whole had done a remarkably good job. Once war-time restrictions were removed, everyone expected prices to go up and inflation to get in its deadly blows. On the other hand, once war-time's feverish activity fell off, everyone expected the spectre of unemployment to have its way. Neither happened.

In the province, economists worried about how to keep all Albertans and their children at work. Some, of course, would be kept busy attending to the needs of the far north, but these would be merely a small sector of the population. In the field of minerals within Alberta, the demand for coal was likely to fall off, and already it was rumoured that the railways were thinking of running some of their locomotives with oil and even of replacing steam with diesel engines. Future employment in the coal mines did not appear good. As for oil and gas, Turner Valley had apparently hit its peak and was ready to decline, while, except for minor oilfields at Vermilion and Lloydminster, none of the numerous wildcat oil rigs had hit anything significant. While everyone was still trying to find oil and, being human, and, therefore, hopeful, would still continue to search, nevertheless, prospects for oil in Alberta began to appear remote. Another of Alberta's resources, its forest lands, had risen to cope with the war's demand for timber and lumber, but after VJ Day that too would fall off.

Even on the agricultural front the future was not bright. Most of the arable land had been settled. What was left was of a lower grade, remote from railways. Even though much land on existing farms could still be broken, the physical volume of agricultural production was expected to flatten out at a figure less than it had been during the war. The trend to more and better livestock and away from complete dependence on grain was good, but, whereas Alberta farmers' cash income had been $338 million at its highest point during the war, it had slumped badly by 1946 to $280 million. This trend, moreover, was likely to continue. On top of that, modern farms employed fewer people, and by 1946 the farm population had slipped to eighty-seven percent of what it had been in 1941. The rural areas were losing people to the cities.

But even in the cities now that the war was over, what would happen? If activities in coal, timber and farming were all going to decline, what would keep the cities from declining? For population-wise Alberta was not holding its own and had not been since 1931. Because its birth-rate was good and its death-rate favourable, the balance between the two — what statisticians called its natural increase — should have resulted in an increase in its population each year. Actually, even though on top of this there had been some immigration, the increase in population had been less than the natural increase — a clear indication that Alberta was dropping into a "have not" position where its young folk had to leave in order to make a living. Between 1931 and 1936 the natural increase had been about 55,000, but the increase in population had only been 41,000; 14,000 people had moved on to greener pastures. Similarly, for 1936 to 1941, while the natural increase had been 52,000, some 29,000 had sailed for other shores. Then in the more recent period, out of a net increase of 60,000, all but 7,000 had moved away!

Economists studying the figures shook their heads. Merchants in Alberta's cities, probably not knowing of the figures but seeing what their cash registers were ringing up, wondered at that lack of progress. Actually, during the five years ending 1946, Edmonton's population had climbed to 113,116, an increase of some 19,000 as against Calgary's population of 100,044, where the increase had been less marked. Though for the time being Edmonton could lord it over Calgary, now that the war and the Alaska road activity were over everyone felt that its population must also slip back.

A drive around the city did little to impress a visitor. It is true that Edmonton had many nice homes and many householders and institutions maintained the marvellous gardens of which everyone was proud. But the homes themselves were a generation out of style. Out of 28,000 of them, 11,000 had been built before 1920. Hardly any new office buildings or schools freshened the streets. Except for the addition of fluorescent lighting, which had come in during the war years and had done much to brighten store interiors, the stores were nearly all of the same old 1910 vintage. One step forward was the new Waterloo Motors layout on Jasper Avenue at 107 Street which pepped up the street and which, with its used car lots spread out under strings of lights, gave a foretaste of the future.

As for the streets themselves, they were a mess. Of 400 miles of streets only 70 were paved, an increase of 12 miles in ten years! Two hundred and eighty-seven miles of sidewalks carried the pedestrians, and while their length had increased from 255 miles a decade ago, only 59 miles were of concrete.

For this state of affairs, of course, the boom years were to blame, for they had thrown off satellite subdivisions with gay abandon, leaving vast empty spaces like the Hudson's Bay Company Reserve. Across these empty spaces transit system lines had to be built, as well as streets and sidewalks. In area, the city was big enough to hold some 300,000 in comfort, and yet its 113,116 people hallo'ing to each other across the gaps had to maintain its far-flung utilities.and services.

Both the city council, under Mayor Harry Ainlay, and the Chamber of Commerce did all they could to attract new industry. Since, however, like the rest of Alberta, Edmonton had to depend on one dominant resource industry which accounted for over fifty percent of the province's population, and since prospects for expansion of that industry were not rosy, there was little the mayor or the chamber could do. During the war, small manufacturing ventures had started up, and some diversification of the city's interests was evident, but its economy, like that of the province, was still based on agriculture and was still relatively simple in structure.

Worse than that, its prospects appeared dull. It was expected that though the area and production of farms would increase, the number of farmers would decrease, and with that decline the population of the province and of Edmonton would fall off. No one seemed to want two of Alberta's well known resources, its 25,000 million tons of mineable coal and its 171,000 square miles of forests, and physical resources are only valuable when someone wants them and will pay for their production. Alberta's great rivers slipped silently off to the sea. No one could foresee mills to turn or wheels to whirl with their several million horsepower of potential hydro power. Sealed into the Athabasca Oil Sands were at least 300 billion barrels of recoverable oil, but since no one needed them, no one had come forward with the magic millions of dollars that would liberate them. For decades up and down Alberta, venturesome drillers had probed the underlying rocks searching for the oil and gas, but they continued to elude them. So it appeared that Alberta and Edmonton would have to fall back into the old routine based on agriculture.

Jasper Avenue after World War II.

Oil Under Every Stook

1947-1956

chapter *19*

O N FEBRUARY 13, 1947, seventeen miles south-west of Edmonton's post office, a black smoke ring belched out of the flare line of Leduc Oil Well No. 1 and floated off into the wintry sky. A smoke signal of amazing portent. A signal that ushered in the province's oil era. Alberta had hit the jackpot and Edmonton scooped up the take.

Leduc turned out to be a field of 1,278 wells, containing two hundred million barrels of recoverable oil. Even in the world famous Texas area this would have been considered a major oilfield. With the Turner Valley field running down so quickly, just when Alberta's demand was rising so rapidly, local refineries were making desperate bids to import crude oil from the States. And then in November 1946 Vernon Hunter spudded in Leduc No. 1.

Early in February 1947, with the bit down some five thousand feet, the well showed indications of oil, and, acting on a hunch, Hunter set February 13 as the date when company and government officials, nosey newspaper reporters and prattling radio performers could come and witness the final proof of the well's success or failure. His hunch proved correct; Leduc No. 1 was co-operative.

A decade later, when reminiscing for a *Journal* reporter, Hunter recalled that: "By the morning of February 13 — the date set — we hadn't started to swab and that operation sometimes takes days . . . By noon a crowd was gathering. By four o'clock the less hardy had shivered their way back to town . . . Shortly before 4 p.m. the well started to show some signs of life. Then with a roar the well came in, flowing into the sump near the rig. We switched it to the flare line, lit the fire and the most beautiful smoke ring you ever saw went floating skywards."

And smack in the middle of that smoke ring sat Edmonton's fairy godmother.

By the end of 1947, in the Leduc field, Imperial Oil brought in twenty-three wells, and within a fifty-mile radius of Edmonton dozens of other companies drilled frantically at hundreds of wildcat wells. Then on January 18, 1948, some fourteen miles west of Edmonton's post office the first Woodbend well swooshed in, and that fall as Alberta's leaves were turning yellow, thirty miles north and east, Redwater came in. The fairy godmother, still astride her ring, circled Edmonton and strewed the farmers' fields with derricks, valves and oil tanks.

During 1948 in the Leduc-Woodbend area, companies drilled 147 wells. Five of them produced gas and oil, eleven were dry, and 131 fairly spouted oil. None of these, however, made such a fuss about it as Atlantic No. 1, a mile away from Leduc No. 1. On March 8, 1948, it went out of control and "blew out". Oil and gas gushed out, and, because they could not escape fast enough from the well-head, formed craters in the surrounding cultivated soil and flowed off in streams to form puddles and pools. Atlantic's employees scurried about throwing up dikes to prevent the oil from spreading farther and laying pipes to conduct it away. Since the small pipe line from the field to the railway eight miles distant could not cope with all this oil in addition to what the other wells were producing, most of the others were shut off so as to allow Atlantic's oil to be saved.

Instant death faced any driller unwary enough to strike a spark. Trucking tons of feathers, sawdust, wheat and cement, and stuffing them down Atlantic's maw failed to stanch the flow. Two other wells had to be drilled so as to slant in from a distance to tap the pool which was erupting so copiously. In September, before they succeeded in bringing Atlantic under control it caught fire. For days a great column of fire visible at night for nearly a hundred miles lured thousands of spectators from all over northern Alberta.

The summer-long excitement culminating in the great pillar of fire drew the eyes of the world to Alberta — to the Leduc field and to Edmonton. Now, everyone knew Alberta had an oilfield.

But the Leduc-Woodbend field was just starting. By 1949 it had 363 producing wells, by 1951 it had eight hundred, and went on to reach its full development in 1954 with 1,278 wells. Similarly, by 1949, Redwater had 278 producers and reached its maximum of 926 three years later.

Even then the godmother, still bobbing about on her smoke ring, had barely begun her benefices. The Joarcam field, twenty-five miles from Edmonton, came in during 1949, and before long had 475 wells. The Stettler field, one hundred miles away, proved up the same year with over a hundred wells, to be followed by the adjoining Big Valley field the next year with its three hundred wells. Then came many another smaller field; Golden Spike, Excelsior, Bon Accord, Acheson, Duhamel, Calmar, Wizard Lake, Bonnie Glen and Westerose, the farthest of these only fifty miles from Edmonton.

It looked as if these discoveries would never stop, and even now it still looks that way. In 1953 the Sturgeon Lake field, 120 miles north and west, came in. That year also, to top all other fields, the huge Pembina reservoirs were tapped, and three years later were yielding from 1,680 wells. As if to make up for the seventy years when time after time Edmonton's oil seekers suffered failure and frustration, now, month after month fate filled their flare lines with oil and gas.

Edmontonians lived in a dream world. Every month brought some fresh discovery, and every month saw more drilling rigs and seismic trucks coming in, more low-boys and more pipe and casing rumbling by on huge trucks. Every week saw some new warehouse going up in frantic haste to service the new fields. Every month saw some more mud carried in to add to that churned up by the big trucks on the endless miles of streets still not paved — black, sticky mud smelling like rotten eggs. But it was the smell of an oil town, and no matter how it offended the nostrils, it contented the pocketbook.

In Alberta, 1956 ended with 7,390 wells gushing oil where ten years earlier only 418 wells had trickled, and three-quarters of these thousands were in territory tributary to Edmonton. A favourite Edmonton pastime was to load two or three

The earth yields its second harvest.

visitors from less fortunate cities like Winnipeg, Toronto or Montreal, into a car and drive them through the oilfields. During the early years of the boom, one could pass a dozen derricks in as many miles, and they were even more impressive at night when every one of them, rattling and clanging away, was lit up like a Christmas tree; gazing away across the flat fields scores of similarly bejewelled structures receded far into the inky darkness.

After the drilling was over and the derricks came down, the land was dotted with oil pumps resembling prehistoric monsters in neatly fenced plots the size of a backyard garden, sixteen of them to a square mile, standing out of the rich green or gold, or the silent snows of the farmers' fields. And night and day on each plot, bobbing up and down like so many boys' hobby-horses they kept up their regular beat, teetering up and down, up and down, to bring up from thousands of feet below the black riches stored millions of years ago.

Moreover, like the pulsing pumps, the fairy godmother's wand kept waggling. Only now it began to point out gas fields, and a new out-pouring of riches fell into Alberta's lap. Natural gas, long regarded in oil circles.as a troublesome by-product, began to be recognized as an exportable commodity, and then it was sought for its own sake. Soon too it was found, and in tremendous quantities, and a new search sent drilling rigs and seismic crews and truck-loads of drill-stem scurrying hither and yon across Edmonton's bailiwick.

In 1946 there had been a production of fifty billion cubic feet, and by 1956 that had quadrupled. Names of new gas fields began to be bandied about on Jasper Avenue — Home Glen-Rimbey, Bonnie Glen, Westerose, Westlock, Gilby and Fort Saskatchewan, Wizard Lake and Morinville, and by coincidence, the area labelled in derision long ago by the fur traders found its name most appropriate for its new riches — Windfall. And although the smell emanating from these oil and gas fields and their processing plants left much to be desired, Alberta's one-shot economy, shivering on the cot of agricultural adversity, awoke to find itself tucked into a bed of roses. What Professor Eric Hanson, an economist at the university, dubbed Alberta's "Dynamic Decade" had arrived.

Oil and gas wells by the hundred tapped scores of fields; gathering lines and transmission lines began to stretch across the province to feed raw material to refineries and many varieties of petro-chemical industries. Then, since Alberta had become the fountain-head of Canada's vast reserves of energy, more gas and oil lines, this time three feet in diameter, began carrying the province's surplus fuel east to Ontario, west to Vancouver, and south to Los Angeles; Interprovincial Pipe Line, Trans-Mountain Pipe Line, and Alberta Gas Trunk Line.

For the godmother did not stop at any mere waving of wands but went the whole hog, through carriages, slippers and princes — not singular but plural. The carriages began to roll along Jasper Avenue as Edmonton broke out in a rash of Cadillacs. As for fairy princes, they naturally looked in to see if the magic slipper really fitted, and, finding that it did, and to boot was filled with oil and floating on natural gas, they went home for their money bags.

And such money bags.

In 1946 the money being invested in all phases of Alberta's development was some $122 million, of which perhaps one-fifth was going into dry holes in the futile search for oil. During the ten-year period after Leduc, the petroleum industry alone invested nearly $2½ billion directly. On top of that, because of the rapid rise of the oil industry, other billions poured into Alberta. They were used to set up the host of new well servicing industries, the new manufacturing plants, the new homes to house the thousands who flocked in to work in the new petroleum industry, the new utilities to service these homes and the great variety of stores, institutions and government capital expenditures necessary to cope with the new era. Scores of millions rubbed off on the agricultural industry and were invested in more land and equipment. All these investments totalled some $6 billion, and all were due to the arrival of the oil age, because without it Alberta would have plodded along losing population and with investments of about a quarter as much. All of it, moreover, was new money poured in, pennies from Alberta sources, a pittance from Canadian sources, and a potful from the United States.

All this new investment swept every Albertan to a new and undreamed of standard of living. The average man, woman and child in the province in 1946 had an annual income of $666; in 1956 it was $1,539. The farmer in his field, the cook in his cafe, the businessman in his board-room, and the provincial treasurer in his palace, all shared in the new prosperity.

The provincial treasurer, ever a cool customer, was indeed nearly overwhelmed as bank bills, bonds and cheques began to pile up in his sanctuary. In 1946 he had collected $45 million in taxes, and owed some $145 million in various quarters. In 1956 he collected more than $250 million in taxes, and, instead of owing anything, had some $250 million bulging his vaults. Starting in 1947, he looked down from his eyrie tower, pricked up his ears, and during the next decade, by way of lease rentals, sale of royalties and indirect taxes, all of which sprang from the oil industry, plus various sundry taxes, set his hooks into $1,540 million. By 1956 Alberta was in fact debt free, had spent millions on roads, farm electrification, hospitals, schools and universities, and was still rolling in wealth.

In the meantime, the province's population leaped ahead, and from 1946 to 1956 the Dynamic Decade swept it from 803,000 to 1,123,000, an increase of forty percent. Only once before had the province seen such a compounding of population — fifty years previously when knowledge and demand had made possible the utilization of Alberta's soil.

In the cities particularly, thousands of workers came to labour in the wholesale trade catering to the oil industry. Many others found work transporting oil equipment or servicing or repairing it. To them were added hosts of others to build the thousands of miles of pipe line, the new factories large and small and new office buildings all directly tied to the oil industry. Other workers swelled the ranks of those providing financial or professional assistance to that industry, of those retailing groceries and supplies to the thousands of new people, and all those employed by the enlarged government departments trying to gear up to cope with the new era. Finally, hundreds more found their livelihood in building homes, hotels, motels and apartments for the new temporary or permanent population.

The result was that there was a drastic shift from the rural areas to the towns and cities, and a new dimension had been added to the province's economy. Now Alberta had two strings to its bow. Now it could rely on two great industries, oil and agriculture, instead of one, and when the farmers' crops were hit or their prices slumped, the province could still carry on. Before 1946 agriculture had generated four-fifths of all personal income; by 1956 it generated two-fifths, with oil supplying an even greater amount.

By 1956, with the tremendous influx of capital and population, metropolitan Edmonton had grown to 254,800, and it shared with Calgary the honour of being the fastest growing metropolitan area in Canada. From being Canada's eighth largest city in 1946 it now ranked sixth; Calgary had jumped from ninth in 1946 to eighth. Within Edmonton's city limits its population had doubled from 113,116 in 1946 to 226,002 in 1956 — a leap of one hundred percent in ten years. Oil had done that.

A great proportion of the oil investment, however, had taken place outside its city limits, sometimes well beyond them. A quick rundown will show the major developments. Between February 1947, when Leduc No. 1 came in quietly, and the day thirteen months later when Atlantic No. 1 blew its top, a line of second-hand pipe eight inches in diameter and eight miles long was built to the railway at Nisku, some twelve miles south of Edmonton. That was a start.

Next, by August 1948, the Imperial Oil Company began operating the first part of its refinery. In its haste to get going, the company acquired the White-horse Refinery which had been built in conjunction with the Canol project and after dismantling it and trucking it down the Alaska Highway, re-installed it at Clover Bar. By a curious coincidence in Edmonton's contribution to Canada's energy supply the refinery which had been built to process oil from Norman Wells, one of its earliest and remote fields, came to roost in sight of the city to refine oil from its Leduc field a few miles away.

A British American Oil Company Refinery, also in Clover Bar, was rushed to completion in 1951. Then, a few months later and across the highway from the Imperial installation, the McColl-Frontenac Company brought its new refinery into operation. Within three years Edmonton had become a major refining centre.

Even so, there was a surplus of crude oil. By December 1950, to carry it to other markets, Inter-Provincial Pipe Line completed a 1,129-mile line to Lake Superior, most of it eighteen inches in diameter. Hard on its heels came 718 miles of twenty-four inch pipe to the west coast — Trans-Mountain Pipe Line. To deliver oil to the Edmonton pumping stations, or to feed these lines at different points, many other lines were laid in from nearby fields. The Pembina Pipe Line, finished in 1955, was followed by 106 miles of the Sturgeon Lake-Bickerdike line. In addition to all these, several natural gas lines were laid, including one from Edmonton to serve the new pulp mill 160 miles west at Hinton.

But the millions and millions of dollars invested in refineries and pipe lines was only part of the total capital spent by this sturdy industry. A host of subsidiary companies went into all the variety of new enterprises needed to service all aspects of oil and gas production. On top of that, petro-chemical plants selected Edmonton as the ideal spot to start up. Accordingly, out in Clover Bar on a 433-acre site, the Canadian Chemical Company's $70 million plant for producing cellulose acetate and yarn came on stream in 1953. In its wake came the Canadian In-dustries' $15 million polyethylene plant, and a year later at Fort Saskatchewan, Sherritt-Gordon completed its plant for using natural gas to leach ores. In the Clover Bar area alone the capital expenditure on plants of one sort or another totalled some $400 million, as much as was spent on the Canadian portion of the St. Lawrence Seaway.

Each of these plants required hundreds of employees to operate them and each was to foster many smaller satellite plants. Now Edmonton had industries second to none. On its eastern outskirts an area of some ten square miles was filled with huge terminal oil tanks, refineries and petro-chemical plants.

About 1949, as soon as oil was assured and Edmonton began its conversion to an industrial city, Mayor Ainlay seized an opportunity to substitute a new design for the original city crest in which a sheaf of wheat had been the central motif. In the new crest, the figure on the left is an early fur trader with his hand above his eyes as if looking to the future. On the right is Athena, the goddess of wisdom, and she carries a book, emblematic of education and signifying the presence of the university. Across the top is the rising sun for Alberta. Below this a flying wheel signifies industry and aviation. Through the middle, a wavy line represents the North Saskatchewan River, and below it is a sheaf of wheat. Around the base are three new words, "Industry, Integrity, Progress". Back of the crest, in the vertical position, is the Mace, as a symbol that the seat of provincial government is in Edmonton.

By 1948 Edmonton's population had jumped to 126,609. The new workers, many of them highly skilled, needed additional factory and office space, their families had to be housed and their children created an immediate demand for more schoolrooms. While these were being provided and more homes built, the changes in downtown Edmonton were perhaps the most noticeable. There, to provide more office space and to modernize office buildings that had become sway-backed and unsightly during their drab existence since 1914, a campaign of revamping and face-lifting took place. The refurbishing, however, was not confined to office buildings. Stores too were remodelled and their show windows jazzed up and set ablaze with modern lighting. Leading the way came the centuries-old Hudson's Bay Company which extended its relatively modern store to take in the whole block.

Cafes too brightened up as new arborite counters and tables in many colours began to replace the dowdiness of restaurants long since run down. About 1948 a group of Chinese built the Seven Seas Restaurant, the first of Edmonton's new up-to-date dining-rooms and lunch counters. During this era Bob Kashower opened his Airlines Hotel on the site now occupied by the Edmonton Inn. By converting some old H-huts into rooms and into an ultra smart dining-room, he met the rising demand for tasteful and tasty meals. At the other end of the scale, hamburger stands sprang up and coffee shops mushroomed. In between the Seven Seas and these hamburger roosts were many clean, well conducted family type restaurants, and many of them, such as Johnson's Cafe, the Shasta, and some of the hotel dining-rooms, had been in business for decades.

Food in a small city catering to an agricultural clientele is invariably copious, monotonous, and swimming in artificial brown gravy — a cornucopia of calories devoid of culinary art. Increased wages and more money in circulation demanded better and diversified restaurants. An occasional pizza parlour appeared, and a number of steak houses began stirring their charcoal fires. Their steaks, cooked in a variety of ways, enticed a large clientele, especially amongst the American oil workers. The cooking was excellent, but in advertising 16- and 24-ounce steaks they started a fashion somewhat novel to Canadians, who had been in the habit of eating to live rather than living to eat.

Brighter cafes, stores and display windows, however, were only part of the change that was rejuvenating Edmonton. During 1947 the city electrical department, the first in Canada to do so, embarked upon a plan of replacing obsolete street lights with mercury vapour fixtures. As a start, they lit up about three blocks of Jasper Avenue from 100 Street east. By 1956 the department decided that henceforth it would instal these fixtures in all new subdivisions, and that year established another record by being the first city in the world to order a quantity of an even better mercury vapour luminaire. Within a few years Edmonton had become the brightest lit city in Canada.

Though all these changes were taking place in the heart of the city, changes equally significant were filling in the large untenanted spaces that had been blank since before the First War. The *Edmonton Journal* for June 12, 1948, reported that since the end of the recent war Edmontonians had built 4,040 houses, thirty-five new apartment blocks, and twenty duplexes. Moreover, Edmonton citizens owned eighty percent of the houses in which they lived. "So far in the boom," the *Journal* said, "they have completely housed-over within-the-city farms, dairy farms, shooting grounds, sloughs, skating ponds, thick bush areas, former dumps, a penitentiary site as well as by-gone railway grades and street car barns."

While this spate of new homes left no part of the city untouched, it was most in evidence in the west end; in New Glenora, West Glenora and West Grove, and spilled over into adjacent Jasper Place. At the time Leduc No. 1 came in this hamlet held a few hundred people. By January 1, 1950, when it was incorporated as a village, however, Jasper Place had a population of 7,100. Five years later that had vaulted to 13,594. In the meantime, on November 6, 1950, it had been incorporated as a town, and at that point was larger than half of Alberta's eight cities. Its valiant town council struggled manfully to cope with the fact that it was not really a town with a proper balance between residential areas, business section and industrial area, but was merely a residential suburb of Edmonton.

The old Hudson's Bay Company's Reserve, part of which for years had contained the Prince Rupert Golf Course, had begun to be built on, and the *Edmonton Journal* commented nostalgically about the proposed loss of the "last remaining farm on the Hudson's Bay Reserve" at the corner of 111 Avenue and 116 Street.

Many new homes were going up in King Edward Park, Ritchie and Bonnie Doon, and promoters were beginning to talk of draining the McKernan Lakes. Several new apartments were built on Connor's Hill, and Wartime Integrated Housing schemes and National Housing Act financing were making the purchase of a home almost painless. On the grounds of the old penitentiary the new spread-out Highland Court apartments sprang up. Considerable building was going on around the Highlands, which for so long had been a pleasant isolated little community.

East of this area lay the old mining town of Beverly, which had been incorporated as a village on May 22, 1913, and as a town on August 5, 1914. For a long time Beverly, with its small miners' cottages, was a quiet backwater. When in 1952 its last coal mine closed down, many of its people transferred their labours to the new oil-based industries that had sprung up across the river. In 1946 Beverly's population had been 1,171, but during the next five years it grew to 2,159, and reached 4,602 by 1956. In 1954 alone, its population increased twenty-one percent, and such a rapid growth in a town without industries of its own and scarcely any business section presented difficult financial problems.

Even Edmonton, however, the beneficiary of all this explosion of population and of the new oil industries outside its borders, had many problems, because it had to build new streets and provide new water, sewer and other utilities. One offsetting satisfaction was that the thousands of lots to which the city had fallen heir so long ago were now being sold to people who built on them, lived on them, and, what was much more desirable, paid taxes on them. In fact, the city only sold them subject to a building commitment. Now, with the new boom, Edmonton's vast empty spaces filled up rapidly. In 1949 Edmonton hired Noel Dant, its first town planner. Under his direction, old subdivisions which for so long had been pasture land for dairy cows or had even felt the husbandman's plough, were resurrected and once more marked off into building lots. In many cases the street lines, surveyed forty years earlier and marked by steel posts and the lot corners marked by long since rotted wooden pegs, were disregarded, and the areas were re-subdivided. The old streets which had been projected to run in a regular rectangular grid were ignored, and new plans were drawn for the areas. These, made to conform to the best in current city planning, became a jig-saw puzzle of curves and crescents, dead end streets and service roads, the last word in modernity and in confusing complexity.

These formerly vacant areas filled up so rapidly that the city was forced to annex land on its south-eastern flank from the municipality of Strathcona. In 1947, under Mayor Ainlay, the first annexation for thirty years took in the Pleasantview subdivision, to add a quarter of a square mile to the city. A minor adjustment of boundaries in the Whitemud Creek area followed this in 1950, during Mayor Sid Parson's regime.

In 1951, a relatively young Ukrainian, William Hawrelak became the first of his descent to reach such a high office in any major Canadian city when Edmonton elected him mayor. The son of pioneer parents, he emerged from a farming background but after moving to the city soon became a successful businessman. As a mayor, he had youth, boundless energy, great ability and ambition, and a capacity to command — qualities which the city needed sorely during its decade of unprecedented growth.

Hawrelak's election marked a new era in the city in so far as he was the first businessman in nearly a decade to direct its affairs. In several other respects, however, 1951 was a minor turning point in Edmonton's career. The early Fifties saw a spate of office buildings that rapidly changed the city's skyline. Scores of three-storey buildings appeared here and there all over, with a special concentration of them on the downtown streets flanking Jasper Avenue. One of the most spectacular changes, however, came as the red steel skeleton of the sixteen-storey Macdonald Hotel began to rise above the old chateau type building. For a brief interval, once the cluttered row of drab one- and two-storey structures, that hid the old hotel from Jasper Avenue, were brushed aside to make room for the new edifice, most Edmontonians got their first view of what the older building had really looked like as its architects had planned it. Only then when it was about to be dwarfed by its addition they came to appreciate it and to raise their voices in protest against its submergence by its rectangular extension. The new hotel turned out to be but the forerunner of other similar structures, and before long the Gas Company's twelve-storey Milner Building and the eleven-storey Financial Building began to give Edmonton a new vertical dimension.

While no one regretted the loss of the small shops in front of the Macdonald, the changing years were pressing hard against other old institutions which had spanned most of the lifetimes of the city's pre-Leduc residents. Many an old-timer, however, remembering the relative quiet of former days, was inclined to regret the changes which rapid progress had brought, and looked back nostalgically at some of the things that had been lost. One such loss had come about in 1951 when the *Edmonton Bulletin* ceased publication. Remembering how in 1880 Frank Oliver had brought in his first press by Red River cart and how for the next quarter of a century the *Bulletin* had been the only paper in the community and how faithfully it had fought the West's early battles, many felt that it had deserved a better fate.

The old street railway met a similar fate. Even before the war, the City Transit System had started to scrap its rattly old cars and its rusty bent rails. The major change in the street railway began in 1939, when the first trolley coaches arrived from England to be placed on the 95 Street and Low Level Bridge routes. Their arrival marked the beginning of the end for the street cars, although the final one was not taken off the streets until 1951. By 1953 the system owned eighty-seven trolley coaches and one hundred buses. Moreover, the change to trolley buses saw the end of the McKernan Lake line, which in 1948 fell before the march of progress. The change to trolley buses also meant the end of the rather spectacular street car ride over the top deck of the High Level Bridge to which two generations of Edmonton had thrilled. Edmonton was changing rapidly.

As part of this change, in 1954, the city annexed more land. By taking over from the municipality of Strathcona 1½ square miles in the Hardisty and Coronet areas, and two years later by taking in another square mile in the Gold Bar district, Edmonton once more had some room to expand towards the east and to close the gap between it and the oil refinery area.

These annexations eased the tight land situation and permitted residential expansion mainly in an easterly direction. In all, by 1956, they had increased the city's size by 2.91 square miles, and now Edmonton embraced an area of 44.07 square miles as compared to 41.16 at which it had stood since World War One. Looking back over the past decade, the city fathers were well pleased. Sizing it up, they could see that two forces had come into play, one, the oil boom peculiar to Alberta cities, and the other, common to all Canada, the post-war change.

All Canadian cities experienced the post-war boom, which swept them into a new era and caught them and the whole country completely by surprise. Canada emerged from the war as a new manufacturing nation. As C. D. Howe said, Canadians had learned to make "at least a hundred major products never before made in Canada." This fact, and many others, gave Canadians a new outlook. Part of it was turned in the direction of the welfare state, and when, after the 1945 election, the government brought in its baby bonuses, it set in motion a train of welfare of which we still cannot see the end. While so much social security may have its drawbacks, there is no doubt that it smoothed many a depression out of our economy and did its share to build a better Edmonton.

The end of the war, baby bonuses, and many another item, all combined to bring about a demand for more and better housing. Edmonton contractors, like builders everywhere, were swamped by returned soldiers eager for houses, by workers anxious to move out after living with relatives for the war years, and by many others wanting houses to escape from the high rents which had vaulted upward when war-time controls were lifted. There had been so little house building for so many long years that a whole generation had been brought up in the old-style front porch houses built by their fathers and grandfathers. The new generation of Edmontonians, conditioned by the war's changes, was determined to have nothing but the newest ideas in homes. Their new homes were to have kitchens with tiled floors and built-in breakfast nooks, a rumpus room in the basement, and legless bathtubs. They were also to be air conditioned inside and open to the world outside, without fences to cower behind or hedges to hide them.

Moreover, both within and without these new picture-window houses, everything had to be modern and to conform with the new fad which had really begun as the war started — streamlining. In cars, Studebaker set the streamlining pace in 1946. But everything else had to follow, toasters, radios, vacuum cleaners, all had to be transformed. Then too, the new dream homes had to have electrical servants; deep freezers, and washers and dryers, represented the larger items, and with them came a host of small appliances of doubtful labour-saving value but of the utmost prestige value — nut choppers, ice crushers and teapot polishers. Then came roll-on paint brushes for the do-it-yourself decorator, pressure cookers, V-master cigarette rollers for the man with the make-it-for-him wife. Where possible, everything was wrapped in the new plastic bags and was fastened up with the new zippers. Ballpoint pens made their mass sales pitch, and in all of Edmonton's new residential areas power lawnmowers began picking up gravel and hurling it through five by seven-foot plate glass windows. Everything was new or different or merely streamlined, but in the decade after the war, during Alberta's Dynamic Decade which was afloat on a freshet of folding money, nothing was too novel or too expensive. In fact, because mass production, hurrying to supply a market-place full of anxious buyers, turned out goods as never before, it kept their unit price down. New types of market-places also appeared, and in 1955 Woodward's Westmount Shopping Centre became Edmonton's first.

It came about in a roundabout way as an aftermath of the scheme to rejuvenate the heart of the downtown area and to create a Civic Centre. In 1915 such a centre had been mooted, only to be forestalled by the First War. At various times after that the idea had been examined wistfully but it did not come to figure in public consciousness again till in 1942, when with a revised plan, Cecil Burgess, the distinguished architect, resurrected it as a dream which might bear fruit when the Second War was over.

In 1947, city architect, M. C. Dewar, realizing long before the populace did that Edmonton's heart must follow the pattern experienced by all other American cities and die unless something was done, submitted a proposal for a new centre. It was to start with a civic auditorium capable of holding 2,300, an art centre, museum and ancillary services. It was estimated to cost $1,500,000, and although the proposal received a majority of the burgesses' votes, it failed in obtaining the necessary sixty-six percent.

In 1950, seeing that Edmontonians would not start a Civic Centre for themselves, a New York group presented a privately financed proposition which came to be known as the Detwiler scheme or the Miracle Mile. While it suffered from some drawbacks, they were probably less than the blindness suffered by Edmonton's burgesses who, in common with the electorates in most cities, could grasp the impact of laying a block of sidewalk but failed to grasp the significance of the death of the city's downtown area. In any event, the Detwiler proposition, like so many others in Edmonton's history, failed to obtain the approval of sixty-six percent of the burgesses.

Even though Edmontonians turned it down, the New Yorker who was behind Detwiler, Clarence Y. Paylitz, retained his faith in the city's future and ironically, by doing a complete reversal of his former policy of building up the city's centre, applied his talents and his capital to building at the outskirts. As a result, and in due course, the Westmount Shopping Centre came into being.

The war payrolls had been good to the movie industry and all theatres played to full houses. The post-war years, however, brought problems, one in the form of outdoor movies, which merely hurt the picture-show houses downtown, and the other, the new TV broadcasts, which hurt them all. The first outdoor screen, the Starlite Drive-in, was set up in Jasper Place in 1949. As part of its campaign to combat television, the movie industry introduced wide screens during 1953. The first CBC-TV broadcasts started in 1952, but it was not until October 1954 that CFRN-TV started and Edmontonians could see this new marvel. During

Civic Centre as proposed 1915.

Scale model of Civic Centre now under development.

1958, after millions were spent spanning Canada with micro-wave towers, CFRN brought in national broadcasts. In October that year a CBC television station opened in the city.

There were other indications that the new era had come. The older set became the victims of a craze that swept the late Forties and embraced Canasta. The younger group set out on a teenage crusade that sent them into screams of laughter and swoons of pretend anguish, and sent their parents into a seething tizzy from which they have not yet recovered and probably never will.

At the same time, however, the more serious side of cultural life suddenly found that the increased piles of folding dollars, combined with a rapid influx of immigrants from the music-steeped cities of Europe, allowed it to flourish as never before. Alongside the discovery of oil, the arts; theatre, ballet, music, opera and painting, each found new strata to tap and new heights to scale.

The Edmonton Community Theatre resumed operations in 1946 and two years later Elsie Park Gowan won the Kerr trophy for acting. In 1951 the Edmonton Community Theatre and the Edmonton Recreation Commission formed a Children's Theatre Group. Next year the Studio Theatre and the Civil Service Playhouse began seeking and receiving public acclaim. During the next four years the Mercury Players and Circle 8 stalked the stages, and the Orion Theatre, a group devoted to developing musical talent, numbered Robert Goulet amongst its devotees. Paralleling the expansion of the performing arts, 1953 saw the organization of the Edmonton Chamber Music Society, and 1954 witnessed the formation of the Edmonton Ballet Company.

All the while the old standby, the Edmonton Civic Opera, under Mrs. Carmichael, continued its high standards and over the years delighted larger and more critical audiences with Rio Rita, The Student Prince, Blossom Time and Brigadoon. Starting in 1949 the Recreation Commission put on a series of Pops Concerts. They were so successful that eventually they became associated with the Edmonton Symphony Orchestra, which during the next several years, under the direction of Lee Hepner, made good music an integral part of Edmonton's life. The Women's Musical Club, which supported all facets of music, brought in top performers and aided local artists, started giving musical scholarships in 1951, when the winner was Marek Jablonski. Through these years the Musical Club still sponsored the Celebrity Concerts.

Money and art go hand in hand, and by 1951 Edmontonians' affluence enabled the Edmonton Art Gallery to buy the old Secord house for $40,000 and to begin enhancing its notable contribution to the graphic arts.

In 1955, in a ceremony attended by Prime Minister St. Laurent and many dignitaries, Albertans rejoiced as they recalled the inauguration of the province and unveiled a cairn in front of the Legislative Building. Several retired employees who had joined the civil service fifty years earlier turned out for the occasion. So did Vernon Barford, who, duplicating his performance of half a century earlier, conducted the musical portion of the program. Present too and in fine fettle as he delighted the audience with his witty reminiscences of 1905 was Col. F. C. Jamieson, one-time CMR trooper in the Boer War.

It is not memories, however, but money that makes the mare go. Money also attracts football and hockey players, and by 1948 there was lots of it around. That year a hockey team, the Edmonton Flyers, won the Allan Cup and gave Edmonton sports fans such a lift that for a while the city became a rabid hockey centre. The next year saw the Edmonton Eskimos revived. After long, careful and costly preparation, they went east in 1952, seeking the Grey Cup, but were defeated by the Toronto Argonauts, 21 to 11. That merely whetted Edmontonians' appetites.

Two years later the Eskimos once more represented the West in the Grey Cup games. Before the showdown, Jack Kinsella, the unbeliever, writing in the *Ottawa Citizen,* opined that: "Edmonton couldn't beat Montreal if they brought along the other four clubs in the league as support and supplied each player with an anti-tank gun."

With less than three minutes to play, Edmonton was down 25-20, and Montreal had the ball deep in Edmonton territory. Those three minutes saw the most famous play in Grey Cup history. Chuck Hunsinger either tried to pass or fumbled, Jackie Parker picked up the loose ball and ran eighty-five yards for a touchdown. Score, Eskimos 25, Montreal 25. For the next awful seconds the fate of the West rested on the toe of Bob Dean — Bob Dean, who during the year had kicked fifty consecutive converts. He kicked and scored, and Edmonton won its first Grey Cup!

The Montreal Alouettes and their supporters passed the result off as "Just one of those things" and were delighted when Edmonton and Montreal met in the 1955 Grey Cup game. But once more the Esks won, and the score was 34-19. Then in 1956 the two teams met again; this time with the betting in favour of Edmonton. This time, too, the Esks won, to the tune of 50-27.

Money had made the mare go, and it had lashed thousands of Edmontonians into a frenzy of enthusiasm. The players it had hired, however, justified every bit of it. For these were the great days of Jackie Parker and Johnny Bright, both of whom won the Schenley Award as Canada's outstanding football player and who followed in the steps of Billy Vessels who had won it during 1953. Jackie Parker won it three times and many fans across the country consider him the best player ever to perform in Canada. Normie Kwong was selected as Canada's athlete of the year, and Rollie "Old Folks" Miles, who came to Edmonton to play baseball, became one of Canada's finest football players.

All these changes in football, music and painting, houses, ballpoint pens, plastic bags and zippers, hubba-hubba and hula hoops, hit Edmonton in the years after the war, and the weather-worn city wondered what had struck it. On top of that came the oil boom with its refineries and its 24-ounce steaks, its chop suey houses and its chemical plants, its hamburger joints and outdoor movies.

With the oil drawing so many vigorous young workers and their equally vigorous young wives to the city, and with the teenage boom doing its share, the city fathers were soon faced with the need to add a new and capacious maternity wing to the Royal Alexandra Hospital. This was not completed until 1951, but about the same time, both the General and the Misericordia hospitals doubled in size. In 1950 the provincial government completed its fine new TB facility, the Aberhart Hospital.

Although the provincial government was waxing wealthy on oil leases and royalties, it was hard pressed to keep up with all the new buildings that were needed. During 1950 it started work on a new Land Titles Building and began its Administration Building at the corner of 109 Street and 98 Avenue. This, the first modern structure to be built in the complex north and east of the Parliament Building, was to be the forerunner of many more buildings. The next year the Alberta Government Telephones' multi-storied, multi-coloured glass conception at the corner of 97 Avenue and 107 Street began to further alter the skyline.

The provincial government wisely poured much of its new-found money into the university. There, by the fall of 1946, as returned men, envisaging the world ahead of them, bent over their books, the registration had jumped to 4,300. By the 1952-53 university year it fell back to the more normal figure of 3,337, but with Alberta in a new era, everyone knew that would soon double.

From 1921, when the main Medical Building had been completed, until a west wing was added to it in 1947, no significant new construction had fallen to the university's lot. Then with a rush, during the interval 1951 to 1954, the attractive Rutherford Library and the Engineering and Agricultural buildings followed. The university too was getting its share of Alberta's windfall.

In other government spheres, the new Federal Building at the corner of 107 Street and 99 Avenue was nearly ready for occupancy at the end of 1956, and Edmonton's new City Hall was completed. A structure worthy of a re-born city and the first modern building in Edmonton, it marked the real start on the Civic Centre. Remembering how the burgesses had recently treated the Detwiler scheme and fearing what they would do to a money by-law for a new city hall, John Hodgson, the Finance Commissioner, pointed out how the coffers could scratch up the necessary $3½ million without having to put the matter to a vote. Then, to insure that the project got away to a good start, Bill Hawrelak sold the idea in private talks with at least thirty-five civic groups.

The architect's plan called for the construction of a fountain in front of the building, and an artist imported for the occasion fabricated its sprays. These, made up of interwoven bronze pipes, turned out to represent five attenuated geese sitting with outstretched vertical beaks, interlaced with four skeletal geese flying with outstretched horizontal beaks, all squirting water. Around it for months the fires of controversy raged. Its proponents found it graceful, alive, sharp, clean and wild, typifying all these qualities which they liked to attribute to Alberta and its capital city. Its opponents, unaware of the artistic wave which for weal or woe was lifting Edmontonians' eyes above their dinner plates, called it a burned out aeroplane carcase, a tempest-tossed bicycle rack, and finally, in what was perhaps its most apt and lasting epithet, "The Spaghetti Tree." But it weathered the storm, and with luck, may well outlast the city hall it adorns.

At this period the huge sprawling groups of three- and four-storey apartment buildings, such as the Bel Air out on the St. Albert Trail, the Strathearn Heights apartments, and many others, sprang up about the city. Then, too, to accommodate all the small industries incidental to the oil business, the city began laying out industrial areas such as that near Kingsway, and along 103 and 104 Streets near the railway tracks in South Edmonton, and the Dominion and Bremner Industrial areas. There were so many buildings that all structural materials became scarce, deliveries of steel could not be promised for a year, and contractors switched to concrete, until that too ran short, and along with it concrete blocks which had become an economical way to put up small structures. To try to cope with the call for concrete, the Canada Cement Company and the Inland Cement Company built plants immediately outside the city.

The best indication of what was happening to Edmonton is illustrated by the building permits issued year by year at the city hall. During the 1912 boom, the permits had totalled $14,447,000. The next high year was at the peak of the booming Twenties, when, after a long decline, they rose once more to $5,670,000. In the depths of the Hungry Thirties they had dropped to a low of $428,000 a year, and by 1947, the first post-war year, they had soared to $13,183,000. For the

Edmonton's City Hall.

year 1956, after a steady climb, they stood at $69,406,000, and during the province's Dynamic Decade had totalled $452,000,000. For comparison, the total of all building permits from 1910 to 1940 was only $79,496,000. During the ten years since Leduc No. 1 had come in, five times as much building took place in Edmonton as that city had seen in all its previous history. In the year 1956 alone, nearly as much building was going on as had taken place from 1904 to 1940.

In 1954 Edmonton had been an incorporated city for fifty years. Taking stock of itself it found that from a frontier distributing centre which had arisen to serve a rapidly awakening agricultural economy it had developed to a burgeoning industrial giant. Its area of some forty-three square miles, once so wide-spread and empty, was now bursting at the seams with new housing projects and industrial areas. The recent demand for more space for small industries had called for considerable expense in providing roads, trackage and other amenities to service these new areas — expense which the city fathers did not begrudge.

Nevertheless, the dramatic and swift changes which had swept Edmonton into such a whirl of activity placed an enormous strain upon its finances. High on the list of its capital outlays was a greatly enhanced program of building new streets and up-grading existing ones. While from time to time some money had been spent in filling in or draining old mud holes, all through the long years since the 1912 boom very little additional work had been done. At the beginning of the war the sixty-two miles of paved streets and the remaining 285 miles of graded, gravelled or oiled streets were essentially what they had been a quarter of a century earlier. The war years added eight miles of paved and forty-one miles of unpaved streets. The Dynamic Decade saw the mileage of streets increase from 396 miles

Aerial view of University of Alberta, 1967.

to 853, and what is more significant, the amount of paving more than tripled, from seventy miles to 266.

Sidewalks more than doubled, from 287 miles to 666, but more important than that, the great bulk of the new sidewalks laid were of concrete, so that by the end of 1956 the mileage of concrete walks had jumped from fifty-nine to 348. Sewers too had kept pace with the far-flung subdivisions and had extended from 234 miles in 1946 to 722 in 1956. During the same period, the miles of water main had stretched from 273 to 653. All in all, the city engineers' department had done a magnificent job on a gargantuan scale.

The city telephone department had also expanded at a terrific pace, but due to an almost incredible demand for phones, coupled with a drastic shortage of equipment, that decade is remembered as the era when many hundreds of residents had to wait as much as a year for a telephone. Trying desperately to keep up with the demand, the department doubled the number of instruments in service during the five-year period ending 1954 and at the end of that time 63,000 users cleared through its exchanges.

The city-owned electric light department, the power plant, and the water-works, forecasting the terrific post-war demand and keeping abreast of the oil boom, did a superb job. By 1951 the power plant had nearly doubled the capacity it had boasted five years before and then doubled it once more by 1956, to reach a size of 120,000 KW — one of Canada's largest steam plants. Bowing before Alberta's new status as a gas reservoir, all its new boilers burned that fuel, and in doing so wrote finis for the time being at least to Edmonton's sixty-year-old coal industry. Inadvertently too, the plant, sucking in huge gobs of gas through equally huge pipes, put the finishing touches to the fifty-year-old E Y & P Railway. While the plant continued to burn some coal until 1954, what little it did use came by truck, and in 1952 the train tracks wiggling down Mill Creek Ravine and crossing the Low Level Bridge were taken up. So too were the tracks which for nearly half a century had wound around below the Parliament Building and the High Level Bridge and desecrated the magnificent hillside above the Municipal Golf Course.

The city's health and hospital facilities expanded enormously. Its fire and police protection, keeping up with the growth of the city and the growth in technology, established most favourable records. Edmonton's Public Library system, always cramped for funds, did its best to cope with the rapidly increasing needs for its facilities. In 1947 the city council set up a Municipal Parks Department to make sure that the new subdivisions provided sufficient space for parks and recreation. One-tenth of the city's total area was devoted to public parks.

During the decade the public and separate school boards spent many millions of dollars on a building program to relieve the overcrowded conditions that arose from Edmonton's sudden and overwhelming growth. As fast as they built new schools, more and more pupils came to crowd them. Improving in quality as well as in volume, Edmonton's new classrooms incorporated every modern innovation, including swimming pools in some cases. In the late Forties Victoria Composite High School opened, in 1953 the new Eastglen Composite High School was completed at a cost of $2,300,000, and the school board had let tenders for a third such high school on the South Side.

In spite of gas rationing during the war, the number of motor vehicles in use in Alberta had risen from 114,000 in 1939 to 130,000 by VJ Day. Then with the coming of the oil era they had spurted ahead to reach a figure of some 380,000 by 1956; that is, the number of motor vehicles nearly tripled in ten years. Of these, in 1956 Edmontonians operated 80,200. This explosion of cars and trucks not only proved a problem for the city engineers' department in the way of highways, underpasses and traffic circles, but also dotted the city with service stations. For a few years these seemed to spring up on almost every corner and in many a location two or even three of them confronted each other across intersections.

Of Edmonton's 80,200 cars, some 30,000 were owned by South Siders and cross-river traffic started to be a problem. At rush hours, the four traffic bridges, the High Level, the 105 Street, the Dawson Bridge and the Low Level, which had been twinned in 1949, were heavily taxed. Perhaps the best indication of the rapid build-up of traffic is the fact that as soon as the second bridge was built beside the Low Level the city engineers closed the 105 Street Bridge for well over a year while they repaired and revamped it, and few motorists felt aggrieved. Just a few years later, if some mishap disrupted the flow of cars over the 105 Street Bridge, all Edmonton's cross-river traffic was thrown out of gear.

By 1954 the council obtained estimates of the cost of a new bridge to be built in the west end at the mouth of Groat Ravine. The city had reached a new milestone in that it began to need to use some of its scenic ravines as routes for crossing its magnificent valley. In rapid succession, the Gallagher and Groat ravines were converted to traffic arteries.

Control of the rapidly increasing traffic also called for a continuous program of installing traffic lights. The city's first traffic light had been installed at Jasper and 101 Street in 1933, and by 1950 seventeen sets of them were operating. By

1954 the traffic had become so heavy that fifty-five of these were helping to speed its flow and the program had really only begun.

The associated problem of parking had also raised its head. Prior to Leduc No. 1, parking places were easy to find. By 1948, however, the city felt constrained to install eight hundred parking meters, and by 1954 two thousand of the one-armed bandits impeded pedestrians. Even then there was not enough parking, and a new phenomenon occurred — one that had begun to appear in all the continent's cities — parking lots. Here and there, empty lots still sported their annual crops of sow thistle and dandelion. As parking started to pinch, owners laid them out into off-street parking lots. In other locations downtown, where old buildings had reached the end of their usefulness or had been gutted by fire, their owners demolished them and made a reasonable return on their investment from shoppers looking for a place to park. Before long all formerly empty lots became sales yards for second-hand car dealers or custom parking lots, and, except on downtown Jasper Avenue and 101 Street, the two main streets, one or two of these lots appeared in every block. All buildings of ten stories were separated from their neighbours by a fringe area devoted to parking — like cathedrals towering over their cemeteries.

With all these changes, Edmonton ended its Dynamic Decade. As in 1956, Edmontonians, twice as many of them as there had been ten years earlier, sat back to think it all over, the nearly incredible transformation that oil had wrought was real. Although some bad had come with all the good, in every way the city had made marvellous progress. Now that Edmonton had become the sixth largest city in Canada, many amenities that make their way to centres where dollars abound came homing in on Edmonton; travel agencies, better drama, better music, better food, costlier cars, costlier sports, and both better and much more costly schooling. Few who lived in Edmonton during that exciting decade would have traded its thrill for anything else in the world.

This, however, had been no temporary boom, because Edmonton present and Edmonton future were both based on diversified activities having their foundations on the solid support of farming land and flowing oil. Even if no more oil or gas should ever be discovered, Alberta was wealthy, and Edmonton had waxed fat. For in petroleum products alone, Alberta had 7,390 oil wells producing 144 million barrels per year and reserves of 2,966 million barrels, as well as more than three hundred natural gas pools producing two hundred billion cubic feet and reserves of 18.3 trillion cubic feet.

Even if Alberta's fairy godmother had gone into well earned retirement and had gone to live in Hawaii, so that oil rich Edmontonians could only spend the winter with her, Edmonton's future was secure.

Gas Under Every Grain Field 1957-1967

chapter 20

BUT EDMONTON'S new era had merely started. The next decade was to see growth just as fantastic and changes just as far reaching. By 1967 the population of metropolitan Edmonton exceeded 400,000. During that decade the population of the city increased sixty-three percent and that of the metropolitan area fifty-four percent.

Figures for metropolitan areas, however, should be used with caution. The Dominion census, the Board of Trade and the city council all have differing definitions of what that area is. The 1966 Dominion census defined Edmonton's metropolitan area so as to include St. Albert (population 9,736), Sherwood Park (5,800), Griesbach Barracks (4,300), and Namao (2,200). The population within Edmonton's city limits was 376,925.

But the city's limits keep changing too and stretching out. These enlargements of its boundaries are shown on the accompanying map on page 294. From an area of 41.16 square miles in 1947 when Leduc No. 1 came in, various annexations had increased it to 44.07 square miles by 1956; from that point on to the end of 1966, the city's area was nearly doubled to 85.59 square miles.

In 1958 the Alexandra Park subdivision was taken in. This was followed the next year by the acquisition of nearly twelve square miles from the Municipal District of Strathcona, part of it in the Ottewell area but most of it stretching as a band about a mile wide along the south boundary. During 1960 more than another square mile was added in the Ottewell area. During 1961 eleven more square miles were taken in. Part of this was the former town of Beverly with its 9,041 people and its one and one-quarter square miles. The rest consisted of some nine sections of land adjacent to the north-east corner of the city. The largest single annexation, however, took in the 16.92 square miles added in 1961 when the town of Jasper Place threw in its lot with Edmonton and when the city's boundary was pushed farther south and east. By the time Jasper Place came in its population was 38,441.

This amazing expansion gave the real estate agents plenty to play with and they laid out new subdivisions by the score. In the north-east, Summerville, Glengarry and Londonderry, all near Griesbach Barracks, began to fill up, while new paving and sewer lines spread out in the vicinity of Beverly into Steele

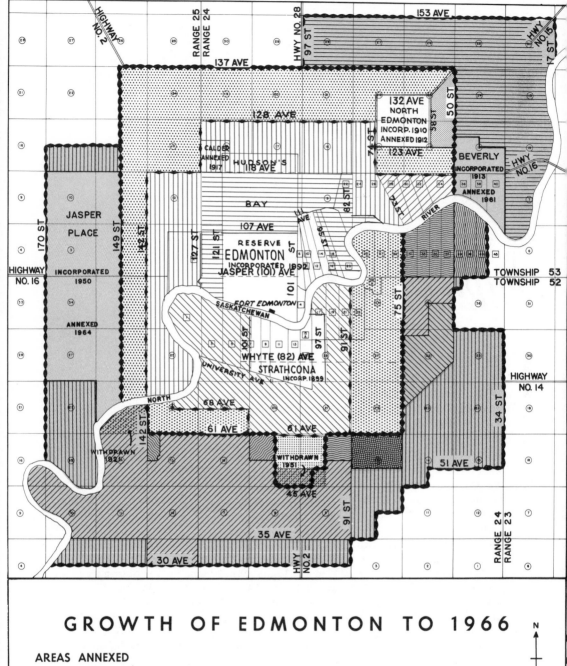

GROWTH OF EDMONTON TO 1966

N

AREAS ANNEXED

Before Amalgamation   **After Amalgamation**

ANNEXED IN 1904	ANNEXED IN 1912
ANNEXED IN 1907	ANNEXED IN 1913
ANNEXED IN 1910	ANNEXED IN 1914
ANNEXED AT AMALGAMATION IN 1912	ANNEXED IN 1947

ANNEXED IN 1950	ANNEXED IN 1959
ANNEXED IN 1954	ANNEXED IN 1960
ANNEXED IN 1956	ANNEXED IN 1961
ANNEXED IN 1958	ANNEXED IN 1964

CITY BOUNDARY 1922   CITY BOUNDARY 1923   CITY BOUNDARY 1966

SCALE IN MILES

0   1   2

Heights, Belmont Heights, Beacon Heights and Rundle Heights, which took in the bend of the river upstream from the Clover Bar bridge. Across the river hundreds of new homes with their lawns, flowers and shrubbery made beautiful residential areas of Gold Bar, Hardisty, Capilano and Ottewell. To the south, Lansdowne, Lendrum Place and Malmo Plains reached out towards Royal Gardens, Greenfield and Aspen Gardens, which looked across the valley of Whitemud Creek to Westbrook Estates. West of Grandview Heights and across the deep gorge of the creek where it cut its way down to the river, Riverbend, Glamorgan Heights and Terwillegar Heights began to take shape. South-west of the core of Jasper Place, Lynnwood, Rio Terrace, Hillcrest and Meadowlark Park filled in rapidly. On crescents and service roads new homes by the thousands sprang up.

As well as these subdivisions, other towns within the metropolitan area served as residential adjuncts to the city. Griesbach and Namao were strictly army and air force towns. St. Albert, Father Lacombe's old mission centre, which for decades had remained around the seven hundred mark and then with the advent of oil had doubled by 1956, took the bit in its teeth and during the next decade jumped to a population of 9,800. Most of its expansion was south of the Sturgeon River, and that portion which extended along the old St. Albert Trail finally came to within two miles of Edmonton's boundary. By 1965 Sherwood Park, a new satellite town three miles east of the city limits, where construction started in 1955, blossomed into a town of almost 6,000. As well as these, small acreage subdivisions sprouted here and there in the pleasant farming countryside within a radius of thirty miles of the city, and the area became dotted with groups of a few dozen homes.

All the incorporated towns and villages lying near the city but outside the metropolitan area became dormitories for major industries near them or for those in Edmonton. Fort Saskatchewan grew from about one thousand people in 1947 to well over three thousand by 1965. Spurred on by the presence of the oilfield practically at its doorstep and by the establishment of Edmonton's new International Airport a mile or so to the north-west, Leduc grew from about nine hundred in 1947 to 2,500 by 1965. Winterburn, Spruce Grove and Stony Plain also felt the bulge of a burgeoning Edmonton.

Nearly all this growth in area, population, buildings and factories was attributable to oil. One economist estimates that without oil Edmonton's 1967 population would have been around 200,000 instead of 400,000. The decade ending 1966 saw continuing oil discoveries: 1957, Kaybob, Swan Hills and Virginia Hills out along the trails the Klondikers had taken; 1958, Carson Creek and Simonette; 1959, Judy Creek; 1960, Fenn West; 1961, Judy Creek West and Kaybob South, adjacent to No. 43 Highway leading to the Peace River Country; 1962, Snipe Lake; 1963, Goose River; 1964, Mitsue, near Slave Lake; 1965, Nipisi, and 1966 saw the discovery of the Rainbow Lake field far to the north-west of Peace River which was thought to be one of Alberta's largest. Almost all were north of Edmonton; all were significant, and some major finds. By 1965, with all these discoveries, Alberta had 12,771 wells capable of producing over 185 million barrels of oil annually. Moreover, where in 1956 there had been 300 gas pools producing 200 billion cubic feet per year, there were now 800 pools producing 1,290 billion cubic feet per year.

During the decade to 1967 the huge Alberta Gas Trunk Line came into being to gather the gas and deliver it at the Saskatchewan border for Trans-Canada Pipe Lines to take on to Ontario markets; and at the British Columbia border to deliver it to other companies, who in turn send it to the Pacific coast and California. Alberta Gas Trunk constructed 1,945 miles of pipe line, much of it three feet in diameter.

Moreover, as well as these gas lines, oil pipe lines were joined into a common interconnected system spreading east and west across the province and extending from Calgary's old Turner Valley in the south, 550 miles north to Rainbow Lake. From this system, Trans-Mountain Pipe Line leaves the province through the Yellowhead Pass on its way to tidewater, while the Inter-Provincial Pipe Line, delivering oil to Ontario, leaves the province over 300 miles to the east near Chauvin.

The many sulphur plants dotted here and there over the province are integral parts of this whole petroleum products production and the extensive system of pipe lines. They produced 1½ million long tons of sulphur in 1965. As well as these, many other plants producing propane, butane and other liquid petroleum products added to Alberta's industries and Edmonton's coffers.

As 1967 opened, Edmonton's bailiwick was studded with sulphur plants, pock-marked with well sites, and criss-crossed with pipe lines, while its one-time untouched forests to the north were scored by a complex grid of seismograph lines and gravelled roads.

Then too, tucked away into the province's vast and once silent north, the sleeping oil sands had been stirred. Known to white men since 1719, reported in Peter Fidler's journals of 1791, and promising to reach the point of development yearly for the last sixty years, the sands began coming into their own. Lying nearly 200 miles north and underlying 15,000 square miles, they contain over 340 billion barrels of recoverable oil. In 1964 Great Canadian Oil Sands Limited started constructing a special plant estimated to cost over $300 million which was expected to come into operation in Canada's centennial year. Then it was slated to produce the first really commercial oil ever to come out of the sands, at the rate of 45,000 barrels per day. In 1966, to handle that oil, the company began building some 250 miles of large diameter pipe line to Edmonton. Exhibiting the versatility of such line, it was to be used first to pump oil from Edmonton to the plant at Tar Island in order to fuel it until it could process enough of its own fuel to keep itself running. After that the flow of oil would be reversed and the product of the oil sands would start its long trip to Edmonton.

In a manner similar to the oil sands, the Pine Point lead and zinc mines lay untouched for over sixty years after their discovery. There, about ten miles south of Great Slave Lake, a great metallic deposit lay waiting until world markets asked for it and transport was available. In November 1964 the 377-mile extension of the Northern Alberta Railway, from the Peace River country to Great Slave Lake, carried its first south-bound shipment of the shiny metal, and as the yellow gondola cars passed through the city yet another vision of the North had begun to pay off for Edmontonians.

During the ten-year period ending 1966 the petroleum industry alone poured over 4½ billion dollars into exploration, drilling and producing activities and into land costs and royalties in Alberta, of which over 1½ billion were paid to the provincial treasurer. As a result of increased construction, manufacturing, trade and services brought about largely by the input of the oil industry, Alberta's per capita personal income increased from $1,456 in 1956 to $2,306 in 1966, and its population grew from 1,123,000 to 1,463,203.

Over the years since the Leduc discovery—from 1947 to the fall of 1966—the province collected two billion dollars from the sale of crown oil reserves, rentals and royalties. Of this, two-thirds had accrued to the provincial treasurer during the last ten years. Of the province's 1966 budget of $682,000,000 its petroleum resources were expected to produce $248,000,000.

This budget was approximately equal to the sum of all provincial expenditures from 1905 to 1947, the year of the Leduc No. 1 smoke-ring. In 1947 the budget had been $34 million. This one in 1966 was twenty times greater and was equal to $455 for every man, woman and child in the province. It gave Alberta the third biggest budget in Canada, exceeded only by Ontario and Quebec.

While the provincial government could take no credit for the presence of oil in the province, it did take pride in the way it administered the oil industry and the way in which it handled the resulting revenues. Moreover, the government's very stability was regarded by some as one of Alberta's greatest assets. This stability was represented in the person of the premier, the Honourable Ernest Manning, who assumed office in 1943, four years before the oil strike at Leduc, and continued to hold it.

The influx of oil money and of the thousands of people of the new era was enough in itself to revamp Edmonton. But this influx coincided with a world-wide change in orientation to life and in the conception of cities. About 1957, when Edmonton entered its second inspiring decade, it also entered a livelier, more exotic world where cities had to gear up to the accelerated pace which the pleasure-loving citizens of the era of affluence demanded. The fact that Edmonton was growing rapidly may have made the transition somewhat easier.

While scores of new buildings had sprung up in response to the doubling of the population by the end of 1956, they had all been more or less conventional. If before their erection the city had been somewhat moth-eaten and uninspiring, the new buildings, with a few exceptions, had done little to lift its face. Over the years, in spite of better lighting, arborite and some brilliant show windows, the downtown area had become dingy and drab. Then, about 1957, the change to the new city got underway. More and more of the old business blocks were torn down and replaced with modern structures of stainless steel, aluminum and glass. As each of the fifty-year-old buildings toppled, those left standing, weather-worn, cracked and patched, stood out more and more like isolated stumps of teeth long since chipped and stained.

Suddenly the city's fringes woke up. With Woodward's shopping centre leading the way in 1955, many of the city's conveniences were taken out to the customers in the new suburbs. Other shopping centres began locating in the outskirts in easily accessible spots and with ample parking room — Bonnie Doon, Northgate, Meadowlark Park and the Capilano Shopping Mall.

Around the fringes and along one or other of the many highways entering the city, new types of accommodation geared to the country's new mobility sprang into being. Motels and trailer parks occupied acres, while not far to seek were all manner of drive-in hamburger and fried chicken establishments. A new type of hotel also made its appearance as the Highway Motor Hotel, the Riviera, the Bonaventure, and the Saxony in Jasper Place were built. Adjacent to another access to the city rose the imposing Edmonton Inn near the Industrial Airport where it had unfettered parking space.

While all this was going on the airport itself had been experiencing changes. To cope with Edmonton's expansion, it became necessary to build an altogether new airport well out in the country. Accordingly, the authorities selected a 7,500-acre site a mile or so north-west of Leduc and at the eastern fringe of the Leduc oilfield. There, in 1957, after some $25 million were spent on runways and terminal and on a huge painting (which raised a storm of disapproval but was intended to honour northern flyers) the escalators of Edmonton's International Airport began to carry travellers.

The new airport, with its spacious lounges and its aluminum trimmings, threw the old one into the shade. Originally the Hagmann farm, then Jimmy Bell's air harbour and Blatchford Field, and, later on, the scene of so much war-time activity, the old air terminal still continued to play a busy role under its new name of the Industrial Airport.

Downtown, the old warehousing establishments and minor manufacturing plants, finding themselves outmoded and overcrowded, began building anew at the city's outskirts and along Kingsway Avenue, as well as along the main highways entering the city. Cleaning establishments, printers, car accessory depots, and a host of other service institutions, spread out around Edmonton's edges. Service stations began to mushroom in the suburbs; new churches, flinging away their orthodox lines, began to exhibit all the modern architectural skills with new spires, crosses and the flying buttresses of this innovative age of design. Banks, too, began to proliferate in the suburbs.

In the heart of the city, the old-time banks, usually rather fine two-storey examples of classical architecture, came tumbling down to be replaced by ten- and twelve-storey glass and steel structures, while their adjacent areas sported surface or tiered parking lots. One of the first of these casualties was the old Imperial Bank, which half a century earlier had been built at the corner of 100 Street and Jasper Avenue as a symbol of the faith financial institutions had in Edmonton. While the classical columns of this old show-piece of Jasper Avenue were demolished and replaced by a multi-storied structure the bank carried on its business in a Quonset hut which it threw up across the street near the Macdonald Hotel.

More and more the downtown area became the idea and decision centre of a vastly expanded business community. And each of the modern, multi-storied buildings provided pleasing space for smart stores. Leading off their foyers, clean, attractive shops and cafes took their place in the new scheme of things, with music by Muzak, potted plants, diffenbachia and philodendron, fountains and fancy chandeliers, and well-conceived interiors giving a sense of repose to their clients. All of these new ideas were costly, but with a growing population which had waxed wealthy, the old dinginess would do no longer.

The trend had been started by the ten- to fourteen-storey structures, the Milner, Devonian and Financial buildings. It was carried on by the Professional Building opened in 1962, near the corner of Jasper Avenue and 109 Street and McDougall and Secord's Empire Block (1963) at Jasper Avenue and 101 Street, the city's main intersection. The Empire block started the revamping of that busy corner and was followed by the new Bank of Montreal (1964), and in 1965 by the striking, floodlit Royal Bank.

Falling in line with this new mood, the last vestiges of prohibition finally disappeared. In Alberta cities, men and women were not allowed to sit together to sip a sociable beer—which was all that anyone could drink in a public place— but had to drink in separate rooms. The country points, strangely enough, permitted mixed drinking, and the result was that after work or on Saturdays, Edmonton couples or parties, in order to drink together, had to drive out to the overcrowded beer parlours in St. Albert, Spruce Grove, Fort Saskatchewan or Leduc. At these places the hotel owners waxed fat, and when, an hour or so before midnight they had to close and eject their patrons, the highways into the city were strewn with tipsy drivers.

Eventually public pressure succeeded in relaxing the rigorous rules, and in October 1957, during a plebiscite, Albertans overwhelmingly endorsed mixed drinking in the cities and the provision of lounges for spirituous liquors. Soon a number of well-appointed beer parlours came into being and some of the better hotels obtained licenses permitting them to serve liquor with meals. Shortly afterwards various lounges opened to cater to the demand for this amenity. Strictly regulated by the Alberta Liquor Control Board, their excellent appointments conformed to a high and pleasant standard, and within a few years many of these outlets added their touch of sanity to Edmonton's life. In them too, architects and interior decorators found much scope for their creativeness.

Keeping pace with the new wave of hotels and dining lounges, high-rise apartments, ten, twelve and fourteen stories high, began to tower over the older drab residences, adding touches of lightness to the skyline by day and columns of light by night. For a start, while some were built on the slope of the valley or on the flats, most of them clustered around what had once been a trail along the brow of the hill, the old High Street leading from Fort Edmonton to McDougall's mission. Among them were Carlton Towers, the Royal Park, the Palisades and Rowand House, named after the man who nearly a century and a half earlier had constructed the wonder of the West, the Big House.

But the spate of high-rise apartments had only started. They progressed west along the brow of the hill all the way from the High Level Bridge to about 124 Street; Jasper House, twelve stories, Regency Apartments, fifteen stories, and many others. While the main cluster of them took advantage of the view looking south over the magnificent river valley, some had begun to view it from the south side. The two prominent ones, Kennedy Towers and the Starlight Towers, added interest to the south side's skyline. These were followed by high-rise apartments along Whyte Avenue near the university property and by the twenty storey Garneau Towers. Then, as an indication of coming change, far off to the east, three miles from its nearest competitor, the Imperial Towers thrust its apartments high above Highway 16.

Adding to the south side's architectural interest, the university completed its ten-storey Education Building in 1963. By the summer of 1966 the slender Henry Marshall Tory Social Sciences Building, with its fifteen stories looming over the vast valley, added another dimension to the sprawling campus and another headland to the city.

The two most impressive buildings, however, both completed during 1966, rose on the north side. Downtown, replacing the old railway station, the CNR building with its twenty-seven storey tower became a landmark visible for miles. Four or five blocks away, built on the slope of McDougall Hill and forming a backstop for 101 Street, rose the Chateau Lacombe, with its offset circular tower. Between the uptown level and the valley floor, its eleven levels of parking space, built to be entered from the level of 101 Street or from the valley floor over a hundred feet below, were indicative of the new age. Viewed from the north, it soared twenty-four stories over 101 Street. Viewed from the south, however, it loomed over the valley which the good Father Lacombe had known so well.

All these apartments, office structures, university classrooms, the CNR tower and the Chateau Lacombe transformed Edmonton's skyline. And nowhere was this more marked than when seen from the tiny stern-wheeler pleasure craft which operated up and down the river. From there, adding their height to the uplift of the hillside, these slender shafts of white masonry formed the profile of Edmonton's sky.

The most striking transformation, however, was in the old heart of the city in what Edmontonians were to regard as their Civic Centre. This major accomplishment was the fulfilment of a dream of some fifty years' standing. As a start, the new and attractive City Hall was completed by the end of 1956. Then, during years of turmoil in the city council, the civic centre idea made little progress. For many years, various plans for a coliseum occupied the press and politicians, but it, too, fell by the wayside. All the while, however, the city commissioners and their staff were doing what they could to advance the cause, and in June 1962, under Mayor Elmer Roper, the council passed a $150 million Civic Centre scheme. As a start, a few months later council approved a $1½ million building east of the Macdonald Hotel, which, when completed, was called One Thornton Court. At the other end of the centre and in August 1963, the CNR undertook to tear down its station and to substitute for it a twenty-seven storey structure.

In January 1964, plans for a new library began to take shape. When they were approved, they marked the knell of the decades-old farmers' market which occupied part of the proposed site. A new market was built two or three blocks to the east and work began on the library. Hard on its heels, in March, the twenty-four-storey, $4½ million Avord Arms building began to define the Civic Centre on the west. Shortly afterwards, on the centre's eastern flank, a $2 million building, Chancery Hall, received the signal to go ahead. Then, in September, the city gave the Art Gallery six lots on which to get under way. In March 1965, to honour the Empire's greatest leader, the council bestowed Winston Churchill's name to the Civic Centre square.

In August 1965, the city council took one of its longest looks at urban renewal and talked about clearing out much of the drab and decaying fringes which bordered the Civic Centre. Two months later the $5½ million nineteen-storey Centennial Building received council's approval and the following March, at the corner of 100 Street and 103 Avenue, Mayor Dantzer turned its first sod.

All this new construction whirled the tally of building permits to a new record of high-rise figures. From the previous oil-generated record of $69,406,000 established in 1956 they climbed up and up; $72,517,000 in 1958, $90,345,000 in 1962, and $135,407,000 in 1966. During 1965 alone, Edmonton's construction firms added 4,300 new living units, including 2,619 new homes.

In another field of construction financed by city coffers during this decade, the miles of streets increased from 850 to 1,416, and the miles of pavement from 266 to 730. Not only were there more miles of streets, but, in a large measure, now that cars had become a substitute for human legs, they were better streets, geared to handle the amazing upsurge of traffic. By 1961 Albertans operated over 500,000 vehicles, that is, one for every 2.6 Albertans — the highest vehicle-to-population ratio in Canada. By 1966 Edmontonians owned over 150,000 cars or trucks. Moreover, while Edmontonians had enough cars to keep the streets humming, the city's thoroughfares also had to cope with all the cars of northern Alberta. While once upon a time farmers and folk from the surrounding area had driven into the city once or twice a year, now, along the first-class paved highways leading to Edmonton, they popped in and out all the time — to shop, celebrate or play bingo.

Elaborate level intersections and traffic circles came into being to handle not only the cross-town traffic but that of the main highways which focused on the city. These had to be linked up by means of such ring-roads and thoroughfares as Argyll and Groat roads. Since nearly forty percent of the population lived south of the river, traffic problems, while scarcely noticeable as compared to those in larger eastern cities, grew too. The problems of moving traffic back and forth across the river multiplied, for after the Groat Bridge was completed in 1955, no others were built until 1968. The traffic engineers advocated others but the council vacillated. Amongst the factors causing delay, the conflict between parkland and space for freeways was probably the most difficult to resolve.

Edmonton's Parks and Recreation Department, working away with little fanfare, has done a fine job of developing the many city parks, and year by year, almost unnoticed by the citizens, has beautified area after area. The fascination of its Storyland Valley Zoo, opened in 1959, attracts thousands of delighted visitors, and on any summer's day their parked cars fill much of Miner's Flats where a hundred years ago Jim Gibbons and his fellow gold panners shoved up their shacks. A year after Queen Elizabeth opened Coronation Park in 1959, the citizens, working together, financed and built the Queen Elizabeth Planetarium there, the first planetarium in Canada. And there are so many other parks, including the one named in 1960 in honour of Emily Murphy, one-time author and magistrate, which forms such a delightful picnic spot near Groat Bridge.

Part of Edmonton's growth was due to a rising birth-rate and part was due to an influx from the surrounding country, for the flight from the farms to cities had really got under way. In 1941, 68.5 percent of Alberta's population had been rural; by 1961 that figure had dropped to 36.1 percent. During that period, of Edmonton's population of 281,027, some 37,500 were immigrants from mainland Europe who had come to live in the city since the start of the boom in 1947.

In theatre, the Court Players, The Edmonton Alumni Players, Edmonton Theatre Associates and the University drama department in such makeshifts as the Yardbird Suite, Walterdale Play House, and the Torches Theatre gave a new impetus to the art and a new encouragement to the players. In 1965, Alberta's first professional theatre, the Citadel, opened. On top of all these, the Theatre for Children, which started in 1953, was extremely successful in presenting plays designed for young audiences. With all these, as well as the Playground Players, Edmonton witnessed some of the most progressive work in Canadian theatre.

In the whole field of arts, one of the highlights of Edmonton's progress and one which acted as a bit of comic relief to the serious business of money grubbing, centred around the provincial censorship exercised in banning the film

Tom Jones. This hilarious movie received the acclaim of the whole world, and vetoing it pointed up some of the follies inherent in censorship. The resulting uproar, which ended in May 1964 with the release of the film for showing to "adults only," brought about a broader outlook on the part of the government.

Ballet also made great forward strides. In 1962, the Edmonton Ballet Company was formed with Ruth Carse as director. Two years later the group presented an abstract dance called "Kaleidoscope," which was created expressly for them by Hans Van Gijn, a Hollander stationed in the army. The highlights of the company's career were the premieres of two original ballets performed on Boxing Day 1966.

In the field of music the bands of military units stationed in Edmonton during the fifties made major contributions, especially the RCAF Tactical Air Command Band, whose members for the most part had been recruited in England, and the Princess Patricia's Band, mostly recruited in Holland. Many of their members played in civilian groups and they had a notable effect on the standards of Edmonton music.

The Edmonton Symphony Orchestra went on from success to success. Under Brian Priestman, who had been with Sadler's Wells Opera Orchestra, the Edmonton group became one in which all Edmontonians took a justifiable pride. Similarly, the Edmonton Chamber Music Society grew with the times and catered to a larger population and an audience growing more appreciative and enthusiastic all the time. So, too, the Edmonton Civic Opera, under Mrs. J. B. Carmichael, who had been its inspiration for so many decades before her death in 1964, achieved continuing success in *Show Boat, Kismet, Can-Can,* and others.

In another operatic field, the Edmonton Professional Opera Association, which was formed in 1963, outshone many imported companies. Through *Madame Butterfly, Pagliacci, Carmen* and *La Boheme,* amongst others, it fostered an increasing interest in grand opera. The Edmonton Light Opera Society also stimulated Edmontonians with its magnificent performances. Meanwhile, the Women's Musical Club continued its meritorious work, bringing the finest performances to the city and starting many talented young Edmonton artists on their way to success.

In the performing plane also, but inspired by motives more mercenary, came Klondike Days. In their tourist and other promotions a few cities in Canada were fortunate because they had a colorful indigenous activity upon which they could capitalize. Calgary's Stampede, for instance, has become a glamorous version of that city's past and present as the centre of the range and cattle area. Edmonton, looking back upon a history filled with colour, with voyageurs and fur traders, explorers and gold panners, lumbermen, pioneer farmers and bush pilots, dragged in a theme based upon a trivial period which had occupied a brief twelve months of its history. In the early 1960s the Exhibition Board and the Chamber of Commerce, seeking a symbol with which to glamorize Exhibition Week, hit upon Klondike Days, and set about to mark their city with its brand.

The theme, barely more indigenous than the St. Nicholas which we imported from Holland, caught the citizens' fancy, and like Santa Claus, became a success. Students of history and other sober-sides called Klondike Days a fake, similar to the two or three west coast Indian totem poles which had been erected in the city.

It may have been a fake, but it stuck. During Exhibition Week the Klondike theme has become the unofficial but best known symbol of the city. The advertising boys did their job well, and the vast majority of Edmontonians got behind them as they had never before rallied behind a light-hearted idea. During Klondike Days women dress in the fashions of the Nineties and in all the feathers and finery flashed in the theatres and saloons by the dance-hall girls of the Yukon. As set off by the women of Edmonton, young or old, these usually expensive costumes are beautiful and add a striking touch to Edmonton's Exhibition days and one which visitors are not likely to forget.

Perhaps the secret of the success of Klondike Days is as deep rooted as a little girl's irresistible impulse to deck herself out in her mother's cast-off dress and a pair of her high-heeled shoes. But the men dress up too, and bedeck themselves in top hats, brilliant vests, gold watch chains, and arm bands. Their preparations start weeks before when many of them stop shaving, and grow all the variations of hirsute adornments so prevalent during the Nineties.

The whole performance is make-believe, as make-believe as drug store cowboys or Calgary's ten-gallon white hats, but it's fun and it's human, and its thousands of participants enjoy it. For a week, in their gay costumes, they become not only spectators during Exhibition days but whole-hearted participants. Klondike Days appear to have become a permanent feature of the city's life.

Aside from Klondike capers, Edmonton offers spectators three or four choices of entertainment or cultural enrichment any evening of the week. The city's mixture of ethnic groups has been a major factor in this great cultural advance. The year 1964 saw the culmination of a ten-year dream when the Scandinavian Centre opened. The Ukrainian people made a major contribution with their outstanding choirs and in the part they played in the development of every branch of the city's culture, singing, acting, orchestral work and dancing. The growing Italian colony, with its traditional love of and skill in opera, also made major contributions to our cultural life. Edmonton's Jewish community has always given strong support to the city's cultural development. Religious and political differences may remain but in these fields they have been submerged in a tremendous cooperative effort.

Arising to meet its greatly enlarged opportunities, the Edmorton public has welcomed the up-grading of the arts with a perceptive awareness that bodes well. The province's contribution of the Jubilee Auditorium gave immense impetus to most of the performing arts. It was opened in 1957 when an audience greeted Mrs. Carmichael's Edmonton Civic Opera performance of *Carmen* with enthusiastic applause. Seating 2,700 people in plush comfort in its main auditorium and equipped with every known facility, it forms a centre about which much of Edmonton's life revolves. In spite of the city's geographical location which has made it more difficult to attract good professional people, Edmonton has made remarkable progress.

Hand in hand with progress in all these other facets of Edmonton's life, the public library made great strides. By 1967, as well as entering new fields, it administered six branch libraries. Due in no small measure to the promptings of Morton Coburn, the city centennial project was the new and imposing public library in the Civic Centre.

Expenditures on the fine arts, however, were small when stacked up against the cost of up-grading health, educational and traffic facilities. On them millions had to be paid out and these millions sorely taxed the burgesses' ability to pay. Decades earlier a city had been a more or less autonomous unit bearing and expecting to bear the costs of the facilities it provided, but by 1966, since some sixty-four percent of the province's population had moved to the cities, the load of providing all these amenities became too great. Edmonton, like all other cities, reluctantly at first and then persistently as a right, appealed to senior governments for help. Asking for help with one hand and flaunting its independence with the other strained the financial friendliness existing between the provincial and the municipal governments. In any event, the province of Alberta began sharing much of the load of municipal government and paying a growing share of its cost.

For instance, whereas when the province was created in 1905 the official in charge of welfare explained that during the year his department had found it necessary to "extend assistance to two females," that situation had changed, and some sixty years later welfare needs began to loom large in the province's budget. By a paradox, as the province's, the city's and the ordinary man's wealth increased, so did the number of what Jesus called the poor ye always have with you.

Quite justly, a large part of the city's costs for education also fell on the shoulders of the provincial treasurer. Over the years, Edmonton's educational facilities had been of a relatively high order, and fortunately during its halcyon years kept up with the trends elsewhere. As the years went by and it became evident that the world bestowed its major benefits on those with education, more and more students passed their Grade 12 examinations and went on to the university. And due to more money spent on facilities and a rapid up-grading of teaching personnel, the knowledge acquired by a modern Grade 12 student is head and shoulders above that of his counterpart in the previous generation.

During the decade, more and better schools of various sorts were built; composite high schools, schools for the retarded, and schools tending to segregate the highly intelligent and ambitious pupils. The increasing need for Albertans to produce their own technicians instead of importing them mainly from Europe, led to the province creating its $12 million Northern Alberta Institute of Technology.

No segment of the field of education gave as clear an indication that Alberta was devoting all possible effort to preparing its people for the new era as did the university. On March 31, 1957, the province had nearly $15 million invested in buildings and equipment at the three branches of the university at Edmonton, Calgary and Banff. Three years later that figure had risen to $30 million, of which some $28 million had been expended on the Edmonton campus. Five years later, by March 31, 1965, the capital expenditure on the Edmonton campus alone had jumped to over $62 million.

By 1963 additions and new buildings had sprung up all over what sixty years previously had been River Lot 5: buildings for Physical Sciences, Physical Education, and the new Cameron Library. These were followed by the ten-storey Education Building, a structural engineering lab and the two residences towering over Lister Hall, which was named, by the way, after a rare janitor, Reg Lister, who during four decades was more widely known than some university presidents. Then came the towering Henry Marshall Tory Social Sciences Building, while at mid-summer 1966 tenders of the order of $24 million had been received for a new biological sciences complex to be built at the north-west corner of the campus.

River Lot 5 became so jammed with structures that the university had to have more land, and acquired that part of the old Garneau residential area north of 87 Avenue and west of 110 Street. By 1966 the Edmonton campus alone had increased its full-time staff to 850 from the 240 ten years earlier. The university's enrolment rose from some 4,600 in 1955, which included 1,600 summer students, to 11,515 full-time students.

But buildings, equipment, staff and students are only part of the criteria by which the world judges the quality of an educational institution. Not only must a university lay its fare before a larger segment of the public, but it must also produce graduates more highly trained. In all its history to the end of 1965, the university had graduated some 29,000 students, and since over 13,000 of them were the product of the last ten years, it was fulfilling one part of its duty. On the score of more intensive training, however, in 1965 it granted 184 masters and 44 doctoral degrees as compared to 51 masters and one doctorate ten years earlier, and thus was facing up to the other part.

The 1966 provincial budget included $22,510,000 ear-marked for construction at the Edmonton campus of the university. Out of a total provincial expenditure of $682 million, $145 million was to be spent on the health of Albertans, not that they were a sickly lot but to keep them as fit as a generation of car drivers could be kept. Education, however, in one form or another, topped even that, at $155 million, to place it in the position of having the largest single slice of the government spending pie. A survey report issued in 1966 by an Ontario institute indicated that out of the sixty Canadian and American areas studied, Alberta placed first in educational effort in the percentage of its budget which it spent in that field.

While the university was the province's sole responsibility, and while it spent large sums on all other phases of education in Edmonton, nevertheless the city had to match them with other sums. Edmonton's city council, even with a 1966 budget of $109 million, was hard pressed to accomplish, even with provincial aid, all the things that needed doing. Trying to spread their money around so as to keep the city operating and at the same time providing works to accommodate the ever growing population, it had a difficult time.

Compounding the confusion came a struggle over the mayor's chair. William Hawrelak, who from 1951 to 1959 had filled that office with a measure of distinction and, by being re-elected twice by acclamation, established a record, tripped over a line which he either did not see or ignored in his private real-estate dealings. Charges of mal-administration led to an enquiry before Mr. Justice M. M. Porter. When his judgment came out in September 1959, reporting that the mayor was guilty of "gross misconduct," Hawrelak resigned. The city sued the ex-mayor and a number of companies and their officials for $226,000, but in May 1961 the action was settled by a payment of $100,000.

On September 9 that year the council officially elected F. J. Mitchell, a long-time and respected alderman, to the mayor's chair. When it was time for the next regular election, he chose not to run and Elmer E. Roper, distinguished politician of long standing, who for years headed the socialist faction in the provincial legislature, assumed the empty chief magistrate's chair. For four years he carried on a well-run regime, and when he declined to carry the burden any longer and stepped down, he was a man respected in all quarters.

In the ensuing election, Hawrelak, strong willed like Shakespeare's Richard the Third, determined to regain the office, fought a memorable campaign and was re-elected. Similarly, he swept the polls at the October 1964 election when he used the slogan "Keep Edmonton Rolling."

Then in December 1964, Roy Anderson, a retired physician, disagreeing with the all too prevalent view that to the victor belongs the spoils, charged Hawrelak with a new and recent contravention of the City Act. As a result, the following March, Chief Justice C. C. McLaurin ruled that the mayor was disqualified to hold office. Though Hawrelak appealed the case to the Supreme Court of Canada, he nevertheless lost. The balance of his term was filled by Alderman Vince Dantzer. Then during the 1966 election when Hawrelak tried to regain the mayor's chair, Vince Dantzer defeated him to the tune of some 64,000 votes to 54,500.

Despite the mayoralty fracas, Edmonton kept growing, annexing more land, laying out more streets, building new schools, adding new cultural activities and pressing ahead with the Civic Centre. The very fact that it made such progress during a time of upheaval in the council chamber is perhaps no surprise, for mayors come and mayors go, but a city's momentum, continuously impelled by a permanent staff, keeps it growing.

Edmonton, 1956.

Edmonton, 1966.

Continuing Prosperity
1968-1974

chapter *21*

T HE NEXT eight years to 1974 turned out to be a continuation, but on an ever rising scale, of the unprecedented activity and growth on which Edmontonians had floated into Canada's centennial year of 1967.

At the end of 1974 the population of Edmonton's metropolitan area had increased to an estimated 530,000. However, that figure will bear watching because in 1971 the area was enlarged once more so as to bring into the fold the town of Fort Saskatchewan and the villages of Bon Accord, Gibbons and Morinville. Bringing these in immediately added their combined populations of over 8,000 to the city's total, as well as several hundred farm families hitherto considered as rural. Even without these additions, however, the growth in the metropolitan figure was still a significant one and amounted to an increase of thirty-five percent during the eight-year period.

It should be noted that even though the city limits, as opposed to the metropolitan limits also had been expanded, the population within the enlarged city limits grew only twenty percent. In proportion, more people were going to the satellite towns. The growth of these is indicated by showing the 1974 population figures and following them with those for 1966; St. Albert 20,500 (9,736), Sherwood Park 25,572 (5,800), Fort Saskatchewan 7,890 (4,152).

And just outside the metropolitan area but within thirty minutes or less driving time from the city centre, a number of growing towns serve as residential adjuncts to the city. These with their 1974 and 1966 populations are: Spruce Grove 5,610 (598); Stony Plain 2,316 (1,397); Devon 1,500 (1,283); Beaumont 450 (300); and Leduc 8,000 (2,856). Outside of these towns but still within easy commuting distance of the city are scores of rural residential subdivisions. Within these on plots of twenty acres or less live several hundred families whose breadwinners work in the city. They have greatly increased the density of the rural population.

Except for 1973, each year since 1969 witnessed some major extension of the city's boundaries. During that time they were extended west of old Jasper Place by three annexations totalling over twelve square miles. In 1971 two huge additions of about equal size, the Mill Woods area at the southeast and the B.A.C.M. block extending north towards the Namao airfield, added some thirty-four square miles. As an indication of the rate of growth of the city, these two annexations nearly equalled the total area which had made up the Edmonton of 1947. During 1974 the Kaskitayo area between Blackmud Creek and the Calgary highway at the south edge of the city added a little over a square mile to the area within the municipal boundaries. By the time all these annexations had been achieved, the area within the city limits totalled 122.61 square miles.

During this eight-year period new subdivisions proliferated. The civic committee charged with selecting names succeeded in producing names that had some historical meaning. They included Oleskiw, an outstanding figure in the great Ukrainian migration to Alberta around the turn of the century. Paying heed to other leaders of an earlier generation who were of three other ethnic stocks, the committee named the subdivisions of Gariepy, Jamieson and Lymburn. Then as a well-merited gesture to the people who had migrated to the Edmonton area a generation or two before the advent of white men, they called several Mill Woods subdivisions by Cree names: Ekota, Kameyosek, Meyonohk, Satoo and Tipiskan. As one year succeeded another new crescents and service roads were laid out in these areas and new schools and churches came into being to serve scores of multi-cultural newcomers who had come to Edmonton to share in its oil wealth.

Just as for twenty years oil had played a predominant part in the city's development, it continued to furnish payrolls, to create jobs and to induce immigrants to come to Alberta. The fact that by 1967 the twenty-year wave of well drilling had crept across Alberta's boundary into the Northwest Territories did not diminish Edmonton's or in fact Alberta's prosperity. Though the rigs had been swallowed up in the mists of the far North, the North to which Edmonton had been the handmaiden so long, their payrolls and their servicing jobs kept finding their way to the city.

Even though Alberta failed to turn up any major new fields and the wave of exploratory drilling had worked north as far as the Arctic Ocean, it had not taken all the drilling rigs with it. Whereas in 1965 Alberta had 12,771 wells capable of producing over 184 million barrels of oil per year and 1,800 producing gas wells, as well as 1,515 capped gas wells, each of the next eight years was to show an increase in these figures. So great was the increase that at the end of 1973 Alberta had 14,368 wells which, because of rapidly growing demand, produced 523 million barrels of oil. Similarly the number of producing gas wells had reached the figure of 4,536 with 2,551 others remaining capped. In the case of these wells also, most of the men working at them spent their pay cheques in Edmonton.

To cope with the oil from new wells and an increasing flow from the old ones and with greater volumes of gas, more and larger pipe lines came into being. A number of new separation plants also began to dot the landscape. Located here and there from the great geese breeding marshes of Hay Lakes to the antelope-cropped grasses of the Sweet Grass Hills 750 miles to the south, scores of processing plants had to be fabricated and welded together — plants costing millions of dollars. Though costly, they soon started paying their way. While the increasing amounts of butane, propane and other products remained largely invisible, the sulphur which they produced became increasingly obvious as great rectangular blocks bigger than skating rinks were exposed to the atmosphere. In the process of preparing some 498 million barrels of oil and some 1,962 billion cubic feet of gas for market during 1974, for which we have only a preliminary estimate, these plants turned out amazing amounts of by-products. The following figures which show the quantities of these products during that year also show the corresponding quantities for 1966 in brackets: propane 33 million barrels (11); butane 21 million (7), and of "pentanes plus" some 57 million barrels (27), as well as 7 million (1.7) long tons of sulphur. Oil, Edmonton's fairy godmother, was still hovering over her.

Oil helped Edmonton to make the transition from an agriculturally based economy to one in which manufacturing has come to play a major part. While other metro areas attempting to make the change encountered many transitional difficulties, in Edmonton's case these were drowned out by a beneficent flow of oil and Edmontonians eventually discovered that they had bridged that gap without the usual dislocations. In any event, at the present time Edmonton and Calgary, its rival, are well along the road towards being industrial cities.

Without going into further details to prove that statement perhaps it will be enough to note that in the last twenty-five years Alberta's annual net value of production added by manufacturing has increased to over $2 billion as compared to a quarter of that to begin with. As for the contribution of the construction industry, it rose from some $279 million to $2,200 million during the same period. While these figures are for all of Alberta and while Alberta's economy was expanding on all fronts, Edmonton received at least its share of that expansion and possibly a greater portion than its population might seem to have justified. Although oil's impact on Edmonton was so great that it has appeared to be the sole cause of the city's prosperity, these other industries have played a vital part. Moreover, in the rest of the industrialized world the last twenty-five years also saw major changes in orientation to life that remade cities and to some extent revamped the outlook of rural areas.

In Alberta, to keep pace with this change in orientation and all the increase in construction, manufacturing and trades and services, some of it based directly on the oil industry and some not, the province's population increased 17 percent from 1,463,203 in 1966 to 1,709,000 in 1974, while during the same period Edmonton's city population jumped 17 percent to 445,691 and its metropolitan population jumped by 30 percent. Moreover, during that same period Alberta's per capita personal income rose from $2,306 in 1966 to $4,929 in 1974. That, of course, was the income of the average Albertan and that of the average Edmontonian was undoubtedly about the same. During that period unfortunately, inflation's invidious hand had reduced its real purchasing value by over 35 percent.

With a metropolitan population of 530,000 and a per capita income of $4,929, it is no wonder that Edmonton's construction industry flourished. During 1966 the value of building permits had been $135,407,000 and by 1974 it had climbed to an estimated $316,000,000. The number of dwelling units erected from 1967 to 1974 inclusive was 54,677.

But for the time being that is enough of dollars and figures and statistics, and of provincial or civic economics. While it is true that it takes dollars to get things done and statistics to evaluate them and keep track of them, people and events are much more interesting.

While the figures for the number of vehicles are still fresh in our minds, however, it might be well to look at one aspect of the traffic problems with which they confronted the city council — bridges. Since roughly half of Edmonton's citizens lived on each side of the river, bridges had become bottlenecks in the flow of rush-hour traffic to such an extent that in the space of five years after 1967 four major new bridges were built across the mighty Saskatchewan River: Quesnell, 1968; Capilano, 1969; James MacDonald, 1971; and the twinning of the Beverly bridge in 1972.

All these bridges had to span the river which flows in a magnificent valley some two hundred feet deep and varying from half a mile in width to perhaps a mile. This valley is one of the gifts which providence has bestowed on Edmonton. Entering the city at its southwest corner and sweeping along in great bends, the river traverses it diagonally to leave at its northeast corner after winding a distance of over twenty-five miles. Much of the city's 8,918-acre area of park-lands and playgrounds is located in this splendid valley. As a result, any en-croachment of highways or traffic structures on this parkland area is watched jealously.

Such an encroachment which battled its way into council deliberations and set the city at sixes and sevens was the McKinnon Ravine roadway. After one or two millions of dollars had been expended on the throughway and when many motorists looked forward eagerly to its imminent completion, pressure groups within and without the council stopped further construction. Once more the engineers and the environmentalists, never having much confidence in each other's ability or stability, played a seesaw game.

The popularity of these parks and open spaces is the result of Edmon-tonians' increased wealth and mobility which permits them to escape some of the pressures of the growing city. It is also a result of the influx of Europeans who are accustomed to the magnificent parks and commons in their native cities. While these recreation areas are being expanded all the time, the rapidly mush-rooming population runs the Parks Department a neck and neck race.

Because the Edmonton metropolitan area's birth-rate per thousand had decreased steadily from 22.0 in 1966 to 17.5 in 1973, the natural increase in its population has dropped to about five thousand per year. The city's amazing growth has come mainly from immigrants from the rural areas, from less indus-trial provinces and from the United States and Europe. Those coming from the rural areas have been continuing the trend of the last two decades which by 1974 had resulted in a mere 26 percent of the province's people being rural. One matter of interest about the city's present population is its multi-cultural back-ground. Ethnically 45 percent of it is British, 13 percent Ukrainian, 12 percent German, 7 percent French and 5 percent Scandinavian, while several countries of origin make up the remainder. Another matter of interest is that Edmontonians are predominantly young; 65 percent of its people are under thirty-five years of age.

Edmontonians are becoming increasingly able to support a whole range of artistic and non-academic cultural events. A growing population enjoying ever-increasing personal income in conjunction with a rapid influx of immigrants from the music-steeped cities of Europe has allowed such events to flourish as never before. Profiting by the discovery of oil, ballet, painting, opera, music and the theatre, have gone on to scale new heights.

In the theatre many groups are broadening the scope of the activities they were carrying on in Canada's centennial year. If progress can be measured by improved accommodation, both the Walterdale Players and the Citadel groups are moving ahead. The former has emerged from its cramped quarters to a more desirable theatre in the revamped South Side Fire Hall. The latter is in the process of watching the erection of its new $5,000,000 theatre immediately east of the Centennial Library. Besides being a boon to its players and patrons, it will become one more addition to an ever-developing Civic Centre.

Ballet continues to attract larger and more appreciative audiences, while bands of various kinds increase in favour with Edmontonians and improve the standard of music in the city. Under the baton of Lawrence Leonard, successor to Brian Priestman, Edmonton's Symphony Orchestra continued to please a critical but enthusiastic audience. In 1973 he moved to Europe and turned the orchestra's direction over to Pierre Hétu, a colleague of rare talent. In similar fields the Women's Musical Club of Edmonton, the Edmonton Opera Association, the Edmonton Light Opera Society and several other very worthwhile groups strive successfully to increase Edmonton's livability.

Fostering all these arts called for considerable subsidies in one form or another from both city and provincial purses. Although scarcely noticed by the general public, the money so expended probably brought more real value per dollar than many a million spent on material needs. It was such financial help which during 1967 brought into being the enthralling Provincial Museum in Edmonton.

But governments, municipal or provincial, each with assists from the Canada Council, were far from being alone in their aid to the arts. Oil and associated activities had made many Albertans rich and a fair number of them millionaires, and often these expressed their gratitude by endowing various cultural activities and edifices. In such a manner, as a bequest from Mrs. Abigail Edith Condell, the seed money for the Edmonton Art Gallery became available. Bringing in exhibits from the National Gallery and from private collectors, it is serving Edmontonians spendidly.

Such cultural structures, however, have been only a minor part of the profusion of buildings which has given Edmonton its dramatic modern skyline. For during the years since 1967 oil and related money has continued to flow and to thrust up high-rise construction cranes, particularly in the old area five or six blocks wide and thirty blocks long which contained nearly all of the pre-1914 city.

Between 1967 and 1974 the annual value of building permits in Edmonton rose from $135 million to $316 million. As the magic wands of the construction cranes moved over it, the city, which had already been transformed during the decade starting in 1956, found itself transformed once more.

During 1969 four major projects were developed near the city's extremities, from the western edge of Jasper Place to Clover Bar a dozen miles away. In Jasper Place as the builders' forms rose storey above storey Edmontonians began to see what the architects had in mind for the new venture undertaken by the Misericordia Hospital authorities. Not only was it to be a high-rise project, but it was being built at the extreme west end of town, miles away from where for nearly seventy years the old hospital had served so faithfully. Then, not far away, a group of entrepreneurs having an eye to one of the directions in which the city was expanding, began constructing an assembly of apartments called the West Meadowlark Complex. It was estimated to cost $13,500,000, was to contain 320 high-rise suites and as well was to include a battery of 288 town houses. As the years passed

Edmontonians found they needed increasingly ambitious and costly projects to keep pace with the city's growth.

In an endeavour to do so but in an entirely different field, the city itself began fabricating one of the province's major gas-fired electric power plants in the area that had once been Clover Bar. Downtown, about half way between the two extremes of the power plant and the Misericordia Hospital, in a slum clearance area, the provincial government started construction of a new court house. Scheduled to cost over $10 million it was planned as one of the city's growing number of architecturally striking buildings.

Also during 1969, along the old Stony Plain Trail, construction started on another major apartment block, the eighteen-storey, 297-suite, $6 million Crescent Place. This huge building was only one of many residential structures which, in all the various far-flung sections of the city, began to tower over their lowly two-storey neighbours. Some of these high-rises were built as condominiums as a new idea began to make itself felt in the city. That arrangement, under which residents of a large building buy an equity in it instead of paying rent, resulted in more and more swinging cranes lifting and whisking material into place.

The next two years produced some structures equally as interesting and varied as those of the preceding year or two but on a grander scale. One of these was the completion of the Woodward's-Hudson's Bay Company $25 million shopping complex in 1970. Called the Southgate Shopping Centre, it appropriated a large cultivated area near 111 Street and 51 Avenue and proceeded to cover a forty-acre field of black soil with concrete and tarmac. The result was a covered mall containing scores of shops carrying goods of all sorts from the more conventional grocery, hardware and clothing goods to the most exotic wares shipped from all over the world to titillate the taste of a people grown wealthy and wasteful.

It was to be in the heart of the city, however, that two exciting new structures came to completion. One, down the slope from the Chateau Lacombe, was the 341-suite Edmonton House apartment building. Built on the east side of Bellamy Hill, it towered thirty-five stories above Macdonald Drive and by starting on the flats below and building up that far it worked in ten levels of parking space to end up as a forty-five-storey structure.

Even more spectacular, however, was the Alberta Government Telephones complex which came into being a stone's throw east of John McDougall's old house. Extending from Macdonald Drive to Jasper Avenue, it was fittingly named McCauley Plaza in honour of Edmonton's first mayor whose house and barn had once occupied the site. Before construction could start it was necessary to demolish several older structures. Among those were the hoary Edmonton Club and the Canadian Legion Hall, built after the 1914 War, as well as the fine old Public Library of somewhat later vintage. Before construction of the complex could commence the occupants and contents of these revered old structures had to find other homes; the Legion in an attractive new building on the fringe of the re-vamped city centre, the library in the new Centennial Library facing City Hall across Sir Winston Churchill Square, and the Edmonton Club which came in for special treatment. Its members had long prized the site of their aging brick structure which gave them such a choice view over the wide river valley. Before they would allow the AGT complex to encroach on their location, the developers had to undertake to provide them with a separate structure on the same site but built to conform to the decor of the whole plaza.

Once all these arrangements had been completed and the construction had been finished, the thirty-five-storey AGT tower became the showpiece on Edmonton's skyline. Associated with it on the plaza the twenty-storey Oxford Leaseholds building (now renamed the Imperial Oil Building) carried the complex north to Jasper Avenue. After the plaza was open, Edmontonians flocked in to see its underground mall occupied by a restaurant, shops, boutiques and even by a liquor store, and they were greatly pleased. For one thing, the liquor store soon embarked on the innovation of speeding up deliveries of its product to impatient Albertans by introducing self-service transactions.

For another, Edmontonians were entranced by being able to do their shopping below grade level in the beginning of what some day soon must become an underground network of stores such as those in the new plaza. Indeed, in preparation for that day, passing under the streets from the labyrinth of shops were pedways crossing Jasper Avenue to the north and 100 Street to the Macdonald Hotel. Both the maze of stores and these passageways were intended to be but the forerunners of a future central core of the city where during winter's blasts pedestrians could move about underground leaving the blizzard-swept streets over their heads to cars and other unfeeling mechanical monsters. And if hardy old-timers who had taken part in Edmonton's development and for eighty years had defied blizzards sneered at the new ways of a softer generation, the younger ones, knowing that our modern wealth had found a way to ease the rigours of Alberta's winters, were glad to let them.

Although inflation had sent building costs soaring, it failed to slow up the construction industry. While during 1972 that industry continued to erect scores of office buildings, warehouses and apartments, three or four of its major projects were on an even larger scale than previous years had seen. The Pepper Tree building on Jasper Avenue west became one of the largest units in a rapidly expanding region of high-rise apartments. Over near the university the three units of College Plaza dominated the whole area. Moreover, in the wondrous world of shopping centres the $24 million Londonderry Mall took shape at 66 Street and 137 Avenue and became the focal point of the whole north-eastern area of the city. Though each venture was notable, nevertheless, even if the sums expended on all three of these projects — the Pepper Tree, College Plaza and the Mall — were added together, the cost of the Clover Bar refinery would have far outstripped them. Imperial Oil Limited was spending $200 million to create a spanking new 140,000-barrel-per-day plant.

1973 saw more activity on an even greater variety of fronts. The twin towers of the Petroleum Plaza started on their way up, and construction commenced on a controversial structure involved with the planning for the 1978 Commonwealth Games. When the builders turned the first sod of the $12,500,000, sixteen-thousand-seat coliseum everyone was relieved that the wrangling had ended. Then, also in the civic field, the needs of Edmonton's burgeoning population for more water made it necessary to start the new water treatment plant. When construction began at the extreme upstream corner of the city (about 170 Street and 35 Avenue) it was estimated to cost $21 million. Because in recent years Edmontonians had become increasingly aware of their history, the city fathers chose to name it after the late E. L. Smith, a long-time, highly respected and well-liked superintendent of the water treatment plant.

During 1973 also, when the core of the city took up the challenge presented by the suburban shopping centres, a major stride saw work start on the Edmonton Centre complex, one of the largest commercial projects ever undertaken in Alberta. By joining forces with others, Woodward's Stores Limited and the Toronto-Dominion Bank were investing a hundred million dollars which by 1976 were expected to produce an aggregation of buildings which would include the following:

A 400,000-square-foot, 5-storey, Woodward's department store, 90 retail businesses, a 25-storey and two 30-storey office towers, as well as a 322-room, 22-storey hotel and parking for 900 cars.

Built at the western edge of the Civic Centre it has added new zest to an area which had become run down and dreary.

About the same time that the cranes were swinging over Edmonton Centre, other builders started to erect the twenty-storey Edmonton Plaza Hotel immediately south of the Centennial Library. Since then, excavation has started on another adjunct to the area — the $5,000,000 Citadel Theatre located east of the Centennial Library.

Work went forward so well on the Edmonton Centre project that many of the fundamental units of the complex were open to the public during the fall of 1974; Woodward's store, one twenty-five-storey tower, many retail stores and much parking. Then the contractors began clearing another old building out of their way. As soon as Woodward's had transferred all their stock from their old store to their new shiny shelves and counters, the demolition crews started on the original building on the corner of 101 Street and 102 Avenue. For some fifty years it had served Edmontonians well and now, day by day, scores of older citizens assembled to watch ruefully as for weeks the wrecker's ball pounded it to pieces. It had been a sound building and, to the last battered brick and bent beam, it resisted the blows of the persistent swinging ball.

While the carpenters and welders who had assembled the Edmonton Centre carried their work into 1975, scores of other craftsmen in all parts of the city were clambering about new buildings of many sorts. In the outskirts, Westbrook Shopping Centre was evolved and near the Industrial Airport the Kingsway Shopping Centre began to take shape. Within sight of it construction on a new $4 million terminal building began to hold out hope that passengers could enjoy a measure of comfort while they waited for Pacific Western Airlines' airbus. All over town scores of structures kept coming into being to serve industries old and new. One involved with television and its younger associate, cable television, brought into being Edmonton's third television station CITV. Built near the Calgary Trail and 55 Avenue at a cost of $6 million, Allarco Developments Limited put the finishing touches to it early in 1975.

To introduce another new idea into the midst of a continuous calvacade of new apartment buildings marching west from the core of the city, various promoters began building high-rises specifically ear-marked for senior citizens and old age pensioners and found a steady stream of prospects waiting for their projects to open their doors.

To cope with an ever increasing flood of people flocking into and out of the downtown area, the city council authorized a start on the first phase of a long-debated and controversial rapid transit system. This phase, estimated to cost $54,700,000, will serve the northeastern sector of the city. Starting at 129 Avenue and 66 Street, this leg of the future project will have three rapid transit stops before reaching one of its terminals near the Centennial Library. Currently under construction is the underground portion from there to Jasper Avenue and 101 Street.

One of the buildings of the future to which rapid transit will give easy access has already been started. This is the first phase — the $800,000 dome — of the most northerly botanical conservatory in North America. A gift from the Muttart Foundation, it will be enlarged from time to time. It will also be associated with the proposed $12 million convention and cultural centre which will be built a few blocks east of the Macdonald Hotel. It is designed in descending levels which will drape themselves down the valley wall from the level of Jasper Avenue to near the water's edge.

Now that we have embarked on a flight of prophecy with the convention centre, perhaps it will be just as well to continue our look into the crystal ball to dream of some of the projects which almost certainly lie immediately ahead of Edmontonians. For a start, the provincial government has announced a proposal to develop the Saskatchewan River valley within Edmonton's boundaries, and the project is estimated to cost about $35 million. It is proposed to put a weir across the river near the Beverly bridges. This will raise the water level as far upstream as the High Level Bridge so as to make the river more amenable to water sports. At the same time other facilities will be developed in this riverside park which it is hoped will be completed by the end of 1978.

Furthermore, the provincial government has initiated a competition to consider ways and means of developing Alberta Centre, a major project contemplated for the area up the slope from the present Legislative Building. The project will cost between $30 million and $50 million and will consist of landscaping, parking and office facilities. It is expected that all of the several phases involved will be in operation within ten years.

On the city's part it is hoped that construction soon will get underway on the $21 million, 45,000-seat Commonwealth Games stadium. Although initially designed for the Games events during 1978, it should serve Edmontonians' recreation needs for a generation or two to come.

If in all this discourse on building we have appeared to be preoccupied with money — with increasing millions — and therefore seem to be looking only in a mercenary direction, it is because there has been little alternative than to tally up the city's progress in dollars. After all, they are but a measure of man-hours and when a city gets to the point where its people can produce results measured in billions of man-hours, it has reached a noticeable step on the ladder of growth.

But many of these new structures have cost more than can be measured in man-hours or dollars. While on the one hand these boom years enriched all Edmontonians materially, on the other hand they have impoverished them by the loss and destruction of some of their treasured landmarks. The Woodward building which was battered down in 1974 was not alone. While the new edifices of the Civic Centre and Edmonton Centre have all done so much to modernize and brighten the area, their improvements have not been gained without the loss of some important historical buildings. One of the first victims of the Edmonton

Centre was the architecturally interesting and historically significant court house which over the years had looked down on the comings and goings of generations of Edmontonians. Another victim which stood in the way of the Edmonton Plaza Hotel and fell to the wrecking crews was Edmonton's old memory-filled post office. About the same time and some blocks away, the splendid seventy-year-old example of the style of life enjoyed by a rich pioneer merchant — the John A. McDougall mansion — was carted away in a welter of rubble and broken bricks.

Not so the Rutherford house just outside the original boundaries of the university's property, the one Alberta's first premier, the Honourable A. C. Rutherford, built while he was in office. When in recent years the university was scheduled to enlarge its holdings to erect more buildings, it too was slated for demolition. But its cause was taken up by the University Women's Club which, by reprieve after reprieve, prolonged the mansion's life until the group could enlist sufficient support within the provincial government to spare the beautiful home and convert it into a museum.

An older Rutherford house, the more modest one in which the premier lived before he was elected, has also been preserved by being moved to a park which was the brainchild of a number of history conscious citizens. The park came into existence because of concern over the practice of demolishing old landmarks which had been going on at least since 1915 when the government of the day destroyed the old Hudson's Bay Company fort as soon as the new Legislative Building was completed.

Amongst old-timers the loss of the fort rankled. During the sixties some of them like the late Sam Dickson inspired such men as the late Merrill Wolfe and Henry Ward, who in turn incited the Downtown Rotary Club to take up the Fort Edmonton Park project and to carry it through until the old fort had been authentically rebuilt. The park, however, went much further than that and with a major assist from the Edmonton Parks Department and a gift of 178 acres from the city, has enlarged its scope. Work is presently progressing towards making the park a living museum which will depict not only what life was like in the fort but also along such typical recreated streets as those of 1885, 1905, 1915 and so on. The older Rutherford house has been reincarnated on the 1905 street.

In a somewhat similar way, many forces have coalesced to prevent the destruction of a few blocks of what was the earliest built-up portion of the city that lay along and adjacent to Whyte Avenue. Brought into focus by the Strathcona Historical Group, approved by the city council and financed by a number of benefactors, the project aims to preserve the buildings so as to retain the sense of identity of old Strathcona.

One of the many knotty problems that has to be solved is how to preserve this area and at the same time work out some way to allow an increasingly heavy flow of traffic through it from the Calgary highway to a new and enlarged 105 Street Bridge which is soon to be under construction. Unfortunately while both the traffic artery and the project are highly desirable, they conflict.

To help projects like the Strathcona preservation, the Fort Edmonton and the Saskatchewan River valley parks, it is fortunate that the provincial government has displayed a growing interest in Alberta's arts, culture and history. It is also most fortunate that it has the financial ability to help all these matters along.

In December of 1968, after keeping unchallenged control of his cabinet and his party for twenty-five years and thus establishing a record for longevity in the premier's office unparalleled in the British Empire, and entirely of his own volition, Premier Ernest Manning stepped down from office. Soon afterwards, by an ironic spin of fortune's wheel, the Liberals at Ottawa appointed this one-time Social Credit radical and small *c* conservative to the Senate.

Then with a nudge from Manning, the Social Credit party chose Harry E. Strom, a southern Alberta farmer, as his successor. First elected in 1955, Strom held the portfolio of Minister of Agriculture from 1962 to 1968, and that of Municipal Affairs until he took over the premier's job. Although Harry Strom was one of the finest gentlemen ever to hold the premier's office, his party's grip on the electorate was loosening and in less than three years the Progressive Conservatives swept his government out of office. When on the night of the 1971 election the votes were counted, out of seventy-five seats, the Social Crediters had won a third, the New Democratic party had elected one member and the Conservatives had come to power with a handsome majority.

Heading the revived Conservative party was a dynamic young lawyer, Peter E. Lougheed, the grandson of Calgary's Senator James Lougheed. Since his election to the provincial house in 1967 he had not only headed the official opposition, but had striven so mightily in reorganizing his party that for the first time in Alberta's history the Conservatives were able to form a government.

Since the election of 1971 fortune has continued to shine on the new premier and his party. As the Social Crediters were cleaning out their desks on the hill for the last time probably none of them paused to remember that from this very location 120 years earlier one of the early West's greatest men, the aging John Rowand, sat writing about himself to a friend and said: "people after being so long in the service get useless. . . ." Times had changed and most of the Social Crediters who had tended the province so faithfully and for so long had grown old. The ways of the world had changed and fresh ideas and fresh methods had come to the surface.

Lougheed was aggressive. One of his first official acts was the institution of a large increase in oil royalties. Though on the whole the oil companies — not entirely the villains some would paint them — resisted, they soon came around and began paying the new Lougheed levies.

The election had been in the summer of 1971, the reassessment of royalties followed in 1972 and by 1973 the province's net oil and gas revenues had jumped from an average of some $260 million during the previous four fiscal years to $328 million that year, and to some $560 million for the next full year.

But fortune continued favouring. Within a few months the Arabian countries, deciding to charge a much higher price for oil, demanded and got a whopping increase in their selling price. Immediately the value of Alberta's oil jumped to a level which previously had been inconceivable, and at a rate hitherto undreamed of the dollars began to pour into the provincial treasury. Because of his stand on the price Alberta should get for its oil, Premier Peter Lougheed immediately became the bête noire of eastern Canada. The old rift between the East and the prairie province widened. A slogan supposedly invented in Calgary, but actually originating in the U.S., voiced Alberta's vexation at the people of Ontario and Quebec — "Let the Eastern bastards freeze in the dark." A similar but perhaps less hastily expressed slogan of distaste, classed Lougheed with the Arabian leaders who had upset the oil pricing apple-cart, calling him the Blue Eyed

Sheik of Alberta. He and Prime Minister Trudeau squared off for a battle of political strength.

Edmontonians, like thousands of other Albertans, supported their premier in his stand and re-elected him in 1975. When the polls closed, sixty-nine Conservatives had been elected out of seventy-five constituencies and only four Social Crediters made the grade.

In the meantime, Alberta's provincial treasurer has been scooping in the dollars and by the time he made his 1975-76 budget address oil and natural gas revenues were expected to reach $1.6 billion. Well may the treasurer have added that Albertans were now the "lowest-taxed citizens of Canada in every major individual tax." Out of the province's total income of $2,490 million from all sources, it proposed to spend $2,439 million on current needs. But over and above that, by setting aside some of its accumulating surplus and looking to the future, the government expected to be able to channel $1.5 billion into an Alberta Heritage Trust Fund "to ensure the prosperity of future generations of Albertans." Fortune had indeed continued to favour Albertans, and nearly one-third of them were Edmontonians.

Albertans were determined to ensure that such prosperity would be shared by future generations. When, early in 1975, it appeared that the gigantic oil sands project being built by the Syncrude Company near Fort McMurray was on the point of financial failure, the provincial and federal governments joined hands to provide the additional hundreds of millions of dollars needed to allow Syncrude to carry on. It would take a large book to tell the story of the chain of events leading from 1966 to this situation. Briefly, on September 30, 1967, the world's first commercial oil sands venture, Great Canadian Oil Sands Limited, started turning out synthetic crude oil and piping it off to Edmonton. By 1972, after teetering along in a shaky financial position, GCOS' ledger figures began to emerge from the red. Thenceforth, partly as a result of the eruption in the world price for conventional oil, its prospects began to look rosy.

In the meantime, the Syncrude Company had been busy planning and building a plant that was to be much larger and was expected to come into production during 1977. The increase in the cost of conventional crude oil worked in its favour but the cost of labour and material, inflated beyond what anyone could have forecast, made it impossible for the Syncrude Company to carry on without government financial aid. Since it was essential to Alberta's economy and to Canada's energy security that the oil sands be developed, both governments cooperated in extending help. Fortunately for Albertans and Edmontonians who stood to benefit directly, the Lougheed government had the money necessary to play its part.

That investment, of course, was of an extraordinary nature. Year by year in the routine operation of the province, however, other governmental responsibilities, health, welfare, traffic facilities, education, etc., all clamoured for increased amounts. One segment of the education front, the university, and especially the university in Edmonton, called for more and more money.

By the end of March 1965 in capital alone the province had invested over $62 million in the University of Alberta in Edmonton. Between 1965 and 1974 another $147 million had gone into construction on the Edmonton campus. In January 1972, for instance, it was reported that there were eight either spacious or towering buildings rising on the campus or in Michener Park. Of these the main ones were the new arts, chemistry, education, engineering, fine arts and law buildings, as well as a magnificent new library.

In 1966 the full-time academic staff had been 850; by 1974 it had grown to 1,350. In 1966 there had been 11,515 full-time students; by 1974 there were 18,524.

The province, whose sudden progress had sprung from an up-grading of know-how which had made it possible to find oil that had always been there, could appreciate the need for more specialized knowledge. In a province abounding in rich resources, it had come to light that the greatest resource of all was a highly educated populace which could perceive and develop resources which less penetrating eyes would overlook. The Indian had not cultivated the soil; the farmer has not discovered the oil wealth; the oil driller had passed by the Athabasca oil sands. On Albertans' ability to penetrate nature's secrets and to step into partnership with her ecology hangs their future. By ploughing much of today's oil riches into education, what crop of riches, material and spiritual, may we not expect in the future?

Including that portion of the 1975-76 provincial budget being spent at the university at Edmonton, it was proposed to spend some $722 million on education in the province as a whole. Directly or indirectly nearly $90 million of this found its way to furthering the cause of education in the capital city. The rest of the money needed to operate the public and separate schools in Edmonton, of course, had to come from taxes levied by the school boards, about $30 million in 1974.

Spending by school boards, however, is only a portion of the money a city like Edmonton needs to try to keep abreast of the demands made on it. In other fields during 1975 the city expects to spend $124 million to meet its current expenses and over $200 million on its capital budget.

With such a record spending year it is little wonder that the aldermen should groan and even bicker under the loads laid on their shoulders or that the mayor should keep pressing the provincial government for new forms of financial assistance such as a definite share of the provincial income tax. In view of the provincial treasurer's prosperity, it is probable that council's hopes for more help may soon be realized at least partially.

Mayor Vince Dantzer declined to seek re-election when in 1968 his term was up. It was during that year that the provincial government passed a new municipal act which provided that elections should be held at three-year intervals and that the whole slate of elected officials should take their chances at the polls at the same time. That same legislation made it possible for a city to decide whether or not to divide itself into wards for electoral purposes. After some consideration and a plebiscite, Edmonton adopted a ward system.

As mayor, Dantzer was followed by Ivor Dent, who like his predecessor did his best to maintain some order in the council and to expedite the city's business. Throughout one three-year term he served faithfully and was re-elected by a good majority in 1971, but a second term eroded his popularity. As the election of 1974 neared, it seemed possible that any strong contender might shake Dent's hold on the electors' sympathies.

It turned out that such a man, a keen businessman, a forceful individual and a former decisive mayor, stood by sifting the political wind. Finding it right, he jumped into the fray, stressing the fact that bygones of some ten years' standing should be forgotten and declaring that he could bring some order out of chaotic council meetings.

Order and decisiveness were apparently what Edmontonians wanted. While many had qualms about forsaking the rapidly eroding British principle that once a man was disqualified from office he was honour bound not to offer himself for election again, they nevertheless voted for the strong contender. When the ballots were counted, William Hawrelak obtained 67,741, Ivor Dent 28,297 and Cec Purvis, a newcomer to the mayoralty race, 32,674.

With a new mayor in what may be a new phase of a new era where more money is spent on a child's toys than was spent on his father's education, the city has reached the place where its resources will sweep it on to greater growth. Like the rest of the world, Edmonton is caught up into an age which fires projectiles at the planets and in which men walk on the moon. Moreover, the trip to the moon took only two or three days — a far cry indeed from the time just seventy-five years earlier when by Red River cart the trip from Winnipeg to Edmonton took some fifty days, and a farther cry from that day one hundred years earlier when Angus Shaw built the first Fort Augustus in the midst of a "rich and plentiful country abounding in resources."

Just as the modern city of over half a million people with its colour and cable TV, its increasing bank robberies and its topless and bottomless dancers, is a far cry from the first Edmonton House with its pemmican, paddles and pack horses, so are the known resources upon which the city grows. Then, Edmonton had been a couple of log hovels where a handful of men sought shelter in a clearing beside the mighty, forest-locked Saskatchewan River. Now it is a city of many mansions commanding the resources of a rich Alberta, directing their harvesting and ordering their disposition. Now that in population Alberta has grown to be Canada's fourth largest province and Edmonton its eighth largest metropolitan area, the city, with its tremendous resources, looks forward with confidence.

That confidence, however, has a slightly different feel about it than the unbridled optimism which all Edmontonians and all Canadians felt a decade ago. Since then on at least three fronts some of the facts of life have begun to sink into the common consciousness, and a cooling breeze has cast some doubt upon a few aspects of our previously unquestioned North American philosophy.

Our very wealth has made available to us such a glut of material goodies that it has dulled the edge of the enjoyment they used to bring. Too frequently possessions or desire for more possessions have become enough of a burden that many have come around to a frame of mind similar to that of Tacitus when Rome was sinking into its decline. Writing of "arcades, amenities, baths and sumptuous banquets" and the Romans' reaction to them, he said, "They spoke of such novelties as 'civilization' when really they were only a feature of enslavement."

That, of course, is only one facet of our wealth about which we are beginning to wonder. Another which is perhaps of more immediate import is how increasing prosperity has brought increased crime and lawlessness in its train. For decades we attributed these conditions to poverty and felt that if we could eliminate it we could go a long way towards curing them. It is now beginning to appear that our wealth has not decreased the number of "the poor ye always have with ye."

Our lavish wealth, moreover, has been at the expense of our diminishing resources. Suddenly we have awakened to a realization of how wasteful we are being of our finite resources and of our decreasing stores of energy. So Edmontonians are beginning to doubt some of the so-called self-evident truths, such as the theory of limitless resources.

Even with these relatively new doubts, the citizens of Edmonton are looking forward to the approaching decades with confidence. For, aside from anything else, the city is the metropolitan gateway to Alberta's remaining 20 million acres of untouched arable land and through it passes an annual cut of timber which could be increased six times.

Then, on the provincial energy scene, in addition to millions of untapped hydro horse power, Alberta has tremendous reserves of other forms of energy. In recent years the Energy Resources Conservation Board has been taking a longer and closer look at the province's energy supplies and has drastically revised previous figures. In its *Energy Resources of Alberta,* December 31, 1973, it has presented the following estimates for ultimate recoverable resources: coal, 70 billion tons; crude oil, synthetic crude and pentanes plus, 267 billions of barrels; propanes and butanes, 2.1 billion barrels; natural gas, 93.0 trillions of cubic feet. These are tremendous reserves of energy. With them Alberta has over 85 percent of all the sources of fossil energy in Canada. Which, God grant, we may use wisely.

And Edmonton, the control centre of the vast continent-wide network of petroleum products pipe lines, sits in the middle of all this energy. Edmonton, which at various times has been the main fur-trade depot of the West, the gateway to the North, the crossroads of the world and Canada's oil capital, is now the core of Canada's energy empire.

And yet, as of old, indifferent to the fact that hurricanes of gas and rivers of oil course through cavernous pipe lines on their way to Vancouver, Toronto, Chicago and San Francisco, fur bearers still haunt the river's bank. Every summer evening when shadows stretch far across Edmonton's beautiful river valley, heedless of the capitol and the marts of commerce on one bank and the university on the other, beavers clamber ashore to cut their winter's wood supply.

As they do, old men, still hale, talk of the old men they knew in their youth — old men who had been born when the bark of the fort's first palisades was still green. They talk, too, of the magic of the days of their own youth seventy years ago, the days of horses, coal mines and log drives, when the smell of wood smoke from the busy mills below seeped over the bustling new city. They recall the mighty men who, often muddle-headed and often at cross purposes, nevertheless, each in his own sphere, created the city. For, though cities grow only where resources abound, they grow only when men build them.

While old men, sitting on the benches facing south over the vast valley, dream of the days that are gone, young men and women at the university, looking north across the river to Edmonton's business section, see visions of the days to come. Their visions skip lightly over the past, but based on an Edmonton already great and on an Edmonton surrounded with the Creator's riches, concentrate on the future.

For it is written that "Your old men shall dream dreams, your young men shall see visions."

The old dreamers have witnessed a vivid past. The young visionaries will see a vital future.

appendix I Historical highlights

1795	First Edmonton House established.
1802	Edmonton House moved to within present city.
1810	Edmonton House moved downstream to near Smoky Lake.
1813	Edmonton House moved back to 1802 site.
1823	Edmonton House becomes the most important depot in the West.
1825 & 1830	High floods at Edmonton.
1830	Edmonton House moved to site below present Legislative Building.
1840	Reverend Robert Rundle arrives.
1842	Reverend Father Thibault arrives.
1852	Reverend Father Lacombe arrives.
1857-9	Palliser Expedition.
1858	First Gold panner.
1859	Grey Nuns arrive.
1861	Father Lacombe establishes St. Albert.
1862	Brother Scollen starts a school.
1862	Arrival of Reverend George McDougall.
1867	Confederation.
1868	A. J. Snyder opens Methodist day school.
1870	Alberta legally becomes part of Canada.
1870	Last Indian battle at Edmonton.
1870	Smallpox epidemic.
1871	Arrival of American Whisky traders.
1871	Reverend George McDougall builds house in hamlet.
1873	McDougall Church consecrated.
1873	Dr. George Verey, Edmonton's first resident physician arrives.
1874	North West Mounted Police arrive.
1875	First steamboat the "Northcote" arrives.
1876	Donald Ross builds first hotel.
1879	Telegraph line extended into Edmonton.
1880	Hamlet of Edmonton surveyed.
1880	Edmonton Bulletin starts publication.
1881	First public school.
1882	Edmonton Settlement surveyed.
1883	C.P.R. reaches Calgary.
1885	Northwest Rebellion.
1886	First telephone service.
1891	Calgary and Edmonton railway completed to south side and South Edmonton started.
1891	Alex Taylor starts first electric light plant.
1892	Edmonton incorporated as a Town.
1893	Scott Robertson builds his hall.
1896	Edmonton Golf and Country Club established.
1897	Klondike Gold Rush.
1899	South Edmonton incorporated as a Town and called Strathcona.

1902	Low Level Bridge opened and Edmonton gets Railway connection to South Edmonton.
1903	New Alberta Hotel built.
1903	Edmonton Journal started.
1904	J. H. Morris brings first car to Edmonton.
1904	First Performance Edmonton Operatic Society.
1904	Edmonton incorporated as a City.
1905	Alberta becomes a province.
1905	Canadian Northern Railway transcontinental enters Edmonton.
1906	Edmonton confirmed as capital of Alberta.
1906	Cecil, Castle and King Edward Hotels opened.
1906	Robertson's Hall burned.
1906	Hamlet of Beverly began.
1907	Strathcona incorporated as a City.
1908	Street Car System started.
1908	Edmonton installs first automatic dialing telephones in North America.
1908	University of Alberta started in Strathcona.
1909	Reginald Hunt builds and flies Edmonton's first aeroplane.
1909	John Walter launches "City of Edmonton" steamer.
1909	Grand Trunk Pacific transcontinental enters city.
1910	North Edmonton incorporated as a village.
1910	Abe Cristall opens Royal George Hotel.
1911	New Exhibition Grounds opened.
1912	Edmonton and Strathcona amalgamated.
1912	Hudson's Bay land sale.
1912	Dawson Bridge opened.
1912	Women's Canadian Club branch organized.
1913	Pantages Theatre opened.
1913	High Level and 105th Street bridges opened.
1913	Beverly incorporated as a village.
1913	Legislative building opened.
1914	City Streets renumbered.
1914	Commercial Grads basketball club formed.
1914	Viking Gas field discovered.
1915	49th Battalion goes overseas.
1915	Macdonald Hotel opened.
1915	River floods out flats.
1915	Fort Edmonton torn down.
1916	Prohibition comes to Alberta.
1917	City annexes Calder.
1918	Epidemic of Spanish flu.
1918	Wop and Court May organize May Airplanes Ltd.
1919	Jock McNeil and K. Tailyour organize Edmonton Airplane Co.
1919	Edmonton Airforce Association started.

1920	Gorman and Fullerton fly Junkers north to Imperial Oil's Fort Norman discovery.
1922	C.J.C.A. Alberta's first radio station starts operating.
1923	Edmonton begins using natural gas.
1923	Prohibition rejected.
1923	The Art and Historical Museum Association starts.
1926	Council authorizes $400.00 to be spent on a runway at airfield.
1926	Ottawa designates airfield an official "Air Harbour".
1927	City spends another $200.00 and calls it Blatchford Field.
1927	Northern Alberta Aero Club set up to train pilots and Ottawa provided two Moth planes.
1927	First class of Edmonton-trained pilots graduate.
1928	Wop May, Cy Becker and Vic Horner set up Commercial Airways Ltd.
1928	First airmail schedule started by Western Canada Airways.
1929	Emily Murphy and other women victorious in having women declared "persons".
1929	Wop May and Vic Horner of Commercial Airways obtain Lockheed Vega with first enclosed heated cabin.
1929	Punch Dickins completes first air trip to Aklavik.
1929	Council authorizes expenditure of $35,000.00 for airfield.
1930	Jimmy Bell appointed Master of Blatchford Air Harbour.
1930	Punch Dickins of Western Canada Airways flies first northern plane to be equipped with shortwave radio.
1931	Leigh Brintnell starts Mackenzie Air Service.
1932	Maurice Burbridge wins McKee Trophy.
1935	Social Credit government elected.
1936	Canada Packers build new plant.
1937	Grant McConachie incorporates Yukon Southern Transport Ltd.
1937	Federal Government finances proper runways at airport.
1938	Clarke Stadium completed.
1939	Blatchford Field transferred to Dominion jurisdiction.
1940	U.S. airlift to Alaska starts.
1942	Americans build Alaska Highway and in one day 500 planes pass through Blatchford Field.
1943	North American record set September 23 when 860 planes pass through.
1943	Namao Field started.
1945	General Griesbach dies.
1947	Leduc Oil Field discovered.

1948	Edmonton Flyers win Allan Cup.
1948	First refinery (Imperial Oil Ltd.) established in Clover Bar.
1949	Low Level Bridge twinned.
1950	Inter-Provincial Pipe Line built to Lake Superior.
1950	Jasper Place incorporated as a village.
1951	Edmonton Bulletin ceases publishing.
1953	Canadian Chemical Company's plant built in Clover Bar.
1955	Groat Bridge opened.
1955	Sherwood Park started.
1956	Eskimos win Grey Cup for third successive year.
1956	New City Hall completed.
1957	Edmonton International Airport opened.
1964	N.A.R. extended to Pine Point Mines.
1964	Great Canadian Oil Sands plant started.
1966	C.N.R. Tower and Chateau Lacombe opened.
1967	Provincial Museum opened.
1967	Great Canadian Oil Sands starts production.
1968	Quesnell Bridge built.
1968	Ernest Manning steps down from premier's office and Harry Strom succeeds him.
1968	Ivor Dent succeeds V. M. Dantzer as mayor.
1968	New Municipal Act provides for wards.
1969	Capilano Bridge built.
1970	Huge Clover Bar power plant opened.
1971	James McDonald Bridge built.
1971	City takes in 35 additional square miles in Mill Woods and B.A.C.M. areas.
1971	Alberta Government Telephones Building in McCauley Plaza opened, including networks of underground stores.
1971	Social Credit government's 36-year life span ends.
1971	Peter Lougheed becomes premier of Alberta.
1972	Beverly Bridge twinned.
1972	Imperial Oil Limited Clover Bar Refinery under construction.
1973	Sod turned for 16,000-seat Coliseum.
1973	Construction started on E. L. Smith Water Treatment Plant.
1974	William Hawrelak re-elected as mayor.
1975	Syncrude Oil Sands plant well under way.
1975	Major upgrading of Industrial Airport nearing completion.
1975	Work continues on first phase of rapid transit system.

appendix II   Officers in charge of Edmonton House

(The fur trade year started in the fall.)

1795	William Tomison	1847	John Edward Harriott
1796	George Sutherland	1848-1853	John Rowand
1797-1798	William Tomison	1854-1856	William Sinclair
1799-1815	James Bird	1857	John Swanston
1816	Hugh Carswell	1858-1871	William Joseph Christie
1817-1820	Francis Heron	1872-1882	Richard Hardisty
1821	James Sutherland	1883-1884	James McDougall
1822	Colin Robertson	1885-1888	Richard Hardisty
1823-1840	John Rowand	1889-1891	Harrison S. Young
1841	John Edward Harriott	1891-1910	W. T. Livock
1842-1846	John Rowand		

appendix III   Mayors

THE FOLLOWING list of Mayors of Edmonton and Strathcona is taken from the report compiled for the City of Edmonton by Julian G. Suski.

EDMONTON

(Town)		(City)	
1892-1894	Matthew McCauley	1905	K. W. MacKenzie
1895-1896	H. C. Wilson	1906	Charles May
1896	C. Gallagher	1907	W. A. Griesbach
1897	John A. McDougall	1908	John A. McDougall
1898-1899	W. S. Edmiston	1909-1910	Robert Lee
1900-1901	K. W. MacKenzie	1911	G. S. Armstrong
1902-1904	William Short		

STRATHCONA

(Town)		(City)	
1899-1900	T. Bennett	1906	W. H. Sheppard
1901	R. Ritchie	1907-1908	N. D. Mills
1902-1903	J. J. Duggan	1908-1910	J. J. Duggan
1905	A. Davies	1911	A. Davies

EDMONTON AFTER AMALGAMATION

1912	G. S. Armstrong	1935-1937	J. A. Clarke
1913	W. Short	1938-1945	J. W. Fry
1914	W. S. McNamara	1946-1949	H. D. Ainlay
1914-1917	W. T. Henry	1950-1951	S. Parsons
1918	H. M. E. Evans	1952-1959	Wm. Hawrelak
1919-1920	J. A. Clarke	1959	F. J. Mitchell
1921-1923	D. M. Duggan	1959-1963	Dr. E. E. Roper
1924-1926	K. A. Blatchford	1963-1965	Wm. Hawrelak
1927-1929	A. U. G. Bury	1965-1968	V. M. Dantzer
1930-1931	J. M. Douglas	1968-1974	Ivor Dent
1932-1934	D. K. Knott	1974-	Wm. Hawrelak

Population Statistics

Year	Notes	Edmonton	South Edmonton	Strath-cona	Beverly	Jasper Place	Metro-Edmonton	Source
1878		148						Unofficial
1881		263						N.W.M.P. Census
1887		350						Author's estimate
1892	At incorporation	700						Town Census
1894		1,021						N.W.M.P. Census
1895		1,165	505					N.W.M.P. Census
1899	At incorporation			1,156				Town Census
1901		2,626		1,550				Dominion Census
1904	At incorporation as City	8,350						City Census
1907	At incorporation as City			3,500				City Census
1908		18,500						Henderson's Directory
1911		24,900		4,500				Dominion Census
1912	After Amalgamation	50,000		5,579				Author's estimate
1913		63,000						Henderson's Directory
1914		72,516						City Census
1916		53,846						City Census
1919		54,000						Author's estimate
1921		58,821			1,039			Dominion Census
1926		65,163						Dominion Census
1929		75,000						Author's estimate
1931		79,197			1,111			Dominion Census
1936		85,774						Dominion Census
1939		90,000						Author's estimate
1941		93,817			981			Dominion Census
1946		113,116			1,171			Dominion Census
1951		159,631			2,159	9,139	176,782	Dominion Census
1956		226,002			4,602	19,957	254,800	Dominion Census
1961		281,027			9,041	30,530	337,568	Dominion Census
1966	June 1st	371,265					393,428*	Dominion Census
1971		436,264**					495,915	Dominion Census
1974		445,691**					530,000	Dominion Census
1975		451,635**						Estimate

*Includes St. Albert, Sherwood Park, Griesbach Barracks and Namao.   **City Census.

appendix V Summary of records established by commercial grads.

The tally of the Grads' achievements over the years from 1914 to 1940, the year they disbanded, stands out uniquely;

Alberta Provincial Champions, 1914 to 1940, except for 1921.

Canadian Champions, 1922 to 1940.

Winners of the Underwood International Trophy from its inception to 1939 when the trophy was retired.

From 1920 to 1940 they played 61 Canadian exhibition games against Saskatoon, Victoria, Winnipeg, Toronto, Montreal, etc., and won 59 of them.

When in 1925, moving on to the United States scene, they played 18 exhibition games in such varied places as Fort Worth, San Francisco, Chicago and New York, etc., they won 15 of them.

In 1924, 1928, 1932 and 1936, they attended the Olympic Games and although girls' basketball was never an official event, they played exhibition games against teams from Paris, Strasbourg, and other cities, and won them all.

In 1940, with the war on and having no more worlds to conquer, after being champions for a quarter of a century, the Grads disbanded. Since for such a long span in Edmonton's history they had been so outstanding, this record would not be complete without a tabulation of their performance from 1922 to 1940.

Title	Played	Won	Lost	Pts. for	Against	Av. Score
North American	14	9	5	593	577	42 to 41
Underwood Trophy	120	114	6	5386	2844	45 to 24
Canadian Finals	31	29	2	1402	649	45 to 21
Western Finals	21	21	0	1104	580	52 to 28
Alberta Finals	38	36	2	1629	709	43 to 19
Canadian Exhibition Games	93	93	0	5411	1431	58 to 15
American Exhibition Games	25	22	3	908	522	36 to 21
European Exhibition Games	24	24	0	1722	263	72 to 11
Men's teams	9	7	2	343	295	38 to 33
	375	355	20	18174	7638	48 to 20

appendix VI *Street names*

TABLE showing the old street names and the numbers assigned to them in 1914 when a numerical system was adopted.

NORTH SIDE

Old Name	New Name	Old Name	New Name
Abernethy Ave.	111th Ave.	Columbia Ave.	105th Ave.
Ackerman St.	71 St.	Connaught Drive	Unchanged
Ada Boulevard	Unchanged	Coot Ave.	108th Ave.
Adrian Ave.	115th Ave.	Corby Ave.	108th Ave.
Agnes St.	128th Ave.	Crescentwood Ave.	95th Ave.
Agnes St.	79th St.	Cristabelle St.	101A Ave.
Albany Ave.	110th Ave.	Currie St.	100th St.
Alberta Ave.	118th Ave.		
Allen St.	49th St.	Darroch St.	75th St.
Appleton St.	42nd St.	Denver Ave.	97th Ave.
Athabasca Ave.	102 Ave.	Donald St.	100A St.
		Douglas St.	78th St.
Bailey Ave.	114th Ave.	Duprau St.	68th St.
Beatrice St.	102nd Ave.		
Beaver Ave.	135th Ave.	Earl St.	67th St.
Beech Ave.	117th Ave.	Edmiston St.	110A Ave.
Bellamy St.	102A Ave.	Elizabeth St.	102nd Ave.
Belleville St.	74 St.	Elm Ave.	113th Ave.
Bolton St.	84 St.		
Boyle St.	103A Ave.	Fort Road	Unchanged
Brandon Ave.	127 Ave.	Fox St.	89th St.
Brazeau Ave.	113th Ave.	Fraser Ave.	98th St.
Brigham St.	71st St.	Fraser's Lane	74th St.
Brown St.	48 St.		
Brown St.	68 St.	Gallagher St.	109A Ave.
Buchanan Ave.	Unchanged	George St.	56th St.
		Gerald St.	89th St.
Calgary Ave.	96th Ave.	Gibbard St.	57th St.
Cameron St.	Unchanged	Gibson Ave.	111th Ave.
Campbell St.	61st St.	Gordon St.	72nd St.
Carey St.	94th St.	Government Ave.	92nd St.
Carle	76th St.	Grace St.	62nd St.
Cavan St.	88th St.	Gracey Ave.	109th Ave.
Charles St.	77th St.	Graham St.	70th St.
Chown Ave.	116th Ave.	Gray St.	58th St.
Churchill Ave.	108th Ave.	Green Ave.	109th Ave. from 121st St. West
Clara St.	103rd Ave.		
Clare St.	45th St.	Grierson St.	101st Ave.
Clark St.	105th Ave.	Griesbach St.	105A Ave.
Cleave Ave.	119th Ave.		
Cliff St.	100A Ave.	Hamilton Ave.	90th St.
College Ave.	McDonald Dr.	Hardisty Ave.	98th Ave.
		Harrison St.	78th St.
		Hart St.	71A St.

Old Name	New Name	Old Name	New Name
Harvey St.	84th St.	MacDonald St.	47th St.
Hastings	87th St.	Magrath Ave.	113th Ave.
Heiminck St.	107th Ave.	Marjorie St.	Rowland Road
Henderson	36th St.	Martin St.	88th St.
Henry St. (Beverly)	44th St.	May St.	102A Ave.
Henry St.	91st St.	Montgomery St.	55th St.
Hill	102A Ave.	Morris St.	106A Ave.
Hillhurst St.	50th St.	Moser St.	65th St.
Holgate Ave.	109th Ave.	Mount View St.	43rd St.
Houston St.	64th St.	Murray St.	73rd St.
Howard Ave.	100A St.	Muskoka Ave.	111th Ave.
Inkerman Ave.	126th Ave.	Namayo Ave.	97th St.
Irwin St.	63rd St.	Nelson Ave.	107th Ave.
Isabella St.	104th Ave.	Nelson St.	63rd St.
		Nipigon Ave.	112th Ave.
James St.	81st St. from 112th Ave.	Normandale Ave.	117th Ave.
		Norton St.	66th St.
Jasper Ave. E & W	(Retain original name) Also known as 101 Ave.	Norwood Blvd.	111th Ave.
		Oak Ave.	116th Ave.
John St.	80th St.	Okanagan Ave.	115th Ave.
Johnston St.	83rd St. from 112 Ave.	Ottawa Ave.	93rd St.
		Otter St.	90th St.
Julia	94th St.		
		Paul Ave.	129th Ave.
		Peace Ave.	103rd Ave.
Kemp St.	83rd St.	Pembina Ave.	117th Ave.
Kennedy St.	93rd St.	Phillips St.	76th St.
Kent St.	58th St.	Picard St.	108th Ave.
King St.	86th St.	Pine Ave.	112th Ave.
Kinistino Ave.	96th St.	Pine Place	112th Ave.
Kinnaird St.	82nd St.	Portage Road	Kingsway
Kirkness St.	95th St.		
Kitto Ave.	94A St.	Queens Ave.	99th St.
Knox Ave.	112th Ave.		
		Race St.	38th St.
Lake St.	60th St.	Raymer St.	81st St.
Lee St.	85th St. from 112th Ave.	Regent Ave.	129th Ave.
		Rice St.	101A Ave.
Leggett St.	87th St.	Richard Ave.	89th St.
Lola St.	83rd St. from 118th Ave.	Riggs St.	72nd St. from 112th Ave.
Lorne St.	92nd St.	Riverside Drive	Unchanged
		Robertson St.	74th St.
McCauley St.	107A Ave.	Ross St.	108A Ave.
McDonald Ave.	88th St.	Rowland Road	Unchanged from 95th St.
McDougall Ave.	100th St.		
McKay Ave.	99th Ave.	Ryder St.	64th St.
McKenzie Ave.	104th Ave.		
McLeod Ave.	95th Ave.	St. Albert Road	Unchanged
Mable St.	58th St.	St. Lawrence Ave.	109A Ave.

Old Name	New Name	Old Name	New Name
Sage St.	46th St.	Vermilion Ave.	106th Ave.
Saskatchewan Ave.	97th Ave.	Victoria Ave.	100th Ave.
Saunders Ave.	86th St.	Victoria St.	60th St.
Scott St.	69th St.	Villa Ave.	Unchanged
Shand Ave.	111th Ave.		
Sharp St.	37th St.	Wadhurst Road	Unchanged
Short Ave.	107th Ave.	Wadleigh	67th St.
Short St.	109th Ave.	Wallace	74A St.
Simpson St.	70th St.	Walsh Ave.	94th Ave.
Sinclair St.	95A St.	Waterloo Ave.	125th Ave.
Spadina Ave.	120th Ave.	Wentworth St.	66th St.
Sparling St.	69th St.	Westminster Ave.	121st Ave.
Spruce Ave.	114th Ave.	Willard Ave.	94th St.
	between 121st	Willow Ave.	115th Ave.
	and 79th Sts.	Wilson St. (Beverly)	39th St.
Stephen Ave.	106th Ave.	Wilson St.	110th Ave.
Stewart St.	101A Ave.	Wilton St.	65th St.
Stikeen Ave.	114th Ave.	Woodsworth St.	105A Ave.
Stony Plain Road	Unchanged	Woodward Ave.	122nd Ave.
Sutherland St.	106th Ave.	Wright St.	59th St.
Syndicate Ave.	95th St.		
		Yonge St.	85 St. from
Thompson Ave.	110th Ave.		118 Ave.
Threadneedle Ave.	128th Ave.	York St.	61st St.
Trethewey Ave.	105th Ave.	York St.	96th St.
Tupper St.	41st St.	Yukon Ave.	116th Ave.
Vancouver St.	62nd St.	1st St.	101st St.

The streets which originally bore the numbers 2nd St. to 35th St. were renumbered 102nd St. to 135th St.

SOUTH SIDE

Old Name	New Name	Old Name	New Name
Adelaide St.	92nd Ave.	5th St. S.W. and N.W.	109th St.
Allen Ave.	65th Ave.	6th Ave. S.E. and S.W.	76th Ave.
Bennett Ave.	Unchanged	6th Ave. N.E. and N.W.	88th Ave.
Bertha Ave.	67A Ave.	6th St. E.	98th St.
Brackman St.	95th St.	6th St. S.W. between	
Calgary Trail	106th St.	76th Ave. and	
Clover Bar Road	Unchanged	University Ave.	110A St.
East St. (Walterdale)	106th St.	6th St. N.W. and S.W.	
Findlay St.	87th St.	north of University Ave.	110A St.
Highland St.	95th St.	7th Ave. S.E. and S.W.	75th Ave.
King St.	108A St.	7th Ave. N.E. and N.W.	89th Ave.
Main St.	104th St.	7th St. E.	97th St.
Park St.	103A St.	7th St. W.	111th St.
Phoenix St.	96th St.	8th Ave. S.E. and S.W.	74th Ave.
Rupert St.	105A St.	8th Ave. N.E. and N.W.	90th Ave.
St. Paul St.	90th Ave.	8th St. S.E.	96th St.
St. Placide St.	91st Ave.	8th St. S.W. and N.W.	112th St.
Saskatchewan Drive	Unchanged	9th Ave. S.E. and S.W.	73rd Ave.
Strathcona Road	99th St.	9th Ave. N.E. and N.W.	91st Ave.
Swansea St.	94th St.	9th St. E.	95th St.
Thomas St.	91st Ave.	10th Ave. S.E. and S.W.	72nd Ave.
University Ave.	Unchanged	10th Ave. N.E. and N.W.	92nd Ave.
West St. (Walterdale)	107th St.	11th Ave. S.E. and S.W.	71st Ave.
Whyte Ave. E and W	82nd Ave.	11th Ave. N.E.	93rd Ave.
1st Ave. S.E. and S.W.	81st Ave.	11th St. S.E. and N.E.	91st St.
1st Ave. N.E. and N.W.	83rd Ave.	12th Ave. S.E. and S.W.	70th Ave.
1st St. S.E.	103rd St.	13th Ave. S.E. and S.W.	69th Ave.
1st St. S.W.	105th St.	13th St. S.E.	87th St.
2nd Ave. S.E. and S.W.	80th Ave.	14th Ave. S.E. and S.W.	68th Ave.
2nd Ave. N.E. and N.W.	84th Ave.	15th Ave. S.E. and S.W.	67th Ave.
2nd St. S.E. and N.E.	102nd St.	15th St. S.E.	83rd St.
2nd St. S.W. and N.W.	106th St.	16th Ave. S.E. and S.W.	66th Ave.
3rd Ave. S.E. and S.W.	79th Ave.	16th St. S.E.	81st St.
3rd Ave. N.E. and N.W.	85th Ave.	17th Ave. S.E. and S.W.	65th Ave.
3rd St. N.W. and S.W.	107th St.	18th Ave. S.E. and S.W.	64th Ave.
4th Ave. S.E. and S.W.	78th Ave.	19th Ave. S.E. and S.W.	63rd Ave.
4th Ave. N.E. and N.W.	86th Ave.	19th St. S.E.	76th St.
4th St. S.E. and N.E.	100th St.	20th Ave. S.E. and S.W.	62nd Ave.
4th St. S.W. and N.W.	108th St.	21st Ave. S.E.	61st Ave.
5th Ave. S.E. and S.W.	77th Ave.	22nd Ave. S.E.	60th Ave.
5th Ave. N.E. and N.W.	87th Ave.	25th Ave. S.E.	57th Ave.
5th St. S.E.	99th St.	30th Ave. S.E.	52nd Ave.

Acknowledgements

IN COMPILING this history the author has been fortunate in being able to rely on help generously given by many departments and individuals. Foremost amongst these have been the many libraries with which Edmonton is blessed and all of these have been most kind in extending their facilities.

I am most grateful to the Edmonton Public Library and particularly Mrs. Dowling and her associates there. The University Library contains a large amount of information bearing on the City's history, particularly the microfilm of the Edmonton Bulletin, and it has always been most helpful. I am indebted to Mrs. Taschuk of the Edmonton Journal Library who kindly made her clippings file available and was always ready to help. Much of the information used in great portions of the book came from scores of hours of research which Margaret Collins did in poring over the Edmonton Journals and the Edmonton Bulletins in the Provincial Library. On these, Mrs. Collins did a meticulous job, and Eric Holmgren, the librarian, was most kind and helpful in digging out material as it was required.

Mrs. Ragan of the City Archives always stood ready to help and from her files produced much material including a number of valuable photographs.

On the score of photographs, of course, the Ernest Brown collection was invaluable and Ken Hutchinson of the Photographic Branch of the Department of Industry and Development kindly made it available and had his staff search out interesting pictures. Moreover, he also placed at my disposal his collection of more current photographs. From their extensive files, the McDermid Studio, the Kensit Studio and the Glenbow Foundation also supplied photographs.

As usual, Hugh Dempsey of that Foundation always graciously allowed me to tap his vast personal reservoir for background material. So, too, did Tony Cashman, who allowed me to quote extensively from his "Edmonton Story" and his "More Edmonton Stories." Moreover, he read the manuscript and made many most valuable suggestions.

Various civic departments helped in supplying information and I am particularly indebted to the late J. D. A. MacDonald, the city engineer, who allowed me to study his department's records. Mr. Docherty, city clerk, was also most kind and ready to help. As usual, Mrs. Shirlee Smith of the Hudson's Bay Company in Winnipeg provided answers to many questions. Bill MacDonald, whose father, Heath MacDonald, did so much work on the problems of trying to restore Fort Edmonton, kindly permitted me to use the copy of the Vavasour plan. Mrs. June Sheppard was most helpful in bringing to light advances made in the fine arts.

Many other individuals helped, particularly Ian Paterson from his knowledge of postal history; D. Istvanffy, Director, Alberta Bureau of Statistics; Bob English, who is a walking encyclopedia of agricultural history; Lieut.-Col. B. D. Stanton, who kindly granted me permission to quote from "A City Goes to War"; and Jim Falconer who revealed some of the history of the liquor trade in the province. Many others too numerous to mention have been most helpful.

I am indebted to Les Collins who bore with me while we decided what to include in some of the maps and then drew them so carefully. The map used in the end cover owes its excellence to Mrs. W. Wonders. To her, as well as to all who have helped so generously, I am particularly grateful.

Finally, much of the credit for this work is due to my wife Frances, who by her typing and constant assistance has helped immeasurably.

Photo Credits

Page 26 Royal Ontario Museum; Page 27 W. MacDonald; Page 39 Public Archives of Canada; Page 42 Public Archives, Victoria, B.C.; Page 51 Alberta Government Photographs, Ernest Brown Collection; Page 64 Glenbow Foundation; Page 72 Alberta Government Photographs, Ernest Brown Collection; Page 73 Geological Survey of Canada; Pages 85, 87, 99, 103, 108, Alberta Government Photographs, Ernest Brown Collection; Page 116 Public Archives of Canada; Pages 117, 119, 128, 129, 133, 136, 137, 145 Alberta Government Photographs, Ernest Brown Collection; Page 149 Top: McDermid Studios Ltd., Bottom: Alberta Government Photographs, Ernest Brown Collection; Page 160 Alberta Government Photographs, Ernest Brown Collection; Page 161 Top: University of Alberta, Bottom: John F. McDougall; Page 174 McDermid Studio Ltd.; Page 175, 181, 187 Alberta Government Photographs, Ernest Brown Collection; Page 192 Top: Tony Cashman, Bottom: Alberta Government Photographs, Ernest Brown Collection; Page 193 Alberta Government Photographs, Ernest Brown Collection; Pages 199, 203, 207 University of Alberta; Page 220 Kensit Studio; Pages 221, 228 McDermid Studios Ltd.; Page 231 The Hon. Percy Page, McDermid Studios; Page 237 Tony Cashman; Page 252 Top: McDermid Studios Ltd., Bottom: Denny Ranson; Page 253 Top Left: McDermid Studios Ltd., Bottom Right & Left: Alberta Provincial Museum and Archives; Page 257 Blyth Studios Ltd.; Page 271 McDermid Studios Ltd.; Page 275 Alberta Government Photographs; Page 285 Top: Glenbow Foundation, Bottom: Alf Gardenits; Page 288 Alf Gardenits; Page 289 Parker Studio, The City of Edmonton, Industrial Development Department; Page 309 Alberta Government Photograph.

Index

337